Centuries of Child Labour

To Ville and Otto

Centuries of Child Labour
European Experiences from the Seventeenth to the Twentieth Century

MARJATTA RAHIKAINEN
University of Helsinki, Finland

Routledge
Taylor & Francis Group

LONDON AND NEW YORK

First published 2004 by Ashgate Publishing

Published 2017 by Routledge
2 Park Square, Milton Park, Abingdon, Oxon OX14 4RN
711 Third Avenue, New York, NY 10017, USA

First issued in paperback 2017

Routledge is an imprint of the Taylor & Francis Group, an informa business

British Library Cataloguing in Publication Data
Rahikainen, Marjatta
  Centuries of child labour : European experiences from the
  seventeenth to the twentieth century. – (Studies in labour
  history)
  1. Child labour – Europe – History 2. Children – Europe –
  History
  I. Title
  331.3'1'094

Library of Congress Cataloging-in-Publication Data
Rahikainen, Marjatta
    Centuries of child labour : European experiences from the
  seventeenth to the twentieth century / Marjatta Rahikainen.
        p. cm. – (Studies in labour history)
    Includes bibliographical references and index.
    ISBN 0-7546-0498-5 (alk. paper)
      1. Child labor–Europe–History. I. Title. II. Studies in labour
  history (Ashgate (Firm))

  HD6250.E8512R34 2004
  331.3'1'0940903–dc22

                                                              2003063542

ISBN 13: 978-1-138-26354-3 (pbk)
ISBN 13: 978-0-7546-0498-3 (hbk)

Contents

List of Tables

Studies in Labour History
General Editor's Preface

Labour history has often been a fertile area of history. Since the Second World War its best practioners – such as E.P. Thompson and E.J. Hobsbawm, both Presidents of the British Society for the Study of Labour History – have written works which have provoked fruitful and wide-ranging debates and further research, and which have influenced not only social history but history generally. These historians, and many others, have helped to widen labour history beyond the study of organised labour to labour generally, sometimes to industrial relations in particular, and most frequently to society and culture in national and comparative dimensions.

The assumptions and ideologies underpinning much of the older labour history have been challenged by feminist and later by postmodernist and anti-Marxist thinking. These challenges have often led to thoughtful reappraisals, perhaps intellectual equivalents of coming to terms with a new post-Cold War political landscape.

By the end of the twentieth century, labour history had emerged reinvigorated and positive from much introspection and external criticism. Very few would wish to confine its scope to the study of organised labour. Yet, equally, few would wish now to write the existence and influence of organised labour out of nations' histories, any more than they would wish to ignore working-class lives and focus only on the upper echelons.

This series of books provides reassessments of broad themes of labour history as well as some more detailed studies arising from recent research. Most books are single-authored but there are also volumes of essays centred on important themes or periods, some arising from major conferences organised by the Society for the Study of Labour History. The series also includes studies of labour organisations, including international ones, as many of these are much in need of a modern reassessment.

Chris Wrigley
British Society for the Study of Labour History
University of Nottingham

Acknowledgements

The academic community has a feature that I have learned to appreciate and for which I have been grateful when writing this book. In the spirit of collegial solidarity, for the love of history, or out of the kindness of their hearts, but always without profiting themselves from it, all the people I asked were prepared to give their time and effort to answering my questions and commenting on what I had written. I am also grateful and much indebted to the hundreds of scholars without whose work this book would not have materialised. The notes and bibliography fail to do justice to all of them.

The person to whom I owe my warmest thanks is Colin Heywood. He did such a good job reviewing the entire manuscript, the kind of job that only a few busy academics would or could do in addition to all their other obligations. His comments were always to the point and his criticism justified. Riitta Hjerppe and Klas Nyberg also read and commented on the entire text, and I am most grateful to them for their wise observations and critical remarks. Others who commented on some parts of the text include (in alphabetical order) José M. Borrás Llop, Laura Guidi, Sakari Heikkinen, Ottavia Niccoli, Matti Peltonen, Tarja Räisänen, Carmen Sarasúa García, Jürgen Schlumbohm and Richard Wall. All of them came with fruitful insights and valuable feedback, and helped me to correct a number of errors and misinterpretations. Discussions with Leonid Borodkin and David Ransel helped me to understand better the conditions of children in Russia. Furthermore, Serge Chassagne helped me to find the nineteenth-century French statistics I needed and Ola Honningdal Grytten did the same concerning Norwegian statistics.

The first embryonic version of this work was read and commented on by Aura Korppi-Tommola, Panu Pulma and Johan Söderberg, and parts of it by Kaisa Kauranen and Toivo Nygård. The first version focused on the history of child labour in Finland and Sweden. It would never have changed into a history of child labour in Europe had not Jo Campling and Rauno Endén been there just in time to push me to write for an international readership.

Discussions with my Finnish friends and colleagues were most important in the slow shaping of this work. Beatrice Moring first introduced me to the family-history approach, and generously shared with me her profound knowledge of rural life, while Kirsi Vainio-Korhonen equally generously shared with me her knowledge of early-modern urban life. My former and present colleagues at the Department of Social Science History, University of Helsinki, have patiently answered my questions on various issues, and discussions around the coffee table have been a constant source of information and pleasure.

The long bibliography is an indication that I have bothered a great number of library staff. I am particularly grateful to those at the Library of the Finnish Parliament and at the Helsinki University Library. Terttu Turunen at the Social Science Library of the University of Helsinki first helped me to find my way in the international library databases, and Liisa Koski at the Helsinki University Library then performed miracles in terms of interlibrary loans.

I am also greatly indebted to Joan Nordlund for her skilful and patient correcting of my home-made English to produce a much more readable text.

For financial support I wish to thank the Academy of Finland and the Council for Research in the Humanities (NOS-H). The Academy of Finland also financially supported my participation in the 1988–1989 Annual Training Programme at the International Institution for Educational Planning (IIEP/IIPE) in Paris. While working on this book I came to realise that what I learned of present-day child labour during that academic year in Paris influenced my historical perspective.

Jouni Peltola professionally turned the manuscript into print. Tom Gray at Ashgate Publishing Ltd was of great help in the many practical questions that popped up during the process of finishing the manuscript for publication. I am happy that my book is included in Studies in Labour History because this is just where I wanted it to be.

Finally I wish to thank my sons Ville and Otto for their unfailing solidarity. I dedicate this book to them.

Helsinki, June 2003
Marjatta Rahikainen

Introduction

Even paradigmatic works are children of their time. In the 1950s, when Philippe Ariès finished his *Centuries of Childhood*, a study of childhood and the family under the French *ancien régime*, children of school age in Europe went to school, and child labour had become a marginal phenomenon. The *ancien régime* children, as Ariès described them, appeared as schoolchildren, not as working children.

Centuries of Childhood was a highly innovative piece of scholarship. This makes it all the more puzzling that Ariès had nothing original to say about working childhood under the *ancien régime*. He passed over child labour with a short remark:

> We know too that the concept of childhood found its most modern expression in these same circles of enlightened bourgeois who admired Greuze and read *Émile* and *Pamela*. But the old ways of life have survived almost until the present day in the lower classes, which have not been subjected for so long a period to the influence of the school. We may even ask ourselves whether, in this respect, there was not a retrogression during the first half of the nineteenth century, under the influence of the demand for child labour in the textile industry. Child labour retained this characteristic of medieval society: the precocity of the entry into adult life. The whole complexion of life was changed by the differences in the educational treatment of the middle-class and the lower-class child [*traitement scolaire de l'enfant, bourgeois ou populaire*].[1]

In his book Ariès put forward the thesis that the discovery of childhood, *la découverte de l'enfance*, took place among the bourgeoisie in early modern Europe, while in the quotation above he appears to suggest that the nineteenth-century practice of industrial child labour should be seen as a legacy of medieval society that continued among the lower classes. Since his description of medieval child-rearing practices was not without certain nostalgia, it appears paradoxical that he saw nineteenth-century industrial child labour as a partial retrogression to medieval society.

I submit below that child labour was discovered under the *ancien régime*. Child labour was, of course, nothing new – no more than childhood – but in early modern Europe the efforts to set children to work became systematic and intensive as never before. The élite and bourgeoisie of the *ancien régime* took the children of the poor and labouring classes as a resource to be disciplined and mobilised. In this respect, there was an analogy between the coming of manufactories under the *ancien régime* and the coming of factories during the industrial revolution. In both cases, the well-off saw the children of the poor as a pool of labour to be tapped, and those who strove to increase the wealth of the nation as well as their own did not hesitate to use children for that purpose.

* * *

Philippe Ariès is today a standard reference in any study of European childhood, past and present. The debate on whether childhood, or rather the concept of childhood, was or was not discovered under the *ancien régime* has been presented many times, and there is no need to repeat the arguments here.[2] Novel conceptions of children no doubt did emerge under the *ancien régime*. For example, in the new doctrines of witches' Sabbath and malicious magic, children were thought capable of and were charged with evil magic and relations with the Devil.[3] Nonetheless, the debate on the *concept* of childhood appears somewhat scholarly. After all, what mattered to medieval and early modern common people was the concrete task of bringing children up into adulthood. Furthermore, medievalists have presented ample evidence that people in medieval societies made a clear distinction between children and adults, were sensitive to children's distinctive characters and took active measures to ensure the survival of infants and children.[4]

Ancien régime France was a warlike society in which riches and power were accumulated at the very top. For many children it must have been a hard society to live in. In that society, Philippe Ariès argued, a new sensitivity to children emerged. If it was so, then it is indeed an irony of history that children who had grown up into adults in that society in the end guillotined the *ancien régime*. I suggest that if attitudes to children and educational practices in Europe changed from late medieval to modern times, this may rather have been because the established hierarchies were challenged, and handing over status and power to the next generation became more problematic than it had been under feudalism.

Moulding characters for a modern élite turned out to be a more hazardous enterprise than had been the military training fit for the feudal élite. The difference appears striking if one compares the instructions for an élite boy's education set out on a few pages by Machiavelli with those given in extensive treatises by his contemporary, Erasmus. For all its timelessness, Machiavelli's *The Prince* is, in this respect, medieval. Bringing up a future prince aimed first of all at military competence, tailored to help him in his two main concerns: how to acquire for himself a principality, and how to maintain his rule. There was not a word on how to imprint on a boy of high birth the right kind of personality, morality, way of thinking or even faith. The inner life, or the soul of a child became an object of education only with Humanists such as Erasmus.[5]

As social mobility and competition increased, channelling their sons successfully into a suitable career and their daughters into an advantageous marriage became a much more complicated and demanding task for the establishment than before. It was no wonder that the market for educational manuals expanded. An intangible good like social position could not be inherited like a piece of land. To secure such an immaterial inheritance, as Giovanni Levi calls it, required the right kind of individual qualifications, characteristics imprinted during childhood and adolescence in the family circle and in educational institutions. It was not in vain that a noble man commissioned Erasmus to produce instructions on how to educate a boy of high birth. Young men who failed to acquire the required characteristics ended up as losers, like the exorcist in seventeenth-century Piedmont or a Behaim boy in early seventeenth-century Germany. For gentry girls, good behaviour and irreproachable manners paved the way to advantageous marriages (as we learn from Jane Austen's novels), and proper manners may have been acquired by systematic training in, say, being able to sit still.[6] Reflecting a new attitude to the creation of wealth, sumptuary laws were enacted 'to prevent the blurring of the hierarchy of birth by one of wealth'(J. Casey).[7]

If parents took their responsibility seriously, they had to invest plenty of time and resources in bringing up their children to have the right kind of personalities with manners *comme il faut*. Moving this burden over to other persons appeared a fine solution, and parents do not seem to have hesitated to send young children away to be brought up in other households or boarding schools. Reading John Locke gives the impression, correct or not, that in late seventeenth-century England, well-off children spent most of their time with servants and tutors. By and large, the same held true for upper-class and bourgeois children until the early twentieth century, if not later.[8] Nevertheless, Rousseau's theories of how to bring up an élite boy or girl made the enlightened bourgeoisie obsessed with problems of education. What the *ancien régime* bourgeoisie and pedagogic authorities discovered was not childhood but childhood as a problem and a project.

For about three centuries now, adequate formal education has been central to middle-class family strategies. For those with little or no property to inherit, the right kind of schooling opened a gateway to comfortable living, while hard labour awaited those with little or no schooling. Pierre Caspard argues that long before the system of public education had developed, the desire for instruction had spread across social hierarchies. In early modern societies, with advanced commercial and service economies, 'instruction was clearly perceived as a profitable investment, independently of one's social position'. According to Caspard, one idea stands out in eighteenth-century literature recording middle-class, and even popular, ideas on education: 'The time of youth is short; the best use the child can make of it is not to do directly productive work, but to learn in order to reap later, with interest, the fruits of his study.'[9]

Nonetheless, in all of Europe the élite were always clear about the risk that education would alienate the children of popular classes from manual work and awaken their social ambitions. Thus the admittance of boys of lower orders (girls were not admitted or did not count) to the education that opened a way up remained limited until the second half of the twentieth century. Likewise, providing children of the poor and labouring classes with proper school education was not only extremely costly but also potentially subversive.[10] In hindsight, the early laws of compulsory education appear – as Otto Uhlig characterises the first German laws – 'almost a fiction', while their implementation was 'almost a farce'.[11] Yet it is clear that the introduction of popular education indicated, as Marzio Barbagli writes of pre-unification Italy, that 'beside the old model of social control through the ignorance of the people, little by little there emerged one of social control through education'.[12]

Our knowledge of the ideas, attitudes and practices prevailing among the lower orders in past times is sporadic and biased by the perspectives of the middle and upper orders, who produced virtually all of our early modern sources. They serve to prove, say, that in *ancien régime* France the lower classes were almost by definition the last to show signs of affection for children.[13] In the same vein, Edward Shorter argues that the fact that peasants gave a new-born son the same name as his brother proves the peasantry's indifference to new-born children.[14] However, the genealogical tables of the nobility show cases in which successive new-born sons of noble families were given the same name until one of them survived infancy. Why, then, should the nobility not be accused of indifference to new-born children?

In early modern France, mothers may have sold their children to beggars or jugglers or the like, but even some foundling hospitals were accused of 'selling' children to beggars.[15] Stories of children being sold to beggars were circulating in Russia as late as the 1840s.[16] On the other hand, the peasant Andreas Huhnholtz from Hohenlandin deeply grieved at the death of his children in 1551.[17] In Värmland, Sweden, when eleven-month-old Petter died in 1826, the father, a peasant called Gustaf Persson, described this in his diary as the most sorrowful strike of fate he had ever been through. When five years later his little daughter Anna Maria died at the age of two and a half, this man, who otherwise wrote in his diary two or three lines about his day's work, wrote several pages, filled with deep sorrow.[18] In the parish of Virolahti, Finland, peasant parents were especially fond of their last-born children, whom they pitied because they were less likely than their older siblings to stay in the land-owning class, and would face the hard fate of the landless.[19]

References to the consent of children's parents to child labour, and to cases in which skilled workers took their own children as their assistants in heavy or otherwise hard work, 'sweating their own children' (E.J. Hobsbawm),[20] have been interpreted as indicating that lower-class parents lacked the sentiments of motherhood and parenthood.[21] Perhaps they acted this way because they saw it as a better alternative, or even as a benefit for the child. A comparable case is offered by the British nobility, gentry and upwardly-mobile middle classes. In order to guarantee the right kind of future for their offspring, they sent their sons and daughters to boarding schools, no matter what they themselves experienced there in their childhood or what their children might expect to experience. That life in a boarding school could be repressive or even a misery for a child has been recorded in several autobiographies.[22]

* * *

The history of child labour has parallels with that of adult labour. Those who hired children treated them as a category of the labour force that, no doubt, had its distinctive characteristics just like other categories, say, lads, young women, skilled male workers, and old men and women. Like other workers, working children adopted various strategies, although they had a more limited scope of action.

Even though medieval sources offer plenty of evidence of child labour, the lack of quantitative data rules out systematic comparisons over centuries. Medieval miracles feature working children: a nine-year-old girl spinning, a six-year-old housemaid, a little serving girl, a nurse aged about fifteen.[23] In Derbyshire, England, many children of families with a loose attachment to the land may have taken up industrial employment at an early age, working on the looms or excavating ore in the mines of their fathers, in order to get cash to buy land.[24] In late medieval London, some large commercial firms only accepted boys aged at least sixteen as apprentices, whereas in fifteenth-century

Barcelona, a quarter of apprentices started between ten and fifteen years of age.[25] The Ospedale degli Innocenti in fifteenth-century Florence placed out boys and girls for apprenticeship and household service at the age of six or seven.[26] In Italian cities and among the middle classes there were numerous 'little servants', girls as young as eight, whose masters owed them only a dowry (a bed, linen and clothing) when they reached marriageable age, usually sixteen. In 1428, a poverty-stricken sharecropper gave his three daughters, aged eleven, twelve and fourteen, to three different citizens in Pisa. Perhaps he received some money in exchange, a kind of clandestine sale of children.[27]

According to Danièle Alexandre-Bidon, in the Middle Ages, 'working children were an undeniable social reality', with children constituting a supplementary work force.[28] However, as virtually all evidence is drawn from feudal societies, the validity of such a conclusion in non-feudal peasant societies remains an open question. Peasant children perform various tasks for their parental households in Swedish medieval, hagiographic miracles, whereas the feudal practice of taking young boys as pages was found in the upper echelons of society: the son of a scrivener in the castle of Stockholm was a servant in a noble household at the age of ten.[29] Thralls, or slaves, were used in Scandinavia until the early fourteenth century,[30] but we can only guess how much labour was required of thrall children in medieval farmsteads in the north.

Given the patchy nature of the evidence, conclusions remain equivocal. Ivy Pinchbeck's and Margaret Hewitt's discussion of late medieval child labour serves as an example. They quote an English statute of 1388 – associated with a scarcity of labour after the great plague – which ordained that any boy or girl '... which used to labour at the Plough or Cart, or other Labour or Service or Husbandry till they be of Age of Twelve Years, that from thenceforth they shall abide by the same Labour, without being put to any ... Handicraft'. They conclude that 'the assumption that labourers' children were "used to labour at the Plough or Cart" under the age of twelve itself suggests that probably few of them had other opportunities'. However, they also quote landowners who, at the same time, begged the king to ordain that 'no bondman nor bondwoman shall place their children at schools, as has been done, so as to advance their children in the world by their going into the Church'. Such regulations were re-enacted, which, as Pinchbeck and Hewitt agree, shows that it was difficult to enforce them.[31] But does not this fact itself suggest that labourers' and bondmen's children had other opportunities than the plough and the cart?

From the early sixteenth to the early nineteenth century, inequality in living standards increased in Europe, in real terms even more than in nominal terms, according to Philip Hoffman, David Jacks, Patricia Levin and Peter Lindert. The prices of staple foods, consumed by the poor, 'rose much more than the prices of what the rich consumed'. The relative cost of 'a high-income lifestyle' declined in England and France, while 'the relative cost-of-living hardship of being poor' was particularly felt before 1650 and again after 1750. What is important here is that in the early modern centuries in Europe, the price of unskilled labour fell, and the costs of keeping servants also declined. 'So the lower the real wages sank before 1820, the cheaper became high-income lifestyle', whereas 'the poor faced growing scarcities of food, housing and land'.[32] This opens up interesting perspectives on the new educational ideals among the upper ranks and the bourgeoisie, on the one hand, and the frequency of child labour on the other. It suggests that the élite could afford more of the luxury services of private tutors and governesses, and the bourgeoisie or middle class more educational services for their children, while the poor found it difficult to meet the expense of life-sustaining staples. How much did this contribute to the supply of child labour?

The State and the propertied classes emerged as promoters of child labour in early modern Europe, and in the last decades of sixteenth-century Elizabethan England it was explicitly encouraged by the relevant legislation. In practice, it was used in industries, even though at times the policy failed because of 'regular seasonal unemployment and, in the towns, lack of employment of children', as Pinchbeck and Hewitt put it. According to Hugh Cunningham, it was the idleness of children that 'worried contemporaries, and had been worrying them since at least the sixteenth century'. He argues that, in England, spinning schools were a response to the idleness of children. A contemporary clergyman, R.G. Bouyer, urging the establishment of spinning schools, complained that 'children, until they become thirteen or fourteen years old, *at least*, continue to be nurtured in idleness…'.[33] This suggests that the demand for and perhaps also the supply of child labour was limited.

Placed in a longer time perspective, nineteenth-century child labour appears as a legacy of *ancien régime* labour policies, moulded and eventually abandoned by the new economic and political order. It is often associated with factory children, a dominant form of child labour in England, but agriculture was probably the largest employer of children in most of Europe. For example, in 1882 there were 291,300 children aged under fifteen in agriculture and gardening in Germany, which was more than double the number of children in manufacturing, mining and construction (143,300).[34] Per Bolin-Hort argues that, in Britain, 'early wage labour was a fact of life for most working class children',[35] but was that so? According to other scholars, 'it looks as if by 1870 the percentage of children aged five to nine in England

and Wales who were gainfully employed was less than 1 per cent of the age group'.[36] If this was the case in England, then there is surely reason to ask whether young children's work was equally rare in the rest of Europe.

The phenomenon of child labour could be approached schematically from the perspective of supply and demand, or in terms of the institutional, cultural and general socio-economic factors conditioning supply and demand. One influential approach in historical writing on child labour in Europe sees the curbing of the demand for child labour and the introduction of compulsory education as decisive, giving the State a prime role in the making of 'the new childhood'.[37] This approach is supported by Hugh Cunningham, Harry Hendrick, Michael Lavalette, Pierre Pierrard, Lee Shai Weissbach and Myron Weiner, for example. Even though Per Bolin-Hort, Colin Heywood and Eric Hopkins put forward a variety of approaches, they seem to belong to this tradition, too, because of the emphasis they give to the role of State actions and the efficient implementation of child-labour laws. Göran Therborn, although not a historian of child labour, must be added to the list because of his firm belief in the law: 'Law ... is a major determinant of childhood.'[38] Contributions following this approach focus on factors outside of production, such as actions taken by public authorities, educational professionals, progressive persons and charity organisations; working-class culture; the motivations for and attitudes of parents to setting children to work; and, most importantly, the family economy. Despite the fact that curbing the demand is presented as crucial, much of the discussion deals more with the reasons behind the supply.[39]

A slightly different line of reasoning, directly inspired by Ariès' idea of the discovery of childhood, interprets the disappearance of child labour mainly as an outcome of a new concept of childhood. The promoters of this interpretation, including Bengt Sandin and Viviana Zelizer, argue that child labour came to be regarded as a social evil because it did not conform to the new sensitivity towards children or to the new ideal of 'proper' or 'normal' childhood, manifested in the victory of school over work. The enactment of child-labour laws would then appear to be an outcome of the new idea of childhood.[40] Cultural factors are dominant in this approach.

Some Western historians have recently come to the conclusion that it is time to rehabilitate the factory child. The vanguards have been Clark Nardinelli with his eulogy on industrial child labour, which according to him liberated children from being exploited by parents, and Viviana Zelizer with her plea for a new 'campaign *for* child labour'.[41] This new turn in a long discourse raises the question why intellectuals at times argue against, and at other times for child labour.

Family composition and household strategies have been at the core of historical writing on child labour for over a quarter of a century, if we start from Tamara Hareven's *Family Time and Industrial Time*.[42] Applying a neoclassic model, Clark Nardinelli considers child labour even more strictly in the context of family economy.[43] Today the family-economy approach is established to the point that it offers itself as almost the natural one.[44]

Proto-industrial theory emphasises the role of the family economy and women's and children's contributions to family labour. According to this theory, the supply of and demand for family child labour tend to merge, while the fact that children remain net consumers until their early teens, if not later, appears secondary to the argument. The discussion on the so-called industrious revolution made consumption, rather than production, a key concept of proto-industrial family economy.[45] The theory was derived from A.V. Chayanov's concept of 'self-exploitation' of family labour on family farms, which he presented as part of a more comprehensive theory of non-capitalist economic systems. He argued that 'the degree of self-exploitation is determined by a peculiar equilibrium between family demand satisfaction and the drudgery of labour itself'.[46]

According to the proto-industrial approach, demographic behaviour is the key, particularly the opportunity to marry at an early age and the resulting nuptial fertility. According to Franklin Mendels' original contribution to proto-industrial theory three decades ago, 'the development of labor-intensive industry by peasants made it possible for them to multiply in their villages without corresponding increase in arable surface'.[47] This idea was further elaborated by Hans Medick, who argued that high numbers of children in proto-industrial families meant 'a maximal number of child labourers'.[48] This line of reasoning has been pushed to the limit by Randolph Roth, who suggests that the decline in child murders in New England between 1630 and 1800 resulted, among other things, from the greater importance of children as a productive resource and, correspondingly, the rise in child murders between 1800 and 1900 from the smaller significance of child labour for the family economy.[49]

The Swedish historians Bo Malmberg and Lena Sommestad connect child labour, past and present, with child abundance and the state of poverty. They argue that population growth is followed by an age transition that first leads to a high child-dependency rate, a demographic 'child phase'. Historically, England entered the 'child phase' around 1800, Sweden from the 1820s. According to Malmberg and Sommestad, in nineteenth-century Sweden, 'child labour was widespread during the child phase, and regional analyses indicate that the incidence of child labour peaked in different regions when the proportion of children in the population was at its highest', and further that the proportion of children in Swedish counties was 'strongly correlated' with the poverty rate. They conclude: 'Today, when child labour is no longer an issue in Sweden and other ageing countries, child labour has instead become very important in poor countries in Africa, Asia and Latin America, where child dependency rates are still high.'[50]

Such generalisations may have a heuristic value but they need to be qualified. First, Swedish studies of poverty at the local level suggest that the rural poor were typically old persons living alone, or widows with children, while married couples with children were not dominant, even though large families were more likely than small ones to be found among the poor.[51] Second, the line of reasoning pursued by Malmberg and Sonnestad approaches child labour from the supply side only, while ignoring the demand side. Implicitly, it assumes either that supply creates its demand or that the demand for some other reason matches the supply. Furthermore, they offer no explanation for the recent return of child labour in 'ageing countries', from Britain to Russia.

The approaches presented above direct our interest towards the supply of rather than the demand for child labour. An alternative approach calls attention to the demand from employers, rather than the reasons behind the supply. Jane Humphries, following Carolyn Tuttle and Christine MacLeod, emphasises that 'the technological innovations of the industrial revolution, particularly in the textile industries, were designed to increase the employment of children not only as helpers but also as substitutes for adult works in the principle process.'[52] The Swedish historian Lars Olsson discusses the demand for industrial child labour in terms of changes in the organisation of production, technology, productivity, management, and the relations between capital and labour. Here, family strategies are of less interest than managerial strategies. Olsson is critical of any effect of child-labour laws or governmental interventions, while changes in attitudes, say, awakening compassion or sensitivity, are useless in explaining the decline of industrial child labour.[53] Parallels between past and present child labour have also been approached from the demand side.[54] Furthermore, the widespread use of child labour in poorer countries today and the recent return of waged child labour in many European countries challenge received ideas.

* * *

This book focuses on working children and the demand for child labour. Since much of the historical writing on child labour, particularly concerning Britain and France,[55] has dealt at length with the nineteenth-century debate about industrial child labour, as well as with the question of whether or not the relevant legislation was crucial for its disappearance, such well-known issues are considered here only briefly. For more than twenty years now numerous scholarly contributions applying the family-history or proto-industrial approach have highlighted various aspects of the role of child labour in the context of the family economy. Therefore it seems that little remains to be said about this issue. Studies on household and family strategies have delved into the factors behind the supply of child labour, but have often passed lightly over the demand for children in the labour market. To complete the picture, child labour is discussed in this book chiefly in terms of demand, while the supply is treated in the context of farm labour.

'Child labour' primarily means here the work children do in the labour market, rather than in their parental household. However, children's work in or for their parental household embodies borderline cases. The theory of proto-industrialisation suggests that, in market-oriented cottage or home industries, children may have been seen first as a labour force. In the context of present-day child labour, a Council of Europe study group defines work as 'all activities done by children ... which provide a necessary contribution to the family or the child or lead to profit for a third party'.[56] The merit of this definition is that it implicitly refers to demand too.

The groups of child workers that are discussed here include hired children, children who worked for their keep, and children who were forced to work, such as indentured and workhouse children. The economic activities performed as family work, where children may have been considered sources of labour first and children second, include market-oriented cottage or home industries, children of tenant farmers and underlings who performed labour services for their landlord, and children used like farm servants on family farms. Nevertheless, since children's work in their parental household is not of central interest, the family and household are given relatively little attention here.

Some of the jobs done by children in their parental household are not discussed here, including gentry children's work, looking after younger siblings, and household chores. Gentry children in country manors may have done some productive work: for example, in the summer of 1800 in south-eastern Finland, thirteen-year-old Jacobina Charlotta Munsterhjelm and her nine-year-old sister Beata – as we read in Jacobina's diary – sowed peas, radishes and marigolds, planted strawberries and weeded in the kitchen garden, and in winter carded, spun, spooled and sewed.[57] Looking after younger siblings to allow 'other family members to be productively employed' has often been defined as child labour. This appears justified, given that the job was often tedious for older siblings.[58] Nevertheless, it tends to water down the concept of child labour. For example, it was considered natural in Scandinavian towns and cities in working-class quarters that child care was provided by older children taking their younger siblings with them to play when the mothers were working away from home.[59] During the centuries dealt with in this book, household chores were very different from today. What appears to us now to have been child labour was for contemporaries ordinary household work, and in this sense comparable to present-day household chores performed by children in middle-class homes.[60]

The concept of 'child' suggests an age criterion. Ages such as seven, twelve, fourteen, fifteen and eighteen have been recognised as turning points in Europe for centuries.[61] For example, the age of seven has been thus recognised among peasants from Spain and France to Scotland, Sweden and Russia.[62] Such widely-applied ages were probably not just cultural constructions but were connected to the child's physical, cognitive and intellectual maturing. Nor were they only characteristic of Christian Europe. For example, Chinese scholars and educational institutions recognised fairly similar ages. Under the Han dynasty about 2000 years ago, the boy was thought ready to begin elementary education at the age of eight *sui* (seven years), the study of the 'Five Classics' took place between the ages of ten and fifteen *sui*, and the study of Confucian classics between the ages of fifteen and eighteen *sui*. In late imperial China, the girl was thought to come into her reproductive capacities at the age of fourteen *sui*, the boy at sixteen *sui*.[63]

The notion of 'children' here refers to boys and girls aged under fifteen years, unless the sources used give other age limits, which in most cases vary between fourteen and sixteen. Fifteen years was established as the age limit for children in international comparisons in the second half of the twentieth century,[64] but fifteen years enjoys historical backing too. After turning fifteen, a young person in the early modern kingdom of Sweden, which covered a much larger geographical area than the Sweden of today, was judicially competent to enter into an employment contract, and became subject to the poll tax. In the early modern kingdom of Denmark too, which then included Norway, individuals were entered in the poll-tax registers at the age of fifteen. First communion (confirmation), which took place between fourteen and sixteen, came to mark the end of childhood in early modern Protestant Germany and Scandinavia, and after this a young person was fit for proper farm service.[65] Correspondingly, in traditional English society, according to David Levine, children at the age of fifteen 'began to leave home to become boarders, lodgers, or servants ...'. Early modern English musters counted males over sixteen years, and in Scotland in the 1690s, children under the age of sixteen were exempted from the poll tax.[66]

Should we talk of boys and girls, rather than children? First, there is a major practical problem that many sources refer to children without specifying their sex – which may be indicative. In languages such as French, Italian and Spanish, sex can often be deduced from the grammatical gender, but this is not possible when children are referred to in the neuter, as is often the case in German and Scandinavian sources, and even less when the language has no grammatical gender, as is the case with Finnish. Second, even though the division of labour by sex was known everywhere, and was certainly relevant for children too, many forms of child labour were common for boys and girls. Both boys and girls spun in workhouses, orphanages and manufactories, in cottage industries all family members were involved in production, piecers could be both boys and girls in cotton mills, both boys and girls were used for herding in agriculture, both boys and girls sold newspapers in cities. There were certainly jobs that were reserved exclusively for boys, and the range of occupations available to girls was more limited. Nevertheless, as long as they were regarded as children, the division of labour between boys and girls appears to have been more flexible than in the case of adolescents or the adult labour force.

Paradigmatic cases of child labour in Europe have been offered by nineteenth-century Britain, France and Germany, the then leading economic powers. The received picture is completed below by examples of child labour in Italy and Spain in the south, Russia in the north-east, and the Scandinavian countries[67] in the north. The long-term perspective, starting from c.1600, serves to highlight the controversial role of the State and the establishment as promoters of child labour. To undermine sweeping generalisations of the kind suggesting that, in the past, parents in poor families readily set children to work at a tender age, contrasting cases are presented: poor parents who refused to send their children out to do arduous work and children of the poorest families who had plenty of time for play and no heavy labour burden. Only brief discussion is given to well-worn topics such as child labour in the British textile mills and the introduction of child-labour laws.

Focusing on child labour necessarily implies that élite and solid middle-class children receive very limited attention. Yet it is essential to keep in mind children who never worked if we are to understand why, at a given point in time, some children worked while others played or received school instruction. Access to formal education has for centuries been crucial in streaming children into different life courses. Children's educational opportunities under the *ancien régime*, during the agricultural and industrial revolutions and during the urbanisation period are thus briefly overviewed.

Chapter 1 presents child labour in early modern manufacturing work. It was far from the dominant form of child labour, but it begins the story because children performing industrial work in charitable and penal institutions, and in manufactories, was an innovation of early modern Europe.[68] The chapter first takes up the issue of massive early modern warfare, which Ariès chose largely to ignore (was it because the Second World War was so fresh in the 1950s?). It is suggested that warfare had an impact on children's workload in many parts of Europe and, furthermore, may have contributed to the readiness to set children to work. Compulsory child labour in workhouses and orphanages serve as examples of unfree labour, so characteristic of early modern Europe. The changing conditions of urban crafts are then briefly touched on, particularly concerning the introduction of the system of parish paupers apprenticed with crafts masters. Manufactories applying the division of labour are given as examples of new kinds of industrial child labour, new compared with medieval crafts. The discussion then moves on to developments according to which education or schooling became consolidated as élite and bourgeois strategies for social distinction and upward social mobility. At the other extreme were the schools offered for the lower classes, such as pauper schools and different kinds of work schools. Finally, tentative explanations for the more intensive use of child labour are discussed. Since there is very little direct evidence of parental attitudes among the labouring population, this question is mostly left open. The attitudes of the establishment, on the other hand, deserve critical comment.

Chapter 2 deals with peasant children as a labour force in pre-industrial Europe. The manpower policy of early modern states is first briefly outlined. Institutional factors, such as feudal dues and mercantilist labour policies are presented as relevant for children's farm work in continental Europe. Three forms of peasant children's work are then discussed. The first is herding, which seems to have changed from being chiefly men's work in medieval Europe to chiefly children's work by the early nineteenth century. The second issue to be taken up is life-cycle service and the use of children as servants. The aim is to qualify the idea, derived from early contributions to family history (by John Hajnal, Peter Laslett and Michael Anderson, for instance), that parents routinely sent their children into service at an early age. The third example of peasant children's labour consists of cottage industry and proto-industry. It seems that these three forms of child labour underwent interesting changes during the early modern centuries. In terms of peasant children's opportunities for education, it is suggested that contemporaries saw them as being of relatively little interest, since school education was still clearly secondary, compared with landed property, in establishing social distinctions, nor did it serve well for upward social mobility. Two questions close the chapter. When did time-consuming jobs became children's domain in the rural labour market? What was the workload of peasant children in early modern Europe?

Chapter 3 focuses on child labour during the agricultural revolution. First, the changing composition of rural labour force (away from living-in servants to more flexible labour) and the increasing economic and social stratification are briefly discussed. Several types of agricultural child labour are considered. The first covers indentured and farmed-out child workers, in other words foundlings and abandoned children, in southern Europe and Russia, and parish pauper children in England, Germany and Scandinavia. The second concerns farm work typically done by children in different countries, including work by peasant farmers' own children, and 'outside' children – who in this context include employed children as well as children of underlings and tenant farmers who had to contribute to the labour service. As far as educational opportunities are concerned, it is suggested that the potentials of school education began to dawn upon country people during the nineteenth century. Lastly, the treatment of peasant farmers' own children and 'outside' children is compared, and questions to do with the amount and intensity of agricultural child labour are raised.

Chapter 4 then deals with child labour in manufacturing industry, on which subject thousands of pages were written in the nineteenth century. This well-worn subject is considered here from the perspective of labour productivity and employers' efforts to cut labour costs. The demand for industrial child labour is connected with the availability of adult workers for factory work. The industries covered are those that employed the largest numbers of children in their respective countries. Industrial child labour was concentrated in a limited number of sectors (about a dozen), which suggests that we should take a closer look at the demand. As the textile industry, alone or together with clothing, was generally the largest or second largest employer of children, it still deserves attention, although the focus here is away from the most familiar case of Britain. The other industries taken up include mining (again mostly outside Britain), metalwork and machinery, paper, glass and brick manufacture, and tobacco and match production. Educational opportunities are discussed with reference to the role of compulsory education in the decrease in industrial child labour. Contemporary ideas are compared with the current view that child-labour legislation was a series of steps towards abolition. Finally, it is suggested that increasing consciousness of productivity, promoted by factors such as profitability problems during the period of long deflation in the second half of the nineteenth century, may offer some explanation for the decline of child labour and the increase in school enrolment.

Chapter 5 moves amidst busy urban life. Migrant child workers are presented as a small, vulnerable group among the young labour migrants who typified urban life. Examples of urban working-class children, boys in particular, earning money by a variety of means in the street and public places are given from various cities. Similarly the harsh policy adopted in Britain concerning children's activities in the street had its counterparts in many countries. The familiar story about the conflict between the school authorities and working-class families over the use of children's time is completed with examples of school schedules rather yielding to the requirements of children's work outside school. Urban home industries, or urban putting-out work (outwork), is touched upon briefly. Here, again, the educational perspective concerns streaming. As a conclusion, typical jobs for children in urban service sectors are considered in the light of the growing importance of services in the economy at large.

Chapter 6 first discusses the breakthrough of compulsory education in twentieth-century Europe. The forms of child labour discussed in the previous chapters largely disappeared from Europe during the two decades between the First and Second World Wars. It is suggested that the two great wars were something of watersheds in this respect. After the Second World War it was generally believed that school was the proper place for children of all social strata, while child labour was thought to belong to the past. It was expected to disappear altogether once the last pockets of poverty had been removed. The future proved different. In the last decades of the twentieth century, Western high-consumption societies witnessed a return of waged child labour. Since this is a recent phenomenon, it is too early to speculate whether it is the beginning of a new phase in the history of child labour, or of childhood. Time will tell.

The concluding chapter summarises the four centuries of child labour in the light of the sporadic and casual examples drawn here from the history of ten European countries. What strikes the mind is that the story could be told in terms of similarities as well as differences. From the historical perspective, child labour in these societies share the same large-scale contours, whereas a closer look reveals great differences in detail. Nevertheless, for all the differences, three general conclusions may be drawn. First, child labour has been strongly connected to adult workers' freedom to choose their work. Second, the forms of child labour and the terms of employment seem to have anticipated changes in adult labour and the labour market. Third, child labour has been closely connected to the lives and options of children who never worked, in other words middle-class and upper-class children. Finally, by way of closing the chapter on four centuries of child labour, the question is raised whether Ariès' *Centuries of Childhood* was the first sign that the owl of Minerva would soon be circulating over the childhood that emerged with the bourgeoisie of early modern Europe.

This book is primarily a contribution to the history of labour, but it could also be read as an alternative story of the emergence of modern Western childhood.

Notes

1.   Ariès 1962, p. 336 (Ariès 1960, p. 376).
2.   One of the best reviews of the discussion is offered by Pollock 1983, pp. 1–32. A more recent resumé is to be found in Becchi and Julia (1998). Other recent contributions include Cunningham, H. 1992; Cunningham, H. 1995; Hendrick 1997; Heywood 2001; Lönnqvist 1992.
3.   Julia 1998, pp. 301–312; Lagerlöf-Génetay 1990, pp. 22, 35–39, 47; Liliequist, J. 1991, p. 399; Roper 2000.
4.   Alexandre-Bidon and Closson 1985; Alexandre-Bidon and Lett 1997; Finucane 1997; Krötzl 1989; Le Roy Ladurie 1990; Myrdal 1994; Shahar 1992; Österberg 1991, pp. 47–53.
5.   Collected Works of Erasmus 1985, pp. 269–346; Machiavelli 1980 [1514], pp. 88–108. See also Alexandre-Bidon and Lett 1997, pp. 43–45, 107–111; Niccoli 1995, pp. 80, 91–111, 129–133; Pullan 1988, pp. 185–186; Shahar 1992, pp. 208–220.
6.   Engel 1978; Flandrin 1980, pp. 138–140; Levi 1988; Ozment 1983, pp. 132–144; Ozment 1990, p. 283; Petschauer 1984; Pollock 1989; Sarti 2002, pp. 42–49; Tovrov 1978.
7.   Casey 1999, p. 71.
8.   Brugger von Nesslau 1991, pp. 137–160; Locke, J. 1988 [1693]; See autobiographies of, e.g., Benjamin 1987; Dönhoff 1988, p. 75; Fraser 1984; Ramsay 1949 [1904].
9.   Caspard 1998, quotations p. 697; Sarti 2002, pp. 58–61.
10. E.g. Ariès 1962, pp. 318–335; Horn 1978, pp. 116–117; Houston 2002, pp. 17–21; Reeder 1998, pp. 104–105.
11. Uhlig 1978, p. 89.
12. Barbagli 1982, p. 51.
13. N. Catan 1971, cited in Weber 1976, pp. 170–171 (note †).
14. Shorter 1977, p. 172.
15. Fuchs, R. 1984, p. 5; Vassberg 1998, p. 445.
16. Rustemeyer 1996, p. 39 (note 79).
17. Enders 1995, pp. 106–107.
18. Cited by Pablo Wiking-Faria in Myrdal 1988, pp. 20–21. See also Larsson 1995.
19. Raussi 1966 [c.1850], p. 317. Eljas Raussi was born in 1800 in a peasant family in Virolahti (see Moring 1999, pp. 164, 174).
20. Hobsbawm 1974, p. 322n.
21. See the discussion in Pollock 1983, pp. 10, 70.

22. See autobiographic writings by, e.g., George Orwell 1953, James Joyce 1993 [1916], Ronald Fraser 1984.
23. Finucane 1997, pp. 103–105, 111; Shahar 1992, pp. 242–247.
24. Blanchard 1984, pp. 245–258.
25. Bonnaissie 1975, pp. 79–80; Shahar 1992, p. 226.
26. Gavitt 1997, p. 241.
27. Klapisch-Zuber 1985, pp. 106–107.
28. Alexandre-Bidon and Lett 1997, p. 95.
29. Myrdal 1994.
30. Martinson 1992, pp. 41–42; Nevéus 1974. A child followed his or her thrall mother's status, even if the father was a free-born man. A free-born father could liberate his unfree child.
31. Pinchbeck and Hewitt 1969, pp. 22–23.
32. Hoffman, Jacks, Levin and Lindert 2002, quotations pp. 323, 335, 340.
33. Cunningham, H. 1990, quotation p. 127; Cunningham, H. 1992, pp. 18–30, quotation p. 21; Pinchbeck and Hewitt 1969, quotation pp. 98–99.
34. Deutsch 1907, p. 67.
35. Bolin-Hort 1989, p. 9.
36. Hendrick 1997, p. 65.
37. E.g. Cunningham, H. 2000; Heywood 1988, pp. 126, 217–236, 260–286; Hendrick 1992.
38. Therborn 1993, p. 243.
39. Bolin-Hort 1989; Cunningham, H. 1990; Cunningham, H. 1995; Cunningham, H. 2000; Hendrick 1990; Hendrick 1992; Hendrick 1994; Heywood 1988; Hopkins 1994; Lavalette 1994; Pierrard 1987; Weissbach 1989.
40. Sandin 1995; Zelizer 1985; See also Davin 1982; Therborn 1993.
41. Nardinelli 1990, p. 102; Zelizer 1985, p. 221, emphasis original. See also Lavalette 1999, pp. 17, 36–42.
42. Hareven 1975.
43. Nardinelli 1980; Nardinelli 1990, pp. 36, 41.
44. Examples include, e.g Borrás Llop 1996, p. 246, Davin 1996; Horrell and Oxley 1999.
45. de Vries 1994a.
46. Chayanov 1966, pp. 5–8, quotation p. 6.
47. Mendels 1972, p. 252.
48. Medick 1976, pp. 304–305; Kriedte, Medick and Schlumbohm 1981, pp. 37–73, 80–93.
49. Roth 2001.
50. Malmberg and Sommestad 2000, pp. 132–138, quotations pp. 136–137.
51. Gerger 1992, pp. 103–123, 139–140; Lundsjö 1975, pp. 86–141; Persson 1992, pp. 265–273; Sandberg and Steckel 1988; Sandberg and Steckel 1990; Söderberg 1978, pp. 99–108, 162–170; Söderberg 1989. See also Winberg 1978.
52. Humphries 2003, p. 258.
53. Olsson, L. 1980; Rahikainen 2001b; Rahikainen 2002b.
54. Rahikainen 2001a.
55. E.g. Cunningham, H. 1992; Cunningham, H. 1995; pp. 134–162; Hendrick 1992; Hendrick 1994; Heywood 1988; Heywood 2001, pp. 134–144; Hopkins 1994; Weissbach 1989.
56. Children and work in Europe 1996, p. 13.

57. [Munsterhjelm] 1970 [orig. 1799–1801], pp. 29, 34, 46, 56–61, 64–65, 75, 80–81.
58. See, e.g. Davin 1996, pp. 88–107; Cunningham, H. 1990, quotation p. 118; Pollack 2002.
59. E.g. Andersen 1985, pp. 158–160; Bjurman 1995, p. 127; Lönnqvist 1992, p. 281.
60. Children in Nordic (Scandinavian) middle-class families contribute considerably to household chores, see, e.g., Solberg 1990.
61. Ariès 1962, pp. 21–25, 115, 153–162, 181, 194–196, 202, 210–211, 238, 300–305; Davis 1975, pp. 24, 107–113; Le Roy Ladurie 1990, pp. 213–217; Mitterauer 1993, pp. 50–59; Niccoli 1995, pp. 6–13; Pastor 1994, p. 45–48; Pinchbeck and Hewitt 1969, pp. 8–13; Rossi 1985, p. 63; Shahar 1992, pp. 23–31, 175–176; Tovrov 1978, 22–24; Trinidad Fernández 1996, p. 462.
62. Brembeck 1986, p. 48; Borderies-Guereña 1996; Heywood 1988, pp. 19, 62; Robson 1984, pp. 74, 82; Semyonova Tian-Shanskaia 1993 [1914], pp. 33, 36.
63. Furth 1995; Kinney 1995; Hung 1995.
64. E.g. Children and work in Europe 1996, pp. 12–14.
65. Brembeck 1986, p. 27; Ehlers 1991; Gaunt 1983, pp. 25, 114–115; Harnesk 1990, p. 13; Jacobsson 2000, pp. 44–47; Johansson, E. 1991; Krogh 1987, p. 71; Löfgren 1974 (note 9); Mitterauer 1993, pp. 52–54; Moring 1996; Nygård 1989, pp. 146–149; Sandin 1988; Schlumbohm 1994, p. 324; Weber-Kellermann 1979, p. 55; Weber-Kellermann 1987, pp. 186–187.
66. Levine 1977, p. 44; Overton 1996, p. 41; Whyte and Whyte 1983.
67. Scandinavia here means Denmark, Norway, Sweden and Finland, which was part of the kingdom of Sweden until 1809.
68. See Chassagne 1998, pp. 236–238.

CHAPTER 1

Children in Early Modern Manufacturing

Children and war

The endemic early modern warfare had many consequences for children and their work, while communities pressed or ruined by wars must have provided a barren soil for any new sensitivity to children. Neither did the obligation or compulsion of the children of the poor to work give proof of such sensitivity. From the perspective of child labour, these two phenomena, war and compulsion, were more typical of the early modern centuries than any signs of the discovery of childhood, as Ariès presented them. The question raised below concerns whether early modern warfare brought with it not only an increase in the amount of child labour, but also long-term implications for its practise.

War was present in children's lives in many ways in different parts of Europe. Peasant households in Castile had to bear the scourge of billeting the Spanish troops when they were stationed in the Iberian peninsula.[1] Similarly, Russian peasants (serfs) had to billet soldiers in their homes.[2] In France, many women followed their husbands to war and took their children with them, so among armies lived children 'who were thus prepared from childhood to the profession of arms' (S. Loriga). In Adam Smith's time, soldiers' children in Scotland appear to have lived in and around the soldiers' barracks.[3] During the Thirty Years' War (1618–1648), civilian mortality was extremely high in the German regions where the troops moved, as refugees from the ravaged countryside crowded into the towns and cities, where they succumbed to epidemic diseases and hunger.[4] Bologna, although far from the battlefields, nonetheless suffered from devastating epidemics and an economic crisis in the period 1619–1633. This was followed by tensions and conflicts in social relationships. Such hardships probably provoked the rough treatment of children and led to cases of children involved in theft and mendicancy or living the life of a vagabond outside their families. The family of Domenico di Vinceso Ferrarese, aged about twelve, succumbed during the epidemic. The lonely, orphaned boy lived as a vagabond until he managed to hire himself out as a cowherd to a widow, Caterina Pancalda, in San Gioseffe.[5]

The early series of larger battles in the Thirty Years' War took place in Bohemia. Did the movements of the armies drive the German countryside into confusion, so that a new labour market for migrant children emerged? Johan Conrad Kostner, the administrator (*Pfleger*) of the castle of Bludenz, reported to the government in Innsbruck in 1625 that, in spring, many children wandered from the poorest valleys of Vorarlberg to work in Ravensburg and Überlingen (north of Bodensee) and other places, returning home at Martinmas in November.[6] These children anticipated eighteenth- and nineteenth-century seasonal labour migration by children from Voralberg (see Chapters 2 and 3).

Absolutist states 'were machines built overwhelmingly for the battlefield', as Perry Anderson puts it.[7] The kingdom of Sweden was a prime example of this. Sweden was the first country in Europe with obligatory service in the armed forces. After 1620, when Sweden became involved in wars on the Continent, conscription was almost an annual event. To save their sons from being conscripted, people bribed the clergy who kept the population registers, and in order to confuse them, parents gave several sons the same name or lied about their birth years. Boys close to the minimum age for military conscription, fifteen years, did not turn up for their first communion, and youngsters who had passed the critical age were still insistently called boys. People also sometimes claimed that the boy or man concerned was dead. Schoolboys escaped conscription, and therefore many boys in towns clung to school, staying as many as eight years in the lowest form, for instance.[8]

Acquiring substitutes became a well-established practice in the kingdom of Sweden. In the Finnish part of the kingdom, in the province of Pohjanmaa (Österbotten, or Ostrobothia), the price for a substituting man rose so high that it corresponded to the price of a holding or what a male farmhand could expect to earn in thirteen or fourteen years. Therefore peasants began to purchase sons of parish paupers to bring up as conscripts. The trade in substituting boys became extensive, and in the 1660s and 1680s small boys were even imported from Swedish parishes to Pohjanmaa. What the parents received varied according to the boy's age: the younger, the cheaper, thus even two-year-old boys were bought. The price may have been just half a barrel of rye, but if the boy had already turned fifteen, the purchaser typically gave his parents or parent a cow and a barrel of grain. It was even cheaper to take an orphaned or deprived boy in the neighbourhood as a foster child and a future conscript. Purchased boys were sometimes sold to other peasants, or even stolen from other peasants. A purchased boy or a foster child worked in his buyer's household as a shepherd or cowherd, and later as a farm hand, until he left for war.[9]

Russian peasants who could afford it bought themselves out of conscription, while serf owners sold substitutes from among their peasants for high prices. To save their sons from being conscripted, parents sometimes made them crippled while they were still infants. However, infirm serfs risked being exiled to Siberia by their lords who wanted to save good workers from being conscripted. Serf owners received quittances for men exiled to Siberia and used them at the next conscription to meet the recruitment obligation.[10] In France, the pay for a substituting man was equivalent to ten years' pay of an agricultural worker, and the rich in particular resorted to replacements, although in the nineteenth century even peasant parents resorted to *marchand d'hommes* who provided substitutes.[11]

As men were sent to war, the workload of women and children grew. According to Jan Lindegren, who conducted a study on the parish of Bygdeå in northern Sweden, the peasant community survived because 'the men who were left and the women, children and old people worked harder'. The archipelago had to supply men for the Swedish navy, so in Åland as many as half of the male farm servants were, quite exceptionally, young boys aged between twelve and fourteen.[12] When manpower became scarce, noble masters in Sweden introduced the idea of bonded service by children. In 1651, the Estate of Nobility proposed that people in towns and cities who took a child as a servant or apprentice ought to have the right to be served by the child for as many years over the age of ten as the child had been under it when taken. The first proper Swedish Hired Labour Act (*tjänstehjonsstadga*) of 1664 then stipulated that if a master or mistress had at his or her own expense taught someone in crafts or book-keeping, that person was to serve the master until he was 'reasonably satisfied'. Correspondingly, the Hired Labour Act of 1723 stipulated that if a master had agreed to raise a poor man's child, and kept him as his servant or as a substitute for military conscription, then the boy had to serve his master 'until the troubles and costs he had caused to the master' had been met. A contemporary would even have given the master the right to sell his surplus young indentured servants.[13]

During the Great Northern War (1700–1721), the subordinated peasantry in Denmark were ordered to provide soldiers aged from fourteen years up.[14] To meet the shortage of men, the Swedish authorities began to send deprived and orphaned boys to war. This happened to thirteen-year-old Hindrich in 1713, near Helsinki. The same year Russian troops occupied Sweden's Finnish provinces. They captured Jacob, a ten-year-old dragoon's son, in Helsinki and put him to serve a Russian Major. A much harsher fate awaited the Finnish boys and girls taken by the occupying forces to Russia, where they were set to work on the construction of the newly-founded St Petersburg, or put in the

Russian army, and some ended in the slave market for Persia. Very few ever found their way back home.[15] One man did manage to return in 1737, and even established himself as an heir to a farm owner under the false identity – like Martin Guerre in the French Pyrenees – of Jaakko Jouppila, a landed peasant's only son, abducted by the Russians at the age of thirteen in 1714.[16]

In Peter the Great's victorious Russia, the sons of the nobility owed the state universal service obligations from the age of fourteen to fifteen onwards, according to which two thirds of them had to enter the army, the rest civilian bureaucracy. All boys eligible for the military or civil service were expected to begin training for it in special schools at the age of ten, but this proved impossible to implement. During the Great Northern War the Russian countryside experienced a demographic catastrophe, corresponding to that which Sweden had been through. The forced recruitment of young men into the armed forces and state manufactories threatened to leave Russian villages with only old men, women and children to work the fields. According to David Ransel, this policy contributed to the social displacement of women, and evidently to the proliferation of illegitimate children and infanticide.[17]

During the large and protracted wars at the turn of the eighteenth century, teenage servants in England, including boys and girls aged under fifteen, became more common among emigrant servants in Liverpool.[18] A century later, during the Napoleonic wars, workhouse boys aged thirteen who were tall enough passed for the navy, while others went into the cotton industry. 'For parish overseers, with children to apprentice, wars were blessings sent from heaven', according to L.D. Schwarz. When the war was over, the London workhouses were crowded with children, since there was now very little demand for them. As in other belligerent countries, there were communities in England in which the shortage of an able-bodied male labour force 'could only be met by the greater use of migrant workers and of women and children' (P. Horn).[19]

Military models and discipline found their way into schools and educational institutions in the eighteenth century, thus bellicose ideas even touched children who otherwise remained unaffected by warfare. The idea of military training for orphans, foundlings and soldiers' children spread in Europe.[20] A military academy for noble youths aged between thirteen and eighteen was opened in St Petersburg in 1731. Sons of impoverished noble families were sent at the age of nine or ten to new military boarding schools in France. In 1790 in Prussia, Friedrich August Ludwig v. der Marwitz, a son of a noble estate owner, formally joined a regiment at the age of twelve in order to start accumulating years for his officer's career, and joined the army for real at the age of thirteen: he found it very heavy since for some years he remained physically weak and with a small stature of a child. While in 1810, under French rule, the life of a German orphan boy, Peter Bohlen, totally changed for the better when he was given the opportunity to join the army at the age of fourteen.[21]

What makes early modern warfare part of the history of child labour is the fact that countries engaged in the wars witnessed the substitution of women and children for men. The war-time increase in child labour was well in line with the labour policy supported by an establishment that strove to set or force children of the poor to work. How much did the war contribute to child labour in orphanages, workhouses, workshops and manufactories? Did the war-time use of child labour also promote a more general readiness to encumber children with work?

Orphanages and workhouses

In many parts of Europe the number of poor had increased since the sixteenth century, a process that has been connected with structural changes in the labour market, unemployment, a long-term decline in real wages, and population growth. A new doctrine spread in Europe of prohibiting begging and rescuing the poor from idleness by compelling them to work in charity and penal institutions.[22] It does not seem to have made much difference whether the country was Protestant or Catholic. In fact, Natalie Zemon Davis asks 'whether businessmen and lawyers in European town councils did not, irrespective of their religious convictions, bring their vocational experiences to bear on difficulties of urban life'.[23] The Great Confinement, as it has been called, was met with resistance from the common people, yet there were also parents who left their children in charity hospitals.[24]

This section describes how the new policy was implemented with regard to children. It starts with France, and proceeds roughly in the order in which the new doctrine spread in Europe, ending with the late *ancien régime* German and French charitable institutions, which were rather like manufactories. In the conclusion, it is suggested that there were no major differences in the treatment of children and adults in terms of compulsory work.

Sixteenth-century French *hôpitaux* for orphaned and pauper children adopted the principle of obligatory work by children. In Lyon the presence of children among beggars may have been a new phenomenon, perhaps associated with the population growth. The pauper hospice there turned out foundlings at the age of seven to beg for alms in the street. In the 1530s, following a famine, the authorities established two new *hôpitaux* for about

300 orphans and foundlings who had been removed from the foundling hospital. Most of the boys were apprenticed to artisans, while the girls were put out as serving girls or trained to work in two new industries, silk and fustian.[25]

The largest charity hospital for pauper and illegitimate children in Florence, Spedale degli Innocenti, was originally modelled on monastic lines, but a new policy was introduced in the sixteenth century. Children's morality was to be improved by intensive training for work and by placement in urban workshops. From the age of seven or eight years, boys were sent to the workshops inside the institution to labour for joiners, shoemakers, spinners, weavers or builders, and some children worked in the institution's garden. Girls were either doomed to remain in the institution, or escaped by going into service with a well-to-do family or, the best option, by marriage. Thus girls were trained in textile work and embroidery, which served as an occupation for some. Most children appear to have succeeded in becoming integrated into urban society, according to Luciano Marcello.[26] Nevertheless, with increasing pauperisation and growing numbers of deprived children, a policy striving for socialisation gave way to one of discipline. Persons caught for vagrancy in Florence of 1590 were punished by expulsion and had to leave within three days. For disobedience, men were forced to become galley slaves, and women and children under fifteen years were whipped. In 1653, a more workhouse-like pauper hospice called Quarconia was established for '*monelli*', that is boys aged between eight and eighteen found roving in the streets, uncontrolled by any family.[27] This new institution observed the principle of disciplining the boys through work and religious instruction. The boys were set to cotton scribbling and spinning, and to silk production. They also worked crushing pine kernels ('*stiaccio dei pignoli*'), paid by the piece. For some decades this brought good income to the institution.[28] Rome had seven institutions for children in 1601, twelve in 1698 and twenty-two in 1842, while the number of orphans and foundlings grew from 1,890 to 2,796 and further to 3,546, respectively. A pamphlet published in 1693 (thought to be a Jesuit work) advertised the fact that in the hospice of Ospizio Apostolico, 'all orphans, boys and girls, who would otherwise lead an idle and wasteful life, can subsequently become good servants and workers for the town and labourers in the countryside after they have been educated and brought up to work ...'.[29]

In sixteenth-century England several laws prescribed the necessity to put 'idle children' of the poor to work, while corresponding local schemes characterised the seventeenth century. For example, poor children aged at least between five and seven were engaged in sewing, knitting, lace making, spinning, pin making, card making, spooling or button making. In 1552,

Christ's Hospital ('The Blue-Coat School') was opened in London. In its first year it had 340 children, boys and girls wearing similar blue uniforms, spinning canvas used for clothing and sheets. There was also a shoemaker to train children in the craft. According to Carol Kazmierczak Manzione, in Tudor times children were well fed and dressed, and received basic education. Christ's Hospital apparently put girls out for service, while boys were apprenticed at the age of twelve to sixteen, and a variety of trades were open to them. Hugh Cunningham paints a less favourable picture of the charity and penal institutions in which children worked, at times together with adults. Many such institutions were short-lived. They proved costly, since children produced less than the costs of providing for them, and the products sold badly. Children's earnings were trifling, as in the Bristol workhouse where they were heading pins, or in Stapleton and Gloucestershire where they were spinning flax and hemp. Children in a London workhouse were apprenticed at the age of twelve to fourteen in 1709, and in the Foundling Hospital between the ages of ten and twelve in the 1750s.[30]

The first Danish penal institute was established in Copenhagen in 1605. Following English and Dutch models, this combined a house of correction and a workhouse for children, *Børnehus* ('children's house'), was run as a textile manufactory. After the plague epidemic, in 1621 separate premises were erected for the *Børnehus*, which were intended for orphans and abandoned children but were eventually transformed into a house of correction. In 1632, the two institutions housed some 100 inmates, consisting of men, women and children. Able-bodied, masterless boys who were not schoolboys were sent to the house of correction, and deprived children aged at least six years to the *Børnehus*. The *Børnehus* was a major manufacturer of broadcloth around 1640. The idea was that children would stay at least four years there in order to learn a craft. Between 1620 and 1650, some 400 boys did learn a trade, but in the course of the same three decades as many as 2,300 children died, high mortality apparently being inevitable in all such institutions. The *Børnehus* was closed in 1662.[31] Notwithstanding this failure, in 1670 the Danish king ordered a combined spin-house and orphanage to be built in the city of Christiania (Oslo), but it was not until 1778 that the first orphanage was established for children aged between seven and sixteen. A house of correction was erected in 1738 by order of the Danish king. Its inmates were to be put to cloth production, tanning, tobacco spinning and the like. The house of correction was intended for the 'undeserving' poor, insubordinate servants and children. Until 1771 parents could send undisciplined children there for a shorter or longer time, and even people of standing were said to use this opportunity.[32]

The new doctrine of compulsory child labour had reached Sweden by the 1590s. The most enthusiastic would have liked to have seen a workhouse for children, *barnhus* ('children's house'), in every town where children of the poor would work as soon as they were able. A plan for a *barnhus* in Stockholm was drawn up in 1621 along Danish and English lines. The *barnhus* of Stockholm, the first one in Sweden, started as a combined orphanage-house of correction and a manufactory producing sailcloth (canvas) and broadcloth for the Swedish navy and army. It was intended to lodge 100 children and 50 adult 'rogues, harlots and villains', who would do the rough manual work. Deprived children were to be corrected there in order to be put out at the age of eight to craft work or service, while mischievous children and servant boys were to be placed in the house of correction. With the establishment of the *barnhus* of Stockholm, children became involved in production, to the satisfaction of many contemporaries. It was expected that the institution would be financed by the work of its inmates, but these expectations were never fulfilled, and the financing fell on tax payers.[33]

The number of children in the *barnhus* of Stockholm was initially modest, but the production was increased in 1640 and the number grew to 135, with about as many boys as girls. As a rule, only children able to work, in other words not younger than five or six years, were taken in. Sometimes a desperate mother might apply to place her child there, and in rare cases a child of people of standing was housed. Before the coronation of Queen Christina in October 1650, begging women and children, who were exceptionally numerous because the crops had failed that year, were rounded up to clean the streets of Stockholm. Such round-ups were then repeated several times, when the financial situation of the institution permitted the expansion of production. Two-thirds of the children thus captured were boys, one-third girls, reflecting the situation in the streets and also in the *barnhus* in the 1650s. Many children, boys especially, escaped or tried to escape.[34]

The management of, and daily life in, the *barnhus* of Stockholm followed German models. In 1643 all of the girls and more than two-thirds of the boys worked in spinning, and some boys worked with spooling. In the 1640s, almost all yarn used for sailcloth for the Swedish navy was spun there. The girls span for warp, the boys for weft. The value of the spinning done by the girls was more than double that of the boys, yet the boys were paid more than the girls. Small financial incentives were used to make children work more effectively. They had to pay for their meals out of their earnings, which were often not sufficient for their basic nourishment, however, and they suffered from scurvy. Nevertheless, since they had food, Gustaf Utterström concludes that they must be regarded as privileged poor – which they were compared with their successors in 1810 who, according to a contemporary observer, were starving.[35]

Despite the fact that the cheapest possible labour, children, was used, the production of sailcloth never became profitable, as careful calculations revealed. The Admiralty, under whose supervision the *barnhus* was run, was also dissatisfied with the quality of the cloth, so enthusiasm for *barnhus* work faded. In the late seventeenth century, *barnhus* girls were instructed in stocking and hosiery knitting by German women and an Englishman, and then became out-work knitters for a private putter-out (*Verleger*).[36] The Stockholm *barnhus* then bacame more like an orphanage, while the workhouse continued to house both adults and children aged at least seven until 1884, when the placement of children in the workhouse was replaced by placement with foster parents.[37]

Who were the children sentenced to work in Stockholm? Young Erik Jönsson, the orphaned son of a mason, had escaped from the paupers' hospice of Danviken in 1674. When he was again caught begging, he was first given corporal punishment and put in irons ('*slås järn på*'), and then sent to Leijonancker's broadcloth manufactory.[38] In the early eighteenth century, little Anna Persdotter, who was believed to have been at the witches' Sabbath, was sent to the Danviken hospice, where children were occupied in spinning. Anna Thomasdotter, 'a young, healthy seaman's daughter' from the Danviken paupers' hospice, was found unwilling to work as a servant and was therefore sentenced to corporal punishment and then to Leijonancker's manufactory. Hans Bengtzon, the orphaned son of a seaman, was twice sentenced to the *barnhus* and punished for begging. Caught again in the street, he was whipped and sentenced to Leijonancker's manufactory. Johan Carlsson Swart, another young orphan, had been convicted of begging and was sent first to Danviken and then to the poor house, but he deserted. Again found begging, he was sentenced to flogging, 'to lose his skin from his back' ('*mista Rygghuuden*'), and to work in the house of correction.[39]

The idea of western-style orphanages reached Russia in the 1690s. A decade later, in the midst of the Great Northern War, Tsar Peter the Great took the initiative to built state-sponsored hospitals for illegitimate children. This first order appeared, David Ransel points out, in a decree covering military recruitment and other military affairs, showing 'how closely awareness of child abandonment was bound up with the creation of a standing army ...'. However, it was not until half a century later that the first foundling homes opened in Moscow and St Petersburg. They were modelled on those in Paris and Lyon, and on the *barnhus* of Stockholm. The mortality rates in the Russian foundling homes proved extremely high. Even so, as early as 1796 the administrators could no longer find work in factories or in craftwork for the surviving children. Only a select group, as many as there were placements available for training in crafts and manufacturing, were returned after five years of village care to the city for primary schooling and training in urban skills, to be apprenticed at the age of eight years. Some children were sent to agricultural colonies in thinly-populated outlying provinces – an innovation that did not prove long-lasting. The rest remained in the villages (see Chapter 3).[40]

During the eighteenth century pauper hospitals in central and southern Europe were getting so crowded that the conditions of the inmates presumably deteriorated. For example, the number of inmates in the Ospedale di Carità in Turin, in Piedmont, was still below 600 in the 1720s, while two decades later, in 1740, it was as high as 2,300. The number fell to 1,400 after 1750, but rose again to over 2,000 in the 1770s. As a rule, the Turin hospital accepted only children aged at least seven, since younger ones were regarded as 'useless persons'. In 1758, the majority of children aged between seven and twelve (170 out of a workforce of 921) worked in the woollen workshops, the girls also made stockings and sewed cloth, while the rest worked as cleaners.[41] The number of the poor probably increased in eighteenth-century Spain, and beggars' children appeared to be a problem during the Enlightenment. In 1777 it was ordered that beggar girls should be occupied in spinning and lace-making schools, and boys aged at least ten should be sent to workshops for rope making, the production of military equipment or carpentry at river docks, or put into service as ship's boys or sailors.[42]

The risk of being captured and detained in a *hôpital* varied in eighteenth-century France. The hospital administers in Paris tried the stop the entry of girls younger than twelve years of age. In Lower Normandy, boys from ten to fourteen were arrested more frequently than any other group, while the risk for girls of the same age was much lower. For example, two orphaned brothers, Jean and Pierre Durand, aged ten and twelve, who had wandered from the countryside, were detained in 1728. Yet many desperate children entered the *hôpital* on their own initiative, driven by hunger, while some were deposited by their poverty-stricken parents. For example, in Caen, twelve-year-old Marie de la Tour, a harness tender's daughter whose mother had died, was 'desperate, hungry and unable to find work' when she was admitted to the General Hospital in 1725; she remained there for over six years. The majority of poor children who entered on their own initiative may have been aged around six to eight years. They had good chances of eventually being released (a few escaped), since eight out of every ten children, aged between one and fourteen, survived in the *hôpitaux* of Lower Normandy. Once in the *hôpital*, the girls would live among women, old and young, the boys among men. Young boys and girls worked alongside women in the workshops, either spinning wool and flax or manufacturing hosiery or stockings, or in the case of girls and women, making lace. Around the age of twelve, boys were set to work with the men, either in the gardens or making leather goods or coarse linen and woollen fabrics. They may also have dressed hemp or helped in the construction of new quarters for inmates. In the 1720s, children up to the age of fourteen (in some *hôpital* statistics twelve) formed the largest single group of inmates in the nine *hôpitaux* of Lower Normandy.[43]

Spinnerei, poor houses, workhouses and orphanages proliferated in eighteenth-century German States. Children, old people, lunatics, able-bodied beggars and convicts were all mixed together, but the regulations of the Berlin Poor-House, for example, stated that children should be cared for separately, should receive education, and when working they should be under the charge of some of the deserving poor. The work in such institutes typically consisted of spinning, chiefly wool but also cotton and flax. In the 1780s, the municipal authorities in the town of Neuss in Rheinland contracted a private entrepreneur, Conrad Manuel, to establish a *Spinnerei* for poor children in the paupers' hospice. The children were expected to maintain themselves from their work and the spinning-wheels were provided by the municipality. However, many of them deserted the institution, and no more than a dozen remained. Not even the entrepreneur could make his living out of the *Spinnerei*, and it was closed. At the centre of the broadcloth industry in the Rhine mountains, the demand for yarn was high, hence woollen spinning in the local orphanage and poor house was more like manufacturing.[44]

A workhouse had been established near Cologne under French rule, and some 300 children, constituting about half of all inmates, were employed at spinning in 1813–1814. The majority of the children were aged at least ten, and were grouped together with adults as being of working age; some 40 children were aged between five and ten, and some 20 were still younger. In 1814, a contemporary observer wrote that children in the orphanage of Cologne looked 'pale and sickly' ('*blass und kränklich*'), because of having too little fresh air, since they were obliged to attend to the spinning wheels and looms. Many also had defective vision ('*böse Augen*'), and wool spinning was believed to be the reason. The orphanage was annexed to an *Industrieschule*, industrial school in 1826, where numerous boys were occupied in turning and cabinetmaking, and toymaking.[45]

During the Revolution and the Napoleonic Wars, according to Colin Heywood, in France, 'the first flourish of mechanized cotton spinning coincided with an acute shortage of manpower caused by the military campaigns. The early cotton mills therefore had little choice but to use women and children'. As the supply of child labour was limited, more coercive measures were taken. Orphans were no longer placed out with families, but put in factories. The work in factories was presented as assistance, but 'the *enfants assistés* were employed under extremely onerous conditions' (C. Heywood). At the time of the Terror (1793), large numbers of children were abandoned, and asylums for them became pools from which manufacturers drew cheap labour. Many manufacturers acquired dozens of children from orphanages, foundling homes and hospices for the poor. For example, after the Thermidor (1794–1795), a cardboard manufacturer named Syker had over 100 orphans, aged over ten years. In 1796, a manufactory in l'Epine near Aparjon made a contract with the *ministre de l'intérieur* for 50 girls aged ten to eleven, and 70 aged twelve to fourteen. Those who proved 'wicked and untameable' were removed, while the rest, dressed in a uniform way, were not permitted to leave until they were twenty-one. If a girl deserted, the manufacturers could have her brought back by force. In 1799, the Directorate decided that as many as 500 children aged between eight and fourteen would be handed over to a textile manufacturer in Toulouse. In Strasbourg the wool for manufacturers was spun in the prisons, in the poor house and in the *maison des enfants*. The 100 girls in the workhouse of Lille may have been privileged compared with their companions in misfortune: they were entitled to have meat four times a week, and to receive a trousseau when they were permitted to leave the workhouse at the age of twenty.[46]

In conclusion, in all of the countries discussed above, fairly similar principles seem to have been observed in the treatment of deprived children and adults. In workhouses, *hôpitaux* and other corresponding institutions, compulsory work evidently applied equally to children (past early infancy) and adults. Orphaned and destitute children might first have been treated with less severity than adults, but eventually those caught for begging or vagrancy were liable to the same type of punishment, including flogging and hard labour, even though children escaped extreme forms of punishment, such as the galleys. Since different countries by and large followed the same type of policy concerning children's pauperism, begging and vagrancy, it is evident that innovations in this field travelled from one country to another. Notwithstanding the fact that compulsory work in the institutes never fulfilled the expectations, the policy of confinement continued to have its adherents among the powerful and well-off.

Finally, it is worth noting that, irrespective of the country, the compulsory work performed by children in orphanages, workhouses and *hôpitaux* often involved textile and clothing production, particularly spinning. As will be discussed below, textiles, alone or together with clothing, were also principal consumers of child labour in manufactories, home industries and factories with power-driven machinery.

Workshops and manufactories

In early modern Europe, manufactories, expanding putting-out industries, mechanisation and capital accumulation forced artisan masters and other small producers onto the defence. They were ultimately to lose their position in the market, the respite later offered by the 'consumer revolution' notwithstanding. Along with such changes, parish apprentices, deprived boys (and girls) placed with a master by poor-relief authorities, were introduced in artisan shops. The division of labour in the manufactories made women and children a new and useful part of the work force in old and new fields of production. Labour-intensive consumer-goods industries increased productivity by pressing the advantages of the division of labour, and cut wage costs by the extensive employment of women and children.

This section addresses two issues connected with this development. First, a few examples are presented of the gradual erosion of master artisans' control of entry into trades and the emergence of apprentice-type low-paid wage workers. The more effective exclusion of women from corporations, together with deteriorating opportunities for girls to be apprenticed, are associated with the efforts of masters and apprentices to preserve their status. The second issue concerns the employment of children in manufactories. In several countries, manufactories recruited and maintained their labour force to some extent through compulsion, varying from restrictions on movement to outright serfdom, and this concerned children too. A third issue related to this theme, that concerning home industries and proto-industrialisation, is addressed in Chapter 3.

Birmingham, 'the first manufacturing town in the world' (E. Hopkins) showed the way. From the early eighteenth century, Birmingham metal workers were making small consumer goods from iron, brass and steel: buckles, buttons, snuff-boxes and various kinds of trinkets, followed by tableware, candelabra, vases, statuary and other luxury products. The demand for such products was balanced by falling production costs per item, achieved by technical innovations in machinery (the stamp, the press, the lathe and the drawbench) and by the extensive subdivision of labour. In 1749, Samuel Schröder (Schroeder), an actuary and later a director of the Swedish Royal Mining Department, observed boys in a button manufactory in Birmingham:

'... a small boy makes the blanks red-hot in a small furnace. Another boy puts them under the punch, one by one. The third picks them out of the punch and greases the upper mould between each punching with a greased brush. All this goes quite quickly.' In the 1760s, Lord Shelburne observed that button making had become such simple work that, in most cases, 'children of 6 or 7 years old do it as well as men'. In a more well-informed description, two leading Birmingham manufacturers explained that the introduction of machines and engines 'lessens the manual labour and enables boys to do men's work'. Boys kept the machines working.[47]

In England, some artisan masters strove to maintain traditional methods and quality, while others were ready to use the newest labour-saving technologies, cheap non-guild labour, putting-out and subcontracting to outworkers. The Statute of Artificers of 1562 provided the basis for the two forms of apprenticeship, one for masters-to-be, another for parish paupers. The former, 'hand-picked boys ... tracked for mastership'(J. Farr), witnessed the entry of unfree pauper apprentices into the workshops, while journeymen fought for the right not to be considered servants. In London, a growing number of artisan companies vigorously enforced trade controls, particularly the monitoring of apprentice and unfree labour, for most of the seventeenth century and even well into the eighteenth century – until the system of guild control was abandoned in the 1750s.[48] Many apprentices in eighteenth-century London fared badly, and there were even cases of a parish orphan being killed by the woman and another being beaten to death by the man who had taken in destitute children for correction, discipline and work.[49]

In the late eighteenth century, fourteen was the normal age to enter into private apprenticeship leading to mastership, but even boys as young as ten were taken on, such as Willian Clowes who was apprenticed to the compositor's trade in 1779 for the sum of 30 pounds.[50] The premiums paid by the family of origin varied by trade, from about 13 pounds to as high as 400 pounds in exceptional cases. Parish or charity apprenticeship premiums were lower, normally four or five pounds. Under the Poor Law, parish apprentices could be imposed upon employers. K.D.M. Snell suggests that the supply of such parochially enforced labour probably grew later in the eighteenth century. In any case, the prospects of apprenticeship declined after the 1750s, particularly after the artisan unemployment following demobilisation after the Napoleonic Wars. The Statute of Artificers was repealed in 1814. Nonetheless, as Jane Humphries states, 'working people persisted in seeing apprenticeship in a trade as the key to economic security and social advancement for their sons', while the premiums often indicated 'significant self-sacrifice' on the part of the parents or the boy himself.[51]

The system of pauper apprentices was introduced in Spain through the sixteenth-century laws under which pauper parents had to surrender any children over five years of age for apprenticeship to a trade. Urban guilds managed to maintain restrictive practices until the Enlightenment, when the restrictions were eased in so far as they appeared to hinder improvements in manufacturing. In Spain, as elsewhere, regulations governing access to a trade covered both technical skills and social acceptability. The latter was guaranteed, for example, by demanding higher fees from outsiders. Fees and regulations effectively precluded pauper apprentices from masterships, however skilled they were.[52]

In Italy, for boys (*monelli*) caught in the streets of Florence and taken into the pauper hospice of Quarconia, placement as a pauper apprentice with a craftsman or master artisan 'represented definitely an important opportunity for integration in the urban society', as Filippo Fineschi argues. Placement in a workshop was in itself better than life in the hospice: as apprentices boys had some right of movement, as required by the work. However, many boys had to stay in the Quarconia hospice in economically bad times when few masters wanted to take on a pauper apprentice.[53]

In Italy, the emergence of putting-out and domestic production and later of manufactories, in silk spinning, for instance, promoted the use of young people in low-skilled work producing quality that fell far short of the established standards of the craft corporations. Contemporaries thought that the main competitive edge was in decreasing the wage bill. During the late sixteenth century, contracts for apprenticeship leading to mastership became very rare, while the numbers of nominal apprentices multiplied. For example, the use of female and child labour, 'little specialised and little demanding', in the Florentine woollen crafts expanded in the sixteenth century, and in 1663 the estimated proportion of children under fifteen working in woollen and silk crafts was 43 per cent.[54] The silk industry faced its first serious crisis in Piedmont between 1729 and 1730, and the trouble spread to the trade of tailoring. For example, the Turin tailors' guild lost its pre-eminence and witnessed its prestige diminishing. The guild responded by paying more attention to the payment of apprenticeship and the defence of its boundaries. Previously, the transmission of the trade from father to son had been common, though not the rule. With the vicissitudes of the trade, the sons of the guild's most prestigious members took up commercial activities, giving up the trade of tailoring.[55]

The median age for apprenticeship in sixteenth-century French cities was twelve, higher than it had been in the fourteenth century, and it was to rise still further in the seventeenth century. Yet, in the seventeenth century, towns set wage rates in textile production for boys aged seven years.[56] Did this low age limit apply to pauper apprentices? Apparently, apprentices aiming for mastership preserved their status. In 1751 in Auxerre, Bourgogne, a wealthy farmer's son, Nicolas-Edme Rétif, aged sixteen, started a four-year apprenticeship with master Fournier to learn the typographer's trade. The life of an apprentice was hard, as Rétif described it in his partly autobiographical *Monsieur Nicolas*. The other workers in the printing shop tormented the new apprentice, and the master was brutal and violent. The apprentice only had to suffer and be patient until relief came in the form of a new apprentice.[57] Was the rough treatment of young apprentices a legacy of medieval practices, or was it a new phenomenon? If the treatment of Nicolas-Edme, for whom his father paid, was that bad, one wonders what would it have been like in the case of a pauper apprentice, such as the wigmaker's son Jean Mathieu Croissy, aged eight? He was found asleep in a Parisian boulevard one early April morning in 1763, and he could not say what had become of his father or mother. He was apprenticed to a man named Dagneau.[58]

Sweden followed the German model as regards artisan trades. Privileged apprentices included the master artisans' own sons and boys working in workshops of purveyors of the royal court, for instance. In 1601, these purveyors had managed to make the entry into such trades tightly restricted.[59] Another privileged group of apprentices consisted of the sons of professional ironworkers at the Crown ironworks. These boys were regarded as the monarch's property working for the benefit of the kingdom, hence they were protected against being made to do too heavy work too young by legislation and craft ordinances on the one hand, and by concerns about not letting unskilled boys spoil the iron on the other.[60] In medieval Sweden, entry ages for apprentices varied from twelve to fifteen, while the artisan regulations of 1621 and 1720 put it at fourteen. The Statutes of Manufactories of 1739 dropped the age limit to ten or twelve years, 'depending on the character of the craft', while the duration of apprenticeship was extended from five to eight years. At the same time, the long-standing practice of classifying apprentices as superior or inferior on the grounds of their social origin was given a legal basis. A boy 'who has had a proper upbringing' could serve his apprenticeship in three or four years, and it was enough 'if he only for certain number of hours a day has worked in the workshop'. Thus he escaped becoming indentured, whereas poor men's children, whom the master provided with board and clothes, had to serve him for as long as was needed to work off the costs, and at least for five years. Such poorer apprentices 'must not refuse to do the master's errands', thus in practice they may have been servants rather than apprentices.[61]

Starting from the late fifteenth century, women in continental Europe were increasingly excluded from corporations, but girls could still be apprenticed – albeit in fewer trades than boys, usually textiles and food processing, and evidently never in prestigious ones. For example, craftsmen in the building trades of Brittany had limited female access to skilled crafts since the sixteenth century by excluding them from apprenticeship.[62] According to Elisabeth Musgrave, daughters of master craftsmen were accorded privileges in the statutes of most corporations of Nantes by 1772, and no statute prohibited daughters from working in their father's trade. Nevertheless, none of the Nantes corporations granted masters' daughters privileged entry into the craft in their own right.[63] In England, the Statute of Artificers, although gender-neutral in referring to apprentices as 'persons', did have a discriminating clause, but without much subsequent effect. Even in the eighteenth century, girls continued to be apprenticed in many kinds of trades, such as carpentry, furniture making, clockmaking, clothes manufacture, weaving, hairdressing, wig-making and shoe manufacture, as well as to goldsmiths and jewellers.[64]

In early sixteenth-century Bristol, after serving formal apprenticeship, young women were still entitled to the freedom of the town, but their opportunities for formal apprenticeship were eliminated during the seventeenth century. By that time, almost all indentured females, whether placed out privately or by the parish, were apprenticed as 'servant maids', or in a combination of household service and craft work, usually in clothing and textiles. Male apprentices were also at times required to perform household services. In the late sixteenth and seventeenth centuries, Rye, on the English Channel, used female apprenticeship largely as a means for providing for orphans, and girls were apprenticed as maidservants. Orphaned children were apprenticed, evidently irrespective of their age, within a short time of their parents' death.[65] In the seventeenth and eighteenth centuries, one-fifth of female parish apprentices in the southern counties were apprenticed in agriculture, while one-fifth in the seventeenth century and one-third in the eighteenth century were apprenticed in clothing or food and drink. Housewifery or domestic service accounted for nearly half of all the female parish apprentices in the seventeenth century, almost two-fifths in the eighteenth century, and a good quarter in the nineteenth. The rest were apprenticed in a broad variety of trades, even those considered male occupations, such as with cordwainers, curriers, blacksmiths, butchers, bricklayers, clockmakers and whitesmiths.[66]

In conclusion, it seems that to be placed with masters as parish apprentices was, in spite of everything, the best that could happen to parish pauper children. If apprentices heading for mastership were bullied by other workers, then parish apprentices may have been tormented, and if the masters were brutal to the former, they might have been even more cruel to the latter. Nonetheless, parish apprentices learned skills in craftsmen's shops through which to earn a living, albeit the hard way. Moreover, shops were respected places in which to work, which is evident from the fact that parents paid to get their sons apprenticed. Girls who were apprenticed to textile work and food processing also acquired the skills to make a living, albeit in very poorly paid occupations.

In contrast, recruitment in manufactories took place through fear and by force, and the emergence of factory work was generally connected with workhouses and orphanages. Many people in England saw the manufactories as the best remedy for the 'idleness' of children, despite the fact that life was hard.[67] As Maxine Berg remarks concerning Britain, 'access to cheap supplies of labour, especially that of women and children, was integral to the spread of manufacture from the early modern period'. Women and children were endowed with attributes of 'flexibility, dexterity and discipline', which made them 'particularly suited to eighteenth-century technologies and work organization'.[68]

At the end of the eighteenth century, the leading calico-printing firm of Peel & Yates employed more than 1,000 pauper apprentices in its cotton mills. In its quest for docile and the cheapest possible labour, the mill relocated far into the countryside where it hired mainly local women and children. 'Little boys' were said to be employed pegging pieces of cotton material for bleaching in the sun, and corps of boys were used as messengers, running 13 miles (about 21 kilometres) from the mill to the town. When the local supply of labour ran short, children were imported from London workhouses, about 180 kilometres away. They arrived after several days' journey in carts, many in their charity uniforms.[69]

A leading French textile producer, the Oberkampf calico printing manufactory, which was located in the countryside like the Peel manufactory in England, employed a great deal of unskilled labour. Twelve was the minimum age of apprentices engaged by contract to the manufactory, and the average age was fourteen (some 80 apprentice contracts were recorded between 1768 and 1774). The manufacturer declared that he employed workers of five or six years of age. However, Serge Chassagne points out that, in the censuses of the Napoleonic era, there was no evidence of such young children, and only one aged eight. He also traced child workers in mortality records, and found four, aged between ten and fourteen. Their deaths occurred between 1795 and 1801, 'just at the moment when war increased the scarcity of adult male labour'. As the manufactory did not employ 'tear-boys' (*tireurs*), assistants to the printers, it was difficult to say how the manufacturer used children productively. Chassagne suggests that 'if young children did regularly work in the factory, it was to acclimatise them to the discipline rather than to expect any product from them'.[70] His reasoning appears plausible, bearing in mind that 35 years later, the great concern of Andrew Ure was still the impossibility 'to convert persons past the age of puberty ... into useful factory hands'.[71] Unlike the Oberkampf in France, calico printers in Geneva hired girls and boys as their *teerers* or *tireurs*. The number of *teerers* aged between five and thirteen at the Labarthe calico manufactory in 1811 was the same as the number of printing tables. This suggests that even the youngest *teerers* worked as assistants to the printers in Geneva.[72]

As in England, the Swedish labour force for manufactories was supplied 'more or less by force', as Eli Heckscher put it. Compulsion was used, particularly to increase spinning capacity. Unlike in Britain and France, the manufactories in Sweden remained few in number and modest in size, despite the efforts of the Crown to promote them for the supply of uniform cloth and weaponry. Only those producing broadcloth were of real importance.[73] In the seventeenth century, Stockholm's largest industrial establishment was Leijonancker's broadcloth manufactory, which cooperated closely with the poor-relief authorities: children in the paupers' hospice of Danviken were used as spinners, for example. According to Gustaf Utterström, there is no doubt that the conditions in Leijonancker's manufactory were terrifying. The official records give several examples of children being thrown out onto the street when they fell ill. One such case from 1674 involved two orphaned children, a boy and a girl, who had 'fallen ill and were thus thrown out' ('*sjuknat och alltså utvräkta*'), as the record stated. Children as young as five years old worked in this manufactory as spinners.[74] One wonders about the productivity in a place in which the labour performance of five-year-old children was not considered inadequate.

However, the Swedish historian Klas Nyberg has shown that not all children following their parents into the manufactories represented child labour. Among those who were registered with their father or mother in a woollen cloth manufactory in late eighteenth-century Stockholm, some were too young to be in the labour force, even by contemporary standards (babies and three-year-olds). In 1784, there were 220 children registered with their father or mother in the nine largest woollen cloth manufactories in Stockholm; in 1788, there were 207 children and eleven spooling boys in the seven largest manufactories. There were also some lone child workers without father or mother, almost 60 of them in 1788, for instance.[75]

The Crown in Peter the Great's Russia, as the Swedish Crown, promoted manufactories primarily for the supply of uniforms and weaponry. The Russian state-owned ones 'were run with military severity', while 'privately-owned establishments were far worse' (J. Blum). They faced severe recruitment problems, and bound and forced labour was seen as a solution. A new category of state serfs was created to meet the labour demand, while apprentices in private manufactories were bound for seven to ten years. 'Merchant persons' were granted the right to buy populated villages for their factories and mills in 1721, and any remaining free factory workers were enserfed in 1736. Now the owners had the right to bind all workmen and their families. In the plants of the Urals, assigned workers' children had to follow their fathers' trade, and women and children were widely employed. As a result of such measures, as Mikhail Tugan-Baranovsky wrote, 'the Russian factory assumed the character of a workhouse'. The purchase of peasants for factories and mills was prohibited in 1762, although the gentry maintained its right to use serfs in factories. Despite the measures to secure the labour supply, there were constant complaints of the shortage of workers throughout the eighteenth century. For example, in 1774, Moscow woollen cloth manufacturers reported that they were desperately short of workers, and that there was an especially acute shortage of child workers aged between ten and fifteen.[76]

In striking contrast to the state manufactories in Sweden and Russia, many French establishments produced luxury goods to increase the prestige of the king. Workers in the French royal manufactories were relatively privileged, albeit at the cost of the freedom to move. The apprentices employed by skilled artisans were treated as family members in the royal china manufactory of Sèvres,[77] while the royal glassworks of Saint-Gobain employed boys, *gamins*, who were at the bottom of the occupational hierarchy. In 1751 and again in 1769 there were two *gamins* in each hall with some 30 workers in all. The boys earned three to four *livres* a week, while the best-paid man in the hall earned four or five times that amount. The best jobs, better paid and more secure, were reserved for the sons and sons-in-law of the best workers, who sometimes built up 'dynasties', with their daughters employed as day workers. Family recruitment was a deliberate management strategy, aimed at tying workers, improving discipline and training the young. Claude Pris maintains that sons of workers were employed at the age of four or five for minor tasks from the seventeenth century on, whereas Maurice Hammon and Dominique Perrin suggest that the *gamins* were aged between twelve and fifteen. In 1823 the regulations of Saint-Gobain fixed ten years as the minimum age of employment.[78] It does not seem likely that very young boys would have been permitted to run around in production premises; glass making in

Saint-Gobain was, after all, quite dangerous and exacting work which did not suffer any disturbances. Even the factory courtyard had its dangers. In 1709 the corpse of little Marianne Delapierre, aged about three, a daughter of an employee, was found in the pond.[79] Small boys may have merely been registered with their fathers, without actually working in the manufactory, as was the case in some Swedish cloth manufactories.

Children do not seem to have been widely used in late eighteenth-century and early nineteenth-century German manufactories. A few producers of paper and needles and a glass-button works, had child workers, and a mirror-polishing manufactory had some dozen girls, for instance. It is no surprise that most child workers were found in textiles, cotton printing and spinning even including six-year-old children. Most child workers in Rheinland (aged under twelve) worked in broadcloth and cotton manufactories. According to Joachim Kermann, all German textile manufacturers faced recruitment problems, since no free citizen who was able to make his living in any other way went voluntarily to work in a spinning mill or sent his children there. People preferred home working, even if it was for the manufactories.[80]

In conclusion, early modern authorities and legislators do not appear to have had any scruples about setting children to work in manufactories, where life was so hard that the common people of the time generally did their best to avoid all but the few better ones. British and French historical writing gives the impression that quite large numbers of children worked in British manufactories, somewhat fewer in France, but estimates of the total numbers involved seem to be lacking. Judging from the fact that the Swedish and Russian Crowns were not very successful in their promotional efforts, the number of children actually working in Swedish or Russian manufactories may have remained relatively small. This was evidently true, in any case, in German manufactories. But whatever the numbers were, the number of children in charity and penal institutions should be added, since their work often was quite similar to that in manufactories. It may not have made much difference to deprived children whether they spun in an institution or in a manufactory.

Educational opportunities

Early modern European societies witnessed upward mobility among the offspring of ambitious merchants, manufacturers, a substantial number of landed peasants and an expanding body of non-noble civil servants. The way of life of the leisured class, who despised work but not the rents derived from the work of others, attracted the upwardly mobile, but the future lay in the more harshly materialistic world of commercial and industrial entrepreneurs. The middle strata swelled, while the old nobility found itself losing ground, or worse still its male members were decimated by the wars. It was in the shared interest of the old and of the aspiring élite, as well as of those on their way up, that the children of the propertyless would continue to fill the ranks of servants, workers, agricultural labourers and the army.

This section charts the process in which formal education or schooling became established as élite and bourgeois breeding grounds for social distinction and upward social mobility. At the other extreme were the schools offered to the lower classes, such as pauper schools, industrial schools and spinning schools.

According to R.A. Houston, 'official attitudes to the education of the lower orders were remarkably homogeneous between countries and over time'. There was 'a set of shared assumptions that education for any rank in society should be appropriate to the place of that stratum in the overall polity'. There was a growing concern among the privileged in *ancien régime* France that education would alienate the children of humble people from manual work and awaken their social ambitions, turning them from producing classes to consuming classes. As formal education gained ground as a merit for civil office, common schools for rich and poor, a legacy from the Middle Ages, disappeared. Now upper-class boys at the age of seven were ensconced in *collèges* or placed under a private tutor, while upper-class girls learned reading, writing, sewing and pleasing manners, perhaps in a convent-like *pensionnat de jeunes filles*. In *hôpitaux* there were *petites écoles* for the children of the urban poor. In the century of the Enlightenment, it was claimed that there were too many *petites écoles*, and that teaching the children of the poor to read and write would jeopardise the equilibrium of the social body.[81]

The increasing concern of the establishment in early modern Spain sprang from social mobility. It was feared that merchants, artisans and manufacturers would gain more wealth and power by purchasing governmental offices for themselves or their sons, which had traditionally been reserved for those who, or whose fathers, had never worked with their hands. The role of schools increased in the education of the élite, and disciplinarian Jesuit schools in particular emphasised character formation. At the same time, sumptuary laws limited the number of grammar schools, which were said to lead 'peasant sons into idleness'.[82]

The reformed school system became a solid hierarchical structure in Turin, Italy, after the Jesuit monopoly had been broken. The problem caused by the increasing number of poor who went or wanted to go to school was solved by creating free elementary classes for poor pupils, who would be instructed in reading, writing and keeping accounts. At the close of the eighteenth century, there were but two pauper schools in Turin. The six *petites écoles*, with instruction in Latin, the key to access to higher studies, served the local élite of notaries, well-to-do shopkeepers and the like. To gain access to the Royal Colleges, which were free of charge, pupils had to pass through elementary schools of Latin, which were often quite expensive. According to Marina Roggero, the reorganised school system served the aims of the ruling classes well 'by blocking upstream the danger of inappropriate access to higher education'. She cites a contemporary notion that making the schools of Latin expensive and mercenary 'was reputed to be the most efficient means of populating fields and workshops'.[83]

Linda Pollock's analysis of gentry account ledgers found that schooling for the daughters of the upper ranks in seventeenth-century England was 'surprisingly expensive', in fact, often more expensive than the schooling of sons, yet parents considered such expenditure acceptable. Gentry girls were educated, say, in reading, writing, needlework, French, singing and dancing, but seldom in the Classics or mathematics, which were a basic component in gentry boys' education.[84] Successful commercial and industrial middle-class people, such as were to be found in Birmingham in the English Midlands, may have raised their children in the spirit of commercialism and under the strong influence of religion. For them there was a grammar school with a heavily classical curriculum, whereas for the children of the poor there were Anglican charity schools, Sunday Schools and the Asylum for the Infant Poor, where children were taught trades.[85]

Élite children in German States enjoyed governesses and private tutors at home. At the beginning of the seventeenth century, the education of élite girls resembled that of bourgeois girls, and included practical skills such as sewing and knitting, while at the end of the century it was primarily oriented towards representative and social skills. During the eighteenth century the role of school increased in the education of boys and girls of the middle strata. The wealthy manufacturer Christoff-Philipp Oberkampf sent his nephew Samuel to a boarding school in Paris at the age of sixteen to learn French, whereas as a craftsman's son he had himself started at the age of eleven as a *tireur* in a workshop in Basle. Burgher fathers continued to teach both their sons and daughters a profession, but most girls of the middle strata learned only women's traditional household skills, perhaps first as a servant, which was their only experience of paid work. For the girls of the poorest families, learning household tasks was secondary to the more important need to earn money in home industries, factories or other professions.[86]

The Russian élite differed from its western counterparts by not providing its daughters with any education. Noble boys enjoyed, usually from the age of seven, instruction by private, foreign tutors. Education helped the élite sons to advance in their career in state offices. The uppermost levels distinguished themselves from the other nobles by setting up special schools exclusively for the children of the 'best' noble families. While most noble girls received no education, those who did learned mainly deportment and to speak French, the aristocratic lingua franca, for which foreign-born governesses were recruited. The first élite girls to enjoy the fruits of the Enlightenment, learning to read and write at a girls' school, were those close to the imperial court of Catherine II. She also launched reforms to introduce universal education, but implementation proved difficult, and enthusiasm was lacking at the local level. One of the few exceptions was the hard-working school board of the largely Protestant city of Vyborg, which had been ceded by Sweden to Russia in the Great Northern War.[87]

In the seventeeth century, noble Swedish families started to take their sons away from public schools, preferring instruction at home provided by private tutors and governesses, often recruited from abroad. Other persons of standing who could afford it followed suit, especially if they lived in country manors, as many civil and military officers did. There were prestigious private schools for élite boys in the cities, in the early 1690s 1,900 boys in Stockholm received such private tutoring. At the same time, Stockholm's public schools (legacies of medieval Latin schools) had about 500 boys. They were sons of soldiers, sailors, iron porters, herring-packers, janitors, apprentices, manual labourers, stable hands and the like, and went to school because, as schoolchildren, they were the only group allowed to beg in the street. They were also paid for singing religious hymns and participating in burial processions and annual festivals. When no payments for services were rendered, they deserted the school.[88]

In Scandinavia, as elsewhere, boys in Latin schools had ecclesiastic duties that brought money to the school, and the boys received free board and clothes. Enrolment was originally open to boys of all classes, even though the sons of wealthier families may have enjoyed private preparatory education. Most Latin schools in Denmark were closed down in 1739, while the remaining ones no longer accepted children of the poor, and in Norway they developed into élite schools for sons of people of standing and civil officers. The measures by which this was achieved were simple: the free board and lodging of schoolboys in Latin schools was removed, ecclesiastic duties as a source of money for the school were replaced by school fees, and formal entrance requirements were introduced. The élite and the middle strata no longer sent their boys to community schools (*folkskoler*), which developed into pauper schools exclusively for the sons of means-tested poor.[89]

Charity schools and parish schools catered for the children of disadvantaged people. Whether Catholic of Protestant, they strove first of all to indoctrinate the children in the right faith. A parish pauper school, the first of its kind in Scandinavia was established in Norway in the city of Bergen in 1740. In the Pietist spirit, its curriculum emphasised learning and reading the catechism. During its first year it had 40 children (eight of them girls) aged at least seven, and 80 children four decades later. After leaving school, a few brighter boys might continue in the Latin school, but for others the alternatives were apprenticeship with craftsmen or service in commerce or shipping. For girls, who never comprised more than a third of the pupils, the choice was between domestic or farm service.[90]

In Italian schools, imprinting the right faith was primary while making children literate was secondary, and making them numerate was even less important. The Catechistic schools of Bologna not only instilled the Catholic doctrine and Christian morals, but also taught punctuality, manners and disciplined behaviour. They were attended at least by some 3,300 boys, even up to 4,100 boys. In principle, the same instruction was also available to girls, but families were reluctant to let daughters go to school because it might make then 'too liberal and impudent'.[91] Spain had its *Casas de Doctrinas*, mixtures of schools and orphanages, whose children brought in money by attending at funerals. Following the Italian model, primary schooling for urban children was introduced in Spain in the early seventeenth century in the form of *Escuelas Pías*, 'pious schools', which attained more significance in the next century. In 1783 it was stipulated that all quarters of Madrid should have established schools, free of charge, for girls who would be instructed in religion and good manners. The instruction consisted of manual work, and if a girl wished to learn to read, that was possible provided that the parish priest found her Christian knowledge sufficient, that she passed a work test and that her way of life and manners were correct.[92]

Along with the effective implementation of separate systems of general education for the high and low, industrial schools and spinning schools were created for children of the lower orders. 'Society was becoming more sharply divided and one reflection of this was the growing provision ... of poor hospitals and work schools' (R.A. Houston). Many industrial schools may not have been much more than parish workhouses 'which adopted the more fashionable name of School of Industry' (H. Cunningham).[93]

Spinning schools had a long history in England. There were some in Norwich in 1570, for example, and King's Lynn established a worsted spinning school in 1633. Scholars in King's Lynn were paid fit wages for their work. Eric Kerridge presumes that children's wages were handed over to the parents 'just as if the children had been working at home'.[94] According to M.G. Jones, in the spinning school at Findon in Northamptonshire, in the early eighteenth century, 'discipline was maintained by a life of strenuous toil'. The school enjoyed the reputation of a model working school, as did the school at Artleborough. Its schoolmistress first taught children reading and knitting, and then the use of the spinning-wheel. She received the profits of the children's labour for two months, after which they would retain some of the wages they earned. Contemporaries were fascinated by the idea that children as young as four years of age might be made to be self-supporting. 'Political arithmeticians worked out the sums which would accrue to the national income if the restless energy of the children were harnessed in this way to the industry', as M.G. Jones sarcastically put it. Charity schools were turned into working schools, although some were united with workhouses. The Grey Coat Hospital in Westminster was the first to introduce spinning-wheels and a spinning mistress to train children, but it sold its 30 spinning-wheels in 1734 on the grounds that the money the children earned was so little compared to the great hindrance to education. Jones concluded that the method of combining work with the school curriculum was successful only in girls' schools, 'where learning was combined with domestic labour'.[95]

Italian *conservatorios* for 'threatened maidens' provide an example of such girls' schools. The first *conservatorio* in Naples was established in the fifteenth century by the silk guild for orphaned girls and widows, followed in the next century by goldsmiths, the woollen guild and public scriveners. The most pious *conservatorio* in Rome admitted orphaned or abandoned girls between six and fifteen years of age; in the 1630s about 300 girls lived there, and later about 130. In the seventeenth century, the girls remained in the institution for ten years on average, while in the following century they stayed for 15 years, some for life, and less than a tenth returned to their families. Another *conservatorio* for poor orphaned or abandoned girls was opened in Rome in the 1670s. It was characterised by religious zeal and monastic discipline, therefore it attracted abundant financial support. The girls were kept occupied all day with prayers and domestic or other work. They also made gloves for sale, and as this proved profitable, more girls were sought, but now from more decent backgrounds. The number of girls declined from the original 200 to 100 by the 1840s. The two new Roman *conservatorios* established in the eighteenth century had a markedly production-oriented approach. In the first, the girls, nearly all orphans, were involved in the manufacture of silk ribbons, and received a wage from their work, according to its quality and quantity. This was not enough, and the girls were sent out daily to collect alms. The other *conservatorio* was part of an up-to-date woollen mill. Men were employed in the woollen cloth mill, while girls worked in the linen, hemp and cloth mill located in a separate building. Their working conditions were evidently unhealthy, as both mortality and turnover were high.[96]

The poor relief authorities of Hamburg established an elementary school and a complementary spinning school in 1789, as it had become clear that children in 'ragged schools' and those who grew up in a correction house seldom turned into useful members of society. The Spinning School of Hamburg had 210 pupils, with an entry age of six years. First the children had to learn to sit still, then they were put to spin from dawn until eight in the evening, with breaks for breakfast and lunch. At the end of the week they received their wages. If parents had dutifully sent their children to the school, there was a modest increment of alms, but if they failed to, alms were withdrawn. Supervised workrooms along similar lines were set aside in the orphanage building, in which children were engaged spinning. Those from the Spinning School who had 'improved enough' for more advanced schooling were moved to the *Industrie-Schule*. There boys made canvas and girls wove and spun. By 1793, the industrial school had 354 children, and 441 three years later. Every enlargement brought with it greater outlays. Enrolment in the Elementary School was higher at 647 in 1793, and 842 three years later. There were also evening schools for children already in the labour market. However, 'the workshops struggled with declining productivity and sloppy workmanship' and 'truancy afflicted the schools', as Mary Lindemann concludes. She sums up the history as follows: 'modest beginnings, great expectations, disappointing results'.[97]

Two Directorates were established for improving the efficiency of yarn manufacturing in eighteenth-century Denmark, and spinning schools were established for that purpose. The idea was that general national proficiency in finer linen spinning would come into being via children. However, the spinning schools did not survive long because the pupils found them to be rather like workhouses.[98] Spinning accounted for about a tenth of all production costs in Swedish broadcloth production, second only to raw material, and about a quarter of labour costs.[99] This may have been an incentive for establishing spinning schools. The first ones had been established in Stockholm by 1739, teaching spinning on pedal spinning-wheels, in fact already in use in the Swedish countryside. The schools were open to female servants as well as boys and girls aged between ten and twelve, but before long even girls aged between seven and eight were admitted. The authorities soon complained that the pupils were deserting the schools.[100]

A provincial governor in Sweden's Finnish province of Häme (Tavastland) established a spinning school on his estate to teach children to spin flax for manufactories. The local people had long been renowned for growing and spinning flax for sale. With the help of generous state grants, a bright new building complex for twenty to thirty children was erected in 1760, and a proclamation about the spinning school was read in churches. Not a single child showed up, although the surrounding villages were swarming with children, as a contemporary observed. After repeated failures to employ children, the school was closed in 1767. The Superintendent of Manufactories reported to the authorities in Stockholm that parents had feared that they would have to sell the freedom of their children to the spinning school, and that the material advantages offered by the school could not compensate for this. Eventually this fear had diminished enough for some parents to send or coerce their children to attend the school occasionally, but this was always the result of some *force majeur*, such as high grain prices, poverty, death or sickness, or the inability to maintain the child. For a sack or two of grain per year from the school, one mother promised to send her child there a couple of years later.[101] The rural people associated the spinning school with the spin-house of Turku (Åbo), notorious for its dreadful conditions, yet which at times also housed children.[102] The long work days and the severe discipline in the isolated school were indeed reminiscent of spin-houses. Parents were not willing to set their children to work under such conditions.

In cultural terms, the exclusionary trend in schooling could be seen as an expression of the European-wide general trend of withdrawal among the upper classes. Peter Burke draws a link between education for the upper classes and the great tradition: 'The great tradition was transmitted formally at grammar schools and at universities. It was a closed tradition in the sense that people who had not attended these institutions ... were excluded.'[103]

In economic terms, luxuries such as expensive private schools or foreign tutors and governesses in individual families support the above-cited argument of Hoffman, Jacks, Levin and Lindert, according to which the well-to-do could afford more of the luxury services as the relative cost of 'a high-income lifestyle' declined.[104] This explains to some extent the economic feasibility of the exclusionary educational strategies that served the parental ambitions of the well-to-do. However, it does not explain the establishment of parish pauper schools and working schools. Hugh Cunningham presents the Schools of Industry as 'the most sustained effort to solve the problem of disorder by setting the children of the poor to work'.[105] Does this not better serve to explain the establishment of the parish pauper schools, if they are taken as storing places of future labour, rather than the various working schools? As working schools tended to bring with them considerable and, it seems, often unexpected outlays, a complementary explanation for their economic rationale seems to be needed. Or did the failures and disappointing results in fact indicate that the economic rationale of working schools was illusionary?

Conclusion

The emerging national states of early modern Europe were characterised by an expanding state apparatus and a growing concern for human and fiscal resources, as indicated by the introduction of population registers and statistics, for example. The main productive resource, in addition to land, was human labour, and mercantilist doctrines served well to legitimate a sharper work discipline and the lengthening of the working year. A large population of poor people was regarded as advantageous to the state and the manufacturers, since great numbers of poor meant an abundant supply of cheap labour. It was, as Jan de Vries writes, 'a world without much productivity growth and with a *mentalité* that could not conceive of incentives to labour other than poverty'.[106] Under the *ancien régime* those who supported the mercantilist doctrines wanted to see children employed at the earliest possible age, 'no child was too young to go into industry', as Eli Heckscher put it.[107] In striving to maintain low costs for labour and poor relief, the authorities and the establishment generally overrated children's capacity to work and to earn their keep.[108] I suggest that this was because they ignored their low productivity.

According to Hugh Cunningham many historians referring to high child employment in seventeenth- and eighteenth-century Britain have used statements by John Locke and Daniel Defoe as evidence, although they concern more the wish to see children of labouring people at work, rather than actual child labour.[109] However, does not the very fact that men like John Locke, Daniel Defoe and Adam Smith felt it necessary to present the advantages of child labour suggest that popular attitudes may not have been particularly favourable to it? Intellectuals of their quality would hardly have taken the trouble to write elaborate discourses on something that any villager or worker took as a matter of fact.

One should also ask to what extent the common people were free to decide over their children. In *ancien régime* France, orphaned children's close relatives, and the remaining parent of half-orphaned children, were, as a rule, involved in the decision to board them out, as they generally ended up as apprentices or servants in households of relatives.[110] Nothing similar appears to have gone on in England or Scandinavia, for instance. When the streets were cleared of begging children who were then set to work in orphanages or workhouses, nobody asked whether their parents agreed, or how the children felt about it. How much room there was for the poor to manoeuvre varied, of course, but repressive laws and punishments were characteristic of the time, and the propertyless everywhere were excluded from political life.

The role of the state and the politically powerful, whose interests always came first, appears to have been central in the utilisation of child labour under the *ancien régime*. From their perspective, children of the common people comprised a real or potential labour force, a resource to be exploited. Those who consistently took determined measures to set children of the common people to hard work were the authorities and the politically powerful, whereas the patchy evidence we have of parental attitudes among the common people suggests a wide variety, from those who left their children in workhouses to those who refused to put them to arduous work.

Notes

1. Vassberg 1984, pp. 225–226.
2. Blum 1972, p. 468.
3. Loriga 1997, pp. 19–20; Smith, A. 1973 [1776], p. 182.
4. E.g. Outram 2002. For the impact of the Thirty Years' War on society, see, e.g. Anderson, M.S. 1988, pp. 65–76.
5. Niccoli 1995, pp. 143–147; Niccoli 2000, pp. 87–91.
6. Uhlig 1978, pp. 20–21.
7. Anderson, P. 1993, p. 32.
8. Hanssen 1978, p. 148; Lindegren 1985; Villstrand 1992, pp. 87–116: Wirilander 1982, p. 301. See also Lext 1968, pp. 189–190.
9. Villstrand 1992, pp. 174, 203–224; Ylikangas 1990, pp. 176–188.
10. Blum 1972, pp. 425–30, 467; Dixon 1999, pp. 38, 107.
11. Goubert 1986, pp. 96, 146–147, 182–187; Guillaumin 1983 [1904], pp. 28–31; Loriga 1997, pp. 22–23.
12. Jutikkala 1990, p. 45; Lindegren 1980, pp. 145–168, 248–258, quotation from the Abstract; Moring 1994, p. 64.
13. Harnesk 1990, pp. 50–56.
14. Krogh 1987, p. 104.
15. Kuisma 1992a, p. 346; Kuisma 1992b, p. 9.
16. Davis 1983; Katajisto 2000.
17. Anderson, P. 1993, pp. 215, 340; Blum 1972, pp. 228–242, 346, 466; Ransel 1988, pp. 20–22. See also Dixon 1999, pp. 91–92.
18. Grubb and Stitt 1994.

19. Hopkins 1994, p. 197; Horn 1980, p. 61; Schwarz 1992, pp. 224–227. See also Bowen 1998, pp. 34–36; Humphries 2003, p. 266.
20. Anderson, M.S. 1988, pp. 177–179; Bardet 1987; Fuchs, R. 1984, pp. 260–261; Loriga 1997, pp. 13–20; Pulma 1985; Trinidad Fernández 1996, p. 463.
21. Ariès 1962, pp. 267, 281, 302; Blum 1972, p. 351; Schlumbohm 1983, pp. 188–202; Weber-Kellermann 1987, pp. 330–331.
22. Capul 1983, pp. 50–59; Capul 1984, pp. 68–88; Cipolla 1981; de Vries 1994b; Davis 1975, pp. 18–20; Fineschi 1993; McIntosh 1988; Niccoli 2000, pp. 173–175; Overton 1996, pp. 64–69; Pullan 1988; Schwartz 1988, pp. 14–19; Trinidad Fernández 1996, pp. 464–467.
23. Davis 1975, p. 20; Jütte 1996, pp. 377–378; Sarasúa García 2000, pp. 67–73.
24. E.g. Moch 1992, pp. 88–93; Schwartz 1988, pp. 89–92.
25. Capul 1983, pp. 47–50; Davis 1975, pp. 24–51.
26. Marcello 1993, pp. 244–246. See also Guidi 1999, p. 867.
27. I am grateful to Raffaella Sarti for clarifying the meaning of the word *monello/a, -i/e*, which originally meant poor vagrants, and later also undisciplined children, while modern dictionaries give 'street urchin; scamp, imp'.
28. Fineschi 1993, pp. 252, 257–258, 273–276. I am grateful to Carlo Ginzburg for explaining the meaning of several knotty expressions in old Italian.
29. Sonnino 1994, pp. 95–100, quotation p. 95.
30. Cunningham, H. 1990, p. 132; Cunningham, H. 1992, pp. 24–30; Manzione 1995, pp. 28–34, 55, 111–119, 147–149.
31. Jørgensen 1990, pp. 17–30; Krogh 1987, p. 84; Sigsgaard 1995, pp. 31–36.
32. Sprauten 1992, pp. 234–237, 370–374.
33. Jutikkala 1990, pp. 53–54; Lindberg 1989, pp. 180–192, 234–236, 257; Müller 1906, p. 304; Utterström 1978, pp. 7, 13–19, 22–33, 113.
34. Müller 1906, pp. 21–28, 42; Utterström 1978, pp. 17, 47–63, 112–113.
35. Utterström 1978, pp. 49–56, 67, 73, 98–102, 154–158. After Sweden had ceded Finland to Russia in 1809, the *barnhus* lost 300 taxed barrels of grain from Finland. If this loss had been compensated by new state grants, someone must have pocketed them, since count A.F. Skjöldebrand, the governor of the *barnhus* in 1810–1812, saw in the store only food gone bad. His description of wet nurses' and children's famished appearance (quoted in Müller 1906, p. 135) appears authentic, since it corresponds to that of starving women and children in famine-stricken areas today.
36. Utterström 1978, pp. 51, 92–110.
37. Müller 1906, pp. 262–263, 353–355.
38. Utterström 1978, p. 114. The promoter of the manufactory was a Scotsman, Daniel Young, elevated in 1666 to the Swedish nobility as Leijonancker.
39. Müller 1906, pp. 53, 57–58. The cases are from the first half of the eighteenth century.
40. Bater 1976, p. 66; Ransel 1988, pp. 7, 35–50, 70–76, quotation p. 27.
41. Cavallo 1990, Figure 1, p. 81, quotation p. 71.
42. Sarasúa García 2000, p. 72.
43. Capul 1984, pp. 68–71; Schwartz 1988, pp. 89–100, quotation p. 77.
44. Kermann 1972, pp. 84–102, quotations p. 96.
45. Tausendpfund 1975, pp. 125–126; Order to end begging in streets and houses, Berlin 1774, reprinted in Pollard and Holmes 1968, pp. 166–167.
46. Fauve-Chamoux 1996; Heywood 1981a; Heywood 1988, pp. 121–122; Soreau 1935.

47. Hopkins 1989, pp. 3–38, quotations pp. 7, 9.
48. Berlin 1997; Farr 1997, quotation p. 65; Sharpe 1991; Snell 1992, p. 228.
49. Linebaugh 1992, pp. 101–107, 263, 322.
50. Duffy 2000, pp. 40–59.
51. Humphries 2003, pp. 261, 266; Snell 1992, pp. 233, 244–257.
52. Bonnaissie 1975, pp. 180–181; Casey 1999, pp. 55–65, 123–125; Laslett 1965, pp. 1–3.
53. Fineschi 1993, pp. 273–278.
54. Marcello 1993, pp. 239–240.
55. Cerutti 1991.
56. Davis 1975, p. 113; Goubert 1986, p. 55.
57. Rétif de La Bretonne 1989 [1797], pp. 315–323. The contract is published by the book's editor, pp. 1295–1296.
58. Farge 1992, p. 64.
59. Lindberg 1989, pp. 90–91, 130–132, 149–151, 171–178, 198–223.
60. Vilkuna 1996, pp. 81–83. See also Evans and Rydén 1998.
61. Jutikkala 1986, p. 135; Lindberg 1989, pp. 52, 78, 101–124, 209.
62. Berlin 1997, p. 86; Farr 1997, p. 67; Reininghaus 1986; Musgrave, E. 1997; Simonton 1998, pp. 50–54; Snell 1992, pp. 271–391; Woodward 1995, p. 53.
63. Musgrave, E. 1997, pp. 153–155.
64. Snell 1992, pp. 272–277.
65. Krausman Ben-Amos 1991; Mayhew 1991.
66. Snell 1992, pp. 278–287.
67. Cunningham, H. 1990; Pollard 1968, p. 207.
68. Berg 1994, p. 31,
69. Chapman and Chassagne 1981, pp. 46, 52, 94–98.
70. Chapman and Chassagne 1981, pp. 171–176, 242–243, quotations pp. 174, 243.
71. Ure 1967 [1835], p. 15.
72. Simon, C. 1994.
73. Heckscher 1936, p. 509; Jutikkala 1986; Lindberg 1989, pp. 178–183; Nyberg 1992, pp. 212–235.
74. Utterström 1978, pp. 113–114.
75. Nyberg 1992, pp. 215–231, 275–304.
76. Blum 1972, pp. 292–293, 308–315, quotations p. 311; Dixon 1999, pp. 38, 100–104; Ransel 1988, p. 20; Tugan-Baranovsky 1970 [1907], pp. 14–24, quotation p. 21.
77. Sergene 1972, pp. 9, 205–206.
78. Chassagne 1998, p. 237; Hamon and Perrin 1993, pp. 343–348, 371–396; Pris 1973a, pp. 663–674, Pris 1973b, Tableau 47.
79. The little girl's mother was dead. The Delapierres belonged to the better families in Saint-Gobain (Hamon and Perrin 1993, pp. 98, 223, 522, 551, 621, 698).
80. Kermann 1972, pp. 191–194, 620–742; Pietsch 1979, pp. 43–51; Reuter 1961, pp. 97–98; Tausendpfund 1975, pp. 220–221.
81. Ariès 1962, pp. 309, 334–336; de Viguerie 1978, pp. 33–40, 60–68, 77–78, 137–140; Houston 2002, pp. 15–20, quotations p. 18; Caron 1997, pp. 133–137; Heywood 1988, pp. 3–4.
82. Casey 1999, pp. 6–27, 103, 119–127, 218–221, quotation 72.
83. Roggero 2000, pp. 539–553, quotations p. 542. See also Roggero 1999, pp. 57–59.

84. Pollock 1989, p. 239.
85. Hopkins 1989, pp. 135–143, 157–159.
86. Chapman and Chassagne 1981, pp. 112–118; Ottenjann 1995; Petschauer 1984; Poulsen 1995; Weber-Kellermann 1979, p. 73; Weber-Kellermann 1987, p. 103.
87. Blum 1972, p. 350; Dixon 1999, pp. 103, 152–157; Eklof 1986, p. 22; Engel 1978; Rustemeyer 1996, p. 47; Tovrov 1978.
88. Lönnqvist 1992, p. 113; Sandin 1988, pp. 366–371; Wirilander 1982, pp. 192, 281–307.
89. Degnbol 1991; Dokka 1967, pp. 13–31; Martinson 1992, pp. 105–106; Sigsgaard 1995, pp. 27–30.
90. Fossen 1989, pp. 19–20, 42–43, 54.
91. Niccoli 1995, pp. 120–125, quotation p. 120; Roggero 1999, pp. 86–89.
92. Sarasúa García 2002, p. 552.
93. Cunningham, H. 1992, p. 27; Houston 2002, p. 15.
94. Kerridge 1985, p. 202.
95. Jones, M. 1938, pp. 89–94, quotations pp. 91, 94. See also Cunningham, H. 1992, p. 28; Horn 1978, pp. 116–117.
96. Guidi 1991, pp. 14–16, 23–25; Sonnino 1994, pp. 101–114.
97. Lindemann 1990, pp. 164–168, quotations pp. 166, 168.
98. Hornby and Oxenbøll 1982, p. 16; Sigsgaard 1995 pp. 52–53.
99. Nyberg 1992, pp. 64–70, 234–235, 330; Persson 1993, p. 124.
100. Harnesk 1990, p. 52; Laine 1935, pp. 66–89, 285; Utterström 1957b, p. 33.
101. Laine 1935, pp. 285–296.
102. Nikula 1972, pp. 569–570.
103. Burke 1994, pp. 23–29, 270–281, quotation p. 28.
104. See above p. 7.
105. Cunningham, H. 1992, p. 28.
106. Anderson, P. 1993; de Vries 1994b, p. 42; Hobsbawm 1974; Olsson, L. 1980, p. 38; Malmstedt 1994; Poole 1995; Reininghaus 1986; Schwartz 1988, pp. 21–23; Thompson, E.P. 1967.
107. Heckscher 1955, pp. 155–157, quotation p. 155.
108. Examples of such wishful thinking are cited, e.g., in Capul 1984, p. 93; Cunningham, H. 1992, pp. 24–30; Herzig 1983, p. 313; Kerridge 1985, p. 169; Nardinelli 1990, p. 49; Schwartz 1988, pp. 101–103; Thompson, E.P. 1967.
109. Cunningham, H. 1990.
110. Fauve-Chamoux 1996.

CHAPTER 2

Peasant Children as Part of the Labour Force

Children and manpower policy

In the family history approach, the focus is naturally on the household, while the institutional context in which peasant customs took shape is of secondary importance. Similarly, the law has often received limited attention when discussing the subject of peasant children leaving home for service. Of course not too much weight should be put on laws and statutes, because many of them could be ignored or circumscribed. Early modern states varied in their capacity to implement their aims, but manpower policy generally had a high priority in contemporary affairs of state. Moreover farm service was connected with some form of enforcement in many parts of Europe, much like manufacturing work. To what extent did such institutional factors concern peasant children?

Historians seem to agree that in agriculture children's consumption exceeded their production. Tim Wales observes that it was not until in their late teens that children were net producers, while Clark Nardinelli found support for his hypothesis that 'child productivity in agriculture was relatively low until age fifteen or so'.[1] According to Richard Smith, 'children of either sex remain in deficit until age fifteen when they begin rapidly to produce more than they consume'.[2] Ann Kussmaul suggests that twenty, rather than fifteen or sixteen, could be taken 'as the modal adult age' for male servants, but adds that the age 'reflects a measurement of status, not of productivity'.[3] David Gaunt estimated that, up to the age of eighteen to nineteen years, young persons in the Scandinavian countryside consumed more than their labour produced, while Jan Lindegren estimated that children's consumption exceeded their production up to the age of fifteen.[4] Michael Mitterauer points out that peasant girls and boys reached physical maturity relatively late, and boys gained full muscular power between the ages of sixteen and twenty. In the small family farms, however, the farmers' own children 'were regarded as able-bodied workers' at the age of about twelve or thirteen years when they substituted for a hired maid or a stable-boy.[5] Thus, if and when young children were used for farm labour is something to be explained rather than taken for granted.

The shortage of manpower in agriculture led to forced child labour in farm work, for instance. In Rome, particularly during the plague or other epidemics, urban able-bodied beggars aged between ten and twenty-five were sentenced to work in the countryside, which was always short of labour. Beggars sentenced to farm work constituted a category of semi-unfree farm labourers called *monelli*. In the late eighteenth century, most *monelli* were men and women at their best working age, that is in their twenties, but they also included boys aged from nine years up and girls aged from ten years up. They were at the bottom of the rural wage scale in the vast estates of Agro di Roma in central Italy, and had the poorest food and housing conditions.[6]

Children's workload may have been beyond their parents' control in countries with feudal dues, corvée labour or serfdom. Russian peasants who were indebted to their landlords repaid them with labour. Sometimes such debt-servitude contracts (*kabala*) were entered into by the peasant parents together with their children. If the whole family was the borrower, the debt servitude lasted for two generations. Enserfment among Russian peasants was sealed by the Code of 1649 (*Ulozhenie*) which pushed serfs into forming extended families,[7] which were then traded as chattels. For example, between 1740 and 1801 the tsars gave away over 1.3 million adult male peasants with their wives and children to private proprietors. When serf children reached about fourteen years of age, light work or a reduced amount of regular labour service was often required of them by their owners. Able-bodied male serfs were expected to perform the full labour service from the age of seventeen or eighteen, females from fifteen or sixteen. To stimulate settlement in Siberia, in 1760 serf owners were given the right to banish a serf (and his wife) there. Furthermore, if they allowed the exiled serfs' children to go with their parents, the government paid them an indemnity of 10 roubles for boys aged under five years and 20 roubles for boys aged between five and fifteen, and half as much for girls, while for boys over fifteen the owner received a commission (recruit quittance).[8]

According to Heide Wunder, people in the German states of Bavaria and Westphalia were disinclined to go into service, which led to the introduction of compulsory service for peasant children. In Saxony, the obligation to work for the gentry landlord (*Hofzwang*) covered peasant children who could be forced into service. In 1759, a group of Saxon peasant fathers whose children had been so forced made a formal complaint against the landlord.[9] Serfdom prevailed in Prussia until the French Revolution. Ernst Schubert argues that the abolition of serfdom on the royal domains during the time of Fredrick the Great 'was not much more than an abolition of compulsory servant work by peasants' children',[10] whereas according to Harmut Harnisch, the abolition of feudal dues in 1799 left the subordination of peasant children largely intact. Peasants' children were still not allowed to work outside agriculture without the approval of the authorities, and their obligation to work on the land continued.[11]

After 1619 male and female farm servants (*karler* and *piger*) in Denmark who were dissatisfied with their wages or terms of employment could immediately be put into irons and sent to a public works or to a spin-house. *Stavnsbånd*, a compulsory residence system for males aged between 18 and 36 (intended to secure the supply of soldiers and labour force), was extended in 1742 to cover peasant boys from eight years up, and two decades later the lower age limit fell further to four years. Extreme forms of feudal order were abolished from 1788, while the obligation to be employed by a master was maintained. According to the Danish Poor Law of 1805, this obligation even concerned the poor who were 'partly unable to work', and thus possibly also deprived children.[12]

The Swedish hired labour acts stipulated that propertyless males and females were obliged to go into service, on pain of being treated as masterless persons, but there was no peasant practice of sending daughters into service 'to pay parents' feudal dues', contrary to what has been claimed.[13] The Hired Labour Act of 1723, a response to a shortage of manpower, was the first piece of legislation to refer to young boys and girls (*gossar* and *flickor*) as servants. The Act also ordered peasant farmers who had sons and daughters aged fifteen years or over to use them as farm servants (*drängar* and *pigor*), with no right to hire servants over the quota permitted for peasant farms by the Act. Moreover, all 'extra' sons and daughters over the quota were required to work for people of standing. The Hired Labour Act of 1739 permitted peasant farmers to have only one son and one daughter aged over fifteen at home, while other sons and daughters, after turning fifteen, had to leave home for service. Landed peasants managed to have this repealed in 1747, and were permitted to keep at home as many of their children as they wished, but it was not until 1789 that the law permitted peasant farmers' brothers and sisters to remain in their home farms after the age of fifteen. Peasants in the archipelago and mining district were exempted from such restrictions as a rule.[14]

Children's usefulness as part of the labour force was limited by their physical and cognitive characteristics, and peasants and masters evidently were well aware of this. In the mid-seventeenth century, peasants in the kingdom of Sweden complained that 'the children of poor beggars' they had taken in to bring up as servants deserted as soon as they had reached 'a useful age'. In 1688, a district court in south-western Finland gave a peasant permission to dismiss his hired hand before the contract time had expired because the boy turned out to be too young. In 1726, peasants complained that fifteen-year-old farm servants could work only enough to cover the costs of their food and clothing.[15] When a mill-toll, which later became a poll tax, was introduced in Sweden in 1625, it concerned those aged twelve or over. The Estate of Peasantry[16] declared in the Estates Assembly of 1738–1739 that children and servants should be exempted from paying the poll tax until they had reached the age of eighteen, since before that time they 'were not of such strength or efficiency that they would be of any particular service or would earn anything special of the sort that would be needed for the payment of the poll tax'. The age limit rose to fifteen in 1652.[17] An analogous case occurred in Denmark in 1762, when an extra tax was first stipulated to concern those aged twelve or over, but only two years later the lower age limit was raised to sixteen.[18]

According to Ann Kussmaul, in England 'each Quarter Session appears to have had its own idea of the productiveness of children'. This is supported by the diversity of wages. The mean wage of boys under fifteen was about two-fifths of men's wages, but the youngest servants may not have received any wage, save being maintained by the farmer for the year. Many boys aged fourteen earned less than a fifth of the maximum adult men's wages, while in some cases their earnings were close to them. Wages were set in the Quarter Sessions from the minimum age up, which for males varied from ten to twenty, for females from twelve to sixteen. The minimum age at which adult wages could be paid ranged from fifteen to twenty.[19] According to Robert Allen, the use of boys on large English farms was limited, because, though cheap, they were difficult to supervise.[20] Further, as Peter Laslett remarks, in the early modern English countryside 'too many members of a family were half-busied about an inadequate plot of infertile land; not enough work could be found for the women and children to do round the cottage fire, in some districts none at all, for there was no rural industry in them'. Along the same lines, Hugh Cunningham argues that farmers in eighteenth-century England accepted putting quite young children out to service as a method of coping with child unemployment.[21]

In conclusion, notwithstanding the timeless air of peasant children's work, it is not self-evident that young children were always and everywhere used for labour. After all, even quite ordinary tasks and jobs in traditional peasant farming required certain manual and cognitive skills, as well as physical strength or stature. Nevertheless, children were used for herding, farm service and rural cottage industries or proto-industries, all of which seem to have undergone interesting changes from early modern times until the nineteenth century. How and why did they change?

Herding

Herding is often described as a typical job for children.[22] Yet the shepherds moving with the flocks in medieval Montaillou in the Pyrenees were men, as they were in Castille in Cervante's time (as we know from Don Quixote). Nevertheless, in 1528 a boy had been put to tend cattle illegally pasturing in the *monte* near the city of Soria.[23] Pigs were guarded by men in the November calendar image of a fifteenth-century book of hours, the *Très Riches Heures* of the duc de Berry. Pierre Goubert describes herding in sixteenth- and seventeenth-century France as able-bodied men's work. Professional shepherds and cowherds were chosen by local decision makers. Sometimes a poor labourer may have worked temporarily as a shepherd, while some worked as swineherds.[24] In Elizabethan England, shepherds were about the only male day-labourers of the gentleman farmer Nathaniel Bacon in Norfolk, to whom he paid the top wage of 10 pounds a year. Professional shepherds on large farms in early nineteenth-century England may have stayed on the same farm for most of their lives, while a cowherd was 'generally a man past middle life, and sometimes an old and almost superannuated ploughman'.[25] Correspondingly, the 1834 Poor Law Report returns did not suggest children's use for herding.[26] Nonetheless, there evidently was a shift from men to children for herding in some countries or regions, which begs an explanation. The discussion below is but a tentative introduction to this issue.

Very young shepherds and goatherds were used from an early age in the Alps. In about 1507 in Valais, a poor, orphaned boy Thomas Platter, was obliged to herd about 80 goats belonging to his brother-in-law during his seventh and eighth years. The job was far too demanding for him, and many people expressed their disapproval of a young boy being engaged in such a dangerous employment. The other shepherds, evidently older, came to Thomas' help. He was then placed out by his sister with a rich peasant, whose goats he herded together with his master's young daughter. The two children proved unreliable shepherds, they got lost in play and the goats at least once disappeared from their sight. Trying to find them in the dark, Thomas risked his life, because of the very rough terrain where he was in danger of falling. After this event, he was no longer sent to herd goats, but began to tend the cows on a relative's farm.[27] His history suggests that people's own or kindred children may have been set to herding at a younger age than was, in fact, rational. If this was the case, was it just to save even the little that was paid to hired children, or was the supply of older children willing to be employed as shepherds insufficient? Furthermore, were children and young persons only tending flocks pasturing near villages, as it appears, while men were responsible for the sheep moving back and forth between pastures a long distance apart? What happened to children's herding work when transhumance began to decrease?

Transhumant cattle breeding was a dominant activity in the Montes de Pas in northern Spain. In the eighteenth century, male household heads all declared themselves to be occupied in farming and grazing. They had male helpers aged over eighteen, most of them relatives, including their sons. According to Carmen Sarasúa, children became part of the labour force at the age of ten, and 'evidence on the fundamental importance of children's work since very young ages to run the farm and take care of the livestock is abundant'. Children also followed their parents into wage work, offered by the nearby Royal armaments Factory. The local people carried the coal needed by the factory on their shoulders, thus men, women and children climbed the hill paths carrying baskets loaded with coal. As far as grazing was concerned, the usual family labour organisation was that the father and some children would take part of the herd to the higher pastures, while the mother and the rest of the family remained with the pregnant cows and young calves near the towns.[28] Since transhumant grazing was adult men's chief activity, did this indicate that men rather than children did the herding, save for helping?

In eighteenth-century France, boys and girls worked as shepherds and cowherds, despite the risk of wolves. Nicolas-Edme Rétif had not yet turned ten when he had his first experience of shepherd's work in Auxerre, Bourgogne, in the autumn of 1745. The shepherd his father had hired, a labourer boy called Jacques Guerreau, aged about fifteen, had gone on a pilgrimage for a fortnight. Nicolas-Edme was eager to act as the shepherd in the meantime. His parents did not like the idea, but as there was nobody else at hand, in the end they agreed, on the condition that he would keep close to their farm because of the risk of wolves. Little Nicolas-Edme took three big dogs with him to protect the sheep from wolves. The next summer, ten-year-old Nicolas-Edme substituted for a hired shepherd youngster, because his father had failed to employ one – or was it also because his father, a wealthy peasant, seems to have been a frugal man who carefully calculated the pros and cons?[29]

Jean-Roch Coignet was but eight years old in the spring of 1784 when he escaped with his elder brother from their hard-hearted stepmother in Druyes in the Department of Yvonne. His brother fastened an oak leaf on Jean's cap at a fair, whereby he was hired as a shepherd's helper for a year. He earned 24 francs and a pair of clogs by 'serving as the dog of the shepherd girl'. While looking for run-away goats in the forest, Jean met a wolf. Having never seen a wolf before, it did not occur to him to escape the beast until the shepherd girl told him to. He was hired the following year by two old landowners and served them for three years. In one year he earned 30 francs, a chemise and a pair of clogs by hauling wood on a cart and tending the six driving oxen, while in winter he threshed in the barn, and slept on straw.[30]

In the region of Bologna, younger children irrespective of sex herded small animals, sheep and pigs, while older boys, aged between twelve and fourteen or approaching adolescence were hired for tending cows and oxen. Boys and girls, aged from seven years up, moved around the meadows and pastures, each keeping an eye on his or her flock of sheep or pigs. As children will, they played and scrapped with each other, and squabbled over flocks that had got mixed up. It sometimes happened that their judgement failed, and they met with mishaps. In 1630, nine-year-old Giambattista and twelve-year-old Lorenzo were working in Val di Sambro in freezing weather, so they decided to set fire to an oak tree – with the result that the burnt tree fell onto another little herder, Maria Tavacchina from Valgattara. In the same year, Lorenzo Sagribono, who was only four years old (exceptionally young), was herding with his elder brother Andrea near Palata, in the region of Ferrara. When the boys crossed the Cavemento canal, Lorenzo fell into the water and was drowned. Quarrels sometimes ended in bloodshed, as children threw stones or bricks at each other. In 1630, for example, Domenico Giordano, aged about thirteen or fourteen, was tending cows in Pizzicalvo with Gerolamo, who was younger than he. He became angry and hit Gerolamo on the head so that blood ran from the wound. Also landowners may have used sticks to hit young boys who failed to prevent cows from crossing landmarks.[31]

Both the young and the old worked as shepherds (*pastori*) in the provinces around Rome, Agro di Roma, judging from the figures presented by Giorgio Rossi:[32]

Year		Average age	Lowest–highest ages
	North of Tevere		
1762	Castel di Guido	31.5	
	Torre in Pietra	35.9	
	Sasso	31.4	13–60
1771	Sasso	34.5	13–64
1784	Sasso	29.6	15–60
1823	Sasso	34.2	13–56
1844	Cerveteri	32.8	10–70
	South of Tevere		
1792	Castel Romano	37.0	19–60

Nevertheless, the high average age implies that children were in the minority. The changes in the lowest and highest ages do not exhibit any clear trend, and at most we might say that the case of Cerveteri in 1844 suggests a declining minimum age.

In German villages, shepherds, cowherds and swineherds were hired by the community, but shepherds may also have worked for themselves. According to Ingeborg Weber-Kellerman, these men had a big role in the economic life of the village, but their status and qualifications varied. Professional shepherds were comparable to craftsmen in some areas.[33] For example, Württemberg boosted a shepherds' guild, and its powers and privileges were even extended in 1723. Keepers of sheep also had to have been properly apprenticed as shepherds. Nonetheless, girls aged between seven and ten in the Württemberg region began to be useful to their parents for herding, while for boys it was somewhat later.[34]

In Upper Swabia, the need for cattle herders increased with the 'enclosure' system ('*Vereinödung*') that started in 1715 and expanded towards the close of the century. Individual herds grew too large for a single village herder to manage, but a herder was needed for each peasant farm's cattle. At the same time, the concentration of land around the farm made herding less demanding. Traffic in seasonal child labour (*Schwabenkinder*) emerged during the eighteenth century from Voralberg to Upper Swabia. In 1796, some 700 boys aged between seven and seventeen were told to travel every spring from Tyrol to Upper Swabia to work as herders of horses, cows, sheep, goats, swine and geese. Many landowners acquired a 'Tyrol boy' in Kempen in Bavaria, on the road to Augsburg.[35] By 1820, informal fairs for hiring migrant herding children had become an established practice (see Chapter 3). Likewise in

Denmark, the enclosure of the commons used for pasturage suggest an increasing need for herding and fencing.[36]

Livestock farming increased in many Swedish provinces from the sixteenth century. The need for herding and fencing – both quite labour-intensive activities – was generally diminished by the practice of fencing in sown fields and the better meadows, and allowing the cattle to move freely. It was the practice in central and northern Sweden for everyone, or just the womenfolk, from the farm to move with the cattle for the summer to upland shielings (*fäboden*), while female farm servants may have left on their own or with young boys for the most distant ones. Peasants in Skåne (Scania) followed the Danish custom of jointly hiring men who were professional cowherds.[37]

Close to the village young girls were used for herding. One day in 1662, a ten-year-old girl, Kerttu, was tending cattle with a twelve-year-old boy and a female farm servant in the parish of Säkkijärvi, when a peasant came across them, shouting angrily at the children on his turnip field. The frightened girl ran into the lake and drowned. Her mother brought the case to the district court. The lay members of the court proclaimed that 'it is the custom of the country and of the common people that little cowherds like this found in turnip fields must not be knocked about, but their clothes must be taken from them to be shown to their parents or master so that they could punish the child'.[38] One day in October 1667, in the Swedish province of Dalarna, eleven-year-old girl Gertrud Svensdotter was herding goats with nine-year-old Mats Nilsson. The two children quarrelled over a piece of bread, and Mats became angry with Gertrud. Meanwhile some goats had taken themselves to a little shoal, and Gertrud waded after them. Back at home Mats told his family about this wading, an insignificant episode, but in words that made his father suspect Gertrud of witchcraft (being able to walk on the water with the Devil's help). This launched a ten-year witch-hunt in Dalarna.[39]

The Swedish Hired Labour Acts requiring farm servants to be hired by the year no doubt increased the incentive to use children for herding, a highly seasonal job in the north. Nonetheless, if the risk of wolves and bears was high, herding was considered men's rather than boys' work. In 1736, in the parish of Laitila, six peasants were taken to the district court because they had risked the lives of their sons by sending them alone to tend cattle in distant forest grazing areas. In 1686 the use of boys for herding was prohibited. This was intended to counteract 'the sin of bestiality' (*tidelag*), which was liable to capital punishment. The prohibition was reiterated in 1729, now backed up with a high fine of 40 silver marks, and it was also included in the Law Codex of 1734. Peasants protested against this prohibition. A group of peasants from Småland appealed to the *Riksdag* (Estates Assembly) in 1713 for the right to use boys aged under thirteen, arguing that their daughters and female servants regarded herding as shameful. Boys, however, where thought to be physically strong and thus more capable of driving away wolves and bears. In fact, the prohibition was frequently ignored.[40]

Still, the ban on using boys for herding had some effect. Some parishes did not allow boys aged under fifteen years to be used as cowherds, while others used girls, women, old people or retired soldiers. In 1749, two peasant farmers from Punkalaidun had to pay a fine for using young boys as cowherds, although they pleaded a shortage of manpower, and again in 1771, two peasant farmers were charged with having used young boys as cowherds. In the parish of Pojo, two peasant farmers who had hired an eleven-year-old boy for herding cows in 1780 were sentenced to four days imprisonment with bread and water. In 1739, Captain Aminoff hired a tenant soldier's twelve-year-old daughter for herding on his estate near Helsinki. The girl was obviously unhappy in her employment, because her father took her back home in the middle of the contract period. Capitain Aminoff took the case to the district court which decided that the girl had to return to service because the parents could not prove that Aminoff had hired her against their wishes. Again in Punkalaidun, this time in 1782, a retired soldier Tuomas Dief, who served as a cowherd, had two girls, aged twelve and fifteen, the daughters of another former soldier Tuomas Kempe, as his helpers. Dief paid the girls with some of the rye he himself received as a wage.[41] This was typical of Scandinavia where boy and girl herders were, as a rule, paid in kind, and very seldom if ever in cash.[42]

If the practice of herding by children was on the rise during the early modern centuries (although there is no time-series evidence), was this because the peasant farmers were wanting to use adult labour in a more productive and profitable manner? Were peasant farmers becoming more profit- or productivity-conscious? Or did they want to cut labour costs, or avoid spending cash on paying wages? According to the Swedish historian Janken Myrdal, there was a growing awareness of the effective use of labour in agriculture in Sweden after 1690, and by 1800 the measurement of the working time required for different kinds of agricultural tasks had produced systematic information that was published so that it was accessible for peasant farmers.[43] Swedish productivity-conscious peasant farmers had their counterparts elsewhere in western Europe, and even in Russia there was an interest in rational estate management.[44] Was something like this behind the development of life-cycle service?

Life-cycle service

Life-cycle service seems to have been particularly characteristic in early modern agriculture, even though it existed before and was still prevalent in the nineteenth century. Ever since John Hajnal opened the discussion on the European family and household patterns in 1965, life-cycle service has been deemed to be one of the characteristics of the West European marriage pattern, although somewhat less so in Mediterranean societies, while the age of leaving home has become a standard theme in family and household history. According to this pattern, servants were 'youths hired into the families of their employers' (A. Kussmaul). They did not form a separate social category or class because of the transitional nature of service, which ended with marriage. Life-cycle servants were recruited generally for the year, and presumably from landed as well as landless families. Landed peasants' daughters and sons maintained their social status in principle despite the years spent in service.[45] The British model of putting children into service is described below and discussed in the light of some contrasting cases from continental Europe and Scandinavia. The question is raised whether or not the received picture of life-cycle service is slightly idealised.

'Generally speaking, the incidence of servanthood in the early modern period was inversely related to food prices', Mark Overton argues concerning England. There the proportion of servants fell during the sixteenth century, and the low point was reached in the middle of the seventeenth century. Thereafter the proportion increased, until it reached its peak in the 1740s. 'From the mid-eighteenth century, the sustained rise in prices encouraged a move away from living-in servants, which continued into the nineteenth century'.[46] How did this general development concern life-cycle service by adolescents, and children in particular?

According to Marjorie McIntosh, orphans and young illegitimate children had been commonly boarded with poor widows in England before Elizabethan times, whereas after the late sixteenth century 'young children were more often given into custody of masters who were free to put them to work'.[47] There was 'a probable expansion of adolescent service' in fifteenth-century England, which could have been associated with economic and demographic changes: 'In the decades after 1460 the institution of adolescent service appears to have become more popular in commercialised agrarian sectors and the market towns. ... By 1500 the pattern of service as an interim stage between childhood and self-supporting adulthood ... was firmly established in many of England's small communities.'[48]

This suggests that a fresh demand for young labour was emerging in

Elizabethan England. This evidently happened later in Scotland, judging from the fact that, as Michael Robson argues, hiring fairs 'originated no earlier than the eighteenth century'.[49] After reading recent contributions to the debate, Clark Nardinelli concludes that 'agricultural (and other) service outside the home was apparently much less common for teenagers of the fourteenth and fifteenth centuries than for those of the sixteenth through eighteenth centuries'.[50] To what extent did all this concern children?

Peter Laslett wrote in the mid-1960s that it was the practice in early modern England to send children (at an age that varied from seven to twenty-two) away as servants or apprentices. It was customary in the English countryside to use hired children instead of one's own, and 'a boy or a girl in a cottage would leave home for service at any time after the age of ten'.[51] Grant McCracken offers some explanations for the extensive exchange of children in Tudor England: reciprocity, the demonstration of status difference, and the refinement of 'raw child material'.[52] However, assuming that children consumed more than they produced, as many historians argue, the economic rationale of the employer is not captured by such explanations.

Subsequent studies have qualified the picture. A. Hassell Smith discovered that a gentleman farmer, Nathaniel Bacon, living in north Norfolk in the 1590s, paid wages to just one or two daughters of working-class families aged between twelve and eighteen, while the rest of his staff were older.[53] According to Richard Wall, the process of leaving home was gradual and protracted, and there were great variations in the age at which it happened. The records of a parish in southern England show that over half of the children over fifteen still resided with their parents in the 1690s, and all children aged fourteen to fifteen lived at home. A century later, in the 1780s, a third of the children aged fifteen years or more in another parish lived with their parents. Boys tended to leave home a little earlier than girls, perhaps because of the better work opportunities. Nevertheless, very few children had left home before the age of ten, and at the age of twenty many were still living with their parents.[54] Ann Kussmaul estimates that, on average, 15 per cent of both male and female servants in three English parishes were under sixteen years of age. Since farmers hired servants to help them with the farm work, they were not willing to maintain a young child for a year. Thus young children first worked for the farmers during the day, but continued to live in their parental home. It was only when they were 'old enough to earn their living' that they could expect to be hired as living-in servants.[55]

One explanation offered for hiring-out practices has been the need for poor families to regulate the number of mouths to feed by sending their children into service at an early age (which does not, of course, explain the custom in England to exchange children). Michael Anderson appears to presume that this was generally the case in Europe.[56] However, neither the practice of putting young children into service nor the need to get rid of 'extra' children appears to have been Europe-wide.

The Spanish countryside witnessed social polarisation in the sixteenth century, as the propertied adopted new family strategies aimed at securing their land in a situation of deteriorating prospects. The poor resorted to cottage industries and migration, rather than putting their children into service in peasant households. The rather strict seclusion of unmarried daughters did not promote the practice of girls going into service, although widows in strained economic circumstances were likely to put their children into domestic service. Employed servants were not common in the eighteenth-century Castilian countryside, although this was not the case in the towns. On the other hand, it was quite common to have 'reared-ones' or foster children as servants. In the late eighteenth century, the households of peasant farmers in the Navarre region had, on average, more kin than servants. A child in service may have been an orphaned child of a relative, an illegitimate son or daughter of the household head, or a foundling or orphan placed out by a foundling hospice into indentured service from the age of four to six years until the early twenties.[57]

In Italy, as in Spain, leaving home for service was less common than in England, whereas child abandonment was more common, evidently as a solution to the problem of 'extra' children. Joint families dominated sharecropping in Italy, and these tended to be highly fertile. This not only guaranteed the family labour force, but also gave the possibility of taking over larger farms, as Pier Paolo Viazzo remarks. However, this strategy was in conflict with the interests of the landlord, who monitored the size of sharecropping households. When he came to visit, the sharecroppers were forced to hide 'extra' children. The next step would be abandonment. Tuscany, where sharecropping dominated, was one of the regions in Italy where the abandonment of children was most common.[58]

An 'extra' child or an unmarried sister might easily find a place in large peasant households in seventeenth-century France, while ongoing social stratification among the peasant population increased the misery of poor households. A minority of country children started at the village school at the age of seven, while the majority of children from seven or eight years up worked with the rest of the family in the cottage industries. At harvest time, children followed the men and women to the fields, and wives and children were engaged in unskilled work in the highly labour-intensive vine cultivation. Having turned ten, many boys would start with larger farmers as shepherds, cowherds or servants. French country children took their first communion at the age of twelve or thirteen, and could then work as adults, which they were possibly already doing.[59] In the eighteenth century, share-cropper holdings required a large labour force of up to twenty employed workers. The usual type of holding had about ten persons, including 'one or two child workers, often orphans of whom the share-cropper had assumed the guardianship in order that they should cost him nothing' (J-L. Flandrin).[60]

Rural childhood had a family character in Schleswig-Holstein and the north-west German States. Peasants with solid wealth and good farms carefully followed the lives of their children, their future heirs. According to Jürgen Schlumbohm, there are few references to children aged under fourteen years being sent away from their parental household, and children lived with their parents. A substantial peasant-farming household might have included both servants and family children over fourteen still living at home, whereas landless households very rarely had servants.[61]

In contrast to the general European trend, there seems to have been no pauperisation of the peasant population in sixteenth-century Sweden.[62] This suggests that, before the population explosion in the late eighteenth century, probably only a limited number of children were forced by poverty into leaving home for farm service before their confirmation. For example, peasant sons and daughters in the Åland archipelago did not leave home permanently until their late teens or early twenties. In 1781, the governor of the province of Heinola remarked that boys and girls in his province left home for farm service for the first time at the age of fifteen or sixteen. He considered this to be too late, and proposed that cottagers and lodgers should not be permitted to have their children at home for longer than they needed care.[63]

Perhaps the Norwegian law of 1604, which stipulated that minors could not be hired without their fathers' consent, indicated that young persons were emerging as a noteworthy resource. The structural changes in the Norwegian countryside during the eighteenth century may have brought with them an increasing supply of child labour. The number of poor cottagers, peasant smallholders and squatters multiplied, and thus the number of children who had to work away from home probably increased. Even quite young children may have been employed, and in 1801 in some areas, a tenth of children aged between ten and fourteen were in service. The conditions and prospects of girls in farm service appeared poor when compared with, say, those of boys in service in urban burgher households.[64]

In Denmark, with its feudal order, going into service was more or less a rule, and boys aged between twelve and sixteen years of age were employed as younger farm hands. Children of the landless (*husmænd*) seldom stayed in the parental households after confirmation, whereas sons and daughters of peasant farmers clearly left home later. On the Danish island of Moen, in 1645, a fifth of the children of farmers and a good third of those of labourers aged between ten and fourteen were servants, and the corresponding figures for children aged between five and ten two per cent and eight per cent. Peter Laslett concluded that on this island, 'up to a half of all young people could expect to become life-cycle servants, but the other half never went to service'. The parishes of Kirkerup and Sørbymagle recorded a total of 21 male and 19 female farm servants in 1645, and at least nine children aged under fifteen who were called servants. Two of these, four- and six-year-old boys, were evidently orphaned foster children. Life in the countryside became harder in the late seventeenth century and there was growing impoverishment. Family poverty drove Ellen Hansen from Rosted into service at an early age. She was treated badly whilst in service in a peasant holding, deserted, and was found dead in 1653, hardly twenty years of age. Her brother Nils was but nine years old when he had to leave home for service. He fell ill and died as a beggar in 1667, at the age of 24.[65]

The system of life-cycle servants did not exist among Russian peasantry, which was characterised by large, complex serf families. Nonetheless, nearly half of the children living on serf farmsteads in the Baltic province of Kurland in the 1790s were not relatives of the head of the household. Some were adoptive or foster children, but most of these children had been sent out to work by their landless parents, and were part of the labour force, working as herders and young farm servants.[66] Was their role in the farmstead economy possibly comparable to that of young living-in servants in Western Europe?

Increasing social stratification among the peasant population, which was in some countries visible as early as the sixteenth century, meant that the children of farmers with substantial holdings were becoming reluctant to go into service. Wealthy farmers began to appear on the northern French plains in the sixteenth or seventeenth century. They tended to form a close caste of their own, and their children married only among themselves. Peasant farmers in poorer parts of the country in the south who owned and cultivated over six hectares distinguished themselves from manual labourers, and with very few exceptions their children married within the same group. Further south the *ménager*, 'the master of the farm', was a landowner farming on a fairly large scale. Occasionally the richest of them even married younger daughters of local minor aristocracy.[67] Among vinegrowers in Languedoc in southern France, the rich landowners had extended families tailored to secure the transmission of the family estate. Their children, few in number, did not go into service.[68]

There is some evidence that social stratification may not have increased in sixteenth-century Sweden. 'Nothing indicates that an upper stratum of wealthy peasants in any way systematically began to be differentiated from the other peasants', as Johan Söderberg and Janken Myrdal argue. As in most of Scandinavia, in Sweden too, regions with little social differentiation were generally characterised by low rates of living-in farm servants. For example, in 1570, it was not particularly usual for peasants to hire farm hands in addition to family labour in Norrland. Social stratification was well underway in most of Sweden in the eighteenth century, and it was in 1780 reported that landed peasants in the parish of Nätra in Norrland only reluctantly allowed their children to go into service. In a province north of Stockholm with advanced social differentiation, it was common to work for a few years as a 'little servant' before permanently leaving home for service at around the age of sixteen.[69]

Around or after the turn of the nineteenth century, going into service began to be connected with downward social mobility in the Swedish and Finnish countryside. Of the cohort born in 1770–1774 in the Finnish parish of Punkalaidun, less than half of the children of landed peasants managed to stay in the landed class, and none of the successful ones, neither males nor females, worked outside their parental farm before marriage.[70] In the parish of Hassela in Hälsingland, where only men could inherit land, going into service appeared to predict downward social mobility for landed peasants' sons, but the same was not true for women. Börje Harnesk suggests that this was because daughters did not inherit, thus for women there was not much difference between being landed and being landless.[71] Although children of landed peasants were still to be found as cowherds over the summer, or as young female farm servants, the social gap between peasant farmers and their farm servants grew, and servants increasingly lived separately from their masters.[72]

According to a study on the German parish of Belm conducted by Jürgen Schlumbohm, there is some evidence that leaving home for service may have been the first step towards downward social mobility. Fewer of the children of landed peasants than of landless people left home for service in 1812: 18 per cent of land-rich peasants', 40 per cent of smallholders' and 78 per cent of landless people's offspring seem to have been in service. The proportions of offspring staying at home were the opposite: 77 per cent of the children of land-rich parents, 60 per cent of those of smallholders, and only 19 per cent of children of the landless stayed on their parental (or a close kinsman's) farm. There was also some evidence that *Grossbauers*' sons and daughters avoided service: 'girls from landless families went into service and married late, while land-rich peasants' daughters stayed at home and married early ... propertied peasants' sons [...] usually stayed with their parents as long as they were single'.[73] Around 1840 Jeremias Gotthelf complained that most servants considered their masters to be their enemies and service a misfortune (*Unglück*).[74]

The system of life-cycle service was rapidly disappearing in Britain around 1800, although the pace was slower in some regions, such as the Blean area of Kent, Colyton in Devon, Sussex and south-east Lowland Scotland. The custom of hiring yearly living-in servants was unusual or had ended by the 1830s, in the south of England. By that time in the south-eastern part of the country, most servants were sons and daughters of labourers, destined to remain in the same class.[75] Alastair Orr suggests that the survival of life-cycle service in Scotland was connected with the fact that, on the small farms, 'the social gulf between farmer and servant was a narrow one'. The disappearance of life-cycle servants in England may have been connected with the commercialisation of agriculture. 'Farm servants were no longer welcome in the farmer's family', hence farm servants and labourers were increasingly housed separately, 'which symbolised the new social division between farmer and labourer'.[76]

Michael Anderson rightly questioned the role of cultural factors as an adequate explanation of peasant customs.[77] Nevertheless, one cultural factor, the reluctance to go into service, deserves more attention in the discussion on life-cycle service. The heavy sanctions applied generally in Europe to masterless persons and the repeated complaints about the 'idleness' of the young were, no doubt, connected to labour shortage or unemployment, but does this not also imply a persistent unwillingness to go into service? This seems to have been the case in German States with feudal dues, and perhaps also in Sweden. How else are we to interpret, say, claims such as, 'young people capable of service have wanted to refuse to get into service for a year',[78] found in 1752 in an authoritative Swedish text? Even though leaving home for service was a common pattern in the early modern centuries, there may also have been tacit or open reluctance, or even resistance to following it. Peasant boys and girls were not just bearers of their culture, but they were also actors who changed customs by breaking them.

The discussion on life-cycle service among peasant sons and daughters easily gives the impression of transactions between equal partners: peasant families reciprocally exchanging children. This blurs the fact that much of the flow of juvenile labour went one way only: from propertyless households to propertied ones.[79] The propertyless families gave birth and nursed their children in their infancy, throughout the unproductive years. When the children reached a productive age, they left for service in the propertied households, which then could exploit their full productive capacity. As a consequence, there was an underlying 'resource drain' from propertyless families to the propertied households, remotely analogous to the more recent 'brain drain' phenomenon associated with migration from poorer countries to richer ones.

Cottage industries

Three decades ago, Franklin Mendels suggested that the 'first phase which preceded and prepared modern industrialization' could be called proto-industrialisation, which was marked by 'the rapid growth of traditionally organized but market-oriented, principally rural industry', as well as by 'changes in the spatial organization of rural economy'.[80] Maxine Berg summarises the criteria suggested by Mendels. For example, proto-industrial manufacture developed in symbiosis with commercial agriculture, industry was seasonal, although it could have become a full-time family occupation, and the market for proto-industrial goods was international. Moreover, proto-industrialisation has been connected with major economic and social changes, from the dissolution of the division of labour between the town and the countryside to the emergence of the world market and the rise of the consumer society.[81]

What is of interest here is the work the children carried out in home industries undergoing such major changes. What was the role of child labour in various types of cottage crafts and putting-out or outwork industries, some but not all of which represented proto-industrialisation? Why were children found in largely similar kinds of home industries irrespective of the country?

In Spain, the history of putting-out cottage industries goes back to the Middle Ages. As early as 1462, all spinning for wool manufacturing in Cuenca in Castile was done by rural home-working women.[82] The Cortes of Castile claimed that very few households could get by with just what they grew for themselves in 1579–1582. If this statement is correct, it suggests that subsidiary trades were of vital importance. For example, in sixteenth-century Calig, between Catalonia and Valencia, 200 families were making arquebuses, shotguns and sharp metal tools – and nothing of this activity remained two centuries later. Around the great woollen weaving towns, men and women, boys and girls were involved in putting-out work, and cottage industries for new draperies (serge and worsteds) still gave work to the peasantry in the late sixteenth century. Some villages made excellent raw silk for sale. In others that had specialised in just one handicraft or skill, the women practised it from childhood, but such one-sided specialisation made the villages vulnerable. In 1782, rural manufacturing was still everywhere as villages produced textiles, clothing, hides and footwear, but rural industries were poorly integrated into the market systems and trade was sluggish, depending as it did on itinerant traders. There was not enough employment to retain the young. 'The growing reluctance to invest in domestic manufactures seems to have much to do with its perceived uncompetitiveness', as James Casey wrote.[83]

The embroidery and lace industry around Ciudad Real in the Castilian plains also suffered from the absence of a modern commercial structure. Bobbin lace was incredibly labour intensive, and like embroidery, paid low wages to the women and girls engaged in it. Nevertheless, in the eighteenth century, numerous families as well as lone women lived on lace making. They worked for a handful of powerful putters-out called *randeros*, who controlled the trade and profited from it. An export-oriented lace and embroidery factory was established by the Torres brothers in 1793, but it does not seem to have incorporated mechanised production, and was rather a place for accumulating and finishing the pieces made by women and girls dispersed in the villages. In 1840, there were still more than 30,000 women and girls occupied in commercial embroidery and lace making in the Catalonian countryside.[84]

According to Carlo Marco Belfanti, in the second half of the sixteenth century, Italian urban merchants began to transfer 'the central stages of production from cities to rural areas in order to solve the high costs of labour'. The Genoese silk-weaving industry moved to the countryside in the last few decades of the sixteenth century, but both city and rural putting-out weavers manufactured fashionable luxury materials (damask and black velvet) for the aristocracy and the bourgeoisie. The putting-out system proved persistent, and in 1872 silk manufacturing around Genoa was still dispersed. Merchants in Mantua chose another strategy to cope with the late sixteenth-century crisis of urban woollen cloth and silk manufacturing. They went over to the production of knitwear. Ready-made woollen stockings were a luxury good, manufactured as putting-out work in the countryside, but finished in the city. The guild organisation was enfeebled in the North Italian small territorial states, giving way to rural manufacturing. In the seventeenth and eighteenth centuries, women and children in the small city of Carpi, in the valley of the River Po, twisted together shavings from willow wood into plaits, which the women then stitched together to make hats. Other women and children made the straw plaits used for making straw hats. Production expanded in the eighteenth century, as straw hats became fashionable, and were exported to

England, France, Germany and eventually across the Atlantic. This expansion attracted additional rural producers, and provided work for day-labourers in the Tuscan region, for example.[85]

In the textile regions of seventeenth-century France, labourers usually made warps for cheap material, or coarse linen cloths which they may have sold themselves in a nearby market. In many areas, badly-off people worked for town merchants who provided them with work in the evenings and in the winter. 'It is clear', Pierre Goubert remarks, 'that these merchants were quite shameless in their exploitation of peasant spinners and weavers, paying them as little as possible'. Putting-out work gave the small supplementary income needed to make ends meet, but required a lot of work: 'Most of the family, including children aged seven or eight upwards, would work by candlelight (if they could afford it) or by firelight or daylight, spinning, reeling, and even weaving.' Boys started spinning at the age of seven, and helped their fathers who wove the cloth.[86] The expansion of cotton factories started in France in the decades before the revolution, and by 1805 there were 1,037 spinning workshops and 2,249 weaving workshops. In 1806, the leading firms launched a new system for subcontracting weaving in domestic workshops. Such changes notwithstanding, 'work continued to be done in country people's homes, or in small workshops nearby where wives and children could be employed – the former as jenny or mule spinners, the latter as dressers and trimmers' (S. Chassagne).[87]

According to Adam Smith's description of cottage industry in late eighteenth-century Scotland, stockings were 'knit much cheaper than they can anywhere be wrought upon the loom'. Such stockings, sold in thousands, were 'the work of servants and labourers', carried out during the part of the year when the master otherwise had 'little or no occasion for their labour'. The spinning of linen yarn was carried on 'nearly in the same way as the knitting of stockings, by servants who [were] hired for other purposes'.[88] This description is in striking contrast to present-day historical writing, according to which, 'the nuclear family without servants was the predominant type of household in rural cottage industry', as Hans Medick puts it following the lines of Peter Laslett.[89] In his discussion of proto-industrial families in England, David Levine suggests that living with relatives and lodgers was a way framework knitters increased the number of co-resident wage earners. The women and children in a knitter's family did the auxiliary jobs of winding, seaming and stitching. In the nineteenth century, knitters' children were reported to be smaller and weaker than those of agricultural labourers, and long working hours together with undernourishment were believed to be the cause.[90]

By the time of the 1834 Poor Law Report, wages in lace making, glove making and button making had collapsed in England in the face of foreign competition and machine-made work. Nevertheless, straw plaiting and lace making by women and children were still common in the South Midlands, silk throwing, and button making and glove making in the South West, and lace working in parishes situated near urban manufactories, such as Leicester. According to Nicola Verdon, children's earnings were much more important to the family income than those of women, and this was the case particularly in areas in which there was non-agricultural employment, such as Bedford: 'This suggests the predominance of child labour in the domestic industries and the still considerable sums that could be amassed by labouring in these trades, even at a time of wage depression.'[91] The considerable sums amassed during the wage depression also suggest that children in domestic industries had long and strenuous working days.

Women and children in the German Erzgebirge area were making lace as putting-out work since the late sixteenth century. In the 1740s, a silk manufactory in Krefeld contracted silk winding out to the countryside, where it occupied peasant wives and children. Mechanical silk spooling was introduced at the latest by 1768.[92] It was not the smallholders or the landless, but more the *Grossbauer* who grew most of the flax in the Osnabrück region. The big farmers set servants to spin and weave flax in the slack agricultural season. In the mid-nineteenth century, when the linen industry was in crisis, *Grossbauer* abandoned commercial linen production.[93] Rural households engaged in linen weaving in Oberlausitz, in the borderland between Saxony and Bohemia, could not afford servants or hired hands, but fully used the labour of all household members. Such relatively poor households also had some subsistence agriculture. In the eighteenth century, peasant smallholders increasingly cultivated flax and hemp in the corporate fields, and widespread village spinning by men and women as outwork came into being.[94] In the Oberlausitz weaving villages, as Christian Pescheck reported in 1852, 'men and women, sons and daughters weave. The oldest and the children sit near the looms and wind the bobbins and prepare the spools'.[95] In Krefeld masters began to use also hired children for spooling, half of the master households had at least one living-in *Spulkind* in 1815, and a tenth had more than three. According to the reminiscences of children concerning nineteenth-century domestic industries, spooling was described as a tedious, monotonous and terrible work (*'verdriessliche', 'eintönige', 'schreckliche Arbeit'*).[96]

Beginning in the 1590s, the Nagold Valley in Württemberg experienced a rapid expansion in the weaving of cheaper and lighter new draperies for export. The exclusionary policies of the local communities imposed a set of entry barriers for children. The rural woollen guild controlled entry to the trade, requiring a three-year apprenticeship. Parents were required to instil work discipline in their children, and a child 'who likes to play' was brought before the church court. Proto-industrial weavers had smaller households than the rest of the population, and therefore, as Sheila Ogilvie suggests, may have made greater use of their young children, aged between seven and ten, than parents with other occupations. Children went to school until the age of fourteen (boys) or fifteen (girls). It was normal to include a provision about schooling in the apprenticeship contract. In 1717 in Wildberg, only two out of 156 girls aged under fifteen were servants, and another two were related servants. Three out of 140 boys aged under fifteen were general servants, and two, both aged fourteen, were apprentices; another thirteen became apprentices between fifteen and nineteen years of age. There was no place for illegitimate boys in the community, who left at the age of fourteen or fifteen, while illegitimate girls became maid-servants and generally remained as such for the rest of their lives. Ogilvie argues that the major costs of sending children to school were foregone opportunity costs.[97] It seems that full-time child labour was not very common in these Württemberg communities.

The very opposite was the rule in putting-out industry in the countryside around Zürich, some 170 kilometres south of the Nagold Valley. As the children grew, they would step into a *Rast* relationship with their parents. This meant that the parents or providers would assign a daily or weekly task, the *Rast*, to their children, which was to be carried out in return for their keep, as Rudolf Braun explains. Children did not have to do any other work, and could keep the excess earnings. The adults in the household would urge young children to spin as much as they could, in order to earn money by spinning more than just the *Rast*. Thus outworking families practised parents' *Rast*-giving and children's *Rast*-taking and *Rast*-making, while there was no *Rast* in agricultural families.[98]

Child labour is rather seldom mentioned in connection with cottage industries in Scandinavia, thus its frequency remains an open question. For example, it is unclear to what extent it was used in home weaving, which in Scandinavia was women's work, as putting-out weaving usually was, too. Gustaf Utterström suggests that children were not mentioned because it was so self-evident that they assisted home weavers.[99] This may have been so, but we are still far from any 'self-exploitation' of the proto-industrial family.

An early form of 'proto-industrialisation' in Sweden consisted of domestic arms manufacturing in the countryside. Specialised peasant blacksmith in Närke had been making lighter firearms since the sixteenth century, and the military authorities organised the production in a fully industrialised manner in the 1640s: each blacksmith would specialise in producing large quantities of wholly standardised parts of firearms. Production remained household-based, and within the household there was an advanced division of labour. Each smithy had one journeyman and one apprentice, usually the smith's son, and boys under fifteen as assistants. His wife and other sons were responsible for the agriculture, but the sons assisted in the smithy as well. Therefore all sons had learned the blacksmith's trade by the time they turned fifteen and – as laid down in the Hired Labour Act – had to leave home for service.[100]

Forging skills survived in peasant households in this region well into the nineteenth century. According to Samuel Sahlstedt, the dean of Lerbäck parish, at least 600 parishioners, mostly boys and old men who were not considered good enough for field work, were occupied by tack forging in 1825. Boys started to learn forging around the age of ten, and by the age of fifteen or sixteen they had become fully skilled. It was said that youngsters were the best tack smiths.[101] Large families were common among miners and blacksmiths who followed the German method, while in the late nineteenth century, proletarian peasant blacksmiths following the Lancashire method had even larger families. Given that the Lancashire method could be learned in a shorter time than the German method, blacksmiths' sons gained master's status at an earlier age than before. What evidently also contributed to the higher number of children in forging families was the fact that by then the iron works had taken over from households as far as the training of boys for blacksmiths was concerned.[102]

Wood crafts, widely-practised at home in Norway, Sweden and Finland, were proto-industrial in character in some regions. A newspaper report by A.G. Sacklinius from 1785 described cooperage, or woodworking, home industries in the village of Laitila, Finland, where there was efficient division of labour between the villages and the households, as well as in the households: each male member of the household made just one part of the barrel, while the youngest boys carried ready-cut boards for drying. This facilitated serial production. The peasant producers themselves then sold the vessels, taking them by sea as far as Stralsund, Rostock, Schleswig-Holstein and Copenhagen. After 1830, wooden barrels began to lose market share in the Baltic ports to manufactured products.[103] Nevertheless, there were still product innovations in wood crafts as late as the mid-nineteenth century. A new type of basket made of planed pine proved a success for some time in the Swedish parishes of Göinge and Åsbo, and soon in every other cottage the whole family was occupied in basket making. Large numbers of baskets were exported to Denmark and Germany, for example.[104]

Knitting woollen stockings and other hosiery was practised on a large scale, particularly in Danish Jutland and Sweden's south-western coastal province of Halland. Putting-out knitting, carried out in addition to agricultural work, started in both regions around 1700. The market for Jutland stockings centred around the Baltic Sea, while women in Halland knitted 'soldiers stockings' mainly for the army. In 1796 Per Osbeck, the dean of Våxtorp parish in Halland, noted that children started to learn hand knitting between six and eight years of age. It was customary for those who made stockings to gather together to knit and chat, in a farm house in the winter, and in the open in the summer. These gatherings included children, men, women and farm servants. In Jutland in the 1830s the knitting done by children over six years of age was considered a contribution to the household knitting income. In both Jutland and Halland women definitely did most of the putting-out hand knitting.[105]

Home industries for textiles were common in Sjuhäraldsbygden, south-east of Gothenburg, in the eighteenth century, but there is no evidence of putting out, although it cannot be ruled out. In 1807, Gustaf Krook, the mayor of Borås, praised the economic prosperity that the home industries had brought with them to the region. As with the knitters in Halland, the picture he drew of home spinning in the district of Mark was rather cosy. In large households, women, old and other men and children sat together during the long winter evenings spinning – like peasants in the *veillées* in France or in *Spinnstuben* in Germany. The favourable economic development in the district of Mark is supported by modern historical writing. Christer Ahlberger has argued that the growth in rural domestic weaving led to higher work intensity, rising fertility and larger households employing farm servants. However, this cottage-industry expansion was not associated with impoverishment, but rather with improving material conditions. In the nineteenth century the region was characterised by extensive putting out in textiles, and from the 1820s onwards this system gave work to thousands of people in the district of Mark. As linen weaving gave way to cotton weaving, domestic industry changed from being predominantly subsidiary to a year-round occupation, carried out by purely wage-paid labour. Together with the population growth, this led to declining wages.[106]

In Russia, as in Scandinavia, some of the home-industry product range was intended for the lower end of the market, and some for the upper end. Despite the quite different institutional setting on account of the prevailing serfdom, Russian cottage industries (*kustar*) largely comprised similar consumer goods or semi-finished products as in Western Europe. For example, textiles such as cotton, linen and silk emerged as important putting-out industries in the eighteenth and early nineteenth centuries. Although the extent of child labour is not known, its existence is suggested by nineteenth-century references to 'trained girls' sewing fine kid gloves, skilled cotton printers who worked at home 'with the aid of a small family', and a *kustar* cotton weaver who 'toils together with his family' in his home workshop. As in Sweden, iron and copper articles, as well as nails, were manufactured in small peasant smithies. Again, references to 'the sons and nephews of blacksmiths [who] improved the methods of production in their family smithies', suggest juvenile workers.[107] Russian peasants employed in home industries or with other non-agricultural sources of cash income were often better-off than those living only on agriculture. For example, *kustar* peasants had better-built homes than those who relied entirely on agriculture.[108]

Fairly similar goods and products, particularly in textiles and clothing, were typical of rural putting-out industries from one country to another. This suggests a common denominator of such dispersed but similar cases. The outwork provider's quest for cheap labour appears the most obvious explanation. On the other hand, even rural producers who did not do outwork wove linen and wool for sale, for instance. This suggests that what was produced in the home industries was largely dictated by demand, in other words the consumption of members of middle and upper classes for whom the lace, embroidered goods, silks and worsteds were made. The emphasis is thus on the consumption of those for whom the proto-industrial households produced rather than on their own consumption, which is what de Vries and others focus on.[109] Moreover, the conclusion offered here is in line with Ingeborg Weber-Kellermann's observation that 'home-working women and children worked for the luxury clothes of children from another social stratum'.[110]

When Franklin Mendels coined the concept of proto-industrialisation, child labour was included only implicitly in the collective concept of the rural household.[111] Hans Medick then elaborated on the theme. In his widely cited article, he argues that child labour, 'which both in its intensity and duration went far beyond that of the corresponding labour of farm peasants households, was in fact a vital necessity for the rural cottage workers' families', to the point that 'the material existence of the proto-industrial family depended on child labour as the "capital of the poor man"'. On the basis of A.V. Chayanov's ideas on the organisation of peasant farms, Medick also argues that the transition from 'peasant-artisan subsistence economy' to proto-industrialisation indicated no loss of effectiveness 'because of the inclination of the poor, landless producers to fall back on "self-exploitation"'.[112] The model originally suggested that the proto-industrial marriage pattern was characterised by relatively low ages at marriage and high fertility, as opposed to the West European pattern with relatively high ages at marriage and relatively low fertility. This line of reasoning has been the subject of much criticism.[113] Medick and his co-authors now agree that 'the connection between the work-process and the family as the reproductive unit turns out to be more complex than was assumed in the original model'.[114]

Detailed studies have shown a variety of demographic patterns. Michelle Perrot, who studied home weaving in France, where it continued beyond the mid-nineteenth century, concludes that the 'rural industry encouraged fecundity' in proto-industrial families.[115] According to Sheila Ogilvie, there were in Württemberg 'consistent and repeated indications that people were trying to adjust their demographic behaviour and the size, composition and structure of their families to their ability to afford them ...'.[116] The two Dutch communities studied by François Hendrickx changed from subsistence agriculture combined with weaving (by men) to a society in which agriculture and industry became increasingly involved in international markets. Despite such proto-industrialisation, the two communities continued to follow the West European marriage pattern.[117] According to Orvar Löfgren, the landless in Sweden developed specialised trades and cottage industries 'in which they could compensate for lack of capital by intensive use of family labour, especially that of children'.[118] In Scandinavia families with non-agricultural cash incomes had on average more children than those living only on agriculture, but most historians have interpreted this as a sign that such families were well enough to be able to afford large households.[119]

Finally, given the fact that one of the many criteria put forward for true proto-industry is that it must have 'developed in symbiosis with commercial agriculture',[120] one might expect the use of child labour to be more or less similar as in commercialising agriculture. However, its seems that hired child labour was seldom used in proto-industry. Why was this? Was it because children's productivity remained low, no matter how industriously proto-industrial households made the children work?

Educational opportunities

Formal education or schooling was relatively limited in the countryside before the nineteenth century. This may have been due to a lack of resources, material or academic, but local support may also have proved insufficient. One outcome was that literacy rates in the countryside were, on average, lower than in urban areas, although there were marked differences from one region to another.[121] Peasants involved in commercial transactions were motivated to become functionally literate, whereas for others, acquiring proper reading and writing skills was still of relatively little use. In the centuries of the Reformation and Counter-Reformation, purity of faith seems to have been a stronger incentive for introducing formal education than any intellectual or material gains. What kind of formal education was available to peasant children, and was it of any use to them?

Education hardly served upward social mobility in the seventeenth- and eighteenth-century French countryside, as Pierre Goubert argues. It was 'impossible to escape from the position of labourer ... except by very gradual steps'. If a priest came across a pious and gifted boy whose education he wished to assist, 'this was likely to be the son of a rich farmer'. In the early seventeenth century, a few provinces, including Normandy, the Loire to Artois and the Vosges, had village schools where boys and even girls aged at least seven were taught religion, reading, writing and sometimes arithmetic. In the vine-growing areas, children came to school after the vintage, and left at Easter or haymaking. In the late seventeenth century, the Catholic Church introduced rigid segregation of the sexes after the age of seven, one outcome of which was that girls were generally excluded from education altogether.[122] In the eighteenth century, anxious about the purity of the faith, it supported *petites écoles* in the villages.[123] Nonetheless, at the beginning of the nineteenth century, an abandoned boy like Jean-Roch Coignet had no chance of going to school. At the age of twelve, when he left the inn where he worked as a servant for a new master, he did not even know the first letter of the alphabet.[124]

Literacy remained rare in the Italian countryside. The church bell told children the time to leave for school, but few attended. Apparently, not even the Catechistic village schools gave country children a real opportunity to acquire literacy.[125] According to Carmen Sarasúa, the 'schooling of female children was almost nonexistent until 1816' in the Spanish countryside. The lace-producing regions had lace-making schools, which also trained girls in embroidery and textile work, but that seems to have been all. Schooling for boys also remained limited among the transhumant cattle-breeding peasants of the Montes des Pas, because of the nomadic lives of their families. A merchant donating a large sum of money to the establishment of an elementary school in San Roque in 1784 did not expect children to attend school in August at all, while at other times of the year the elementary school and its teacher would follow the movements of the transhumant families. This school was to teach reading, writing and arithmetic, which were needed in the commercial activities that were so central in the local economy.[126] Wealthy peasants, *labradores*, sent their sons to Latin schools and universities in the ambitious hope of seeing them as canons or employed in the administrative apparatus, but such expensive projects could have been considered a waste of the family fortune, if the sons failed.[127]

In England, the increase in endowed elementary schools in the second half of the seventeenth century was closely associated with the new preference for the vernacular as the language of instruction instead of Latin. Endowed grammar schools were not intended exclusively for children of any particular class or location, and the doors were kept open for the reception of poor men's sons, too. Children in early elementary schools may first have been taught to read, and only a few years later to write, when those of the poor may already have left. In the eighteenth century thousands of schools were endowed by charitable men and women for the education of the children of the poor. Fear, punishment and religious instruction were the disciplinary methods applied in charity schools. These schools were strongly and constantly attacked by 'the vast army of persons who were opposed to any form of education for the poor'. They argued that schools 'unfitted the children for their function in society', that is cheap labour. The farming middle class in particular opposed all forms of instruction for the children of the poor, who were there 'to supply casual labour when required' (M.G. Jones).[128]

In Schleswig and Holstein, the peasants themselves established small schools for their children, whereas in some German States the *Hofarbeit*, corvée labour to the estate owner, had absolute priority, hence the children were able to go to school only occasionally. According to Ingeborg Weber-Kellermann, notwithstanding the fact that compulsory education was introduced in Prussia in 1717, school attendance in the countryside remained poor.[129] The church court in the heavily pietistic rural Württemberg tried to bring the youth under its control with the help of compulsory school attendance and Sunday schools. In 1641, the pastor of Wildberg exhorted parents to send their children to school more diligently. As this was 'the last, terrible decade of the Thirty Years War', as Sheila Ogilvie observes, 'it is not surprising that the parents of less than one-tenth of the youth between 7 and 15 ... could afford to send their children to school'. Nonetheless, in the late seventeenth century, school attendance began to be considered essential for all children. Parents who did not send their children to school were fined or gaoled. Nevertheless, the level of attainment may not have been high, since parents found it useless to send their children to school to learn little more than religious rituals and hymns. Some preferred to send them to a private night-school run by an under-employed weaver, for example, while others asked to be allowed to teach their children at home. There was a demand for education that the official schools failed to meet.[130]

In the Protestant Scandinavian countries, the head of the household was made responsible for ensuring that all household members were able to read set religious texts, primarily Luther's Small Catechism. Passing confirmation (first communion) was a condition for legal marriage, and for that boys and girls had to be able to read the given texts at least tolerably well. Common people's ability to read, or rather to memorise, the given texts was controlled and registered by the local clergy by means of public interrogations, which peasant children attended for the first time at the age of at least seven, usually between nine and twelve. Girls and women generally did at least as well as boys and men in these interrogations. Peasant children learned rudimentary reading skills in the household or at modest parish schools, while their opportunities to learn to write were limited, thus few men and still fewer women had this ability. In Denmark, local clergymen organised parish schools for pauper children, including orphaned and abandoned children who had been placed with rural households by the poor-relief authorities of Copenhagen. More advanced education was available only in towns and cities. Only ambitious, wealthy peasants who wanted to see one of their sons in the pulpit would make such a costly investment.[131]

Catherine II wanted to reform the Russian educational system, while she also consolidated and expanded serfdom. The final enserfment of the rural population undermined any improvements in the educational standards of the Russian peasantry. 'Most peasants saw no point in schooling' (S. Dixon), which was hardly surprising, given their serf status. According to Simon Dixon, there was some interest among the peasantry in the kind of mechanical reading skills needed in church services, and some young people on the large estates were taught to read and write for the purposes of administration. In 1807, probably less than 0.5 per cent of the Russian school-age population was enrolled, and most of the children who were dropped out. By 1825 no more than about 300 parish schools had been established in the whole, vast Russian countryside. 'Russia entered the nineteenth century with fewer than one in two hundred of its school-age population under instruction', as Ben Eklof notes.[132]

In conclusion, land ownership among the peasant population remained the core of social distinction, while being literate served to make the land-owning peasantry even more dominant in the local context. Social mobility was 'a phenomenon that would be out of place in a hierarchically structured society', as Jean-Claude Caron observes.[133] Nevertheless, proper reading and writing ability did occasionally serve a peasant boy in changing his life. Peter Hansen, aged about nineteen, left his native village of Bylderup in Tønder (Tonder), northern Schleswig in 1643. As a younger son, excluded from inheritance, he had probably been encouraged by his parents to learn to read and write, and to study some arithmetic. These skills proved valuable to him first in getting a job at the royal warehouse in Copenhagen, then in the service of the Dutch West Indian Company in South America. After returning home, he eventually become a burgher and an assistant teacher at a parish school in Flensburg.[134]

Jean-Claude Caron presents 'a simple shepherd' Valentin Jamerey-Duval (born in 1695) as a rare example of upward social mobility in France: 'This "wild child," who had run loose in the days of Luis XIV, died in Vienna at the court of the Empress Marie-Thérèse.'[135] Anyone reading Jamerey-Duval's *Mémories* would be touched by the way this neglected child discovered the world outside his small village. Valentin, who was terrorised by his stepfather, ran away from home around the age of thirteen. This was the beginning of his journey from ignorance to the world of learning, and at first he was guided by the little he knew: he had heard people speak about Paris and wanted to see it.[136] Only by becoming functionally literate, and provided there was some instructive reading at hand, could peasant children enlarge their intellectual horizons beyond the familiar.

Conclusion

The Swedish historian Mats Sjöberg, in line with some other historians, has suggested that country children typically performed time-consuming tasks. He argues that in agriculture time was the main competitive edge or 'capital' of children.[137] Nevertheless, it is considered a scarce resource only in a society in which time is money, or, as E.P. Thompson put it, where 'time is not passed but spent'.[138] When did time become the 'capital' of country children? Was it with the emergence of market-oriented commercial farming, with the breakthrough of the cash economy, with the social stratification of the rural population, or with the whole complex development called the agricultural revolution?

There was evidence of market-oriented agricultural production, monetary thinking and a sharp social separation between peasants, cottagers and day-labourers in Holsteinian Elbmarshes, north-west of Hamburg, as early as the fifteenth century.[139] Were there also child workers? In Castile, the royal revenue-raising schemes of Philip II led to enclosures and, more importantly, to the selling of common land, *tierras baldías*. Contemporaries believed that this contributed to the growing numbers of beggars and landless rural labourers.[140] How much did the individualisation of land ownership, foreshadowing the rise of capitalism, increase rural child labour in Castile? In sixteenth-century England, the lives of those working on the land 'were regulated by the rhythms of nature and the vagaries of the weather' (M. Overton), and in the absence of commercial consumer goods there was no pressure to work more than necessary in order to make a living. This seems to suggest a limited number of child workers. Eric Kerridge suggests that the Elizabethan times offered the first of 'the great inventions of the agricultural revolution', such as the establishment of large farms from smaller ones, which turned petty farmers into servants and labourers. How much did this contribute to the supply of child labour? Given that some 34,000 families in England were dispossessed by enclosure and encroachment between 1455 and 1637, what consequences did this have for the children of these families?[141] Commercial farming dominated most of the English countryside after the seventeenth century, but does this explain the use of children as farm servants?

Were children burdened with labour in peasant farmsteads? Many certainly were. For example, those in the Alps who were set to herding at a tender age evidently found the work beyond their capacity. Children working as servants were vulnerable to exploitation if their masters were beyond the control of the parents or if the child had no parents. Many families involved in putting-out production risked overworking their children.

On the other hand, much of children's farm work was casual and undemanding, and could be seen as informal training for their future roles as peasants and peasants' wives. Hugh Cunningham writes of eighteenth-century England, 'the evidence amounts to little more than plausible but undocumented references to crow-scaring and other tasks of a like kind, suggesting that the employment of children was at most casual and intermittent ...'.[142] Along the same lines Colin Heywood observes that 'children gradually drifted into the labour force, mopping up a host of tasks that were appropriate to their size and experience'.[143] Hugh Cunningham offers evidence that there was a clear parental opposition to the employment of their children, 'parents withheld their children from labour'. He cites John Houghton who, in the seventeenth century, wrote about 'our poor' who did not 'think it good for their children to work hard in their youth'. Cunningham set out to prove that unemployment among children, which contemporaries saw as idleness, was more common in England than historians have claimed or believed.[144] It seems to me that the notion of 'idle children' suggests not only child unemployment, but also parental opposition to child labour. However, as evidence of parental attitudes is fragmentary or even anecdotal, the question must remain open.

Notes

1.　Wales 1984, p. 376; Nardinelli 1990, pp. 45–54, quotation p. 53.
2.　Smith, R.M. 1984, p. 69.
3.　Kussmaul 1981, pp. 38, 144.
4.　Gaunt 1983, pp. 113; Lindegren 1980, pp. 248–249.
5.　Mitterauer 1993, pp. 2–5, 66–68, 119, quotation p. 68.
6.　Rossi 1985, pp. 50–53, 106–142, 193–231.
7.　Blum 1972, pp. 262–264. See also Czap 1983, pp. 110–111, 120–122; Sarti 2002, pp. 81–82.
8.　Blum 1972, pp. 243–246, 356, 422–430, 446–447.
9.　Kuczynski 1958, pp. 58–67; Hoppe 1958, pp. 64–66; Wunder 1996, pp. 83–84.
10.　Schubert 1996, pp. 372–373.
11.　Harnisch 1986, pp.62–65, quotation p. 65.
12.　Frandsen 1988, pp. 133–134, 196; Krogh 1987, pp. 105, 139–153; Østerud 1978, pp. 104–105.
13.　Cf. Simonton 1998, p. 29.
14.　Harnesk 1990, pp. 88–91; Jutikkala 1990, pp. 47–51; Utterström 1957a, pp. 249–257; Wilmi 1991, pp. 79–89, 246, 290.
15.　Kuisma 1992a, p. 255; Nygård 1989, p. 101; Wilmi 1991, pp. 216, 226, 246.
16.　'Peasantry' as an Estate of the Swedish Estates Assembly, *Riksdag*, represented crown tenants and peasant farmers who paid taxes directly to the State. Other categories of the peasant population had no political rights.
17.　Lext 1968, pp. 21–22, 43–44, quotation p. 43.
18.　Krogh 1987, p. 111.
19.　Kussmaul 1981, pp. 38, 143–146, quotation p. 144.
20.　Allen 1988, p. 135.
21.　Cunningham, H. 1990, p. 120; Laslett 1965, p. 31.
22.　E.g. Heywood 1988, pp. 27–28; Martinson 1992, pp. 81–83; Mitterauer 1993, p. 68; Sjöberg 1997, p. 109; Weber-Kellermann 1979, p. 74.
23.　Vassberg 1984, p. 74.
24.　Goubert 1986, pp. 141–143.
25.　Allen 1988, p. 138, quotation from J.M. Wilson 1847, p. 136; Hassell Smith 1989a, p. 31.
26.　Verdon 2002.
27.　[Platter] 1999 [1572], pp. 85–92.
28.　Sarasúa 1998, pp. 180–186, quotation p. 181.
29.　Rétif de La Bretonne 1989 [1797], pp. 67–77, 100–101, 1203. According to Rétief, his father did not disregard any economic opportunity, '*Il n'était pas homme à negliger aucune des parties économiques*', (p. 67).
30.　Coignet 1923 [1851], pp. 6–8.
31.　Niccoli 1995, pp. 144–151.
32.　Rossi 1985, pp. 107, 114–116, 123, 136.
33.　Weber-Kellermann 1987, pp. 111–115, 254.
34.　Ogilvie 1986, pp. 298, 317.
35.　Uhlig 1978, pp. 15–16, 25, 149.
36.　Raaschou-Nielsen 1990, pp. 54–59.
37.　Gadd 2000, p. 175; Hanssen 1976, p. 41; Söderberg and Myrdal 2002, pp. 159–170.

38. Matikainen 2002, p. 121. I am grateful to Olli Matikainen who kindly provided me with details of this case.
39. Lagerlöf-Génetay 1990, pp. 20–21.
40. Gadd 2000, 174–175; Liliequist, J. 1991, p. 415 and passim.
41. Kuisma 1992b, p. 165; Niemelä 1989, pp. 82–83; Nordström and Nordström 1966, p. 121; Wilmi 1991, p. 217.
42. E.g. Gadd 2000, p. 174; Wilmi 1991, p. 203.
43. Myrdal 1981, pp. 41–43.
44. E.g. Allen 1988; Czap 1983, p. 111; Thompson, E.P. 1967.
45. Hajnal 1983, pp. 92–99; Kussmaul 1981, pp. 3–9, quotation p. 3. For a recent owerview, see Dribe 2000, pp. 8–17. For differences between Northern vs. Mediterranean Europe, see Reher 1998.
46. Overton 1996, pp. 181–182.
47. McIntosh 1988, quotation p. 232. See also Blanchard 1984, p. 251 (note 51) for some evidence of an increase in life-time service as well.
48. McIntosh 1988, p. 219.
49. Robson 1984, p. 79.
50. Nardinelli 1990, pp. 45–57, quotation p. 52.
51. Laslett 1965, pp. 13–16; Laslett 1977.
52. McCracken 1983.
53. Hassell Smith 1989b, p. 370.
54. Wall 1978; Wall 1987. See also Krausman Ben-Amos 1988; Macfarlane 1984; Mitterauer 1990.
55. Kussmaul 1981, pp. 70–78; 146.
56. Anderson, M. 1980, pp. 70–71.
57. Casey 1999, pp. 28–31, 58–59, 204–212; Molas Ribalta 1988, pp. 153–156; Reher 1990, p. 202; Vassberg 1998, pp. 443, 452–453.
58. Viazzo 1994.
59. Goubert 1986, pp. 54–73, 100–101, 176.
60. Flandrin 1980, p. 60.
61. Poulsen 1995; Schlumbohm 1994, pp. 197–211, 233, 296–298.
62. Söderberg and Myrdal 2002, pp. 135, 148–153, 214–218, 223, quotation p. 132.
63. Gaunt 1983, pp. 112; Jutikkala 1990, pp. 44–45; Moring 1993; Moring 1996.
64. Hajnal 1983, Table 2.13; Martinson 1992, pp. 81–83; Slettan 1984, p. 66; Sprauten 1992, pp. 77–78.
65. Frandsen 1988, pp. 45–6, 170; Hajnal 1983, Table 2.12, 2.14, 2.15; Krogh 1987, pp. 37, 52; Laslett 1977, p. 104.
66. Plakans 1978, pp. 88–90.
67. Goubert 1986, pp. 110–117, 176; Jones, P.M. 1988, pp. 10–14.
68. Smith, H. 1984, pp. 70, 74–76.
69. Harnesk 1990, pp. 26, 186, 212; Söderberg and Myrdal 2002, p. 153.
70. Niemelä 1989, pp. 51–57.
71. Harnesk 1990, p. 29. The information refers to people who died in 1785–1788 and 1836–1855.

72. J.O. Björkman 1974, cited in Wilmi 1991, p. 298; Ehlers 1991; Gaunt 1977; Gaunt 1983, p. 113; Hanssen 1978; Harnesk 1990, pp. 26–31, 115, 186, 209–212; Löfgren 1974; Moring 1993; Moring 1996.
73. Plaul 1986, pp. 118–121; Schlumbohm 1996, pp. 84–85, quotation p. 88; Reay 1996, pp. 25–26; Snell 1992, pp. 69–71, 81–88, 101–103; Walton 1998, pp. 79–80.
74. Scharfe 1986, pp. 34–35.
75. Horn 1980, p. 47; Kussmaul 1981, pp. 10, 120–133; Levine 1977, pp. 109–110; Snell 1992, p. 71.
76. Orr 1984, p. 30.
77. Anderson, M. 1980, p. 63.
78. The phrase is from a proposed new hired labour act (*Project till en förnyad stadga om legofolk 1752*), which would have 'introduced virtual serfdom' in Sweden (Harnesk 1990, p. 52). See also Utterström 1957a, p. 275.
79. For this discusssion, see Kussmaul 1981, pp. 76–78; Laslett 1977; McCracken 1983; Schlumbohm 1994, pp. 341–342; Schlumbohm 1996; Smith, R.M. 1984, pp. 69–72.
80. Mendels 1972, p. 241 and passim.
81. E.g. Berg 1994, pp. 66–72; de Vries 1994b; Kriedte, Medick and Schlumbohm 1981.
82. Iradiel Murugarren 1974, p. 218.
83. Casey 1999, pp. 55, 61–65, 203.
84. Sarasúa García 1995, pp. 155–168.
85. Belfanti 1993, pp. 255–259, 266–267, quotation p. 255.
86. Goubert 1986, pp. 54–55, 101–102.
87. Chapman and Chassagne 1981, 165–170, quotation p. 170;
88. Smith, A. 1973 [1776], pp. 220–221.
89. Kriedte, Medick and Schlumbohm 1981, p. 54.
90. Levine 1977, pp. 27–29, 79, 150–151; Wales 1984, pp. 375–376.
91. Verdon 2002, pp. 304–306, quotation p. 319.
92. Kriedte, pp. 244–248.
93. Schlumbohm 1994, pp. 221–222; Schlumbohm 1996, pp. 84–85.
94. Quataert 1985, pp. 150–151; Schubert 1996, p. 374.
95. Quoted in Quataert 1985, p. 151.
96. Kriedte 1983, p. 243; quotations from Herzig 1983, p. 371.
97. Ogilvie 1986, pp. 281–286, 291–293, 304–307, 313–319.
98. Braun 1990, pp. 54–59, 66, 139.
99. Harnesk 1990, pp. 189–191; Hornby and Oxenbøll 1982, pp. 11–23, 32–33; Schön 1982 pp. 62–63; Utterström 1957b, pp. 66–67, 122–123, 177–178; Vainio-Korhonen 2000.
100. Klingnéus 1997, pp. 32–72, 102–113. See also Evans and Rydén 1998; Florén and Rydén 1992; Florén 1994.
101. Utterström 1957b, p. 239. See also Isacson and Magnusson 1987, pp. 51–67.
102. Florén and Rydén 1992, pp. 56–58.
103. Virrankoski 1963, pp. 266, 276–286.
104. Isacson and Magnusson 1987, pp. 27–28.
105. Hornby and Oxenbøll 1982, pp. 24–30; Johansson, P. 2001, pp. 102–103, 132–135, 145, 183, 199, and passim; Utterström 1957b, p. 73.
106. C. Ahlberger 1988, cited in Söderberg 1989; Persson 1997, pp. 78–81; Utterström 1957b, pp. 122–123.

107. Blum 1972, pp. 301–302, 343; Tugan-Baranovsky 1970 [1907], pp. 171–214, quotations pp. 177n, 186n, 197, 201.
108. Blum 1972, p. 303.
109. de Vries 1994a.
110. Weber-Kellermann 1979, p. 71.
111. Mendels 1972, p. 258, and passim.
112. Medick 1976, pp. 299, 302.
113. E.g. Anderson, M. 1980, pp. 76–7; Cunningham, H. 1990; Cunningham, H. 1995, pp. 84–87; Landsteiner 1999; Nardinelli 1990, pp. 54–56; Pollard 1981, pp. 73–77; Smith, H. 1984; Smith, R.M. 1984, p. 5. Young children as an economic burden rather than an asset is particularly emphasised in Wales 1984.
114. Kriedte, Medick and Schlumbohm 1993, p. 223.
115. Perrot 1997, quotation p. 82.
116. Ogilvie 1997, p. 306 and passim.
117. Hendrickx 1997, pp. 440–441.
118. Löfgren 1974, p. 29.
119. Gaunt 1977, pp. 199–202; Isacson and Magnusson 1987, pp. 20–23; Moring 1993; Moring 1996; Söderberg 1978, pp. 101–108.
120. Berg 1994, p. 67.
121. E.g. Houston 2002, pp. 13–14, 146–150.
122. Goubert 1986, p. 55, quotations p. 108.
123. Capul 1983, pp. 30–47, 88–109; Capul 1984, pp. 15–28; de Viguerie 1978, pp. 41–68; Heywood 1988, pp. 3–4.
124. Coignet 1923 [1851], p. 27.
125. Niccoli 1995, pp. 121, 151.
126. Sarasúa García 1995, pp. 154–156; Sarasúa 1998, p. 188.
127. Sarasúa García 2002, p. 552.
128. Horn 1978, pp. 5–15; Jones, M. 1938, pp. 15–27, 73–96, quotations pp. 85, 95; Overton 1996, pp. 39–41; Spufford 1995.
129. Weber-Kellermann 1979, p. 73; Weber-Kellermann 1987, p. 103.
130. Ogilvie 1986, pp. 304–311, quotation pp. 305–306.
131. Frandsen 1988, p. 199; Johansson, E. 1991, p. 131; Jørgensen 1990, p. 26; Kirby 1995, pp. 68–74; Myllyntaus 1990; Nilsson 1999, pp. 284–285; Pettersson 1996; Sandin 1988, pp. 359–364, Wirilander 1982, pp. 191–193.
132. Anderson, P. 1993, p. 343; Dixon 1999, p. 156; Eklof 1986, pp. 19–25, quotation p. 25.
133. Caron 1997, p. 120. See also Chassagne 1998, pp. 225–226.
134. Kraack 2002.
135. Caron 1997, p. 120.
136. Jamerey-Duval 1981 [1747], pp. 112–121.
137. Sjöberg 1996, p. 137; Sjöberg 1997, p. 117. See also Heywood 1988, pp. 28, 47–48; Nardinelli 1990, p. 40.
138. Thompson, E.P. 1967, p. 61.
139. Lorenzen-Schmidt 1998; Wunder 1996.
140. Vassberg 1984, pp. 169–176, 227–229.
141. Kerridge 1973, pp. 103–104; Overton 1996, pp. 37–38, 180, quotation p. 37, critic of Kerridge p. 198. See also Musgrave, P. 1999, pp. 61–71.

142. Cunningham, H. 1990, quotation pp. 122–123.
143. Heywood 2001, p. 123.
144. Cunningham, H. 1990, quotation p. 120. See also Cunningham, H. 1992, pp. 18–24.

CHAPTER 3

Child Labour during the Agricultural Revolution

Children and the rural labour force

The composition of the rural labour force changed with the agricultural revolution, defined as 'rises in agricultural output and in labour productivity' (M. Overton),[1] and with the rapid population growth that started in Europe around the mid-eighteenth century. The number of living-in servants diminished in the nineteeth century since they expensive to keep during agricultural slack times. Even Russia started moving towards more flexible labour, as indicated by the emancipation of the serfs in 1861. Along with the commercialisation of agriculture came an increasing demand for more flexible or seasonal labour, as specialised cash crop cultivation and livestock farming expanded. It is suggested below that, in its labour-intensive phase, the agricultural revolution probably increased the use of child labour.

After c.1815–1820, the long-term trend in relative real wages in England and France turned upwards, and servants became more expensive.[2] More flexible labour was available in England through the bondage system, whereby male workers were required to recruit female labourers to work on the land for the farmer when they were needed.[3] According to Robert Allen, labour intensity in English agriculture increased over the first half of the nineteenth century, and farmers were instructed to carefully monitor every employee's exact whereabouts and activities. Large farms employed mobile gangs of between six and ten men to perform tasks at high efficiency, and increased labour productivity by using specialised workers and a work-crew system. It is estimated that output per worker in Britain and Ireland in 1800 may have been double that in France and Germany, while French productivity was 40 per cent of that of Britain in 1840. Gregory Clark argued that large farms hiring more specialist and casual male labour per acre, 'would also be hiring more casual female and child labor for such tasks as weeding, clearing stones, and turnip hoeing'.[4] Nonetheless, children who started as casual labourers may have become specialised farm workers. For example, little Joseph Arch, aged seven or eight years, started as a crow-scarer on a twelve-hour shift, earning four pennies a day. After two or three years he became a ploughboy at six pennies a day, and at the age of fourteen a stable boy at eight shillings a week, earning as much as his father.[5]

The French Revolutionary land settlement of the 1790s brought with it a dominance of small peasant farms. Colin Heywood refers to 'archetypal' French family holdings of between 10 and 40 hectares that 'risked being swamped by too many children of working age', although he also draws attention to the attempts of various socio-economic groups to adapt the numbers of children born to the opportunities offered by their family patrimony: 'The small plots held by the *ménagers* encouraged a family strategy of one child, whilst tenant farmers had an interest in producing three or four children.' Nevertheless, between 1830 and 1880 the productivity growth rate in French agriculture was above the European average. Small-scale farming was suited to livestock rearing, fruit growing, market gardening and the production of better wines. 'As the Agricultural Revolution spread, so the work load required to support this diversification of crops increased', as Heywood observes. Eventually, the high density of labour in the countryside led to a slow productivity growth rate and backwardness of a kind in French agriculture. In the late nineteenth century, as many as 75 per cent of the agricultural holdings were smaller than ten hectares, which was too small to support a family.[6]

Servitude to the nobility was lifted in early nineteenth-century Spain, but peasants remained in a client relationship with their landlords. The laws of land ownership were reformed, but the landed aristocracy preserved and expanded its landed property, and eventually the high bourgeoisie followed suit. Well-to-do peasant farmers dominated late nineteenth-century Catalonia, whereas peasants in the south took action to get hold of more land. In its Mediterranean version, the agricultural revolution indicated a shift from wheat fields to vineyards and orchards, but also a decline of transhumant cattle breeding. Agricultural productivity in eastern Spain increased with specialisation.[7] On family farms specialisation in cash crops probably entailed increased work intensity on the part of family members. Representatives of mid-nineteenth-century economic and agricultural societies remarked that it was necessary for children to contribute, in one way or another, to family subsistence. According to them, from the age of seven, peasant children 'earn what they eat, and sometimes even more', while having turned ten, and even earlier, the family's own children substituted for servants.[8] If it really was the case – as these bourgeois writers claimed – that very young children earned more than their keep (in cash or kind?) in Spain, it suggests that children's employers were more concerned about labour costs than about productivity.

Sharecropping, or *mezzadria* farming, in Italy hit a permanent crisis, and social descent into the day-labourer and ploughmen (*boari*) classes loomed large. In an attempt to prevent expulsion from the farm through having too many unproductive members, the heads of sharecropping families strove to maintain the right ratio between consumers, the women and children, and agricultural producers, adult men, while the permission of the landlord was needed for a member of a sharecropping family to get married. Tuscan sharecroppers changed their pattern of early and frequent marriages to one of late and few marriages, but continued to live in complex families. Ploughmen's households were responsible for a great deal of work connected with the animals, and in the region of Ferrara, for instance, were large and complex, comprising several adults, some half-grown boys and two to four younger children. Unlike sharecroppers' and ploughmen's families, however, the families of day labourers did not comprise a productive unit. Increasing mechanisation and commercialisation changed their work, whereas very labour-intensive production methods and non-market production continued among Tuscan sharecroppers. The late nineteenth-century agrarian crisis made the young abandon farming.[9]

Enclosures featured in Denmark, Finland and Sweden in the late eighteenth and early nineteenth centuries, and in Norway in the late nineteenth century. Peasants with substantial land holdings often gained remarkably in the reforms. The commercialisation of the peasant economy roughly coincided with the lifting of migration restrictions and the abandonment of mercantilist labour laws in favour of a free labour market. Now the peasant landowners could afford to imitate the bourgeois or gentry lifestyle, keeping their children longer at home and making sure that they married socially equal partners. At the same time, deep poverty characterised many regions in Finland and Sweden where the lowest agrarian stratum largely comprised the offspring of peasant landowners.[10]

Before the commercialisation of agriculture, there were no incentives in the Scandinavian northern backwoods to press the family's own children to work in order to increase household consumption. For example, in the mid-nineteenth century, lodgers' children in Central Finnish inland parishes seem to have passed most of their time in play, carrying out only minor tasks, while their parents were undertaking contract labour (labour service) for the land owner or doing extra work for cash. Lacking proper footwear and warm clothes, lodgers' children could not even stay outdoors in winter. In spring, every lodger family sent one of its children to tend cattle with a female farm servant of their landlord. This lasted about a week, after which time the cows had re-adopted their daily routine and no longer needed intensive herding.

After haymaking, the cows pastured near the village, and the lodgers' children were needed to keep them away from the rye fields. A lodger household lived on the bare necessities, and thus there were not even household chores for the children to do.[11] Perhaps the poorest parents could not rely on children's work, for whom the responsibility for the family survival would have been too heavy a burden, or perhaps there was very little demand for child labour in these communities.

In Scandinavia, the flexible labour needed by peasant farmers was provided by smallholders, landless farm labourers, day labourers, crofters and cottagers whose wives and children were held in reserve. As early as the close of the eighteenth century, landed peasants with large holdings in Hedmarken in southeastern Norway, who were involved in labour-intensive commercial arable farming, established crofter farms (*plasser*) and extracted labour service from the crofter families. The number of crofter farms stagnated around 1800, so the peasant landowners satisfied their need for more labour by increasing the amount of labour service of the existing crofter families. As the working capacity of men was already fully used, the workload of their wives and children (*plassebarn*) became heavier.[12] Land reform came to a halt in mid-nineteenth-century Denmark for fear of the uncontrollable growth of a class of poor farm labourers.[13] As grain prices fell because of the flow of cheap grain in the international market, there was a general shift from arable to dairy farming. This brought with it higher wages for living-in female farm servants, responsible for cattle and milking, and young women became too expensive for herding. Manufacturing, railway building and forestry competed for roughly the same male labour force as agriculture, hence the wages of male farm hands rapidly rose.[14] Thus there emerged new niches in the rural labour market for children.

Similarly, from about 1860 the wages of farm servants in Germany kept gradually rising as industrialisation, migration and emigration across the Atlantic encouraged young people to sell their labour for a better price. Peasant farmers would have preferred strongly-built servants aged at least sixteen years, but the shortage and price of such servants drove them to employ children, as well as to resort to their own children. There was also increasing social antagonism between farmers and servants, as happened in the Magdeburg region, for example, where servants had separate quarters and lower quality food. Seasonal migrant labour, both children and adults, was increasingly used.[15] Thus there emerged a fresh demand for child labour in German agriculture.

Russian peasants had been pushed by the law and by serf owners to live in extended families for more than two centuries, and they continued with the practice even after emancipation. Serfdom had also encouraged virtually universal marriage, and even this practice was retained in the villages. Simon Dixon suggests that the high population-growth rate in pre-industrial Russia, second only to Britain, did not 'force Russia into the jaws of a Malthusian trap' because of the availability of new land and the eventual mass migration to Siberia which started in the 1890s.[16] Nevertheless, migration did not remove poverty from the villages. The western traveller Howard Kennard blamed the bureaucratic regime, the brutal police and soldiery, and the clergy for it.[17] The birth rate began to fall in the 1890s, and there was a shift in marriage patterns. This change was attributed to the fact that young men and women had had a taste of urban life as migrant workers. Moreover the semi-feudal relations that the former serf owners had striven to maintain deteriorated as a result of agricultural commercialisation.[18] In the early twentieth century, the efforts of peasant families to cope with the changes provided A.V. Chayanov with material for his theory of the peasant economy.

The major changes connected with the agricultural revolution had several implications concerning child labour. Life-cycle service among landed peasant's sons and daughters largely disappeared during the nineteenth century, which meant that children and adolescents in farm service were increasingly of lower social origin than their master's family. Peasant farmers' need for cheap juvenile labour was met by farmed-out parish pauper children, children of farm labourers, underlings, tenant farmers and other subordinated landless families, or by the family's own children. The family's own children contributed to making ends meet in the small farms, while in the larger ones the hired farm servants may have substituted for the family's children.

Indentured and farmed-out children

Large numbers of deprived children signified widespread poverty, and this has usually also been the perspective from which farmed-out children have been considered. However, if we do not take it for granted that the supply of this particular form of child labour created its demand, then the question arises why the demand for farmed-out child labour expanded or came into being in the eighteenth and nineteenth centuries. The fact that the expansion in the numbers of farmed-out children coincided with agricultural modernisation suggests a connection between the two.

This section discusses the terms under which children were farmed out, why foster households took them, and the kinds of work the foster households required them to do. Some tentative ideas why farmed-out child labour was common during agricultural modernisation are suggested. The discussion starts with England because it seems to have been the first country in which farmers lost interest in farmed-out child labour, or parish apprentices, as they were called there.

Placing out orphaned, abandoned and destitute children with private households had a long history in Europe, but large-scale traffic in children did not come into being until the eighteenth or nineteenth century, depending on the country. Being placed out usually meant labour service or indentured labour in the foster household. The traffic in children was managed by foundling homes, orphanages or poor-relief authorities, while in the German and Scandinavian countryside poor children were also put up for public auction, a practice with distant models in *ancien régime* France and in auctions of unemployed labourers in England.[19]

The farming-out of pauper children was evidently routine in eighteenth-century England. Yet the fact that masters were forced to take on such parish apprentices suggests that the demand for farmed-out children was limited. According to Hugh Cunningham, boys in the West Country were put out to farmers at the age of nine, and were bound until the age of twenty-one, so in time they would become increasingly more useful to their employers. Pauper boys and girls in Devon were commonly apprenticed at the age of eight, although the ages varied between four and twenty. The average age of parish apprentices in Southampton was twelve for boys and ten for girls, in Lancaster it was ten or eleven, and the children were bound until the age of twenty-one. In some parts of the country, 'it was a norm to bind out nearly all the children of the poor at the age of eight, nine or ten'.[20] This piece of information suggests that the poor-relief authorities did not much care about the family situation of children who were bound in service.

English farmers' interest in taking workhouse and pauper children as parish apprentices began to die in the early nineteenth century. Apprentices were generally a burden and an expense for farmers, and the unwillingness to take them on spread. Nevertheless, the system continued in some regions, such as Devon. Children aged nine years or over could be taken from their parents by poor-relief authorities without consultation, and apprenticed to husbandry in return for payment from the overseers to farmers who had been chosen by lot. In 1841 in Colyton, Devon, two-thirds of children under fifteen lived away from home, and children as young as ten lived apart from their families.[21] Were these children placed out as parish apprentices or did they go into service so young? The system of boarding out children was revived after the mid-nineteenth century, this time principally to protect the morals of young girls who, if kept in the workhouse, often landed in prostitution. This boarding-out, which was alleged to be better for children's morals than institutional care, survived in Britain until the Second World War.[22]

From the 1740s onwards, seven-year-old children in France were sent from pauper *hôpitaux* to the countryside to live with labourer or other rural households and learn agricultural work. According to Maurice Capul, the new policy was adopted essentially for economic reasons.[23] However, it was not until the early nineteenth century that this activity assumed the proportions of organised mass traffic in children. French rural families taking foundlings were often extremely wretched. To encourage foster parents to keep the children, the authorities in Paris paid a stipend or bonus until they reached the age of twelve. Those caring for infirm and disabled children were paid extra. Payments for other children varied: the older the child, the smaller the monthly amount. Foster children were provided with new clothing once a year, but uniform state-provided clothes effectively stigmatised the foundlings in the village community. The payments as well as all supervision and responsibility for any administration ended when assisted children reached their thirteenth year, but authority over assisted children was extended to the age of twenty-one in 1852. Foster boys aged between seven and twelve worked as swineherds, ploughboys or field hands, while girls usually worked as general domestic helps, including taking care of small children, and as keepers of sheep, goats and chickens.[24]

Marie-Claire (Marguerite Audoux) was five in 1868 when she and her older sister were placed in a convent for orphans and *enfants de l'assistance* in Sologne, at the upper reaches of the river Loire. The two sisters were separated. When Marie-Claire was about twelve, the institution placed her out with a peasant farmer in a village called Sainte-Montage. She was to stay on this farm until she turned eighteen, and at first she replaced an old women as a shepherd. Alone all day with cows and sheep, she felt lost and, after losing two sheep to a wolf, she was also afraid. Although she was not treated badly, she tried to run away. At the age of thirteen she started to milk the cows and feed the pigs while continuing with herding. When she became a farm servant, she found it repugnant to kill chickens and rabbits. Then the peasant farmer suddenly died of a fever, and the landowner wasted no time in turning the rest of the family off the farm. Marie-Claire's only friend now was a neighbour who also had been abandoned in his childhood, and who had been placed out in the village at the age of twelve. Marie-Claire had to remain on the farm, so she became a servant of the new master, the son of the landowner. Her new mistress soon found that she did not want to keep her, so she was placed out as a domestic servant with her mistress' mother, at the grand estate of Gué Perdu. After coming of age, Marie-Claire returned to the convent where she was put to kitchen work. One night she took her sister, who had come to see her, to the railway station from where a train to Paris was about to leave. The money she had with her was enough for a ticket. With the image of Paris guiding her she changed her life – as 'the simple shepherd' Valentin Jamerey-Duval had done two centuries earlier. Marie-Claire was to become a respectable seamstress in Paris.[25]

After the mid-nineteenth century, taking foster children became a livelihood for some people in the department of Alliers in central France. The agricultural revolution, exploited by local landlords, meant that sharecropping families needed to hire more male labour, while their women lost their major productive contribution in that they were forbidden to milk the cows of the new beef cattle. Landlords also substituted pigs and hogs for sheep, and thus children and old people who had worked as shepherds had to be replaced by able-bodied adults. The costs of hired labour rose sharply around 1860, and rural wages were forced upwards as landlords increased the commercial exploitation of forests. In this situation, sharecropping families began to take in foundlings, and eventually nearly half of the population in some villages was raising abandoned children from Paris. Ultimately the foster children profited the landlords, who could increase agricultural production by labour-intensive means, while the costs of the labour fell on sharecroppers and the French state. Day labourers took in foster children primarily because they represented supplementary cash income, and they therefore preferred younger ones, while sharecroppers were more interested in older children, whom they immediately put to work. By the late 1880s, foster children from Paris had replaced local young people as the main source of agricultural labour. Around 1900, when the mechanisation of agriculture began to appear profitable, landlords largely succeeded in eliminating foundlings – whom they now considered troublemakers – in the villages they controlled. Yet Alliers still accommodated thousands of abandoned children from Paris in 1916, and the system survived until the Second World War.[26]

In Italy, the number of abandoned infants began to grow very rapidly in the early nineteenth century. Traditionally, there had been more girls than boys, but this discrimination against girls now completely disappeared. Another change was that there was a massive increase in the abandonment of legitimate children, and in many villages such children were treated as foundlings. Infants placed in foundling homes were placed out with rural wet nurses as soon as possible. Payments to foster parents decreased as the child grew older, and in the 1880s they usually ceased when the child reached eleven to fourteen. In southern Italy they stopped when the child was five or seven, not because such young children would have been considered self-supporting, but because they were expected to be returned to the charity institutions. The payments ceased much earlier for boys than for girls, who were thought to be in need of special protection. The foundling home kept a close eye on the conditions of girls who had turned twelve: they had to sleep separately from the males, and were not permitted to be used for herding, which was solitary work. Girls enjoyed a number of benefits long after the payments had ceased, and some foundling homes even provided them with a dowry, whereas boys were on their own. Boys aged between seven and fifteen who were left to fend for themselves by the foundling home were at the bottom of the social hierarchy and often faced a sad fate.[27]

The high mortality in Russian foundling homes had originally motivated the shift from institutional care to village fosterage. From the turn of the nineteenth century onwards, most of the foundlings were placed out in the countryside, and a little more than one-tenth of them survived. Foster families received stipends, which varied according to the sex, condition and age of the children. A little more was paid for the care of girls. According to David Ransel, taking in foundlings was totally commercialised, offering the women in the villages 'an opportunity to earn needed cash or goods'.[28] It turned out that the main incentive was not the stipend, or the child's labour potential, but, as a secret report explained in 1856: 'Children are taken, for the most part by the poor families, not because of the money they expect to earn but because they plan to use the pay booklet from the foundling home as a collateral for loans to acquire things they need for the household, such as livestock, seed, and buildings.'[29]

Russian peasant families fostering older children frequently complained about the pay which was well below the costs of the upkeep. The pay was cut when the foster child turned seven, but according to the peasants children as old as nine contributed nothing to the domestic economy, but consumed a great deal. Later in the nineteenth century foster families simply returned the children when the monthly pay they received from the foundling hospital lagged too much behind the costs of maintaining the children. There may have been genuine attachment between the foundling and the foster parents, yet poverty forced the poorest to give up the child. In the 1880s, when bread prices were high, the monthly pay for a child aged over seven years was one rouble, while it cost at least three roubles just to feed him or her, to say nothing about clothing which was not, as in France, provided by the foundling hospice. Towards the end of the nineteenth century, it was getting difficult to place foundlings with any but poor families, hence an increasing number of them lived in miserable conditions.[30]

In the early eighteenth century, many foster children in Hessen worked as 'cow boys' or 'chicken girls'. In the 1720s a ten-year-old foster boy called Sebastian herded cows in the summer and gave them fodder in winter, and assisted with ploughing in the fields. He received no wage, was not allowed to go to school, and was not even confirmed before he left at the age of fourteen.[31] In 1830, the poor-relief authorities of the city of Osnabrück began to place out city children with private households in a nearby parish. In 1858, of the some 70 farmed-out foster children in the parish (seven per cent of all children aged under fourteen in the parish), half of them were born outside. After the age of twelve, foster children started to be of real use in farm work, and having turned fourteen they were considered strong enough to be proper labourers. They were relatively more common in the households of substantial farmers (*Grossbauer*) than among other groups. During the worst labour shortage, one farmer even accepted a female servant with an illegitimate child, who was then brought up as a foster child to become a servant. In 1858 in Belm, the 90 *Grossbauer* households had 26 foster children in all (one per 3.5 households), while the 372 households of the landless and day workers had 24 (one per 15.5 households). What was more important for the landless than the work the farmed-out children did was the pay that followed – which, as Jürgen Schlumbohm points out, did not exclude the possibility of an emotional bond between foster children and parents.[32]

Taking foster children paid for by the parish (*Kostkinder*) was a way of making a living in the German countryside, as elsewhere. The business-like character of fosterage was striking in cases in which orphans and foundlings were offered to potential foster parents in public auctions. In one German village, a boy was first offered for an annual wage of five *Gulden*, then for less, yet no farmer was willing to take him, although one made nasty jokes while the boy said nothing himself. A girl was offered for three *Gulden*, and was eventually taken by a farmer for a little over two *Gulden*. When she left with him, he said to her that there was already enough work waiting for her. Foster parents seldom permitted *Kostkinder* to go to school, which would have cost money, and this marked these children out even more clearly as the socially most inferior.[33]

From the 1750s onwards the Swedish Crown made repeated efforts to place out deprived children with peasant households, but with little success, because the parishes were not willing to subsidise foster parents. In 1785, children taken from *barnhus* (orphanages) as fosterlings were exempted from the poll tax for three extra years, that is until they turned 18. Since this did not prove attractive enough, the age limit rose to 21 years for males and 20 years for females in 1796, and in 1804 it rose further to 25 for males and 24 for females. People of standing were first attracted by the poll tax exemptions involved for taking orphan children as indentured servants, but eventually their interest faded.[34] In some parishes, such as Locknevi in the mid-nineteenth century, the parish shoemaker and the parish tailor were obliged to take local pauper boys as parish apprentices.[35]

With the growing numbers of illegitimate children in nineteenth-century Stockholm, 'taking a foster child developed into something of an industry ... and a veritable export of unwanted children took place', as Orvar Löfgren observes. A common saying among crofters and smallholders in south-eastern Sweden run thus: 'A couple of cows, a few acres of land and two foster children [are] enough to support a family'. A similar attitude also prevailed in Denmark. Taking several foster children was a way for many women without means to make a living. The Swedish national railway system provided a special car for transporting children to foster households in the countryside, and in the late nineteenth century such trains left Stockholm five to ten times a year. It was easier to place out girls, who could be used at an early age for various household tasks, therefore foster parents were paid more for taking boys. About 41,500 children were registered as foster children in 1894, one in forty of the child population. The system functioned until 1923.[36]

The expansion of the farming-out system in the Finnish countryside was connected with the breakthrough of the monetary economy. After the mid-nineteenth century, the costs of poor relief were kept down by offering in public auctions parish paupers of every age and condition for one year at a time to the *lowest* bidder, that is to the one who accepted the smallest pay from the parish as compensation. Landless people preferred to take the old, sick, lunatic and crippled because of the higher cash pay that came with them, while peasant farmers usually took able-bodied children who would do for labour, in addition to bringing in the money that the parish paid for maintenance. Most farmed-out children were the orphaned or destitute offspring of the local poor. If the fosterling did not know how to read, someone in the foster household had to teach him or her. Fosterlings were often treated harshly, and they generally had a heavy workload, which may have been too much for them, undernourished as they were to begin with. Nevertheless, against all odds, a genuine attachment sometimes developed between the fosterling and the foster parents. In 1894, about 10,300 children (one in ninety) were registered as farmed-out foster children. The system survived in the Finnish countryside until the late 1920s.[37]

In northern Sweden, as in Finland, local parish paupers, adults and children, were offered out to the lowest bidder in public auctions, which was very humiliating. The less the farmed-out child was given for food and clothes, the more his or her master gained in the deal. Young foster children were first set to mind the masters' small children, a job they disliked, or to herding in the forest, in the first summer two together, and alone the next year. Those who were a little older had a heavy workload. In the late nineteenth century the nine-year-old daughter of a very poor landless settler in Djupdal in the parish of Vilhelmina, was taken, with her father's consent, as a foster child by a richer neighbour, whose own daughters were thus spared from unpleasant and heavy work, such as cow-house work and milking. The little girl was burdened with so much work that she could go to school only occasionally and had no time to do her homework, and thus her teacher proposed that she might as well drop out. She was not allowed to eat with the rest of the household members, and was often so hungry that she shook with weakness. She was not given proper clothes, so she suffered from the cold. She had to work without wages for this household until she came of age, at twenty-one.[38]

In Norway, as in Finland and Sweden, payments to foster parents varied according to the children's ages, the younger the child, the higher the pay. In 1893, Kristiania (Oslo) had about 500 children placed out in the countryside. Unlike in Sweden, it was easier to place out boys than girls with peasant households in Norway. Nonetheless, the proportions of pauper boys and girls of all non-family child labour of the same sex were the same (28%) in 1900. Farmed-out children had seldom been abandoned, but were rather children of parents who had no choice but to give them away. As late as the 1920s, a farm labourer whose wife died had to give away his three children, since he was not allowed to take them to his master's holding.[39]

According to Tim Wales, 'pauper apprenticeship should be seen as a means of transferring children from families which could not support them to families who could'.[40] No doubt this held true in cases in which a foster child had been taken as a substitute heir, for instance, but the poor circumstances of many households taking foster children and the unscrupulously commercial character of the traffic make Wales' argument appear idealised compared with, say, that of the Swedish historian Marianne Liliequist. She suggests that a contemptuous and insensitive attitude among the members of the master households towards farmed-out foster children was a means of creating distance from them, making it easier to exploit them and keep them on a starvation diet.[41] As several historians have observed, up to the age of fifteen, at least, a growing child consumed more than he or she produced.[42] This necessarily led to exploitation whenever fosterage acquired a commercial character whereby masters wanted to profit from foster children. Moreover, cash subventions from public funds to foster parents were needed so that the supply of parish pauper children would create its own demand.

The rise and fall of the system of farmed-out pauper children or parish apprentices seemed roughly to follow the phases of the agricultural revolution. It may not have been merely a coincidence that farmers' interest in parish apprentices first faded in England, distinguished by its unusually high labour productivity in agriculture. In the second half of the nineteenth century marginal farming regions, such as the settler communities in northern Sweden, must have lagged far behind in agricultural labour productivity. In 1896, two English ladies ventured on a tourist trip to the very regions in Finland where pauper auctions were common. 'Farm work is very primitive in Finland', the two ladies noted, while life in the countryside 'seemed to take us back a couple of centuries at least'.[43] The First World War turned out to be a watershed concerning orphaned and deprived children. Within a decade from 1917, modern adoption legislation was introduced in France, England and the Scandinavian countries while in Italy and Spain statutes on abandoned children and in Germany those on foster children were reformed.[44] Modern adoption legislation marked the formal end of the old principle that boarded-out children must work for their masters or foster parents. Would it be an overstatement to suggest that it was not a coincidence that, by that time, the most labour-intensive phase of the agricultural revolution was over?

The family's own and hired children

As long as children and adolescents in farm service were of a more or less similar social status as their master's family, it is plausible to argue that young servants were treated like the peasant farmer's own children, whatever this may have meant in individual cases. However, when they were of lower social status, they were probably not treated as equals. According to Regina Schulte, at the end of the nineteenth century, in Bavaria, 'male and female farm servants were in a similar position to the children of the peasant family on whose farm they were employed', but her reference to 'particularly loud and frequent' complaints by farmers about 'the negligence and apathy' of farm servants suggests a strained relationship.[45] This section discusses the work and treatment of the peasant farmer's own children, on the one hand, and of the children employed by him, on the other. It is suggested that even though the work load of his own children probably increased, their status gave them advantages over the 'outside' children employed on the farm.

As in many parts of Europe, in the German countryside the family's own children were first given easy tasks as part of their play, and gradually more demanding ones.[46] Judging from the fact that the 1812 census called almost all single persons aged fourteen or over servants, Jürgen Schlumbohm suggests that 'adolescent children were equivalent to servants', although there were other major differences in the status of the two groups.[47] One example of a case in which staying on the parental farm did not necessarily make any difference in terms of work was that of Anna Catharina Grein from Hessen. After confirmation in 1852 she remained on her parental farm, which her father had transferred to her half-brother. Close kin though he was, the half-brother evidently did not spare Anna but extorted work from her as if she had been a hired servant.[48]

It was common for peasant farmers in Scandinavia to use their children for labour instead of or in addition to farm servants.[49] The demand for the labour of the family's own children of useful age may have grown among small farmers and crofters in southern Sweden because marginal land was increasingly being taken into use, and this seems to have lead to 'self-exploitation' of family labour.[50] According to Eljas Raussi, (of peasant origin), some landed peasant farmers in Virolahti in Finland put their eldest son to heavy work at too early an age, while others did not have the heart to put their children to work but let them pass their time in play. Landed peasants regarded lodgers' and cottagers' children as ill-bred and even pilferers, and only reluctantly hired them as surrogates for landed peasants' children who were not willing to go into service.[51]

In Jutland, Denmark, at the time when farmhands were evidently difficult to find because of the Danish-German war (1848–1851), Knud and Esper, the two eldest sons of the peasant farmer Peder Knudsen, had to start at an early age on work usually done by a farmhand. Knud, the elder of the two, began as a cowherd the year he turned seven, since in that year his father no longer hired outside children for herding. When he was only thirteen years old, he was already doing a farmhand's work. He helped in manuring the fields and cutting heather and sods on the heath, and ploughed and harrowed the fields on his own. Esper joined him at the age of twelve. Normally boys started doing such heavy and specialised work only after they were confirmed. Knud and Esper were confirmed at the age of fifteen in 1849 and 1851 respectively. Their father managed without any farmhands for the first time in 1849, but for a few years more he continued to hire day labourers for harvesting, threshing, potato picking, carting manure and cutting sods and heather.[52]

Lars Andersson from Flundre, in Västergötland in Sweden, was thirteen when he began to write down his activities in 1860. He was the sixth-born son of a prominent landed peasant. He was set to run errands, fetch firewood and water, give water to animals, take sheep to the meadow and do herding, sow clover, peas and beans, drive a cart and assist with harvest work. In winter, he often worked very hard chopping firewood for the family to sell, while farm work took over in the spring. He had plenty of time to play with his friends in January, February and March, and again in May and July. Lars went to school sporadically at first, but from 1861 more regularly. The peasant farmer Ludvig Wennberg from the province of Uppland followed in his diary the growing up of his son Axel Leonard from the day he was born in 1882. Axel was gradually introduced, first as half play, to tasks and work on the farm, and started helping around when he was seven. He piled chopped firewood, picked berries, and tore up and cut old clothes for re-use (a female's job). At the age of ten his work become more varied, and at twelve he was occupied mostly in farm work, although he apparently never went herding. Every other day he went to school.[53]

According to Colin Heywood, in French peasant households 'there was no difficulty in finding various simple jobs around the farm that were suitable for children'. As elsewhere, a typical children's job was to take the family's animals to graze in village pastures. Other jobs they did 'in order to free adults for more exacting work included minding younger brothers and sisters, picking stones from the fields, collecting dung from the roads, hoeing in the vegetable plots, and ... scaring birds and working beside the haymakers and reapers'. In the highland regions, shepherd boys from the age of twelve were sent up to the mountains for the summer with the sheep, and adolescent boys herded large cattle on their own. In the arable field regions, farm boys began to handle the spade, the plough and the threshing flail. They cleaned out the stables, tended horses and oxen, and eventually led the plough team. Peasant girls working as servants were occupied with women's work: milking the cows, feeding the poultry, doing some cooking, fetching water, taking food to the men in the fields, and spinning at other times. French country children appeared to have entered the agricultural labour market from the age of twelve, the 1851 census listing an increasing proportion of children from that age up with an occupation.[54] Among the vinegrowers in Languedoc in southern France, the children of agricultural labourers started with seasonal work at the age of fourteen, but do not seem to have become regular labourers until three to four years later, whereas landowners' children did not do paid work.[55]

Children on sharecropper (*métayer*) farms may have stayed throughout their adolescence as part of the family labour force. Etienne Bertin from a sharecropper family in Bourbonnais, in central France, started to work in 1830 when he was almost seven. He was first entrusted with the care of the sheep, replacing his sister Catharine who, at twelve, had to take the place of the servant their mother had employed until then. In addition to her domestic concerns, Catharine had to do her share of work in the fields. Shepherd's work was too much for little Etienne in the first summer. Alone with his dog and the sheep in the pasture, he found the days very long, and at dusk he was ready to weep from fear and misery. When he was nine years old, he was given pigs to look after, and had to go to the fields with them in all weathers, however cold. That work, too, was beyond him at first. In spring 1835, after his second year of catechism, he received the sacrament. The same autumn he turned twelve and began to get used to all kinds of work. He was put in charge of the oxen used for ploughing, but was not able to do the ploughing himself. After his fifteenth birthday, he no longer looked after pigs, but began to do men's work, such as threshing with the flail and cleaning out the cowsheds, both very rough jobs.[56]

In mid-nineteenth-century Spain, children of agricultural day labourers were familiarised with various tasks on the home farm at a very tender age, 'as soon as they can walk and talk'. They started to be of use when they were robust enough, boys between six and nine, and girls between nine and eleven. Both boys and girls did similar kinds of work, and both were set to dig in the garden, and pick and sell fruit, for instance. A typical job for boys between six and eight was to collect dung and garbage used as fertiliser, and at the age of twelve they learned to plough light, dry soil. A strong boy of seven or eight may already have been given some paid work. At the age of seven, children of professional shepherds began to be of help in tending livestock, and were paid in kind: four to six loaves of bread a week, olive oil, vinegar, salt and garlic. Paid work was not usually offered until the age of ten years, and from the age of sixteen boys were regarded as able to work as labourers. Family members and living-in relatives comprised the labour force on small farms, while hired servants were common on farms with ten or more hectares of land.[57]

Children were found among all of the main groups of agricultural workers in the central Italian countryside around Rome, although they dominated none. In 1823, the ages of farm labourers used for ploughing (*bifolchi*) varied from 14 to 64, of male *monelli* from 10 to 64, and of female *monelle* from 10 to 45. Twenty years later the ages of the male *monelli* varied even more, from 9 to 66. The *monelli* – old and young, male and female – were used as labour gangs for hard work, and the married *monelli* men had their families with them. Quite young boys were also sometimes bonded as *monelli* without parents. For example in 1858, of a group of 70 *monelli*, nearly half were children: one was aged eight years and one nine, five boys were ten, seven boys eleven, and 18 boys were between twelve and fourteen. *Monelli* labour gangs had disappeared from the Italian countryside by the turn of the twentieth century. Farm servants, *garzoni* ('boys') and farmed-out foundlings, *innocentini* were now at the bottom of the agricultural hierarchy.[58]

In nineteenth-century England, where 'distress was strongly regionalised' (W.A. Amstrong),[59] agricultural labour gangs were used by farmers with large holdings and in areas where men were plagued by very low wages and unemployment and women and children suffered bad health due to sheer want of food. Gangs of women and young children, at times as young as between four and six years of age, were employed in field work, paid by the piece. Where the farms were few and far between, such gangs had to walk several kilometres to their place of work, and then back again in the evening, since the gangmasters organised transport in carts and overnight stays only if the distance was well over ten kilometres. They imposed a routine of sustained hard work and tough discipline. These characteristics made gang work particularly laborious for children, and such work by women and children remained unaffected by the general technological changes in agriculture (the use of the scythe instead of the sickle, mechanised reapers and binders, steam ploughing). Public gangs of this type were prohibited in England in 1867.[60]

Within a decade of this prohibition, international depression and competition from cheap imported grain, dairy products and refrigerated meat cut the demand for labour in the English countryside.[61] Even farmers with large holdings reduced their outside labour force to a minimum and put the children of the family to help before and after school. Farmers generally moved from cultivating arable crops to less labour-intensive pastoral farming, while machinery substituted for labour in hay and corn harvesting. Nevertheless, there remained many labour-intensive jobs for mobile gangs of women and children, now recruited by individual farmers. Children did not usually join such gangs until around the age of seven or eight years. Together with adults, children would be engaged on various tasks throughout the agricultural year: sorting potatoes and picking up stones in January, spreading dung, hoeing and setting potatoes in March, weeding in April, May and June, singling turnips and getting up hay in July, harvesting or pulling flax in August and September, gathering wood and gleaning, spreading dung, picking potatoes and gathering mangolds, turnips and carrots in October, November and December, until the frosts came. Much of the work was onerous and was even worse in the cold season. Turnips (together with clover) were the 'revolutionary crops' paving the way for the agricultural revolution, but one of their advantages as winter fodder – the fact that they could remain in the ground during the first half of the winter – made them particularly hard for women and children to hoe up.[62]

Judging from the census returns, the use of hired agricultural child labour in England increased between 1851 and 1861 and then declined in all categories save gardening (was this associated with the vogue for English-style gardens?). Since the total number of labourers and shepherds, as well as the total agricultural labour force, kept steadily declining, the proportion of children was in fact higher in 1861 and 1871 than it had been in 1851 (Table 3.1). In 1861, of all agricultural child workers, 32 per cent (41,090) were aged under twelve. The great majority of these were boys between ten and twelve (32,580), and even boys under ten were quite numerous (7,000). There were only 1,500 girls under twelve, and less than 300 of these were under ten.[63] The declining demand for hired agricultural labour was felt more strongly among children under fifteen than among older workers: during the twenty-year period from 1861–1881, the number of hired children declined by 43 per cent, and that of workers over fifteen by 22 per cent. In the case of children, the decline was particularly rapid during the period 1871–1881.[64]

According to Eric Hopkins by 1861 'half a century of factory legislation was beginning to have obvious implications for the employment of children in agriculture. This was not so much because of fears that the labour was too hard, but rather because of the effect of child labour on their education'. A commission was set up in 1867 to enquire into the extent to which the principles of the factory acts could be applied in agriculture.[65] Nevertheless, it remains unclear through what kind of mechanisms the factory acts made themselves felt in agricultural child labour before or after the 1860s. Would not structural changes in agricultural production and the international depression of the 1870s offer an equally if not more plausible explanation for the declining demand for child labour?

German children of smallholders and the village poor may have gone into service at about the age of thirteen at an estate, *Hof*, or with a peasant farmer, *Bauernhof*. Local boys and girls aged twelve or even younger were hired for herding, and children of the poor might even have ended up working on far-away farms. Children aged eight to nine, along with their mothers, were hired in the autumn for potato picking in a *Hof*, and were paid about half of what their mothers earned.[66] The daughter of an impoverished shepherd man, Maria Elisabetha Treibert (born in 1871) began as a helper at a peasant farm, *Bauernhof* Krauss in Hessen, when she was still of school age in about 1880. She left home for the *Bauernhof* very early in the morning, and cooked millet porridge for the farmhands before leaving for school.[67] German peasant farmers apparently did not take on children as living-in farm servants. For example, in 1858, of some 220 male farm servants in Belm, only seven boys were younger than fifteen, and of 190 female servants only ten were that young.[68]

Local children in the German countryside may not have been willing to put up with bad treatment, poor food, clothes and wages, or the loneliness that usually went with herding work. The farmers may then have resorted to foreign migrant boys and girls, *Schwabenkinder*, from the poor mountain valleys of the Tyrol and Vorarlberg in Austria. Every March, children aged between seven and fifteen left for work as seasonal herders in Upper Swabia, Bavaria, Württemberg and beyond. After several days' journey, they reached their destination where they either went from farm to farm, offering themselves for hire, or gathered at unofficial hiring fairs, *Kindermarkt*. As early as 1821 in Württemberg, for example, there was an established practice of 'foreign children' waiting in the market place to be hired by peasant farmers, and the practice continued until 1914. The peasant farmers first wanted to know how much the child was asking for wages before hiring him or her for herding, while children learned to recognise and avoid bad masters. Still the risk of bad treatment was always present. When the outdoor herding season ended in the late autumn, the children walked back home. As a part of their wages they had new clothes, to the envy of the children back home, and some money, between 3 and 6 *Gulden* from 1820 to 1860, between 50 and 70 *Mark* from 1890 to 1914, and 100 *Mark* in their third year of herding. According to Otto Uhlig, the poverty underlying the supply of migrant children originated partly from the increased price of food at the beginning of the nineteenth century. The annual number of *Schwabenkinder* support this: they numbered between 2,000 and 3,000 in the early nineteenth century, about 1,500 in the mid-century, and about 400–500 at the end.[69]

The majority of young people in Bavaria with a rural background remained firmly tied to agricultural employment at least until the beginning of the twentieth century. The daughters of agricultural day labourers, cottagers and smallholders took their first job on a farm at the age of thirteen or fourteen, after they had left school. They sometimes started as gooseherds, but usually helped the peasant's wife with household tasks and looking after children. As small servant girls grew, they started to learn farm tasks, then milking and feeding cows, eventually becoming responsible for the animals. Stable boys and dairy maids were expected to perform much the same or complementary tasks. A dairy maid may have spent the entire summer alone, or accompanied by a small boy, on the high Alpine pastures with the cows. The farm maid's existence was oriented towards future marriage, and during her ten or fifteen years in service she saved her dowry in order to attract a potential husband. Becoming a smallholder's wife was her only opportunity to achieve financial security, status and prestige in the village.[70]

In Scandinavia, peasant farmers, like their German counterparts, did

Table 3.1. The agricultural labour force including children under 15 in England
and Wales, 1851, 1861, 1871 and 1881 (in thousands).

		1851	%	1861	%	1871	%	1881	%
Farmers and	total	371.7		357.7		342.9		318.5	
their relatives	children	..		..		1.9		0.2	
	boys	..		..		1.9		0.2	
	girls	..		..		0		0	
Labourers and	total	1,253.8	100.0	1,188.9	100.0	980.1	100.0	870.8	100.0
shepherds	children	118.9	9.5	125.1	10.5	102.2	10.4	70.1	8.1
	boys	105.7		119.0		98.0		68.0	
	girls	13.2		6.1		4.2		2.1	
Gardeners,	total	85.9	100.0	91.3	100.0	112.7	100.0	83.4	100.0
nurserymen etc	children	2.0	2.3	2.3	2.5	2.7	2.4	1.9	2.3
	boys	1.9		2.3		2.6		1.8	
	girls	0.1		0		0.1		0.1	
Breeders and dealers	total	48.2	100.0	59.1	100.0	64.7	100.0	62.3	100.0
(horses and cattle)	children	1.2	2.5	1.9	3.2	1.7	2.6	1.4	2.2
	boys	1.2		1.9		1.7		1.4	
	girls	0		0		0		0	
TOTAL*	total	1,759.6	100.0	1,700.2	100.0	1,503.9	100.0	1,341.0	100.0
CHILDREN TOTAL	children	122.1	6.9	129.3	7.6	108.5	7.2	73.6	5.5
	boys	108.8		123.2		104.2		71.4	
	girls	13.3		6.1		4.3		2.2	

* Including drainage and machinery attendants (all aged over 15).

Source: Occupation Censuses 1851–1881, published in Booth 1886, Appendix A.

not hire children as proper living-in farm servants but typically took on the
children of poorer families for the outdoor grazing season. Around the mid-
nineteenth century, farmers in Virolahti in south-east Finland hired children
from outside for herding only if they had no suitably aged children of their
own. These children's wages consisted of board and lodging during the summer
and a little money. The cowherds were usually either younger womenfolk or
older children of the household, or even professional male herders. Since
cows grazed far from the village, young children were not used as cowherds,
but were only taken on as shepherds tending sheep that were pastured close
to the village.[71] In northern Sweden, none of the 142 male or the 182 female
farm servants in the parish of Bollnäs in 1860 was aged under fifteen, and in
1890 only one each of the 72 male and 114 female farm servants was under
that age.[72] Skåne (Scania) was socially very differentiated, and corvée labour
survived there well into the nineteenth century. The life-cycle service of
landed peasants' sons and daughters continued past the mid-century, but with
few exceptions they were aged at least fifteen when they left home.[73]

Danish crofters' sons aged eight or nine left home in April to serve as
herder boys long into the autumn, returning only for midwinter. They

worked eighteen to nineteen hours a day, and were often paid no other wage than board and lodging.[74] The days spent herding seemed very long, especially if the children were alone, if it was cold and rainy (children often went herding barefooted in Scandinavia), or if the children were hungry. Accounts from Sweden and Finland tell of stingy farmers' wives who gave their young cowherds so little to eat that they tried to satisfy their hunger by eating grass. Many a cowherd was afraid of the wolves that still roamed in the forests used for grazing. Masters who wanted to make sure that their young cowherds spent rather than passed their time ordered them to pick berries and mushrooms, or to do piece work, which meant spinning with the distaff or knitting for the girls, and making wooden whistles, whisks or other such items for the boys. However, if there were many of them around, boys and girls also found the opportunity to play.[75]

Among the better-off settler farmers in northern Sweden, family strategies may have been based on the availability of cheap child labour in the neighbourhood. When the eldest son was becoming old enough to do men's work, at about twelve or thirteen, it was more profitable to hire a young girl of between six and twelve as a childminder, and to relieve the boy from taking care of his younger siblings. Taking care of babies in cradles and small infants who had to be carried around was boring and heavy, and children disliked the job. A small growing girl hired to mind an infant, could become deformed from carrying the infant on her hip day in, day out.[76] More girls than boys had paid work away from home in the Norwegian countryside, chiefly because more girls than boys were employed as servants. According to the census of 1876, two-thirds of servants aged under fifteen were girls. Of all girls with paid work, as many as four-fifths were servants, while one-tenth worked as shepherds or goatherds. Less than half of the boys worked as servants, and one-quarter as herders.[77] In 1890, 23 per cent of Norwegian country boys and 22 per cent of girls aged between thirteen and fourteen had an occupation, in 1900, 22 and 18 per cent, in 1910, 16 and 13 per cent, and in 1920, 10 and 7 per cent, respectively.[78]

In the Scandinavian countryside, hired children were usually paid in kind, in other words board and lodging, perhaps some clothing, and very little if anything was paid in cash, not even earnest- or fasten-penny (*städje-* or *fästepenning*). It was an established practice in Nord-Trøndelag in Norway that if a boy or a girl had served in a farmhouse before confirmation, and had in the meantime gone to confirmation classes, he or she would serve the master without pay for the first year after confirmation. The children of smallholders' children could earn cash by potato picking for other farms; girls were paid 50 øre, boys 80 øre a day, despite the fact (as a women born in 1896 recalled) that girls were quicker than boys.[79] Children of the landless and the poor who were hired as servants by better-off farms had to work hard and had no free time. Their work was often not considered worth sufficient or proper food, lodging and clothes. Being socially inferior, they were looked down upon by the master's family, whereas the children hired by socially equal neighbours or relatives were treated more like the farm's own children. In the latter case, there often existed a sort of reciprocity in that farms exchanged children as they, in turn, reached the age in which they could work as childminders or cowherds.[80]

Russian peasant children began to be of use in their parental household at the age of seven. Their first job was to take care of their younger siblings. Peasant households also hired young girls as childminders. Girls aged between nine and ten tended calves, while boys between seven and eleven years tended sheep or cattle, or grazed horses. Boys may have been given too heavy work, such as fetching tubs of water.[81] Children also contributed to *kustar* work. They cleaned and combed the goat down, and girls and women then spun the goat hair (and women wove it into kerchiefs, then a fashionable luxury product), unwound cotton or were involved in the manufacture of tiny hollow tubes for cigarette factories: the women and girls made the tubes while young boys were hired to pack them into cartons.[82] Nonetheless, Ben Eklof suggests that the 'extent of child labour may have been substantially overstated by historians', and presents evidence that the peak labour demand in agriculture hardly affected children under twelve (that is school-age children), and particularly not children as young as seven or eight.[83]

In the early twentieth century A.V. Chayanov observed that, on Russian peasant farms, 'adolescents work fewer days than adults. The distribution of their labor by farm sectors is according to their sex; in general, boys are more engaged in agriculture and girls spend many days on domestic work'. He estimated that, in Volokolamsk, about a quarter of men's time was 'unused', and well over half of male youths' time was 'unused' free time. The rest of the boys' time was allocated between crafts and trades (17.6%), tillage (14.7%), livestock (5.1%) and domestic work (4.1%). For the women, no more than about a tenth of their time was 'unused', while young women and girls were free for 50 per cent of their time. The rest of girls' time was divided between domestic work (25%), crafts and trades (14%), tillage (8.8%), and livestock (2.8%).[84]

In addition to using their own and hired children, landlords and farmers may have used the labour of their tenants' or underlings' children, a practice that was connected not only to the increasing demand for labour, but also to the deteriorating bargaining position of the landless.

In the late nineteenth century, landlords and landed peasant farmers in the Finnish and Swedish countryside preferred underlings with large families, seeing their children as a cheap and flexible labour reserve. In Sweden it became impossible for a man to get employment as a *statare*[85] farm labourer, unless he was married, while crofter contracts in Finland included extra labour service by the crofter's wife and children at the landowner's request.[86] Landowners accepted the fact that crofters' children assisted their parents when the labour service was based on piece work, on condition that the children did not eat at the landowner's table. As a rule of thumb, two child work days were equal to one woman's work day. Somewhere between the ages of fourteen and sixteen, children's work began to be accepted as that of an adult. Typically children's labour service to the landowner consisted of work other than assisting their parents: they picked berries, minded the landowner's children, weeded root crop fields, tended his cows, and sowed potato seeds and dug up potatoes.[87]

Similar conditions were found in nineteenth-century Italy, where the contracts the landlord made with sharecropper or ploughmen families indicated that families as a whole provided the labour force, even though the landlords saw young children as 'useless mouths'.[88] Despite its more modern labour market, analogous terms of employment were known even in the English countryside. According to Pamela Horn, in Dorset and Northumberland, for instance, 'it was customary for male workers to provide extra labour from among their families when the farmer needed it'. As late as in the 1890s Dorset farmers advertised for labourers 'with a working family', or indicated a preference for men with large families.[89]

At the turn of the twentieth century, from Spain to Russia, life in the countryside could still be very hard and impoverished. In Spain, the wages of male agricultural day labourers were so low that the combined pay of a husband, wife, son aged thirteen and daughter aged ten may not have been enough to make ends meet, and the children had to be sent to beg for alms.[90] In Fougères in Ille-et-Vilaine, France, little Jean Guéhenne, born in 1890 into a shoemaker's family, was sent out to the countryside to live with his poor great aunt, who made her meagre living in an old-fashioned way by spinning wool, and as *la nourrice*, a wet nurse and nurse for children farmed-out by mothers with long working days in factories. Jean loved his *nourrice* great aunt as his mother, and stayed with her until he was almost twelve years old. Apparently, he was not burdened with much work, but he helped his *nourrice* in spooling bobbins and went herding cows with other village children.[91] In 1905, Joseph Allais, a widowed sheep-breeding peasant with six children living in the French Alps, had no choice but to bind Émilie, only five years old, on the back of a mule that she then rode up to their mountain chalet, from where the mule would carry down grass. The Allais family had cows and some sixty sheep in 1910, and it was up to the children to milk and clean them, and to see to the fodder and litter. When Émilie was fourteen, her brother taught her to plough before leaving himself for war. For her, the war years meant hard work on the farm.[92] Wives and children in Norway ran the small family farms while the fathers were away fishing for three or four months at a time. The children wove, spun and knitted for themselves, and helped with the washing, carried water to the cows and horses, and helped with minding the animals and in the cowshed, clearing out the muck, and haymaking.[93]

During the nineteenth century, successful farmers and freeholders in the European countryside accumulated land and capital and gained from the commercialisation of agriculture. At the same time, numerous peasant farmers' children faced social descent into the landless classes, while children of crofters and smallholders ended up as farm labourers. The striking economic and social stratification of the peasant population brought with it huge contrasts in consumption and material standards on the one hand, and in prospects for children on the other. Children of the propertyless seemed to have no other prospects than toiling first for the parental household, then for the landowner, in the hope of one day acquiring a smallholding of their own, which would require its share of endless toiling. They escaped repeating the cycle from one generation to the next only by leaving the village for work in factories or the city.

Educational opportunities

The agricultural revolution had an impact on children's educational opportunities in the countryside. For example, successful peasant farmers now had the incentive to provide their sons with more formal education, as well as the money to cover the costs and to pay for farm labourers substituting for their sons at school. However, as long as children made up an essential part of the cheap rural labour force, sending them to school incurred opportunity costs, either as lost labour input or as lost income, whether in the form of money or the consumption of food and clothing. In practice, the outcome may have been that the education of sons was favoured at the cost of that of daughters, or that the family's own children were sent to school while 'outside' children were kept working full time. What kinds of solutions were attempted in different countries? Which country children were winners and which were losers?

It seems clear that peasant farmers of substance soon saw the benefits to be reaped from proper education. At the beginning of the nineteenth century, in the Weser marshland of Oldenburg, Johann Friedrich Töllner, a future successful large-scale farmer enjoyed as many as nine years of formal education: at the age of six he started learning to read at the village school, he learned to write at the age of eight, and at the age of ten he had lessons in singing and arithmetic, followed by spelling and more arithmetic in evening classes, some Latin and French, geography, history and essay writing in the English and German languages. At the age of fifteen, after receiving religious instruction, he was confirmed. Even the peasant girl he would marry, Caroline Friederike, had been sent after her confirmation to study household and kitchen management in an upper-class family.[94] The late nineteenth-century large-scale farmer, *Grossbauer*, could always make sure that the poorly-paid village school master devoted extra time and effort to his children, if need be at the cost of other children.[95] Likewise, teachers in English rural public schools favoured children of the well-to-do, while some farmers employed governesses for their children or sent the older ones to private school to make sure that they would not mix with the children of their labourers.[96] Danish fishermen who did not want their sons to continue in the same profession kept them at school, and the children of peasant farmers of substance even received education in private lower-secondary schools.[97]

At the other end of the scale were the pauper children. Those on poor relief in England seldom received any school education.[98] In France, foster parents were reluctant to let foundlings go to primary school until the 1882 education act made it free, and the authorities began to pay the foster parents to compensate for the loss of the child's labour.[99] Sharecroppers in the district of Alliers, who used foundlings from Paris for labour, did not send them to school, bribing the authorities to turn a blind eye. Artisans, innkeepers and propertied peasants took foundlings for their labour force, which enabled them to keep their own children in school longer.[100] Austrian migrant child workers, *Schwabenkinder*, went to school only during the winter months between two herding seasons. There were attempts to deny school-aged children a passport, but in practice this was rare, and they could cross the border illegally in any case.[101] Children of the poor in Germany often failed to go to school, compulsory school attendance notwithstanding, because of work or the lack of footwear in winter, or because their parents did not send them. The inferior quality of teachers and school premises tended to further alienate children.[102]

In many English parish schools, children were taught only religion and basic reading skills, since writing skills and arithmetic were considered unsuitable for those intended for manual labour. Rural boys who attended school left at the age of ten to eleven, while in some parishes children were kept at school until fourteen years of age. Schools charged for instruction: for example, in Hernhill in Kent, the fees were 6 pennies a week for reading, but more than double for reading, writing and arithmetic. Sunday schools were often more successful than day schools in teaching reading (of the Bible). Since they were free and did not interfere with the children's weekday work, the number of children in them far outstripped day-school attendance. In areas with plenty of cottage industries, parents put their children in craft schools run by women in their homes. Children aged six may already have been occupied in work such as button making. Small craft schools concentrated on training children in the skills of a particular trade, lace making or straw plaiting, for instance. The discipline was severe, as the women kept the children working as hard as possible the whole day in order to maximise the output and improve their manual dexterity.[103]

According to Michael Robson, parents in the Scottish Borders around the mid-nineteenth century 'made sure that their children received at least a little schooling', provided either by the parish school, which was generally of a high standard, or by teachers with various qualifications hired by several families for the winter. School attendance in winter was higher than during the summer and autumn, when the children were needed for various farm duties. At the end of the century, school log books still regularly listed each year absenteeism for work such as hay-making, potato-lifting, clipping, peat work, lambing, winter foddering, driving sheep, keeping house, beating for shooters and pig killing.[104]

Until the law of 1833 obliged every commune to have a primary school, only a minority of children attended school in rural France. However, in many areas the school system was slow in coming, and primary education for girls was given a low priority both by peasant parents and in official circles. Children seldom attended school in areas with poverty and a heavy reliance on family labour: they worked in the fields during the summer, and in the forests during the winter. In early spring, February or March, they deserted school for farm work, and did not return until October or November. Even though the school year did not conform to this, the village teachers did, restricting themselves to teaching the catechism, reading, writing, arithmetic and some grammar in winter, at low cost. Many parents preferred to save money and their children's time by teaching them some reading and arithmetic themselves. Compulsory primary education was introduced in 1882, but formal schooling still had little to offer to country people who continued to regard experience as a superior form of education for working life in agriculture and the household.[105] The peasant was ashamed of being uncivilised, yet school instruction was in French (most country people knew only *patois*), and learning to write was secondary. 'It was only when what the school taught made sense that they became important to those they had to teach. ... People went to school not because school was offered or imposed, but because it was useful', as Eugen Weber observes,[106] and this applied to primary education in most of the European countryside.

Spain and Italy formally introduced three years of primary education to all children in the late 1850s, but the implementation in the countryside was slow. According to Linda Reeder, agricultural workers and artisans in southern Italy recognised that education was a means to social mobility. The local élite also saw it as a mark of wealth and social distinction, and an educated daughter was a clear sign of social status. Therefore to educate the masses was an attack on the social order, and in Sicily in particular, the élite were deeply hostile to the idea. This made the realisation of educational reforms extremely difficult. Public primary schools suffered by having poorly paid and incompetent teachers, inferior school premises and a very limited curriculum. Absence from school because of farm work or household chores was common. The teaching of agriculture, which was included in the curriculum of the public primary schools in both Italy and Spain for some time, proved a failure, since the rural population only trusted experience.[107]

In contrast, schools in the northern Spanish countryside that functioned only the winter (*escuelas temporales*) proved a success, as they did not compete with farm work. The existence of such schools correlated with high rates of literacy. Even though country girls may also have been employed in household chores in winter, they promoted their schooling and literacy. However, in many areas parents were only prepared to pay for the education of sons, and not for daughters. The segregation of boys and girls in separate schools also worked against country girls. Half of the Spanish villages that had an ordinary primary school only catered for boys. According to Carmen Sarasúa, this was the chief reason for the low average rates of schooling and literacy among Spanish women. However, relatively high rates of female literacy were achieved in provinces where co-educational schools were common, indicating low segregation by sex, as well as in provinces with high segregation but also high numbers of primary schools for girls.[108]

Throughout the nineteenth century, several laws were promulgated and schemes launched to organise rural popular education in Russia, but because of the lack of funding, the implementation was slow. Financial sponsorship and the allocation of tax money (collected from peasants) favoured secondary and higher education, to which serf children had no access. Nonetheless, literacy among the peasant population kept slowly increasing. The demand for education among the peasants was met by local parish priests instructing peasant children to read and write, or by peasant-sponsored and peasant-run domestic or 'free' schools. The teachers were retired soldiers, clerks or other literate villagers, or as in Ukraine, 'peripatetic teachers'. According to Ben Eklof, 'between 1864 and 1890 peasants themselves were the driving force behind the progress in literacy registered in official statistics'. Yet female literacy was given low priority, unless the girl was expected to need it in future as a wife, and since peasant girls were useful at home all year round, the opportunity costs of educating them were higher than for boys. The expansion of the official school system began in the 1880s. On the local level, the school year was adjusted to the need for the children's labour on the farms. By accommodating their schedules to the seasonality of agriculture, village schools enjoyed relatively high enrolment and attendance rates, while avoiding the kinds of conflicts over children's time that were common in Western Europe. As the school system expanded, the enrolment rate increased. Before the First World War, Olga Semyonova Tian-Shanskaia remarked that, in view of the wages paid in Moscow, peasants endeavoured to have their sons learn reading and writing.[109]

Danish school legislation strove to take into consideration the needs of agriculture. Children had to go to school only every other day, that is three days a week, and older children only two days a week in June and July. Periods of high demand for farm labour were free of school, and this particularly concerned children aged ten or over. Local decision makers could decide on further changes in favour of farm work, if the need arose. It was commonly believed that farmers could legitimately keep young farm servants away from school because of work. For example, in 1880–1885, children who worked as servants on peasant landowners' (*gårdmænd*) farms in the district of Merløse-Tuse had higher absence rates (21%) than the landowner families' own children (11%).[110]

In Norway the school year first lasted only 30 weeks and fell during the agricultural slack period. Young girls employed as childminders may have had the opportunity to go to school every other day in winter, as in the case of Johanna Hansdatter from Telemark. In the early 1880s she worked from the age of seven until her confirmation as a herder in summer, and as a childminder in peasant-farmer households in winter. Nonetheless, the peaks of absenteeism in Norwegian coastal parishes coincided with booms in local agriculture and fishing. Bad weather was often a true reason or an apt excuse for absenteeism. In fact, from the 1860s to the 1890s, local school authorities in the northern coastline near Tromsø tacitly accepted just six to seven weeks of school attendance. The Swedish school year overlapped with the outdoor grazing season, when children were needed for herding. In some cases this problem was solved by siblings taking turns, one going herding while the others went to school, but absenteeism was common.[111] In the settler parishes of northern Sweden it was solved by cutting the school year: in Vilhelmina, the school curriculum of 1900 comprised only twelve weeks in the winter.[112] There was no compulsory education in late nineteenth-century Finland.[113] Nevertheless, enrolment in 'ambulatory schools', run by peripatetic teachers, and in ordinary primary schools was increasing in the countryside. The short school year fell during the agricultural slack period, thus attending school had small if any opportunity costs.[114]

At the turn of the twentieth century, English farmers continued to hire children of school age, compulsory education and labour regulations notwithstanding. In 1891, the school enrolment rates of boys and girls in three Kentish parishes were about the same (77–78%), but while all girls out of school worked at home, only half of the boys did, which meant that the rest were working away from home. A boy could take his first job on a farm at the age of eleven, working outside of school hours. Absence from school because of work was still common in the English countryside, and feelings of hostility towards school prevailed. Agriculture employed 39,000 boys in 1911, well over half the number three decades previously. Like other young men, boys aged thirteen continued to be hired as farm servants well into the twentieth century. They were taken on for the year or for six months at hiring fairs in the northern counties of England, in the East Riding of Yorkshire, for instance.[115]

The opportunity to go to school may have placed siblings on an unequal footing. The following example is from Sweden. Axel Eriksson (born in 1864), the peasant farmer's son who became a Nobel laureate in literature, as Erik Axel Karlfeldt, was given the opportunity to go to school and even further to university. He had herded cattle when he was very young, but at the age of thirteen, out of school hours, he also had time to play. During the school break in the autumn of 1879, he was excused from working while his younger brother Per, who was to take over the farm, worked in the fields with a roller.[116] The other example is from Val-de-Prés in France. Émilie, like most of French country children, was five when she started school in 1905. She tended sheep during the noon break, gathered pine nuts and droppings for kindling when returning home after school days and outside school hours she helped on the fields and in the kitchen garden. By obtaining a scholarship for her, her teacher persuaded her father to let her continue at school to become a school teacher herself. Émilie's sisters and brothers felt this to be unjust, since they saw it as a way to escape from farm work.[117]

Compulsory education had been introduced in most of Western Europe by the end of the nineteenth century, but the way in which it was implemented implies that no one seriously thought that the children of the rural poor also had the right to receive proper schooling. Had this not been the case, the school year would have been better adapted to the agricultural work year, opportunity costs would have been taken into consideration (as happened later on when children began to be given school meals), and schooling would have been free for the poor. When schooling was arranged so as to minimise conflict with the economic needs of the family, rural families readily seized the opportunity offered for their children to learn to read and write, as proved by the 'temporal schools' in Spain, the Russian village schools and the 'ambulatory schools' in Finland.

Who were the winners, and who were the losers? The Sicilian élite, who regarded education as their privilege, knew the answer, as did the Danish fishermen who kept their children at school, and Émilie's envious brothers and sisters in France. Then there were the peasants in Brittany who used to say of a child who did not work well at school, 'This one is no good for anything but looking after the cows' ('*Celui-ci n'est bon qu'a garder les vaches*').[118] *Schwabenkinder* and their parents lived in conditions in which children's work was valued more than their school education, but the declining numbers of Austrian migrant children suggest a shift from work to school as the nineteenth century drew to its end.

Conclusion

The commercialisation of agriculture resulted in a farm's own children and outside children being treated differently. The landless may have been pressed by increasing demands from the landowner to exploit family labour, while substantial peasant farms turned to non-family labour, even though the farmers' own children may have made a contribution. Less well-off peasant farmers may have demanded even more from their own children in the way of work than they could demand of living-in male and female farm servants, who were more difficult to come by as industrialisation and urbanisation advanced. Peasant farmers' attitudes appear to have been particularly mercenary in their treatment of foundlings, fosterlings and children of the landless. Such outside children were put to any work immediately, were not given time to play, and were seldom given the opportunity to go to school. Outside children were seen first as labour and then as children, and moral inhibitions about exploiting them thus faded into the background.

There is reason to be cautious about generalisations, since specific information about children's work in agriculture is mostly lacking. Concerning nineteenth-century France, for example, Colin Heywood resorts to mapping child labour in the factories in 1839–1845 in order to 'give an approximate indication of areas where agricultural work for children predominated'. He reasons that agricultural child work dominated in areas with few children in factories, whereas in other areas 'agriculture had to compete with factories and domestic workshops for its child labour'.[119] Since he does not distinguish here between children's work on the family farm and work in other households, in principle all country children aged around seven years or over represented 'child labour'. Implicit in his reasoning is that the demand for child labour in agriculture more or less balanced the supply, actual or potential. Whether this is a reasonable assumption is unclear. For example, according to Hugh Cunningham, in an English peasant family, 'many children, unless there was local industry, were frequently idle'.[120] He maintains that 'children were a dubious asset' in agriculture, and, citing a nineteenth-century writer, adds, 'while there were certainly tasks that children could do, they could very rarely be employed full time'.[121]

The commercialisation of agriculture had brought with it a number of very labour-intensive product lines which increased incentives to cut labour costs by employing women and children. Under pressure to increase productivity with the help of machinery and economies of scale, highly labour-intensive production increasingly gave way to labour-saving solutions. Although such changes were felt in the whole of Europe, they occurred during different periods of time, depending on the country and the region. The changes in the amount of agricultural child labour in the English and Norwegian countryside, cited above, suggest a decline in the incidence of paid child labour away from home towards or after the turn of the twentieth century.

The very labour-intensive phase of agricultural commercialisation was more or less underway in most of Europe at the time when the first ethnologists began to compile oral histories. Thus they heard and noted down stories of heavy work loads for peasant children from a tender age up. These stories then formed our received ideas of peasant children's labour 'in olden times'. What may have escaped the ethnologist's eye was that many of the very labour-intensive methods used in commercial agriculture relatively soon passed into history. As labour-saving technology spread, agricultural child labour would continue only on small family farms where the family's own children made a contribution although this increasingly gave way to school. Thus what appeared in ethnologists' notes as traditional may in fact have been transitional. Have these oral histories led us astray?

Notes

1. Overton 1996, p. 8.
2. Hoffman, Jacks, Levin and Lindert 2002.
3. Horn 1980, p. 48; Verdon 2002, pp. 301, 308–315.
4. Allen 1988, pp. 118, 137–138; Allen 1991, p. 483; Clark 1991, pp. 248–255.
5. Humphries 2003, p. 262.
6. Heywood 1988, pp. 23, 29–30; Heywood 1992, pp. 36–42.
7. Bahamonde and Matínez 1994, pp. 273–287, 448–470, 482–484.
8. Borrás Llop 1996, pp. 235–239.
9. Barbagli 1984, pp. 64–83; Barbagli 1991, pp. 112–117; Karvinen 2001, pp. 98–99, 213–217; Kertzer 1977; Pratt 1994, pp. 31–55.
10. Eriksson and Rogers 1978, pp. 153–155; Gadd 2000, pp. 229–230; Gaunt 1983, pp. 98–102; Hanssen 1978; Kirby 1995, pp. 63–66, 138–145; Lundh 1999; Löfgren 1978; Martinius 1977, pp. 128–135; Peltonen forthcoming; Slettan 1978, pp. 114–116; Østerud 1978, pp. 113–150.
11. Kuusanmäki 1954, pp. 46–55.
12. Eriksson and Rogers 1978, p. 27; Peltonen, forthcoming; Tranberg 1996, pp. 17–18.
13. Christensen, D.C. 1998.
14. Gadd 2000, pp. 326, 359–360; Harnesk 1990, pp. 203–206; Heikkinen 1997, pp. 101–139, 152–158; Kirby 1995, pp. 141–145; Lundsjö 1975, pp. 122–123; Niskanen 1995, pp. 12–35.
15. Assion 1987, pp. 106–113; Becker 1986, p. 39; Plaul 1986, pp. 118–121; Weber-Kellermann 1987, pp. 255–258, 360–383.
16. Dixon 1999, pp. 230–239, quotation p. 230. See also Czap 1983, pp. 105–107, 121, 144–150; Plakans 1983, pp. 204–205.
17. Kennard 1908, p. 33.
18. Gatrell 1986, pp. 52, 57–58, 73–74.
19. Guidi 1999, pp. 864–867; Horn 1980, pp. 104–105; Perrier 1998.
20. Cunningham, H. 1992, pp. 30–31.
21. Cunningham, H. 1990; Hopkins 1994, pp. 14–15, 21; Wall 1978.
22. Pinchbeck and Hewitt 1973, pp. 520–544.
23. Capul 1984, pp. 93–95; Fuchs, R. 1984, p. 156; Goubert 1986, pp. 103–104.
24. Fuchs, R. 1984, pp. 235–260.
25. Audoux 1936 [1910], pp. 9–10, 40–45, 51–71, 77–92, 108–115, 125–126. See also Weber 1976, p. 171n.
26. Fitch 1986. See also Magnac and Postel-Vinay 1997.
27. Barbagli 1991, pp. 122–127; Kertzer 1999.
28. Ransel 1988, pp. 47–48, 70–73, 199–201, 209–210. See also Brugger von Nesslau 1991, pp. 53–55.
29. Cited in Ransel 1988, p. 206.
30. Ransel 1988, pp. 202–207, 262–263.
31. Assion 1987, pp. 103–104.
32. Schlumbohm 1994, pp. 200–202, 276–277, 288–289, 306–319; Weber-Kellermann 1979, pp. 176–177.
33. Weber-Kellermann 1987, pp. 262–264.
34. Lext 1968, pp. 71–72; Pulma 1985.

35. Gerger 1992, pp. 74–75, 94.
36. Löfgren 1974, p. 30; Persson and Öberg 1996; Söderberg, Jonsson and Persson 1991, pp. 59–62.
37. Lönnqvist 1992, pp. 216–217; Rahikainen 2002a.
38. Liliequist, M. 1991, pp. 99–122, 170, 202–218. I am grateful to Bodil Nildin-Wall (Språk- och folkminnesinstitutet, Uppsala) who kindly provided me with details of this case.
39. Folktællingen i Kongeriket Norge 1900, Tab. 12; Slettan 1978, p. 122; Søreide 1991, pp. 78–84.
40. Wales 1984, p. 376.
41. Liliequist, M. 1991, pp. 197, 214.
42. See above pp. 53–54.
43. Tweedie 1897, pp. 133, 232.
44. Adoption was made legally possible in Norway and Sweden in 1917, in France and Denmark in 1923, in Finland in 1925, in England in 1926. Statutes on abandoned children were reformed in Spain in 1919 (e.g. prohibition of the use of *expósito* or other words indicating illegimatcy), in Italy in 1923 (*assitenzia agli esposti*). German statutes concerning foster children (*Pflegekinder*) were reformed in 1922, 1924 and 1927.
45. Schulte 1986, p. 161.
46. Weber-Kellermann 1979, pp. 18–19.
47. Schlumbohm 1994, pp. 213–221.
48. Brockmann 1987, p. 147.
49. Dribe 2000, pp. 110–145; Höck 1987; Lundh 1999; Myrdal 1988, pp. 11–17; Slettan 1978, pp. 113–114.
50. See the debate between Sandberg and Steckel 1988 and 1990, and Söderberg 1989.
51. Raussi 1966 [c.1850], pp. 340–347, 377–383.
52. Gormsen 1995.
53. Kjellman 1997, pp. 19–20, 31–32.
54. Heywood 1988, pp. 18–29, quotations pp. 27–28; Weber 1976, pp. 170–171.
55. Smith, H. 1984, pp. 76–77.
56. Guillaumin 1983 [1904], pp. 7–18, 28–36.
57. Borrás Llop 2002, pp. 504–515; Erdozáin-Azpilicuenta and Mikelarena-Peña 1998, Table 3.
58. Karvinen 2001, p. 37; Rossi 1985, pp. 116–29, 181–193.
59. Amstrong 1990, p. 112.
60. Hopkins 1994, pp. 11–22; Horn 1976, pp. 4, 25–27, 79–84.
61. Amstrong 1990, pp. 113–115.
62. Horn 1976, pp. 7, 79–84; Orr 1984, pp. 39–43.
63. Hopkins 1994, p. 17.
64. Excluding the category 'farmers and their relatives', the decline concerning children under fifteen was 22,900 (18%) in 1861–1871 and 33,200 (31%) in 1871–1881, and concerning workers over fifteen 158,800 (13%) and 105,300 (10%), respectively.
65. Hopkins 1994, pp. 17–18, quotations p. 17.
66. Weber-Kellermann 1979, pp. 170–173; Weber-Kellermann 1987, pp. 248–255.
67. Brockmann 1987, p. 150.
68. Schlumbohm 1996, Table 1.

69. Uhlig 1978, pp. 44, 52–56, 63–73, 104–107, 117–131, 138–147. For household structure and demography in the province of Voralberg, see Landsteiner 1999, Table 1.
70. Schulte 1986, pp. 158–167.
71. Raussi 1966 [c.1850], p. 47. See also Moring 1999, pp. 177–178.
72. Harnesk 1990, pp. 261–262.
73. Dribe 2000, passim; Lundh 1999. Corvée labour or villeinage (*hoveri*) survived beyond the mid-nineteenth century in Halland and Skåne (Scania), both of which were ceded by Denmark to Sweden in 1658. (Johansson, P. 2001, p. 73).
74. Christensen, J. 1988, p. 392.
75. Brembeck 1986, p. 27; Gerger 1992, p. 112; Korkiakangas 1996, pp. 129, 143, 181–183; Liliequist, M. 1991, pp. 144–146; Martinson 1992, pp. 81–83; Slettan 1984, pp. 66–68; Szabó 1971.
76. Korkiakangas 1996, pp. 134, 155–159; Liliequist, M. 1991, pp. 87, 109–111, 170–173; Slettan 1978, p. 91.
77. Resultaterne af Folketællingen i Norge 1876, Tab. 25.
78. Cited in Slettan 1984, p. 69.
79. Gadd 2000, p. 174; Slettan 1978, pp. 29–31, 49; Slettan 1982, p. 146–150.
80. Korkiakangas 1996, pp. 174–178; Liliequist, M. 1991, pp. 171–177, 198–210; Harnesk 1990, pp. 26, 31; Szabó 1971.
81. Kennard 1908, pp. 19–45, 98–101, 129–130, quotation p. 33; Rustemeyer 1996, pp. 66, 100; Semyonova Tian-Shanskaia 1993 [1914], pp. 23–49, 108–142. See also Brugger von Nesslau 1991, pp. 55–64.
82. Glickman 1984, pp. 40–48.
83. Eklof 1986, pp. 319, 353–380, quotation p. 316.
84. Chayanov 1966, p. 180.
85. *Statare* were farm labourers who received their wages principally in kind (residence and food). *Statare* families were the embodiment of rural poverty as long as the system lasted, that is until 1945.
86. Eriksson and Rogers 1978, pp. 151–152; Gaunt 1983, p. 115; Löfgren 1974; Winberg 1978, p. 172.
87. Korkiakangas 1996, pp. 166–173.
88. Barbagli 1984, pp. 66–70.
89. Horn 1976, p. 69.
90. Borrás Llop 1996, pp. 234–235.
91. Guéhenno 1973, pp. 24–27, 44–48.
92. Carles 1991, pp. 29–30, 38, 60, 70.
93. Slettan 1982, pp. 146–147.
94. Cited in Ottenjann 1995, p. 21.
95. Weber-Kellermann 1987, pp. 109–110.
96. Horn 1980, p. 140.
97. Ehlers 1991, p. 71.
98. Pinchbeck and Hewitt 1973, pp. 512–513.
99. Fuchs, R. 1984, pp. 252–253.
100. Fitch 1986, pp. 132, 143–145.
101. Uhlig 1978, pp. 100–103.
102. Weber-Kellermann 1979, pp. 178–180; Weber-Kellermann 1987, pp. 103–110.

103. Hopkins 1994, pp. 130–141; Horn 1978, pp. 23–32, 116–139; Reay 1996, pp. 223–33.
104. Robson 1984, pp. 77–79.
105. Heywood 1988, pp. 20, 40, 62–73.
106. Weber 1976, pp. 7, 303–338, quotation p. 303.
107. Genovesi 1998, pp. 76–99; Guidi 1999, p. 869; Guereña 1996; Palacio Atard 1988, pp. 314–328; Reeder 1998, p. 104–105.
108. Sarasúa 1998, pp. 188–190; Sarasúa García 2002, pp. 556–572. For the number of boys and girls, see Borrás Llop 2002, Cuadro II.
109. Eklof 1986, pp. 24–37, 79–87, 275–289, 315–341, 361–371, quotation p. 84; Semyonova Tian-Shanskaia 1993 [1914], pp. 44–49.
110. Christensen, J. 1988, pp. 393–395.
111. Edvardsen 1992, p. 85; Pettersson 1996; Sjöberg 1996, pp. 58–88; Slettan 1984, p. 65.
112. Liliequist, M. 1991, p. 111.
113. Compulsory education was introduced in Norway in 1739, in Denmark in 1814 and in Sweden in 1842, but not until 1921 in Finland.
114. Myllyntaus 1990.
115. Caunce 1975; Hopkins 1994, p. 225; Horn 1976, pp. 39–52, 85–86; Horn 1989, pp. 29–30; Reay 1996, pp. 226–228.
116. Myrdal 2002, pp. 239–244.
117. Carles 1991, pp. 37, 42–45, 59–60, 78.
118. Hélias 1975, p. 338.
119. Heywood 1988, pp. 20–21.
120. Cunningham, H. 1995, p. 83.
121. Cunningham, H. 1990, quotation p. 146.

CHAPTER 4

A Century of Factory Children

Children and labour productivity

In 1835, Andrew Ure anticipated 'the system of decomposing a process into its constituents', which would make workers interchangeable, while skilled male labourers would be replaced 'by mere overlookers of machines'.[1] Ure knew the early mechanised textile industry, in which machines were designed and constructed based on the fact that there were assisting children 'with watchful eyes and nimble fingers', as he put it. He concluded that 'the constant aim and tendency of every improvement in machinery [is] ... to diminish the costs by substituting the industry of women and children for that of men'. He looked forward to the day when a process would be 'so self-regulating, that a child may superintend it'.[2] That day never came. The first assembly line was designed and constructed for adult men only, and needed no children around. The more automated the production process became, the less child labour it needed.

Why children disappeared from factories has been a subject of endless debate for more than a century, and there is no sign of it settling down. In this chapter the decline of industrial child labour is discussed from the perspective of the demand for child workers. It is suggested that labour productivity – today a topical issue in the economy as a whole, but less so in terms of the history of child labour – deserves reconsidering as an explanation for employers' declining interest in using children. Furthermore, it is suggested that Myron Weiner's conclusion that 'child labor laws proved to be unenforceable unless all children were required to attend school'[3] needs to be qualified.

To begin with, the demand for children stemmed from the recruitment and discipline problems faced by early industrial entrepreneurs. Wherever it was introduced, the factory system was first met with repulsion and reluctance by those who had to submit to it. Ivan Turgenev regarded the coming of textile and other factories to Russia, where owners 'piled in miserable shacks hundreds of their slaves, preferably girls and boys', as a calamity comparable to the prohibition on the movement of serfs. He had overheard Russian peasants talking about factories with horror: 'They said, "There is a factory in that village" as if they had said, "The plague has broken out there".'[4]

According to Sidney Pollard, in Britain 'pauper children represented the only type of labour which in many areas could be driven into [mills]'. Pauper apprentices were taken on 'because otherwise the mills would have been without sufficient labour, or at least without sufficient child labour in relation to the number of adults'. In Scotland 'even the children found the discipline irksome', thus they were much beaten to make them submit to the factory system. Men and women not used to the long confinement and monotonous regularity of factory work found it unbearable. If there was freedom of choice, everywhere people preferred the cottage industries, outworking or undisciplined workshops.[5] Subsequent generations of factory workers were different. Like their predecessors, they may have disliked the hard discipline, yet they stayed in the factory, 'because at the end of the week their wage [was] ... greater than they [could] achieve without discipline', as Gregory Clark puts it,[6] or because there were no longer any alternatives. Children of factory workers learned to take waged industrial work for granted.

Internal subcontracting of the labour force and managerial paternalism were strategies that were adopted to overcome monitoring and discipline difficulties. In the eighteenth century, children were known to have been subcontracted in France in calico printing, in 'sweated' trades in London and in British metal workshops, blast furnaces and in the Wedgwood pottery at Etruria, where parents hired their own children. This practice was adopted by cotton mills in Britain. Spinners recruited, supervised and paid the two or three piecers they needed. In Lancashire, according to Michael Huberman, 'spinners effectively became the managers of production in the factory'.[7] In contrast, the subcontracting of children was rare in Scandinavia, paternalistic management strategies notwithstanding, although according to Edvard Bull, it was common among boys in Norway: 'They helped their parents or other adult piece workers and got their pay from them – if they were paid.'[8] Factories and workshops still employed parents together with their children in early twentieth-century Spain.[9] Cotton factories in northern Italy resorted to paternalism as well as to coercion and military-style discipline to make country people adapt to the factory system. Some mills established dormitories to attract 'good workers' or orphanages for 'skilful and steady spinners'. Nonetheless, as late as in 1911, according to the organisation of cotton industrialists, it was because of people's reluctance to go into factories that domestic manual spinning persisted.[10]

Cheap-labour economy was another factor that made manufacturers rely heavily on a labour force with weak or no bargaining power, such as women and children and tied labour. 'Broadly speaking,' Eric Hobsbawm writes, 'employers assumed that the lowest wage bill for the longest hours meant the lowest labour costs per unit of time'. According to Mary Rose, in Britain 'before power was applied to the mule in the 1790s, the only men to be found in cotton factories were overseers and mechanics'.[11] As far as the entrepreneur was concerned, children and unfree labour were docile and cheap, but the larger British manufacturers who compared pauper apprentices with paid labour found them expensive. One of them explained that pauper apprentices were 'more expensive than paid labour ... and troublesome, inconvenient ... and objectionable in almost every point of view', while another pointed to 'the expense of providing buildings for their reception ... and of being at more expence with their maintenance than their labour would be worth'. The use of parish apprentices began to die out in British manufacturing after 1815.[12]

Any effort to estimate the profitability of child labour or the productivity of children compared with that of adults was hampered by the existing accounting methods. In his seminal study on management and accounting during the first industrial revolution in England, Sidney Pollard portrays the difficulties entrepreneurs and their clerks had in calculating costs and profits, to say nothing of more complicated concepts. Bookkeepers' time was consumed by the extremely detailed and elaborate wage calculations, but the information gained was not used to evaluate labour productivity. Even the large British cotton mills, whose very size forced them to become pioneers in bookkeeping, required their clerks to note a myriad of small entries, a consequence of the system of combining family wages with piecework. According to Pollard, shortcomings in accounting were tolerated because of the easy profit margins and high profits, thanks to the monopolistic position enjoyed by those who were among the early users of new machinery and techniques.[13]

Gautam Sen suggested that in the process of industrialisation six industries form the strategic set: iron and steel, chemicals, textiles, machinery, paper and paper products, and transport equipment.[14] Of these, textiles was the only truly massive user of child labour. Generally speaking, the first industrial revolution was characterised by more labour-intensive technologies than the technologically more sophisticated production processes of the second industrial revolution.[15] The use of child labour echoed this development by and large, as the case of textiles, the champion of the first industrial revolution, aptly illustrates.

Textile producers had been cutting labour costs by resorting to women, children, apprentices and unskilled workers since medieval times, whereas increasing labour productivity proved difficult.[16] According to Franklin Mendels, 'from the invention of the spinning wheel in the twelfth century to the adoption of the flying shuttle – that is not before the 1760's in England – labor productivity did not change much in textile production'. Innovations such as the stocking frame, the ribbon frame and the mechanical silk mill 'were not important enough to outweigh basic technical stagnation in this largest of all European industries'.[17]

It is a well-known historical fact that the mechanisation of spinning and weaving in British textiles after the late eighteenth century raised labour productivity to previously unknown levels, and this was repeated with successive generations of machinery.[18] Clark Nardinelli suggests that there was an increase in the productivity of child labour in textile production as children moved from home manufacture of textiles to the factory, where 'a child could aid the combined resources of man and machine power, rather than human power alone'.[19] This may be a reasonable assumption, but is there any proof, other than an analogy with the increase in adult labour productivity? By the late nineteenth century, the textile industry was no longer technologically dynamic (apart from the sectors included in the chemical industry), as Robert Locke argues. The spinning and weaving of cotton and the dyeing industry now fell into the category of older industries 'less susceptible to the multiplier effect', such as increases in productivity. Nonetheless, Youssef Cassis points out that British textiles, cotton included, continued to yield high profits.[20] Be that as it may, the British textile industry had by then offered a new benchmark for labour productivity.

Cotton was considered part of 'the modern sector' in mid-nineteenth-century France. Nevertheless, as Pierre Sicsic argues, cotton weaving was the sector with the lowest labour productivity, and seasonal unemployment drew it further down in textile firms that used the domestic system. Paper mills (of the traditional kind using textile fibres) also had a lower-than-average labour productivity, while the two most capital-intensive industries, breweries and flour milling, showed the highest levels. However, at the beginning of the twentieth century, French labour productivity was superior to that in British in construction and leather goods.[21]

In Spain, 'it was cotton industry that ... opened the way to modernisation and mass production', as Gabriel Tortella observes. This started in Catalonia, which specialised in consumer goods such as cotton. However, the expansion of Catalan cotton manufacturing was followed by a decline in textile production elsewhere. Moreover, the Catalan textile industry suffered from low productivity and high production costs. The increasing mechanisation of production resulted in the feminisation of the labour force. The heyday of industrial child labour in Spain was over by 1875, having peaked during the decade of 1856–1865.[22] According to José Borrás Llop, Spanish employers resorted to child labour chiefly in order to cut labour costs, and only secondly to have manpower that was willing to submit to the factory system. This contributed to keeping male wages down, thus making children's incomes necessary for worker families.[23]

Cotton was 'another key staple in Italy's first industrial revolution' (A. Colli and M. Rose), together with silk. The supply of the female labour force was helped by the fact that, in sharecropping families, women and girls were the only ones whom the landlords permitted to work off the farm. As the status value of commercial consumer goods increased, these families had strong incentives to send their daughters to work for wages in industry, since it was difficult to raise any money otherwise. Much of the labour force in the Lombardian cotton industry in northern Italy was inexperienced in factory work, and more workers per machine were needed than in other countries. This indicated low labour productivity, which was, however, blurred by the low labour costs. At the close of the nineteenth century, despite the expansion in the mechanised weaving industry, hand-loom weaving survived, and even cotton printing remained as largely manual work. There is some indirect evidence of significant growth in labour productivity in cotton in the decades preceding the First World War, while the growth rate in the Italian industry as a whole remained relatively modest.[24]

Until the 1880s, the majority of the German labour force was occupied in technologically less advanced sectors, in which child labour was also common. One example was textiles, in which 'labor that although cheap, was also unproductive' (J. Brown). Well over half of all industrial establishments consisted of tiny firms of one to ten persons, typically producing labour-intensive consumer goods. Truly large companies were still rare in textiles at the turn of the twentieth century, and a fifth of the firms in metals and machinery, which employed plenty of children, were of the handicraft type. The dominance of handicraft-type firms may explain something of the lower labour productivity compared with that of Britain.[25]

As far as Sweden was concerned, it was not so much the technology, but rather the commercial competence of the cloth and cotton firms, and the sector of the engineering industry producing consumer goods, that characterised the first phase of industrialisation. The Swedish historians who argue along these lines suggest that the same may have been the case in the whole of Scandinavia, which was characterised by scattered, small local markets.[26]

Denmark, Finland and Norway had very little manufacturing production until the 1840s. Danish broadcloth factories tried to solve recruitment problems by hiring German workers and by encouraging parents to take their children with them to work in the mills. Moreover, poor-relief authorities in Copenhagen provided the state-owned broadcloth factory in Usserød with pauper children who were farmed out to worker families. Such foster children comprised more than two-fifths of all child workers in 1812. The same year the mill decided to remove children from foster families to the factory dormitory, housing 80 children.[27] The promoters of the early Norwegian textile mills had acquired their technical knowledge in England, and often hired British foremen, while the management emulated a British model of company paternalism. The majority of permanent workers were women, who did the (throstle) spinning and weaving, while men worked in maintenance and repairs, and as artisans and foremen. Difficulties in recruiting workers pushed some Norwegian textile mills into importing Swedish women workers. Norwegian factory statistics for 1875 list less than two per cent of children aged between ten and fourteen as employed in industry.[28] The evolution of the first Finnish textile mills largely followed a similar pattern, except that the Finnish mills were quite export-oriented thanks to their customs-free access to the Russian market. As in Norway, the proportion of factory children among all children aged ten to fourteen years remained small.[29]

With its prolonged use of unfree labour, Russia was apparently different. The system of bonded labour that replaced the purchase of serfs in factories was outlawed in 1825, but bonded labourers, including young children, continued to be used. Nonetheless, manufacturers increasingly used freely hired workers. Cotton manufacture began to increase at the time when manufacturers were forbidden to buy serfs and therefore relied heavily on freely hired labour; by 1825 almost all cotton workers were freely hired. According to Reginald Zelnik, 'the more that industrialists were compelled to include wages as an important factor among their costs, the more they were tempted to turn to the cheapest available source of labor – women, and especially children'. Labour productivity remained low. In the mid-nineteenth century, the ratio of workers to spindles in the Krenholm cotton factory, which was the largest and most modern, was six per 1,000: it was 10 to 17 per thousand in other Russian cotton mills, and three per 1,000 in the largest English factories. The low wages may not have compensated the low levels of skill. For example, Nobel's factory in St Petersburg managed to produce only a small amount of poor quality rifles, and thus failed to fill government's order, evidently because of the extensive use of child labour.[30]

If manufacturing, mining and construction are ranked according to the number of children they employed (which is different from ranking them according to the proportion of children), it turns out that about a dozen of them – depending on how they are grouped – covered the 'top six' users of child labour in the countries discussed here (for the ten countries, see Table 4.1, for England Table 4.3). The textile industry tops the list in seven out of ten countries, and others include clothing, hosiery and footwear, mining, metals and machinery, food and tobacco, furniture and wood working, match manufacture and the sawmill industry, brick and glassmaking, construction, and paper and printing. The first three industries with the largest numbers of children accounted for between two-fifths and two-thirds of them, while the first six industries covered between two-thirds and nine-tenths of all children occupied in industrial work in each country (Table 4.2). For example, in Italy in 1881, eight out of ten children were occupied in the three, and nine out of ten in the six industrial sectors using the largest numbers of children. In time the concentration tended to become somewhat less marked. The fact that the same industries featured as major employers of children from one country to another suggests that what counted was the demand for child labour in a handful of sectors. It is their use of child labour we should look at.

The textile industry

Children's work in the mechanised textile industries, particularly cotton, has probably attracted more attention than any other form of child labour. Per Bolin-Hort's knowledgeable work on the British cotton industry is a relatively recent example.[31] This much-discussed issue is considered below country by country. What is revealed is not a constant decline of the use of child labour, but a more varied development, with ups and downs until the production processes in textiles became automated enough to make the remaining workers into 'mere overlookers of machines', as Ure predicted.

In the short term, the demand for child labour was probably connected with market fluctuations, but in the long run it followed the development of production processes. A high demand for children was connected with production technology in two ways: either in the 'traditional' labour-intensive sense in that much of the production or stages of the production process were still performed manually using simple equipment, or in the capital-intensive sense in which children were needed as assistants for operatives tending more advanced power-driven machinery. Children were used in cotton mills for carding and as piecers who mended yarn breakages, 'creel fillers' who placed the 'roving' from which the yarn was spun, and as scavengers or cleaners who removed the waste cotton and cleaned the machines.

In Britain the initial enthusiasm for the extensive use of children did not last long, and by 1820 a general decline in child labour levels had taken place. However, this trend was reversed with the introduction of larger mule machines. Fine-spinning firms using enlarged mules had to employ more children as piecers to mend the additional yarn breakages. Thus there was a substantial rise in the demand for child labour in mule spinning. Spinners in Manchester mills with the largest mules had between three and five piecers each. In 1833, most of the boys in the Lancashire mills were occupied in mule spinning, while the girls did weaving, mule spinning and carding. Eight out of ten children in mule spinning were employed by the operative, while subcontracted children were clearly less common in weaving, and rare in carding. With the coming of self-acting mules, employers first tried to get rid of male mule-spinners altogether, staffing the machines with young piecers, but this proved unprofitable. Eventually they managed to replace some of the skilled male mule-minders with women, but generally at the cost of productivity.[32] According to S.J. Chapman, in the Lancashire cotton industry the proportion of children aged under thirteen fell from 13 per cent in 1834 to five to six per cent around 1850, then rose again and was 14 per cent in 1874 after which it fell and was six per cent in 1895.[33]

It has been suggested that the French excelled at the finishing end of textile manufacturing.[34] This matches Louis Villermé's description of child labour in French cotton weaving in 1840: girls aged between twelve and eighteen inspected each piece of fabric, mended the broken threads and smoothed the knots that spoiled *la bonne apparence*. Nevertheless, the majority of children in the French cotton industry worked on similar tasks as those in the British cotton mills, usually as piecers. Girls also assisted the women who prepared the cotton for spinning, while women, children and old people prepared the yarn for the male handloom weavers. Women and children who prepared the yarn were paid 50 to 70 centimes a day. The subcontracting of children was common. According to Villermé, in Mulhouse, for example, spinners who earned two to three francs a day paid the children they hired 35 to 50 centimes or at most one franc. Cotton printers who were on piece rates and earned 1.25 to 3.30 francs a day, paid the children they had subcontracted as *tireurs* perhaps 25 to 33 centimes. In Lille, children aged eight to thirteen were paid 50 to 65 centimes a day in ateliers, half what women were paid in factories. In general, Villermé concluded, children's day wage increased by one *sou* (five centimes) for each additional year of age.[35]

In their quest for low-paid female and child labour, Catalan textile-factory owners found their way into the countryside. Poor families, cultivating their small plots, had difficulties making ends meet, so people thought that going to the mill was better than working the land.[36] In the mid-nineteenth century, about half the inhabitants of the town of Sabadell were employed in the textile industry. Children worked predominantly in cotton, and girls outnumbered boys. According to Enriqueta Camps i Cura, with a shift from home-based production to the factory system, the age at which children started to work could have risen from six or seven years to ten. Although the activity rates of women and children were high (70% for women, 21% for boys and 28% for girls in 1850), she argues that 'both wives and children were a net drain on the household's resources during the large part of the family cycle ... the deficit occasioned by children occurred even when assumed that all children over the age of 10 are employed in factories'. By 1919, children aged under ten had almost disappeared from the labour force, and the activity rate of those aged between ten and fourteen had dropped.[37] Cotton was the largest industrial employer of children in Barcelona, too. The proportion of child workers declined only slightly (from 18% to 16%) during the period 1856–1905, while the proportions of girls of the female and boys of the male labour force increased. Unlike in Sabadell, boys outnumbered girls and were also relatively more dominant among the male labour force.[38]

Foreign proprietors of cotton factories and the supervisors they brought with them imported industrial discipline into Finland. In the late nineteenth century, people in the Forssa cotton mill thought that a heavy-handed English foreman who was notorious for beating child workers with a leather belt out of sight in his office had brought such a behaviour from his home country. Although there was much poverty in the countryside, the cotton mills faced recruitment difficulties at first. For example, the owner-manager of the Forssa mill first failed to get enough child workers because of the hostility of the local rural people. Children did not work with their parents in the Finnish textile mills. There are no records of children being subcontracted by their parents or other operators, but children were hired and paid directly by the employer or a supervisor. In general, it was not difficult for a child to get a job in a mill. For example, many boys and girls simply walked to the main gate of the Finlayson cotton mill and asked the gate-keeper to let them in to see the director or a supervisor. Children seeking jobs were usually about twelve years old, while in the Forssa mill even ten-year-olds may have been given a chance.[39]

The second half of the nineteenth century was a time of great expansion in the Russian textile industry. The prime manifestation of this was the founding of the Krenholm cotton spinning and weaving factory in 1857 in Narva, about 150 kilometres southwest of St Petersburg. Once the Krenholm mill was fully ready, it had over 64,000 spindles and close to 1,000 looms.

Table 4.1. The largest employers of children in mining, manufacturing and construction, by industry, country and year.

	First largest*	Second largest	Third largest	Fourth largest	Fifth largest	Sixth largest
Textiles	England 1851–1881 Finland 1887, 1907 France 1861 Italy 1871, 1881, 1927 Russia 1910, 1914 Spain/B. 1905 Sweden 1875	Denmark 1872, 1897 Germany 1895 Italy 1901 Schl.-Holstein 1865 Sweden 1891	Norway 1870			
Clothing hosiery footwear	Germany 1895 Italy 1901	England 1851, 1861, 1881 Italy 1881, 1927	England 1871 Spain/B. 1905	Finland 1887		Schl.-Holstein 1865
Food drink				Germany 1895	France 1861 Italy 1881 Spain/B. 1905	Italy 1901, 1927
Tobacco	Denmark 1872, 1897 Schl.-Holstein 1865	Norway 1870			Sweden 1875	
Brick making earthenware pottery		France 1861	Denmark 1872 Schl.-Holstein 1865	Finland 1907 Russia 1910	Finland 1887 Norway 1870 Russia 1914 Sweden 1891	Denmark 1897
Glassmaking		Russia 1910, 1914	Denmark 1872		Denmark 1897	Sweden 1875
Matches		Sweden 1875		Denmark 1872 Norway 1870 Russia 1914 Schl.-Holstein 1865		Finland 1887 Russia 1910 Sweden 1891
Wood furniture carriages			Italy 1901	Italy 1927		England 1851, 1861 Germany 1895 Italy 1881
Sawmills	Norway 1870 Sweden 1891	Finland 1887, 1907		Sweden 1875		
Papermaking wallpaper etc. printing trade		Italy 1871 Spain/B. 1905	Denmark 1897 Russia 1910, 1914		Schl.-Holstein 1865	England 1871, 1881 France 1861
Mining			England 1851, 1861, 1881	France 1861 Sweden 1891		
Metals machinery			Finland 1887, 1907 France 1861 Germany 1895 Italy 1927 Sweden 1875, 1891	England 1851–1881 Denmark 1897 Italy 1881	Italy 1901 Russia 1910	Norway 1870 Russia 1914 Spain/B. 1905
Building construction			Italy 1881	Italy 1901 Spain/B. 1905	England 1851–1881 Germany 1895 Italy 1927	

* First largest (Second, etc.) = In the given year in the country concerned the industry had the largest (second largest, etc.) number of children.

Notes and sources: See Table 4.2

Table 4.2. The first three/six sectors* employing the largest number of children as a proportion (%) of all children in manufacturing, mining and construction.

Country	Year	The first three sectors, %	The first six sectors, %
England	1851	76	91
	1861	71	87
	1871	70	87
	1881	71	87
Denmark	1872	65	80
	1897	69	81
Finland	1887	50	66
	1907	39	63
France**	1861	72	88
Germany	1895	56	89
Italy	1881	79	91
	1901	66	89
	1927	62	83
Norway	1870	63	88
Russia	1910	78	93
	1914	76	92
Schleswig-Holstein	1865	73	91
Spain/Barcelona	1905	63	82
Sweden	1875	52	80
	1891	48	68

* The sectors are grouped as in Table 4.1.
** France 1861–1865, incl. Paris (1860) and *établissements de l'État*, excl. Lyon.

Sources: (age limit for child in brackets): *England and Wales* (under 15): Occupation Censuses 1851–1881 (in Booth 1886, Appendix A); *Denmark* (under 14): Christensen, J.P. 2002, Appendix Tab. II.5; *Finland* (under 15): Industristatistik 1887, 1907; *France* (under 15): Statistique de la France, 1861–1865; *Germany* (under 14): Ergebnissen der Berufs- und Gewerbestatistik 1895 (in Agahd 1902, pp. 27–8); *Italy* (under 15): Censimento della popolazione 1881, 1901; Censimento industriale 1927; Ellena 1879, p. 389; *Norway* (under 15): Statistiske Opgaver ... af Norges industrielle Forholde 1870, Tab. 3; *Russia* (under 15): Rapports annuels des inspecteurs de fabriques, 1910 and 1914; *Schleswig-Holstein* (under 14): Hansen 1987, p. 46; *Spain/Barcelona* (under 15), Anuario Estadístico de la Ciudad de Barcelona, 1905 (in Bórras Llop 1999); *Sweden* (under 14): Betänkande 1877, Tab. 3; Betänkande 1892, Tab. 2.

Its labour force, typical of Russian industry, consisted of semirural workers, barely-skilled piecers, highly qualified weavers and spinners, and children from the St Petersburg foundling home, delivered at about the age of twelve. Nevertheless, by the turn of the twentieth century, children had become rare in the cotton mills.[40] The stages of textile production that relied heavily on children were spooling and threading. In 1898–1900, for example, in two districts of Moscow province, boys and girls under thirteen comprised 30 per cent and 24–30 per cent of the male and female labour force respectively in spooling, and 14–33 per cent and 6–18 per cent in threading. At that time,

Table 4.3. The economically active population, including children under 15, in manufacturing, mining and construction in England and Wales, 1851, 1861, 1871 and 1881 (in thousands).

		1851	%	1861	%	1871	%	1881	%
Textiles	total	934.5	100	966.2	100	970.0	100	962.6	100
and dyeing	children	149.3	16.0	149.0	15.4	152.3	15.7	116.5	12.1
	boys	68.0		65.6		63.1		50.5	
	girls	81.3		83.4		89.2		66.0	
Dress	total	868.7	100	929.5	100	916.0	100	954.0	100
(clothing)	children	50.3	5.8	44.6	4.8	36.7	4.0	29.1	3.1
	boys	20.1		18.2		13.3		8.8	
	girls	30.2		26.4		23.4		20.3	
Metals, machinery	total	393.2	100	533.4	100	628.4	100	701.0	100
and tools	children	27.2	6.9	39.4	7.4	31.8	5.1	20.4	2.9
	boys	22.9		33.2		28.0		18.2	
	girls	4.3		6.2		3.8		2.2	
Miners	total	263.0	100	334.3	100	376.9	100	444.3	100
(mining)	children	33.8	12.9	40.5	12.1	36.8	9.8	26.2	5.9
	boys	32.4		39.9		35.9		25.7	
	girls	1.4		0.5		0.9		0.5	
Building	total	460.7	100	538.7	100	664.1	100	796.5	100
(construction)	children	10.7		13.5		13.6		11.3	
	boys	10.7		13.5		13.6		11.3	
	girls	0		0		0		0	
Earthenware,	total	46.5	100	55.9	100	67.4	100	71.9	100
glass etc.	children	8.4	18.1	8.6	15.4	7.5	11.1	5.6	7.8
	boys	6.0		6.1		5.0		3.7	
	girls	2.4		2.5		2.5		1.9	
Wood, furniture	total	189.1	100	216.3	100	233.7	100	240.0	100
and carriages	children	8.1	4.3	7.2	3.3	7.0	3.0	5.0	2.1
	boys	7.5		6.4		5.7		4.3	
	girls	0.6		0.8		1.3		0.7	
Printing and	total	34.5	100	47.5	100	66.2	100	88.1	100
bookbinding	children	1.9	5.6	3.9	8.2	5.0	7.6	6.1	6.9
	boys	1.5		3.2		4.2		5.0	
	girls	0.4		0.7		0.8		1.1	
Paper etc.	total	21.9	100	25.3	100	33.7	100	47.8	100
	children	2.2	10.0	3.2	12.6	3.1	9.2	3.1	6.5
	boys	1.4		1.9		1.8		1.4	
	girls	0.8		1.3		1.3		1.7	
Food, drink,	total	133.3	100	149.0	100	164.2	100	181.2	100
tobacco	children	3.8	2.9	5.3	3.6	5.3	3.2	5.6	3.1
	boys	3.5		4.8		4.5		4.3	
	girls	0.3		0.5		0.8		1.3	
TOTAL*	total	3,550.7	100	4,080.7	100	4,497.2	100	4,957.1	100
CHILDREN TOTAL*	children	306.7	8.6	332.0	8.1	320.6	7.1	243.4	4.9
	boys	183.6		206.9		191.5		145.6	
	girls	123.1		125.1		129.1		97.8	

* Including sectors not listed above or unspecified manufacturing.

Source: Occupation Censuses 1851–1881, published in Booth 1886, Appendix A.

mechanisation of spooling was on its way and so the demand for child labour in that process was probably in decline.[41] Children comprised a mere one per cent of the labour force in cotton in 1911, but still 3.6 per cent in the more labour-intensive linen and hemp industry, while silk at 2.7 per cent and woollen at 1.2 per cent were between these two extremes. There was not much difference in the numbers or proportions of boys and girls, except in silk where girls and women dominated.[42]

The mechanising woollen industry also used children. According to Louis Villermé, those working in the woollen industry in France were more healthy than those working in cotton, despite the fact that they suffered from equally long working days. Generally in textiles, the work day lasted between twelve and fifteen hours, depending on the area, but in winter it may have ended when darkness fell. Children in wool manufacturing were on average two to three years older than those in the cotton industry, had slightly better wages, and were better nourished because their parents were less poor.[43]

Broadcloth manufactories suffered from low profitability in early nineteenth-century Stockholm, then a stagnating city. The number of skilled workers in broadcloth production fell drastically during 1829–1843, thus an increasing proportion of the labour force consisted of unskilled workers and children, usually workers' children aged under ten. A few wool manufacturers even resorted to using prisoners. The Swedish mechanised wool industry would prosper in the industrial town of Norrköping, which grew into a leading industrial city with large numbers of factory children. Often whole families were employed in the cloth factories, the men working up the wool, weaving, and shearing, while the women and children were chiefly engaged in yarn production. In the partly mechanised Finnish cloth industry, boys working in spinning were paid about a tenth and in spooling about two-thirds more than female spinners, and the total wage bill comprised well over a quarter of the total production costs in 1850. Family employment was apparently not prevalent in Finland, nor did the cloth industry use many children.[44]

The woollen industry used more child labour than the cotton industry in late nineteenth-century Denmark. When the first self-acting mule was installed in 1866 in Brede Klædefabrik, the leading broadcloth mill, a contemporary described it as a peculiar sight 'to see a machine spinning thread c.720 ells a minute without any other help but a boy of six to seven years of age'. In one Danish woollen mill, the division of labour between girls and boys in 1872 was such that boys worked in carding and spooling and fed the carding machine, while girls worked in spooling, reeling, bobbing and shearing; children had already disappeared from the spinning department.[45] In Schleswig-Holstein, children prepared the raw wool, and sorted and transported wool. Even though carding and spinning were taken over by machines, the production process still involved many manual work phases, which often fell upon children. Those working as piecers in mechanised wool spinning suffered from sore fingers due to the constant handling of woollen yarn, and by nine in the morning, after three to four hours of work, their fingers may already have been bloodstained. As elsewhere, children largely disappeared from German mills as the repairs of yarn breakages became automated.[46]

Italian silk factories were pioneers in terms of teaching women and children industrial work habits. As in some French silk mills, the girls were made to sing hymns and recite prayers and the *rosario* to keep them from chatting, but girls and women took this as a pastime, and it was better than being required to keep quiet for the whole day. In Italy, as in France, children's work consisted of various tasks connected with silk-worm breeding, the treatment of cocoons and reeling, as well as silk spinning. Silk-worm breeding involved periods of very intensive work, when all hands in the village, 'strong and weak', were busy and occupied, as Louis Reybaud described French raw-silk production in 1856. The silk industry flourished in the less fertile hill zones in northern Italy, Lombardy and Piedmont, where it had long benefited from the part-time nature of agricultural work.[47] The labour-intensive phases in the production of crude silk, such as creating silk knobs, *torcitura* ('silk twisting'), were disconnected from agriculture. The use of children in this process was concentrated in Lombardy in the 1870s, where it occupied more children than women, and 90 per cent of all children engaged in *torcitura* in Italy.[48]

The number of child workers in the Italian silk industry was six times the number working in cotton in the 1870s, and almost double three decades later. The number of women in the silk industry in 1901 was two and a half times that of girls aged between nine and fourteen, and in the Italian textile industry as a whole the number of women was five times the number of girls. Furthermore, there were six times more female than male workers in textiles, while the number of men aged fifteen or over was more than eight times the number of boys. Interestingly enough, the clothing industry, despite its feminine image, employed almost as many boys as girls, while men were more numerous than women. It was chiefly the extensive use of girls in textiles which accounted for the excess proportion of girls (56%) in manufacturing.[49]

At the turn of the twentieth century, a Catalan silk mill may still have employed children as young as eight years old, but they were usually ten when they began to do paid work in a textile mill. Power-loom weavers used to hire two assistants each, one aged ten to fourteen, the other aged fourteen to sixteen. Young women subcontracted their own or relatives' children. Children were also employed together with their fathers or mothers. Parents on piecework often took their children to do auxiliary tasks, without asking the manager. The demand for women grew in Catalan silk mills between 1900 and 1930, and married women now worked longer, while the opposite was true for children. According to Enriqueta Camps-Cura, with the beginning of the second industrial revolution in Spain, child labour in Catalan textiles was replaced by that of married women.[50]

The increasingly streamlined production processes and high-speed automated spinning and weaving that developed in the 1920s and 1930s meant that extra labour, however cheap, was no longer needed or tolerated in textile mills. Nonetheless, the use of child labour in the textile sector continued. It was extensive in and around urban areas in the clothing industry, for example (more on this in Chapter 5). Moreover, the International Labour Review reported for the first time in 1930 and 1933 on the use of child labour in textiles in two British colonies, Egypt and India. Since then such reports have featured on the international agenda.[51]

Other industries

It is difficult to see a common denominator in the other industries that ranked high as users of child labour (Tables 4.1 and 4.3). Some of them, such as mining, metal and, in some countries, paper, which later became capital-intensive were still heavy users of manual labour in the late nineteenth century and at the turn of the twentieth. Others, such as machinery, furniture, earthenware, glassmaking and construction, long preserved their craft character. Tobacco and match production had always relied on the intensive use of cheap labour, and new technology may have been reluctantly introduced.[52] The demand for the flexible labour of women, children, juveniles and unskilled men was also typical of seasonal production.

The history of young boys and girls, and sometimes the colliers' own children, drawing coal in British coal mines is a familiar one.[53] In 1905 a miner's son started at the age of fourteen with an above-ground job in a coal mine in Skåne (Scania) in southern Sweden, but was badly treated and beaten by the smith he was assisting. After his confirmation he moved to a much better-paid but heavy job underground, where the working day was two hours shorter than above ground. His job was to draw and push carts loaded with coal, as boys did in British and German coal mines.[54] Children generally worked above ground in the Swedish mining industry. According to the employers, there were only ten boys aged fourteen in the iron-ore mines and only sixteen in the coal mines working underground in 1891, while younger children worked 'in the open air'. At that time, children under fifteen years comprised five per cent of all workers in the mining industry, while those under fourteen comprised three per cent, which had also been the case in 1875. A typical job for children was grading the iron ore, or in the coal mine taking tools sent up from the shafts to the smith for grinding.[55] In France, mining was the fourth largest employer of children in the 1860s. It was difficult for French mines to keep their work force because of the dangers involved; boys aged fourteen were reported to have died in accidents as late as the 1920s.[56] In the Basque region, boys aged under fourteen hired themselves out as extra day workers in the iron-ore mines, but such employment opportunities decreased after 1890. It was not until after 1919 that ordinary miners' wages were enough to support a family.[57]

Children were even employed in the mercury mines. In the applications sent to Almadén, Spain's largest mine, it was indicated that children's incomes were needed for the family subsistence. Their situation must have been desperate, since the toxic effects of mercury were well known for a long time in Spain. Eighteen children, aged between eight and thirteen, were employed in Almadén in 1851. Thirteen of these were miners' children: seven had become orphaned, two had fathers who had met with an accident in the mine, and four had fathers still working there. The proportion of children and adolescents in mercury mining started to decline after 1900, but increased again during the First World War.[58]

The metalwork and cutlery industries were long characterised by small workshops using traditional methods. In the mid-nineteenth century, a nailing workshop in England employed both boys and girls on the bench, while girls operated the bellows. The metal trades in Birmingham had children arranging buttons for stamping in the stamp, as they had done previously.[59] Johan Carlsson, who lived north of Stockholm in Uppland, was nine years old in 1881 when he started as an oxdriver in a brickworks during the school holiday, and at the age of eleven he was employed as a fire watcher in a hammer forge. He went to school for some hours three days a week, but the other days were divided into six-hour shifts, that is six hours work followed by six hours rest. Eleven-year-old Erik Jansson endured week after week, the whole year round, a similar wearing system of six hours work, six hours rest in an ironworks in Gästrikland. In 1898, John Carlsson from Karlstad started working at the age of twelve as an errand boy in a manor, and at the age of fourteen in the same engineering shop in which his father worked. The father had no time to give support to his son, although John was one of the boys giving assistance in the same work team. The workshop was cramped, dark, cold and dirty, and occasionally in the night John, tired and freezing, found himself weeping.[60]

Starting around 1870, paper making changed from small-scale production from textile fibres to large-scale manufacture from wood fibres in a mechanised operation. This brought about the disappearance of child labour from the paper industry in forest-rich Scandinavia. For example, children still comprised about a fifth of the industry's labour force in Finland in 1867, but in 1887 it was down to two per cent, and in 1907 no more than a handful of children were employed in the paper industry. The number of children in the Swedish paper industry fell by half between 1875 and 1891, while the proportion of children in the labour force fell from six to one per cent.[61] In contrast, paper making remained a child-labour industry throughout the nineteenth century in Schleswig-Holstein. Likewise, in the late 1870s a boy of seven in Spain still worked in a factory making cardboard boxes. The Italian paper industry was slow to change from textile to wood fibres, and evidently remained very small-scale for a long time: in 1901, there were, on average, only 12 employees per employer (*padrone*). The number of children in the Italian paper industry remained high, at between 2,500 and 2,800 in the period 1871–1901, and their proportion of the labour force was 11 and 16 per cent. There were still 2,300 children, or six per cent of the labour force employed in 1927 – a proportion found 50 years earlier in the Swedish paper industry.[62]

The printing trades employed more children than the paper industry in England, but it is interesting that, by 1881 girls had outnumbered boys in the latter (Table 4.3). The Russian paper industry employed fewer boys than the printing trades, while the opposite was true for girls. Printing was a heavily male-dominated industry, and boys comprised 3.6 per cent of the male labour force in 1911.[63]

The sawmill industry was an expanding exporter in Sweden, Norway and Finland in the late nineteenth century. Sawmills were major employers of seasonal child labour in the countryside, although children comprised a relatively small proportion of the total labour force in the sawmill industry. Oral histories have plenty of references to boys following their fathers to the sawmill at a relatively young age, for example around the age of ten in Norway where boys were subcontracted by their fathers. Jobs in the sawmills were quite heavy for both women and children.[64] In 1910, a nine-year-old boy was employed in a Swedish sawmill to push a heavy cart uphill. When he was twelve, the same boy worked piling boards from the steam-driven saw, which was also heavy work.[65]

Tobacco was a child-labour industry in northern Europe, whereas in the south it was chiefly women who comprised the cheap labour force. Women cigar makers in France strove to pave the way for their daughters, as happened with traditional crafts.[66] This echoed the Norwegian tobacco industry, in which the subcontracting of children by their parents was practised. The numbers of children in tobacco factories in Schleswig-Holstein seem to have been very small, almost nil, until the mid-nineteenth century, after which it rapidly increased. By 1865 tobacco had become the largest employer of children, and remained a child-labour industry for the rest of the century.[67] Developments were diametrically opposite in Bremen, where the use of child labour ended with the 1850s recession in the tobacco industry. However, this did not herald the end of industrial child labour in Bremen, but only meant that it moved from the factory to the home.[68] The tobacco industry continued as a major employer of children in Denmark. In the early 1870s, children comprised a third of the labour force in the largest tobacco firm, and two-thirds in the second largest. Boys aged ten were allowed to be employed as half-timers in a tobacco factory. With plenty of cheap child labour engaged in grading and preparing tobacco leaves for adult workers who rolled cigars by hand, tobacco was the least mechanised industry in Denmark in 1872, and the production process was still very labour intensive at the beginning of the twentieth century. As late as 1914, boys aged under fourteen comprised seven per cent of all male workers, while girls comprised just one per cent of female workers.[69]

Children comprised the majority of the labour force (between 70% and 90%) in the first Swedish and Finnish tobacco manufactories applying an advanced division of labour. In 1806 the majority of children in one Swedish tobacco manufactory were aged between eight and eleven, but the practice of hiring children aged under ten then stopped. Nevertheless, children comprised 12 per cent of the labour force in the Swedish tobacco industry in 1872. Mechanised cigar rolling made its breakthrough in Swedish factories in the 1880s, and by 1891 the industry only employed a handful of children. Similarly, the use of child labour in the Finnish tobacco industry declined rapidly after c.1870, but rather because of a change in the product range from cigars to machine-made cigarettes, and women mended the machines.[70] The popularity of cigarettes in Finland is explained by the close contacts with Russia, where cigarettes dominated the market. In Russia cigarette rolling had been a major employer of children, boys aged under thirteen comprising 12–19 per cent and girls 8–12 per cent of the labour force in the Moscow province in 1898–1900. The demand for children was probably in decline by then, since cigarette rolling began to be mechanised after 1896.[71]

Match manufacturing was another child-labour industry shared by north-western Germany and Scandinavia. It was important in Russia as well.[72] Children were employed for the match-making process itself, and women and children were used in the factory for filling the matchboxes, and at home for making match boxes. As long as phosphorus was used in matches, the toxic effects could not be avoided, and the risk of phosphorus necrosis (degeneration of the chin bone) loomed large for children making matches. An alternative method was available, but remained unprofitable until the production technology was improved and mechanised. The mechanising of 'safety-match' production started in Sweden in the late 1860s, while matchbox production and box-filling were mechanised around or after 1880.[73] The entire production process was changed from a manual to a mechanised one over about twenty years. The number of children working in the match industry fell in Sweden by a half between 1875 and 1891, and their proportion of the labour force fell from 16 to seven per cent. Finland followed suit. Children still comprised almost half of the labour force in the Finnish match industry in the 1860s, and well over one-tenth in 1887, while in 1907 it employed no more than a handful. In Schleswig-Holstein, however, children comprised as much as 84 per cent of the labour force in the match industry in 1865, and it remained a leading employer of children for the rest of the century.[74]

Glass, pottery and brick-making were examples of industries with long traditions of apprenticeship which came to be transformed into cheap child labour. By hiring and dismissing children and other unskilled workers assisting the expensive highly-skilled craftsmen, production volumes could be adjusted to consumer demand cycles. Children's jobs in the glass and brick industries were often very heavy, even exhausting. In late nineteenth-century Germany, Nikolaus Osterrat was thirteen when he left school and started in a brickworks. Later he recalled how, in five months, the murderously heavy work turned 'a cheerful, bright-eyed child' into an old man who had lost the zest for life.[75] Danish brick production offered seasonal work lasting from Easter until Michaelmas, and it was the women's and children's job to turn hand-moulded bricks on their sides and smooth them.[76] Oscar Karlsson, aged eight, started as a stoker in a glass works in Småland, Sweden in 1887. He worked six-hour shifts day and night, weekdays and weekends, in all 240 hours a month. Later he recalled how endless the night shifts minding the glass ovens seemed to be for a sleepy young boy. Ester Franzén, a glassworker's daughter, was nine years old in 1900 when she started at another glassworks in Småland. Her job was to close, hold and open a hot iron form into which bottles were blown by glass blowers at a very fast rate. Burning hot fragments of glass flew onto her hands and face. She often wept before she became used to it all, but – as she later recalled – all hardships were forgotten when pay day came and she could bring home money to her mother who needed every single coin.[77]

The glass industry long remained dependent on master glass blowers, since the blowing of even standard products such as bottles proved difficult to mechanise. The industry therefore enjoyed dispensation from regulations concerning child labour and night working. For example, Russian glassworks (along with textile factories) were exempted from regulations prohibiting night work by children, and the industry employed more than a quarter of all children in manufacturing in 1911. Two-thirds of the children in the glass industry were boys, but they were proportionally fewer among male workers than girls among female workers (16.1% versus 25.3%).[78] While glass blowers would continue to introduce their own sons to the trade, outside boys were just cheap labour, and were often badly treated by the glass blowers. Finally, the glass blowers lost their monopoly and their ability to control entry to the trade. As the glass blowing trade lost its privileges and appeal, 'parents began discouraging their children from entering it', as Michelle Perrot notes.[79]

In the second half of the twentieth century, in what were known as the developing countries, children were making matchboxes and working in glassworks and brickyards under terms such as bonded labour, pseudo-apprenticeship and subcontracting. These working children did not appear so very different from their counterparts in industrialising Europe, and the terms under which they worked were familiar from the European past.[80] This may serve as further proof that child labour was and still is a necessity for low-income households from the perspective of the family economy and the supply of child labour. Yet, again, the fact that industrial child labour is also concentrated around a limited number of industries in the developing countries, some even the same as in nineteenth-century Europe, suggests the need to focus on the demand as much as on the supply.

Educational opportunities

In the course of the nineteenth century, mass schooling came to be seen as a tool for reforming individuals and society, and attitudes grew increasingly similar between countries and over time. Even the First International (International Working Men's Association) put on the agenda children's rights to education.[81] In the long run, in all the countries considered here, industrial child labour declined while school attendance increased, although the process and its timing differed greatly from one country to another. This section briefly compares the formal education provided for future general and middle-level managers with that of shop-floor workers. Another issue is the legislation concerning the primary education of working-class children, including the issue of compulsory education.

The popular idea of the rise 'from rags to riches', or 'from errand boy to manager', seldom held true even during the industrial revolution. In Britain, France, Germany and Scandinavia, for instance, business leaders and managers were generally recruited from among the privileged classes and the solid middle class. For boys destined to join the business élite there were private secondary schools offering a traditional academic curriculum that provided them with useful networks and prepared them to assume the role of leader.[82] An élite education may not always have benefited the family firm, as Mark Casson remarks, since 'successful Victorian businessmen who sent their sons away to boarding school may have diminished their sons' willingness to join the family business later on, not only because the sons' social aspirations may have risen, but because their sense of filial obligation may have been undermined by their enforced, if temporary, expulsion from the family home'.[83]

Boys who would become middle-level managers and engineers may have attended various technical secondary schools, well established in Britain, France and Prussia by the time of the second industrial revolution. Early nineteenth-century German States created *Realschulen* to meet the needs of the merchant and manufacturing middle class, while proper vocational education in factory industry was not introduced until the 1870s. Facing the competition of German industrial performance, the French state decided to reorganise apprenticeship training in 1880, and schools of trade and industry were established. Boys entered French technical schools at the age of fourteen. Technical colleges were established in England to complement on-the-job apprenticeship training. Instruction in technical colleges took place mainly in the evenings, but colleges also served as secondary trade schools for full-time students who usually entered them at the age of fourteen.[84] German-type *Realschulen* were introduced in Russia in the 1870s, and the number of pupils, some 8,000 in 1876, grew tenfold by the First World War.[85]

Technical know-how was primarily acquired in Scandinavia via private technical societies and through direct professional contacts, and the establishment of corresponding schools came second. Norwegian textile entrepreneurs first visited textile plants in Holland and Belgium, and later, after 1840, in Britain. In Sweden, iron manufacturing was supported early with the establishment of the Falu School of Mining in 1822. The second Swedish mining school started in 1850, and there were also three more elementary, less technical, schools with instruction in the evenings and on

Sundays. The first technical secondary school started in Stockholm in 1827, and regular on-the-job training was introduced in the Swedish mechanical engineering industry at about the same time. By 1872, nearly two-fifths of Danish industrial leaders had formal technical training, and a good third of them had mercantile training, while nearly a fifth had only on-the-job practical training. The first commercial school, for boys aged fourteen or over, was established in Finland in 1839, followed by the first technical schools and technical Sunday schools.[86]

What kind of education was available for factory children? Those already in the industrial labour force often had little time left for school, given the very long working days, six days a week. However, it seems that, taken as a whole, a minority of factory children started full-time work very young, contemporary references to young children notwithstanding.[87] Most would-be factory children had one to three years when they could attend school, if there was one available.

In England a few mills and factories established their own schools teaching reading, writing and basic arithmetic, but in the 1820s this kind of community building by the promoter of the factory was already in decline. Providing primary education was left to public authorities or philanthropists, even by the mill owners in Lancashire who revived paternalism a few decades later. Working-class interest in primary-school education appears to have been rather limited. In 1857, four in ten children registered as school pupils attended school for less than a year, two in ten for between one and two years. According to Eric Hopkins, 'the children who did attend were usually very young and less ready to go to work than others'.[88]

At the beginning of the nineteenth century, French manufacturers were eager to establish schools applying the Lancaster method (*écoles mutuelles*) for their employees' children. A mining company in Flanders established such a school in 1816, and two years later, Protestant manufacturers in Alsace took the initiative to set up similar schools that proved a success for some years to come. However, in the 1830s and 1840s, in the words of Colin Heywood, 'the expansion of the industrial sector was directly responsible for low levels of school attendance'. In industrialised cantons, 'children were put to work as soon as they could earn a few sous, leaving little or no time for their schooling'. For example, in Reims in the 1830s, a day-worker's eldest son, aged eight years, who did attend school earned only 3 *sous* a day, while a ten-year-old child working full time in the woollen industry may have earned 50 *sous* or more a day.[89]

The French Child Labour Law of 1841 introduced two years of compulsory education before children had the right to be employed, that is at the age of eight years. Employed children aged under twelve should have attended a public or private school. This was, in theory, made feasible by stipulating an eight-hour workday for children, but the practice was different. According to contemporary reports, children continued to work long days, like adults: parents and children cooperated with factory owners to circumvent the law, or then children were moved over to shops not covered by the law. A number of firms fired all their child workers under the age of twelve. 'This unintended result of the law was especially hard on the working families whose children were turned out of their jobs, for the income of children was critical to the families' survival', as Lee Shai Weissbach comments.[90] Other factors offer additional explanations to do with the business situation or mechanisation.[91] The law of 1874 stipulating part-time education for all working children under the age of twelve, and for those aged twelve to fifteen who had not finished the whole curriculum, was an effort to achieve a balance between school and work. The education laws of 1881 and 1882, 'the Ferry Laws', provided for compulsory education, but not compulsory school attendance, since instruction could be given in the home. By 1884, more than two-thirds of working children aged twelve to fifteen, encountered by the factory inspectors had school certificates.[92]

Attending elementary schools was made obligatory in northern Italy by the school law of 1806 and again in 1818. Elementary schools were even intended to offer technical instruction, but this came to nothing, while technical secondary education was successfully introduced in Tuscany. Private evening schools catered for working boys and apprentices, and a well-run evening school had existed in Rome since 1819, for instance. The authorities strove to implement a minimum of three years of school for working children aged between six and nine, but this exacerbated family poverty, and thus enrolment remained low. Even so, from the school year of 1820–1821 to that of 1866–1867, the number of schools in northern Italy increased by a half, and that of teachers nearly doubled, while the difference between boys' and girls' school attendance almost disappeared. Compulsory education was introduced in the 1850s, and the Law of 1877 reaffirmed it, but the statute remained largely ignored by the poor, who also suffered from the inadequate supply of schools. In 1861, two in five, and in 1901 one in five, children of compulsory school age attended school only sporadically if at all. Work and ragged clothes kept them away. Early entry into the labour force was behind the 1904 law offering two-year courses for children destined for manual work, while for others compulsory education lasted until the age of twelve.[93] Nonetheless, there was a relatively marked increase in schooling in the period 1871–1895, and a more modest one in 1896–1910. According to Marzio

Barbagli, 'at least for the period 1881–1913, it can be said that the course of primary education shows some significant variations that correspond to the course of the economic cycle and also that between these two phenomena there is a direct relationship'.[94]

As in Italy, Spain entered the modern era 'with a deficit in terms of human capital formation' (G. Tortella). The 1812 Constitution of Gadiz formally introduced universal primary education with a modest curriculum, while the Law of 1857 formally brought in compulsory primary education for children aged between six and nine. The number of school children increased after the mid-nineteenth century, but in practice, far from all boys and particularly girls who were registered attended: in 1880, as still in 1908, only about a quarter of all enrolled children actually went to school. According to Alejandro Tiana Ferrer, 'economic backwardness resulted in low demand for skilled workers, which did not exactly encourage working-class families to invest in the education of their children'.[95]

The *Schulordnung* of 1814 formally introduced compulsory education in Schleswig-Holstein, but in practice school yielded to work. In general, children's employment in industrial work was seen as a positive phenomenon. Factory children could seldom attend ordinary primary schools, but resorted to special arrangements or were exempted from school education. For example, of the six children working in a mechanised broadcloth factory in the 1820s, four had no school education, while two had not attended school since they had turned eight and nine years. Local authorities and the owner of the factory then agreed that children should attend an evening school nine hours a week for one or two years before their confirmation. The nine hours were not taken from their working hours, but were added to them. In the 1840s, ten children employed in a tobacco factory had their week divided in half between school and work. Children in a glassworks had almost no time for school: in winter they were declared indispensable for work at the ovens, and in summer they attended school only irregularly because they helped in peat work on the moor. In the 1850s, children in cotton printing attended evening school in winter, and Sunday school in summer. In summer, because the daylight, and thus the working day, lasted so late into the evening they were not able to go to school. Factory schools were often the only option, and children paid about one-fifth or a little more of their wages in fees.[96]

According to Arcadius Kahan, the emancipation of serfs in 1861 and the growth of modern industry accelerated the expansion of elementary education in Russia. Nonetheless, primary-school enrolment by girls remained poor, which would later explain the low literacy rate among women in manufacturing. 'Regulations concerning the school instruction of young persons employed in factories and mills' brought out in 1884 stipulated compulsory education for factory children, but implementation proved complex. In 1885, only 112 factory schools (with 3,000 pupils) were registered, while local school authorities had done very little towards constructing public schools that could be attended by juvenile workers. Only a quarter of the young persons employed in the inspected establishments were literate, and another tenth were able to read but not write.[97] According to Kahan, 'schooling dragged back on development' in late nineteenth-century Russia because of the mismatch between the level of education and the basic technology borrowed from Germany. In contrast, Peter Gatrell positively notes the 'substantial improvements in the labour productivity' due to gains in literacy.[98] Gatrell echoes the Russian industrialists and education specialists, who towards the end of the nineteenth century, began to 'elucidate the links between education and productivity in industry and agriculture' (B. Eklof).[99]

Although all children in Scandinavia were expected to learn to read, less so to write, the authorities did not unreservedly give priority to school over work.[100] The Danish committee drafting the first child-labour law in 1873 considered children's employment in industry good in principle, since it was more healthy for them to learn dutiful work than to go idle, and a poor family had use even for the little money that they could earn.[101] The Norwegian governmental committee drafting the Primary School Act in the early 1870s emphasised the fact that, when organising the school system, it was important to keep in mind that children of the poor were sent out to work at an earlier age than formerly because, thanks to industry, they had better chances of finding employment. Moreover, most Norwegian factories were situated in rural districts where school was usually held just two or three days a week. Thus children could work full-time on the other days, as well as during the long summer holiday. As school days were relatively short, it was possible for them to work part-time then, too.[102]

Compulsory education had been introduced in Sweden in 1842, but fourteen years later the Swedish *Riksdag* (the Estates Assembly) gave little support to a proposal to impose a fine on any industrialist employing a child aged twelve or over without a certificate showing that he or she had completed the minimum primary-school curriculum, or at least had acquired reading skills and a knowledge of basic religious doctrines. The majority of *Riksdag* members rather thought like a member of the Estate of Burghers, who observed that such a provision 'would place obstacles in the way of many children who, having attained 12 years of age, [are ready] to be taken on in a factory or a trade'.[103] The Swedish Child Labour Act of 1881 introduced a half-timer system. The same year Knut Fisher, the nine-year-old son of a Småland glass master, started as a half-time heater in a glassworks, attending school the other half of the day. The 1881 Act was soon forgotten in this glassworks, after which children again worked full time. Glassworks employees served on the local school board, so no one protested, not even the teacher, when, short of labour, the factory sent word to the school that boys were now needed.[104]

In anticipation of the establishment of public primary schools, the larger Finnish textile mills, which were few in number, organised elementary school education for their child workers and workers' children. The first factory school was established in 1840 by the largest single user of child labour, the Finlayson cotton mill. Public primary schools were established in towns and cities from c.1870, and on their own initiative, working-class parents then began to send their children to school. The number of factory children continued to vary with business cycles, but the trend was downwards, and the proportion of children in the total industrial labour force had become negligible by 1900. This suggests that the demand for industrial child labour in Finland declined long before the introduction of compulsory education, since the first legislative bill was not presented to Parliament until 1907, and it was another fourteen years before the law came into force.[105]

Other latecomers in implementing universal primary education included Italy, Spain and Russia. It was not only in silk, but also in the Lombardian cotton industry that the number of child workers grew many times over during the period of 1854–1911, while the proportion of children of the total labour force, having once declined, rose again.[106] Enrolment rates in elementary schools in Lombardy grew very slowly or even fell in the period 1901–1907, as they did in Piedmont, another industrialised region.[107] Correspondingly, in 1908, school enrolment in the industrialised province of Barcelona was among the lowest in Spain, while child labour continued to be about as common in the municipality as in the mid-nineteenth century. According to José Borrás Llop, this confirms 'the importance of the supply of child labour, effective or potential, in the labour market of Barcelona'.[108] But do not the two indicators equally well serve to confirm the importance of the demand for child labour? In fact this is implied in Borrás Llop's discussion on the attitudes of employers to the Spanish child-labour law of 1900.[109]

Russian primary school required attendance only between the ages of eight and eleven. According to Ben Eklof, at least in the Moscow province, 'employment in factory and cottage industries for the overwhelming majority of children of both sexes began well after the standard age for completing elementary education'. Of the 69,368 factory workers in the Moscow province in 1908, a clear majority (about 48,460) had joined the workforce aged fifteen or more, and one-quarter (about 16,800) between the ages of twelve and fourteen, that is, in all respects at a legal age. Thus only a small minority (between four and five per cent, or less than 3,100) had begun to work aged under twelve, that is, when still of school age. These numbers include 50 children under the age of eight, all of them from before 1878, some 1,400 starting work aged between eight and nine, all of them before 1898, and some 1,600 between ten and eleven, the last of these (some 200) after 1898. In short, 'after 1888 only about three per cent of entering factory workers were twelve years old or younger and that between two-thirds and four-fifths of the workers had remained free until the age of fifteen'. Eklof concludes that the traditional description of conflict between school and factory 'is an overstated view'.[110] It could be added that the number of children aged under fifteen in manufacturing declined in Russia in the period 1901–1910 from 34,000 to 26,600, but then again rose to 31,500 in 1914 (was this because men were mobilised for the war?). Girls comprised two-fifths of child manufacturing workers in 1901, as they did in 1914.[111]

The Italian and Spanish cases suggest that it was the continuing demand for child labour rather than, or as much as, the supply of it that kept children away from school. As long as attending school instead of working in the factory incurred opportunity costs, the poor could not afford the choice. In contrast, the Finnish and Russian cases suggest that, even without compulsory education, 'schools were proliferating, children were crowding at the doors, and literacy rates were climbing' (B. Eklof),[112] once parents had reason to send children to school and to keep them there. The low demand for children aged under twelve in manufacturing meant that there was very little if any conflict over children's time use between school and factory, since primary school was over before factory work began. In time, the demand for children aged between twelve and fifteen declined as well, while the years spent at primary school increased.

Child-labour laws in retrospect

Contrary to received ideas, not all factory work by children was objectionable to nineteenth-century reformers or legislators. The main item on the agenda was the regulation of industrial child labour. In all of the countries discussed here, the legal minimum age remained low enough to allow the employment of children – generally eight or nine years in the first half of the nineteenth century, and nine, ten or twelve in the second half.[113] The following examples from France, England, Russia, Scandinavia, Italy, Spain and Germany strengthen this argument.

In his passionate plea for the first French child-labour law, Charles Dupin fought for a minimum age of eight years in 1840, which was what employers in Mulhouse had already agreed upon, which was not to their detriment because factory children so young were in any case few in number. The same year, Louis Villermé, another champion of reform, was of the opinion that if the working time were adjusted according to children's ages, so that the youngest ones worked only four hours, then six- and seven-year-olds could well be employed in *les grands ateliers*, while the minimum age proposed by the Minister of Commerce, nine years, would postpone the entry into wage work for too long. Not only did the poor families need the incomes of even young children, but it was also better that children worked in the factories than loitered idly in the streets. Furthermore, Louis Reybaud praised the large silk spinning mills in 1856 for offering girls and women better wages than they had been able to earn in the home silk industry, without risking their moral welfare.[114]

The Children's Employment Commission of 1840 in England was not concerned by child labour as such, but by the demoralising effect of women and girls working underground in coal mines, and the young age at which children started in the mines. Eric Hopkins was puzzled by the fact that English middle-class observers did not find the employment of children objectionable in itself, nonetheless he claims that 'an increasing sensitivity was manifested among the middle classes rather than the working classes'. When the Royal Commission was dealing with the issue of child labour in textile mills in 1892, two factory inspectors were in favour of part-time work by children, because without their earnings the mother would have had to go out to work.[115] As Harry Hendrick remarks, generally, 'observers viewed *some* degree of labour, either paid or unpaid, as desirable', thus the total abolition of child labour was 'rarely seriously considered'. Further, as far as the half-time system of the Edwardian period was concerned, 'there was no mention of bringing it to an end'. Lancashire textile-factory workers were divided on the question of raising the minimum age from twelve to thirteen in 1908, and with family consent, girls continued to be employed as half-time tenters in weaving manufacturing until the 1930s.[116]

In Russia, the mechanised cotton spinning mills in St Petersburg went further than the law of 1882, which prohibited children under twelve from working in factories and limited the working day of children between twelve and fifteen to eight hours. The factory owners 'deemed profitable for themselves the total prohibition of night work for women, the work for juveniles between 12 and 14 to 6 hours a day, and for adult men to 70 hours a week', whereas their competitors in Moscow, relying heavily on cheap labour, vigorously insisted on their right to freely manage their labour. Mikhail Tugan-Baranovsky offered as an explanation the high wages in St Petersburg, as well as the international economic depression in 1883, which made many cotton mills and other factories reduce their output and dismiss large numbers of workers. St Petersburg manufacturers explained that the crisis could only be overcome by 'a general prohibition of night work'. Supporting their interests, the law of 1885 prohibited night working by women and children in the cotton, linen and woollen industries. According to Tugan-Baranovsky, this prohibition 'did not encounter great opposition on the part of factory owners' as long as the depression lasted. Afterwards, in 1890, a new factory act 'fundamentally altered the laws of 1882 and 1885'. Children aged between ten and eleven were again permitted to work in factories, and night working was allowed for children between twelve and fifteen in the glass industry, and in certain cases for women and juveniles.[117]

Corresponding legal revisions took place in Sweden. The first Child Labour Act was enacted in 1881, but iron and timber, Sweden's chief export industries and the largest employers of children, were exempted by royal decree before it came into force. In 1890, the School Board of Norrköping, then Sweden's leading industrial centre, complained that, because the 1881 Act had introduced a six-hour working day for children under fourteen, children now went idle half the day, which had resulted in moral degeneration and the emergence of gangs of pilfering boys. Such complaints bore fruit. The revised Act of 1900 lengthened the working day for thirteen-year-olds from six to ten hours, and that of fourteen-year-olds from ten to eleven hours. In addition, the iron and timber industries were permitted to lower the minimum age of children employed 'for lighter work' to eleven from twelve which had been the norm since 1846. It was not until 1912 that the iron and timber industries lost their dispensation regarding working hours for children.[118]

The Spanish law of 1897 prohibited underground work in mines for children aged under twelve and women of all ages, while the law of 1900 raised the minimum age for underground work to sixteen, but allowed children from ten years up to be employed above ground; night work was prohibited for children under fourteen. Children who applied to work in the large lead and zinc mines of Peñarroya in Andalusia were evidently well aware of such age limits, since whatever their true age – the youngest applicants had not turned eleven – they claimed to be fourteen or sixteen. The company doctor frequently noted that a child had falsified his age, yet according to Arón Cohen, this played no role in the actual recruitment practice. Occasionally even quite young children of eleven or so were taken on, which Cohen takes to be an expression of paternalism.[119]

The Catholic Church in Italy opposed the law of compulsory education (enacted in 1877) and the law restricting child labour (1886), while extreme liberals feared them to be the first step towards the collective, public regulation of all industrial relations. Mario Chiri, advocating a Christian social programme, used many alleviating phrases to veil his support for industrial child labour in 1908.[120] The Instituto de Reformas Sociales of Barcelona in Catalonia, the most industrialised region in Spain, opposed a rigid implementation of the Spanish law of 1900 concerning women's and children's work in manufacturing and commerce. This law stipulated a minimum age of nine for children who could read and write, otherwise ten years, except in subterranean or other dangerous work in which it was sixteen. In 1905 and 1909, the Society's representatives argued that it was not right to exclude children from mines, because they needed an early start in order to get accustomed to them, and that in glass making it was necessary for children to be exposed to the heat of molten glass at a young age so that they would learn to bear it. Likewise, many factory inspectors continued to argue that child labour was a necessity for the survival of many working-class families.[121]

José Adsuar Moreno, an *inspector provincial del trabajo* writing for the Spanish Society of Hygiene in 1916, ranked different forms of child labour from the worst to the best. The worst was work in public places and the best was apprenticeship in factories and large workshops. He had no objections to proper industrial child labour, neither did he criticise the low minimum age for factory work. He did propose, though, that children be provided with the necessary religious instruction and at least two hours daily of primary-school education.[122]

Child labour was justified at the northern end of Europe in much the same way as in Spain in the south. The introduction of industrial child labour was originally welcomed by the Finnish authorities as a means for pauper children to make their living without resorting to poor relief. The first Labour Protection Act was enacted in 1889, but Finnish factory inspectors were disinclined to strictly implement it, while the Governmental Board of Industries generously granted exemption to textile and glass manufacturers, sawmills and other industries still using child labour. The 1905 committee for child protection, like the factory inspectors, blamed the 1889 Act for the declining demand for children in the manufacturing industry. The Finnish committee saw work in public places as the worst form of child labour, while work in factories was the best remedy for 'the idleness' of urban boys.[123]

The German Child Labour Act of 1903, for which the primary-school teacher Konrad Agahd gave the German Teachers' Union the credit, limited daily working time for 'outside' (*fremde*) children aged twelve or over during school terms to three hours in home industry, trade and transport, while that of the industrialists' own children aged ten or over remained unlimited. Julius Deutsch wrote a prize-winning essay in 1906 in which he advocated that all work for wages in industry, trade and agriculture should be prohibited for children of compulsory school age (under fourteen), and only that done by the proprietors' own children should be permitted, since such work had a pedagogic function. Nevertheless, there was still energetic opposition to the 1903 Act in Saxony in the early 1910s. In the Saxon countryside, home industries generating cash income from a variety of saleable products, such as linen and cotton cloth, and bobbin and warp spools, had long been part of the household strategy, enabling people to stay on the land. Perhaps at least a quarter, and in places more than half, of children of school age worked in various home industries, such as making dolls and other toys. Those who criticised the 1903 Act wanted to keep children working.[124]

The above examples suggest that the idea that industrial child labour would or should end altogether was alien to nineteenth-century legislators, reformers and pamphlet writers. Contemporaries evidently did not see early child-labour laws as the first steps towards the total abolition of industrial child labour. They began to appear as such only in hindsight.

Conclusion

Several countries witnessed a downward turn in the number or proportion of factory children and an upward turn in school enrolment during the 1870s and 1880s. Discussing the case of France, Colin Heywood suggests that the problem is 'to explain this radical shift in attitudes and employment patterns concerning child labour'.[125] In my view, in offering such an explanation we should consider the effect of the growing productivity-consciousness of employers, and possibly also the improving managerial competence, both pressed forward by the profitability challenges during the long deflationary period of the 1870s and 1880s. There is also reason to compare the possible impact of child-labour laws with the effect of those restricting women's labour.

Child-labour laws and compulsory education have long enjoyed the status of useful explanations. According to Heywood, by the turn of the twentieth century in France 'the cause was largely won: with the comprehensive system of factory inspection built up after 1874, and free, compulsory primary education in 1882, child labour was clearly on the wane'.[126] According to Hugh Cunningham, 'there is strong evidence in the shape of employment figures to show that some child labour legislation has had a profound impact'.[127] Basically similar conclusions are to be found in other contributions to the history of child labour.[128]

The idea that the effective implementation of compulsory education was decisive in the decline of child labour has been advocated by Myron Weiner, who argues that the enforcement of compulsory education laws 'substantially reduces or eliminates child labor'.[129] Hugh Cunningham backs this up: 'It is widely argued now that the most effective way of ending child labour is by making school compulsory. There is certainly evidence that the introduction of compulsory schooling in Britain in 1880 was associated with a decline in the proportion of children described as in the workforce.'[130] In the same vein, Michelle Perrot suggests that the French education laws of 1881–1882 'removed childhood from the industrial sphere'.[131]

Behind this type of reasoning seems to lie a supposition that the supply of potential child labour was virtually unlimited, hence 'the key to its reduction rested with the curtailment of demand', to quote Hugh Cunningham.[132] Nevertheless, detailed studies have brought to light evidence of a variation in the supply even in Britain.[133] In addition, Clark Nardinelli argued that what was decisive in the long run in Britain in terms of reducing the supply of child labour was mainly rising living standards and the economic value of school investments. Since real wages did rise in nineteenth-century Britain, albeit unequally and with setbacks, on this point Nardinelli's reasoning appears plausible.[134] Nonetheless, Sara Horrell and Jane Humphries are critical of this. In their data the 'weighted averages of participation rates of children in families do not decline despite increases in average adult male real earnings from the mid-1830s onwards, cautioning against an overemphasis on income effects as an explanation of patterns in children's participation rates'.[135]

Moreover should we not give more attention to the fact that, in several instances, we encounter the phrase 'women and children'? Women and children often performed related or similar kinds of work; Nardinelli goes so far as to regard women as children's 'close substitutes'.[136] What was stipulated concerning children and young persons was often applied to women workers, too.[137] This raises a question: if the legislation restricting children's work in industry was an explanation for the decline in or abolition of industrial child labour, why was women's work in industry often largely immune to the legal restrictions associated with it?

Lars Olsson made a strong case against the interpretation that legislation was decisive: 'Child labour was not abolished as a consequence of any legislation or humanitarian ideas. It was abolished as a consequence of changed forms of production and exploitation of the labour force.'[138]

Certainly legislation serves poorly in explaining the curious fact that from the mid-1880s to 1914 in Germany and Finland, different as the two were, the number of child workers in industry followed largely similar curves. The integration of European business cycles and labour markets would appear to be a more likely explanation.[139]

Shortcomings in managerial competence were tolerated in Britain as long as there were 'easy profit margins and high profits' (S. Pollard), whereas increasing competition brought about a more professional attitude towards managerial tasks. It seems that in European industry in general, the time of 'easy profit margins and high profits' for those who had joined the game early came to an end during the long deflationary period of the 1870s and 1880s. Discussing the seasonal industrial and agricultural labour market in France after 1870, Gilles Postel-Vinay speaks of 'the long depression affecting both industry and agriculture and the subsequent restructuring of both sectors', and points out that 'the transformation of the industrial labour market between 1860 and 1890 was particularly striking'.[140] The restructuring of the two sectors was not limited to France, but was a general European phenomenon. Hardened competition required better managerial competencies and keener monitoring of profitability and productivity.[141] In the 1870s and 1880s, when the survival of many firms was at stake, the number or proportion of children in manufacturing decreased. Was the productivity or profitability of child labour weighed up and found wanting?

During the decades of the 1870s and 1880s, new child-labour and educational laws were enacted in many of the countries discussed here, and as a rule their implementation proved less difficult than in earlier cases. This could be interpreted as indicating that entrepreneurs and employers now had use for new rules of fair and unfair competition. The issue of child labour was put on the international agenda in 1889, and the first conference in Berlin agreed on twelve years as the minimum age for boys and girls, except in Mediterranean countries where it was ten.[142] This indicated that the leading economic powers wanted to be sure that each one of them followed the same rules of the game. From this perspective the new child-labour and compulsory-education laws merely confirmed what was already taking place due to market forces in the demand for child labour. Thus in the wake of the industrial restructuring in the 1870s and 1880s, the enforcement of compulsory-education laws, which had previously been so knotty, began to progress. After losing their niche in the industrial labour market, children might as well attend school.

For more than a century now there has been a lively debate on whether or not factory laws and compulsory education contributed decisively to the decline of industrial child labour. Perhaps it is a sign of saturation that both Harry Hendrick and Colin Heywood have recently deliberately kept their distance from this debate by placing industrial child labour into a wider context and a longer time perspective.[143] Whatever the role, if any, of child-labour laws in the decline of industrial child labour, at least we could say that before children left the factory they had rendered service to other factory workers. What had originally been special concessions to them, such as the right to regular breaks, an eight-hour working day and protection against occupational accidents and diseases, were eventually adopted in laws and collective agreements concerning all workers. The price adult workers paid for this was acknowledging industrial discipline.

Notes

1. Ure 1967 [1835], pp. 19, 23. See also Humphries 2003, pp. 258, 266.
2. Ure 1967 [1835], pp. 15–16, 20, 22–23.
3. Weiner 1991, p. 114.
4. Tourgueneff [Turgenev] 1847, pp. 143–144.
5. Clark 1994; Pollard 1968, quotations pp. 161, 165; Rose 2000, pp. 99–105. See also Anderson, M. 1971, p. 28; Hansen 1987, pp. 31–32; Heywood 1988, pp. 8, 132–139; Heywood 1992, p. 22; Hobsbawm 1974, p. 352; Nardinelli 1990, p. 87; Olsson, L. 1980, p. 34; Polanyi 1971, pp. 164–165; Thompson, E.P. 1967, pp. 335–337; Tugan-Baranovsky 1970 [1907], pp. 87, 117, 133, 247–248.
6. Clark 1994, p. 160.
7. Anderson, M. 1971, pp. 114–117; Bolin-Hort 1989, pp. 40–51; Huberman 1991, p. 90; Pollard 1968, pp. 44–45, 81, 185; Rose 2000, p. 119; Schwarz 1992, p. 183; Simon, C. 1994.
8. Betänkande 1892, p. 155; Bull 1982, p. 224; Olsson, L. 1980, pp. 49–50; Rahikainen 2001b; Rahikainen 2002b. For paternalism, see Jansson 1990, pp. 122–141; Kirby 1995, pp. 163–165, 291–292; Rostgaard 2000.
9. Borrás Llop 1996, pp. 274–275; Camps i Cura 1996, p. 70; Camps-Cura 1998.
10. Romano 1992, pp. 305–327, quotation p. 320n.
11. Hobsbawm 1974, pp. 351–356, quotation p. 352; Rose 2000, p. 103–105, quotation p. 103.
12. Bolin-Hort 1989, pp. 22–23, 36–39; Pollard 1968, quotations pp. 164–165.
13. Pollard 1968, pp. 219–249; Rose 2000, p. 123.
14. Sen 1995, p. 59.
15. E.g., Brown 1995; Landes 1991; Locke, R.R. 1984, pp. 59–63; O'Brien 1994; Pollard 1992.
16. E.g. Crouzet 1994; Iradiel Murugarren 1974, pp. 217–231; Kerridge 1985, pp. 11, 236–241; Simon, C. 1994.
17. Mendels 1972, p. 242.
18. E.g. Pollard 1981, pp. 25–26. See also Blaug 1961; Crouzet 1994; Griffiths, Hunt and O'Brien 1994.
19. Nardinelli 1990, p. 60.
20. Cassis 1997, pp. 20, 79–81; Locke, R.R. 1984, pp. 65–66.

21. Heywood 1992, pp. 18–24, 35, 48; Sicsic 1994.

22. Bahamonde and Martínez 1994, pp. 394–398, 481; Borrás Llop 1999, p. 26; Tortella 2000, pp. 75–82, quotation p. 75.

23. Borrás Llop 1995, pp. 630–639.

24. Colli and Rose 1999; Pratt 1994, pp. 37–48; Romano 1992, pp. 9–48, 286–287, 308; Toniolo 1990, pp. 29–30, 42–43.

25. Cassis 1997, pp. 24–26; Fremdling 1991; Hertrich 1986; Peikert 1986; Pollard 1981, pp. 139–140, 223–224.

26. Nyberg et al. 1998.

27. Christensen, J.P. 2002, pp. 36–45. I am grateful to Hans Christian Johansen for bringing Christensen's work to my attention.

28. Bull 1984, p. 79; Kiel and Mjøset 1990, pp. 27–36; Martinson 1992, pp. 90–91.

29. Rahikainen 2001b, p. 44; Rahikainen 2002b.

30. Gatrell 1986, p. 163; Glickman 1984, p. 73; Kohl 1843, pp. 10–23; Tugan-Baranovsky 1970 [1907], pp. 72–73, 133; Zelnik 1971, pp. 17–48, 292–300, 316–317, quotation p. 36.

31. Bolin-Hort 1989.

32. Bolin-Hort 1989, pp. 40–53, 102–110, 208–236; Boot 1995, Table I; Hopkins 1994, pp. 92–94; Huberman 1991.

33. S.J. Chapman 1904, cited in Blaug 1961, p. 368.

34. P.K. O'Brien and C. Keyder 1978, cited in Heywood 1992, p. 24.

35. Villermé 1840a, pp. 4–5, 11–23, 37–46, 63–66, 89–99, 111, 124–125, 145, quotation p. 46; Villermé 1840b, pp. 11, 89, 111. See also Heywood 1992, pp. 18–24, 35; Sicsic 1994.

36. Borrás Llop 1996, pp. 241, 270–275; Tortella 2000, pp. 75–82.

37. Camps i Cura 1996, pp. 58–64, quotation p. 68.

38. Borrás Llop 1999, Tables 3 and 7.

39. Rahikainen 2002b.

40. Gatrell 1986, pp. 92–93, 147–148; Leontief 1906, pp. 19, 62–65; Tugan-Baranovsky 1970 [1907], pp. 75, 296–297; Zelnik 1995, pp. 17–33.

41. Eklof 1986, pp. 372–375.

42. Rapports annuels des inspecteurs de fabriques. Année 1911, p. 27.

43. Villermé 1840b, pp. 89–91.

44. Nyberg 1999, pp. 58, 65, 87, 194; Persson 1993, pp. 15–17, 124–131; Rahikainen 2002b, Table 1; Söderberg, Jonsson and Persson 1991, p. 63.

45. Johansen 1988, pp. 23–27, 338–339; Tønsberg 1997, quotation p. 36.

46. Hansen 1987, pp. 80–81, 104.

47. Heywood 1988, p. 123; Karvinen 2001, pp. 29–31, 68–74, 141; Kertzer 1977; Ortaggi Cammarosano 1991; Reybaud 1856, pp. 107–110; Toniolo 1990, p. 42.

48. Ellena 1879, pp. 389–407.

49. Censimento della popolazione … d'Italia 1901, Vol. IV, Tavola 1B. The numbers for textiles were the following: boys 12,401, men 109,078, girls 105,989, women 555,785.

50. Borrás Llop 1996, pp. 241, 270–275; Camps-Cura 1998.

51. For references, see, e.g., Rahikainen 2001a (note 29).

52. Clark 1994; Locke, R.R. 1984, pp. 62–69; Perrot 1997; Peukert 1986.

53. Anderson, M. 1971, p. 118; Hopkins 1994, pp. 51–61 and his references; Locke, R.R. 1984, pp. 20, 66.

54. Quoted in Bjurman and Olsson 1979, pp. 62–63. For German mines, see Peukert 1986.

55. Betänkande 1877, p. 113, Table 3; Betänkande 1892, pp. 86–87, 119, 129–131, 163–164, Table 1.
56. Perrot 1997, p. 85; Table de mortalité des ouvriers mineurs 1923–1928, Tableau V.
57. Borrás and Cohen 1990, pp. 11–15; Borrás Llop 1996, pp. 245–246; Tortella 2000, pp. 96–109.
58. Borrás and Cohen 1990, pp. 9–11; Borrás Llop 1996, p. 245; Tortella (2000, p. 107) describes Almadén as the richest mercury mine in the world.
59. Hopkins 1994, pp. 22–26, 43–51.
60. Quoted in Bjurman and Olsson 1979, pp. 50–62.
61. Moen 1991. For statistics, see sources for Table 4.2.
62. Borrás Llop 1996, p. 249; Ellena 1879, pp. 471–480; Hansen 1987, pp. 42–49; Censimento della popolazione ... d'Italia, 1901, Volume V, p. xc.
63. Rapports annuels des inspecteurs de fabriques. Année 1911, p. 27.
64. Bull 1982; Martinson 1992, pp. 92–93; Rahikainen 2001b.
65. Quoted in Bjurman and Olsson 1979, p. 55.
66. Bahamonde and Martínez 1994, p. 480; Dubert 1999; Perrot 1997, p. 85.
67. Olsson, L. 1980, p. 50; Hansen 1987, pp. 31, 36–49.
68. Fuchs, S. 1981, pp. 107–112.
69. Andersen 1985, pp. 66, 169; Christensen, J.P. 2002, p. 78 and Appendix table II.7; Johansen 1988, pp. 20–23, 63–66, 106–108, 338.
70. Fellman and Hjerppe 2001; Nikula 1962, pp. 38–40; Olsson, L. 1980, pp. 55–61, 81–85, 119–120.
71. Eklof 1986, pp. 372–374.
72. I have presumed that in the Russian statistics for the years 1910 and 1914 included in the *Rapports annuels des inspecteurs de fabriques* (*Svod otchetov fabrichnykh inspektorov*) 1912 and 1915, children employed in the sub-category 'd' of chemical industries (*d*) *Industries non compris dans les sous-groupes a, b, et c*) were, in fact, employed in the match industry, since also in French industrial statistics, evidently used as models for the Russian ones, match production (*allumettes chimiques*) was included in the chemical industry.
73. Judging from the fact that, up to 1888, matchboxes were made by male inmates in the workhouse of Stockholm (Müller 1906, p. 375).
74. Hansen 1987, pp. 36, 46–49; Olsson, L. 1980, pp. 61–67, 122–129; Rahikainen 2001a; Rahikainen 2001b.
75. Quoted in Peikert 1986, p. 207.
76. Hyldtoft 1991, p. 204.
77. Quoted in Bjurman and Olsson 1979, pp. 68–69, 75.
78. Rapports annuels des inspecteurs de fabriques. Année 1911, pp. x, 27.
79. Bjurman 1979, pp. 28–29; Hansen 1987, pp. 43–49; Johansen 1988, pp. 28–30; Locke, R.R. 1984, p. 69; Olsson, L. 1980, pp. 68–77, 129–132; Peikert 1986; Perrot 1997, p. 84; Pierrard 1987, pp. 10, 70–75, 83–84; Rahikainen 1995b; Sigsgaard 1995, p. 64; Tugan-Baranovsky 1970 [1907], p. 332.
80. E.g. Rahikainen 2001a; Standing 1982.
81. Devreese 1999.

82. Boje 2000, Tabel 1; Cassis 1997, pp. 123–142; Caron 1997; Colli and Rose 1999; Fellman 2001, p. 149; Genovesi 1998, pp. 80, 106–112; Heywood 1992, pp. 54–57; Kaelble 1979; Kocka 1979; Locke, R.R. 1984, p. 35; Palacio Atard 1988, pp. 316–325; Pollard 1968, pp. 104–105, 150, 157; Schlumbohm 1983, pp. 309–312; Torstendahl 1979.

83. Casson 1999, p. 16.

84. Hansen 1987, p. 103; Heywood 1992, pp. 59, 195–202, 297–298; Locke, R.R. 1984, pp. 30–34, 58–65; Pollard 1968, pp. 180–181.

85. Kahan 1989, pp. 174, 238.

86. Boje 2000, Tabel 2; Bruland 1989, pp. 56–68; Bruland 1991; Bruland 1998; Jansson 1990, pp. 27–30, 45–53, 72, 141–146; Fellman 2001, pp. 80, 91; Parmer 1991; Strømstad 1991.

87. Anderson, M. 1971, p. 23; Guereña 1996, p. 370; Heywood 1988, pp. 128–129, 234; Nardinelli 1980; Perrot 1997; Pierrard 1987, p. 53; Pollard 1968, pp. 185–189. See also Adolphs 1972, p. 20; Adsuar Moreno 1916, pp. 4–5; Dupin 1840, p. LIX; Friedländer 1887, p. 12 (on Italy); Hoppe 1958, pp. 70–75, 86; Villermé 1840a, pp. 11, 58, 70, 91, 96–97, 111, 121, 174, 193, 354, 395.

88. Anderson, M. 1971, p. 108; Hopkins 1994, pp. 132, 139; Pollard 1968, p. 179; Rose 2000, pp. 121–124.

89. Heywood 1988, pp. 204–207, quotations pp. 205–206; Pierrard 1987, pp. 42–48; Villermé 1840a, pp. 235, 239–240.

90. Daru and Bournat 1875, pp. 270–281; Dupin 1840, pp. XXIV–XXV; Heywood 1988, pp. 224–230, 240–241; Simon, J. 1875; Weissbach 1989, pp. 12, 63–83, 91–94, quotation p. 92; Villermé 1840b, pp. 124–125.

91. See Heywood 1981b; Pollard 1981, pp. 94–95, 139. Louis Villermé noted in the late 1830s that some manufacturers in the Nord had cut wages because of stagnating business or changes in production (Villermé 1840a, pp. 91–95, 111).

92. Caspard 1998; Heywood 1988, pp. 287–299; Weissbach 1989, p. 221.

93. Albertini 1996, pp. 94–113; Cives 1994; Genovesi 1998, pp. 40–54, 69–70, 84–91; Roggero 1999, pp. 121–126, 140–149.

94. Barbagli 1982, pp. 74–75.

95. Guereña 1996, pp. 351–362; Molinas and Prados de la Escosura 1989; Tiana Ferrer 1996, quotation p. 653, Tortella 2000, pp. 46–49, quotation p. 47.

96. Hansen 1987, pp. 15–23, 106–116. See also Adolphs 1972, pp. 59–61; Meyer 1971, pp. 139–148.

97. Giffin 1967; Giffin 1977; Kahan 1989, pp. 169–175; Tugan-Baranovsky 1970 [1907], pp. 312–325.

98. Gatrell 1986, pp. 161–162; Kahan 1989, pp. 177–178.

99. Eklof 1986, pp. 97–105, quotation p. 99.

100. Boli 1989, pp. 214–248; Kirby 1995, p. 147; Myllyntaus 1990; Nilsson 1999; Nilsson and Pettersson 1990; O'Rourke and Williamson 1995; Sandin 1997.

101. Christensen, J.P. 2002, pp. 77–80; Sigsgaard 1995, p. 63.

102. Bull 1982, p. 226; Dokka 1967, p. 289.

103. Rahikainen 2002b; Sandin 1997. See also Betänkande 1877, pp. 95–98.

104. Quoted in Bjurman and Olsson 1979, p. 70.

105. Rahikainen 1996, p. 326; Rahikainen 2001b; Rahikainen 2002b.

106. According to the statistics, the Lombardian cotton industry employed 1,176 children (most likely underreported) in 1854, 3,130 in 1876, 6,968 (1,650 boys, 5,318 girls) in 1896, 9,307 (1,621 boys, 7,686 girls) in 1903, and 12,400 (2,271 boys, 10,129 girls) in 1911. The proportion of children of the total labour force was 30.9%, 19.4%, 17.5%, 15.9% and 20.2%, respectively (Romano 1992, Tables 35–39).

107. Barbagli 1982, pp. 77–78.

108. Borrás Llop 1999, pp. 34–35.

109. Borrás Llop 1995, pp. 636–639.

110. Eklof 1986, pp. 371–375, 384, quotation pp. 371–372.

111. In 1901, girls comprised 1.9% of the female and boys 1.1% of the male labour force in St Petersburg, 2.4% and 2% in Moscow, and 3% and 1.6% in the whole of the Empire, respectively. In 1911 girls comprised 2% of the female and boys 1.2% of the male labour force in the whole of the Empire. Children comprised 1.4% of the total industrial labour force in 1910 and 1.6% in 1914. (Svod otchetov fabrichnykh inspektorov za 1901 god, pp. 34–35; Rapports annuels des inspecteurs de fabriques. Année 1911, pp. LII, 27; Année 1914, p. XLIII.)

112. Eklof 1986, p. 384.

113. For laws, see Agahd 1904 (Germany, the law of 1903); Bjurman 1979 (Sweden, 1900); Bull 1982 (Norway, 1892); Christensen, J.P. 2002, p. 81 (Denmark, 1873); Giffin 1977 (Russia, 1884); Guereña 1996, p. 370 (Spain, 1873, 1878, 1900); Hansen 1987, pp. 23–25 (Schleswig-Holstein, 1813–1857, Germany, 1878); Bertoni Jovine 1963, pp. 71, 92–93 (Italy, 1886, 1902); Mathias 1995, pp. 182–3 (Britain); Rahikainen 2001b (Finland, 1889); Ritter and Tenfelde 1992, pp. 200–201 (Germany, 1869, 1891); Sandin 1997 (Sweden, 1881); Tugan-Baranovsky 1970 [1907], p. 332 (Russia, 1890); Weissbach 1989, pp. 231–247 (France, 1841, 1851, 1874).

114. Dupin 1840, pp. LVIII–LXI; Reybaud 1856, pp. 119–121; Villermé 1840b, pp. 114–122.

115. Hopkins 1994, pp. 34, 59–60, 223, quotation p. 36.

116. Bolin-Hort 1989, pp. 226–236; Hendrick 1992, quotations pp. 49, 51.

117. Tugan-Baranovsky 1970 [1907], pp. 320–333, quotations pp. 321, 326, 331–332; Rapports annuels des inspecteurs de fabriques. Annèe 1911, p. x. See also Giffin 1977.

118. Betänkande 1892, pp. 86–87, 119; Bjurman 1979; European Historical Statistics, Table E13; Jörberg 1994. The royal degree exempted mining (iron ore), metalworking, sawmills and timberyards.

119. Cohen 2002. Until 1930 children under sixteen comprised six to 14 per cent of all employees found in the medical examination records (that is between seven and 17 for every 100 adults).

120. Chiri 1908 (repr. 1990), p. 81; Guidi 1999, p. 857.

121. Borrás Llop 1995, pp. 632–641.

122. Adsuar Moreno 1916, pp. 5, 19–36, quotation p. 4. In apprenticeship contracts the minimum age was thirteen, in dangerous works it varied from twelve to sixteen.

123. Rahikainen 2001b.

124. Agahd 1904; Bierer 1913, pp. 22, 34, 126–129 and passim; Deutsch 1907, pp. 154–159; Ritter and Tenfelde 1992, p. 201; Quataert 1985.

125. Heywood 1981a, p. 34.

126. Heywood 1981a, p. 34.

127. Cunningham, H. 2000, quotations p. 415.

128. E.g. Giffin 1977; Heywood 1988, pp. 273–280, 287–298; Hopkins 1994, pp. 94–95, 219–220, 258, 316, 320; Weissbach 1989, pp. 161–179, 213–225.
129. Weiner 1991, p. 191.
130. Cunningham, H. 1996, p. 43.
131. Perrot 1997, p. 76.
132. Cunningham, H. 2000, p. 419.
133. Horrell and Humphries 1995; Horrell and Oxley 1999.
134. Crafts and Mills 1994; Feinstein 1991; Holley 1981; Horrell and Humphries 1992; Nardinelli 1980; Nardinelli 1990, p. 8 and passim. See also Bolin-Hort 1989, pp. 102–106.
135. Horrell and Humphries 1999, p. 89.
136. Nardinelli 1980, p. 753.
137. Examples of the parallel treatment of women and children in the legislation are to be found, for example, in Adolphs 1972, pp. 79, 82 (Germany); Betänkande 1877, pp. 13, 25, 74, 87, 113 (Sweden); Borrás Llop 1996, pp. 256, 273 (Spain); Bertoni Jovine 1963, p. 117 (Italy); Chiri 1908 (repr. 1990), pp. 11, 53 (Italy); Genovesi 1998, p. 85 (Italy); Giffin 1977 (Russia); Weissbach 1989, pp. 240–241 (France).
138. Olsson, L. 1980, passim, quotations from the English abstract. A synopsis of Olsson's arguments is in Sandin 1997.
139. Craig and Fisher 1992; Rahikainen 2001b; Ritter and Tenfelde 1992, p. 201; Williamson 1995.
140. Postel-Vinay 1994, pp. 74–75.
141. E.g. Saul 1989, pp. 34–69.
142. For the Berlin conference, see, e.g., Bertoni Jovine 1963, pp. 83–84.
143. Heywood 2001, pp. 121–122, 129–134; Hendrick 1994, pp. 24–27, 67–74.

CHAPTER 5

The Urban Labour Market for Children

Children and labour migration

Until the early twentieth century the population of urban conglomerations grew only because of migration, as natural growth was checked by a high mortality rate. This suggests that, to a great extent, the urban child labour force was made up of migrant children and first-generation city children. Therefore this history of urban child labour begins with children who migrated with or without their parents, and who had to adapt at once to a new job and a new urban environment, sometimes even to a new language.

Behind migration often lay sheer necessity, but also higher wages attracted young people from agriculture to urban and industrial occupations of easy entry, such as general labouring and domestic service. Young men from small manufacturing centres left to try their luck in larger ones. Country girls in central and southern Europe left for the mill or the city in order to save for a dowry, whereas this was hardly ever the reason in Scandinavia. For many juveniles migration indicated emancipation. Labour migration also attracted middlemen who saw the chance of doing business. Migration was facilitated in the nineteenth century by the coming of railways and steam ships.[1]

In early modern Europe, young apprentices migrated over long distances, perhaps alone but more safely in the company of journeymen. From the sixteenth to the nineteenth centuries, young chimney-sweeps from Savoy travelled in England and, with the king's approval, in France. They not only swept chimneys by climbing up the flues, but also entertained passers-by in London and Paris with hurdy-gurdies, marmots and magic-lantern shows.[2] Many children and young teenagers travelled without their parents, or lived precariously as vagabonds, perhaps having been orphaned or abandoned. In February 1629, an unknown boy, aged about twelve, was found drowned in Malalbergo, Italy, and the body of a still younger unknown boy was found in the river, and in June 1630 an unknown boy, aged about fourteen and dressed in black, was found dead in a ditch.[3]

Labour migration undertaken in the traditional way by walking long distances could be arduous for the young. Martin Nadaud, 'Léonard', a peasant boy from Bourganeuf in the region of Creuse, France, set out northwards for Paris with his father and other village men in March 1830. He had taken his first communion the previous spring, and now, at the age of fifteen, left for the first time for seasonal construction work in the capital. His friends started eastwards for Lyon (where they would face premature death as poor, young construction workers). Martin found parting from his friends and family painful, and the long journey became a veritable trial. His father pressed their small company to hurry in order to arrive in Paris before other labour migrants from Creuse, so after a day of walking they continued in the moonlight. By then young Martin could no longer keep on his feet, and one of the village men took to carrying his small bundle. After walking some 60 kilometres, they stopped to rest. Martin's feet were torn and bleeding. Having covered more than three hundred kilometres on foot, they reached Paris. Martin found lodging with his uncle, and started work as a hand for masons making a garden wall. He lacked the necessary physical strength, occasionally falling with the loads he was made to carry. He was teased by some fellow workers for his clothes and cap, and crying with anger and rage, he took to fighting. If he earned the standard wage of an apprentice, he was paid 1.80 francs a day, while his father, a skilled mason, was probably paid 3.50 francs or so.[4]

Being forced to leave home alone and against one's will was hard for a child. This happened to Hulda, a peasant girl from an island in the Åland archipelago, in the northern Baltic Sea, at the turn of the twentieth century. A friend had arranged a servant's post for her in Stockholm. Carrying a small bundle with her clothes in it, at the age of fourteen she left alone for Stockholm, where she had never been before. Her mother rowed her the eight kilometres to the main island and walked with her to Mariehamn where the ship waited. When the ship was about to leave, Hulda wept and begged to be allowed to stay at home. Explaining that there was no food at home, her mother had to force her daughter to depart. The daughter left crying, and the mother cried all the long way back home.[5]

In Britain there was a tradition of boys leaving for manufacturing districts at the age of twelve or even earlier. However, most young people who migrated to Preston in Lancashire, for example, were evidently over fourteen, and the majority of the younger ones arrived with their parents. In 1851 there were 139 migrant children aged ten to fourteen in Preston, but only 16 of them did not live with their parents. They lived either in lodging houses or with relatives, while a few were living-in apprentices.[6] According to

J.W. Walton, adult migrants to the cotton towns in north-west England rarely worked in factories, unless they had previous experience. 'Only children and young adolescents were likely to make both sets of adjustments at once.'[7]

Mills and factories built dormitories to attract young, single workers. There were convent-like dormitories for lone young female silk workers in the French Midi. The first such *internat* for girls from the age of twelve up was established in 1835. They housed 40,000 girls and young women in 1860, some 100,000 in 1900. Recruitment was confined to mountainous areas, where girls were evidently brought up to be even more docile and resigned, and less demanding, than elsewhere in the French countryside. The austere discipline under the supervision of nuns ensured regular work habits.[8]

Dormitories for lone factory children were also known in Finland. Finlayson, the largest cotton mill in Finland, paid girls aged under fifteen less than they charged for their board and lodging in the mill's dormitory. In the case of lone girls aged over fifteen, the mill saved for them what was left of their wage after their rent. The girls had their earnings withheld by the mill the day they left the dormitory, which was usually the year they turned eighteen. Lone migrant child workers who had no place in the dormitory lodged in working-class households. After paying the landlord the rent, and giving the mill the money towards the relief fund and any fines imposed on them by foremen, they had just enough left of their wages to make in the market their Saturday purchases of a large loaf of rye bread and salted Baltic herrings, the two staples of the poor, on which to live the following week.[9] Lone migrant children in textile mills were seldom if ever able to contribute to the family budget back home, except by staying away.

Similarly, children in Sweden were invited to leave alone for factories. In the 1850s, a match factory in Kalmar announced in a newspaper that if parents would let their children come to work in the factory, the employer would provide them with clothing from top to toe for their confirmation. The authorities sent begging children to work in this match factory. The managers of another match factory, also facing difficulties in recruiting child workers, came to the conclusion that parents in the countryside would not send their children to work in the factory unless the employer gave them their meals and assisted them in finding lodgings.[10]

Russian manufacturers used travelling agents to recruit workers. In spring 1859, when the spinning departments were already running, the half-finished Krenholm cotton mill in Narva sent an agent to Finland to recruit children aged between ten and twelve. However, the annual wage he promised, 10 to 13 silver roubles, was less than Finnish cotton mills paid.[11] In the early 1880s Victor Tissot, a Western traveller visiting Kiev, was told that girls and women from the countryside were recruited for the factories by an agent who travelled from one village to another and chose the most robust and healthy-looking ones. Tissot watched barefoot factory girls leaving work for supper in the canteen of the large refinery of Demiewka. Living in the factory dormitories, male and female workers were provided with board and lodging by the employer. Working twelve hours a day, men earned between 10 and 25 roubles a month, women nine to ten roubles, and children, 'employed for easy work', six to seven roubles.[12]

The most attractive destination for Russian migrating children and juveniles was St Petersburg, while Moscow was second best. St Petersburg was one of the largest cities in Europe around 1850, and its consumer and labour markets drew people from far and near.[13] At the turn of the twentieth century, Olga Semyonova asked a village youngster why country boys were so eager to leave for Moscow, and was told the following: 'It seems to me that many of them go there for clothes, too. Here you go around in the same old rags winter and summer, but in town you can get decent clothes and shoes. Why, the way they look when they come back from town, we can't even stand next to them.'[14] The call of the metropolis for Russian juveniles was in the late nineteenth century described as follows:

> It is not only the wages that attract the parents (who send their children to St. Petersburg to apprentice a trade), but also the relative lightness of work in the capital ... Many boys themselves implore their parents to send them to Peter[sburg]. It even happens that parents, against their own desires, send a son away in order to avoid severe reproaches and quarrels later. Several times I happened to hear adolescents complain about their parents not sending them off to Peter early enough. Generally, the local youths here very willingly go to Peter.[15]

Semën Kanatchikov, a peasant's son from a village near Moscow, would also have liked to leave for the metropolis at the age of fourteen, but had turned sixteen before his father let him go in 1895. The father drove the boy by cart to Moscow, and before returning to the village the next morning arranged cheap accommodation and a job in an engineering workshop for him. Left alone, the boy felt abandoned and near to tears. The skilled workers in the workshop looked down on him, pinched him in the ear, pulled him by the hair and called him by insulting names. The twelve-hour working day made him terribly tired, so despite bedbugs and fleas he slept like a log once he fell on the filthy, hard, straw-filled sack that served as his bed.[16] Unlike his elder brother who remained in the village and inherited the farm, Semën, by his departure, which cost him so dear, seized for himself an 'individualised destiny' (L.P. Moch), becoming a revolutionary.

Russian country girls who became domestic servants in urban households were cut loose from any community and had to stand on their own feet, which promoted individualisation as well, whereas those who became factory workers remained members of a collective. Girls, as a rule, did not leave the village before they were fourteen, but even this was rare, since women seldom migrated before they had turned twenty.[17] This appears to have been a more general trend. For example, in the early nineteenth century, the median age at which the young country women migrating to Sundsvall, a small town on the northern Swedish coastline, left home for service for the first time was sixteen to seventeen, but they were generally aged well over twenty before moving to the town.[18] Similarly, in the period 1850–1866, the great majority of newly arrived servants in Frankfurt were aged sixteen or more: two thirds of the female servants were found in the 16–24 age group, while only about seven per cent, and about three per cent of male servants, were aged under sixteen.[19]

Children who migrated without their parents were vulnerable to unscrupulous middlemen. In nineteenth-century Finland, enterprising men in carts travelled around the countryside purchasing children for the St Petersburg labour market. Even the vicar of the coastal city of Vyborg, about 100 kilometres north-west of St Petersburg, provided a manufacturer in the city with Finnish children. Some of these children ran away and returned back home. The deserters evidently said that they had been treated badly, because the Finnish Passport Office in St Petersburg made enquiries at the factory, but the children who stayed did not complain. In the 1870s, Finnish migrant children in St Petersburg were reported to be making their living mainly by begging or factory work, while many girls ended up in prostitution.[20]

Around the mid-nineteenth century, 'exploited begging children' in France were said to be mainly foreigners, those in Paris to be Italian, and those in Lyon children from the mountains. Once in Lyon or Paris, young Italian children sharing a lodging dispersed every morning around the city to beg, and returned during the night with their earnings. Their masters were said to stay in France only over the agricultural dead season, returning to Italy with their earnings in the spring. It was also said that these children paid 20 to 30 francs to their masters for taking them to France. Indignant French citizens claimed that such a 'school of vagrancy and theft' must be closed, and 'the odious trade of these foreigners' must be stopped from providing 'disastrous models to our poor'.[21]

Italian migrant children were found in many cities all over Europe. John Zucchi tracked the origin of this traffic in Italian children to the end of the

Napoleonic Wars. He argues that the post-war economic depression gave the incentive for peasant parents in impoverished mountain areas to indenture boys and girls to a labour agent or a master. Some children, mostly boys, but occasionally girls, worked as helpers of travelling craftsmen, such as stone cutters. Those who became street entertainers were led by their masters, *padroni*, 'on foot from small towns and villages in the Duchy of Parma and from the district of Liguria in the province of Genoa to London, Paris and beyond'. Many children were taken over the Atlantic to New York and Rio de Janeiro, for instance. The young entertainers in the streets were at first exhibitors of small animals, and later on they played an instrument, such as a street organ or a harp, occasionally a violin or fife, or the bagpipes. Passers-by gave money because they pitied such children. Zucchi estimates that at the height of the trade in the late 1860s and early 1870s, there were about 3,000 to 6,000 Italian child musicians around the world. Italian laws of 1844 and 1852 banned children from the street music trade, while Italian consular representatives on both sides of the Atlantic expressed concern about the number of young street musicians. Only the Italian consul in St Petersburg 'did not see the presence of child organists in the streets as a problem'. He successfully appealed to the municipal authorities of St Petersburg to permit the *padroni* with their child performers to stay in the city.[22]

Overseas migration by children was deliberately promoted by the authorities in some countries. In 1750, people in Paris revolted against the rulers and the police, accusing them of abducting their children. It was believed that the kidnapped children, aged from five years up were sent to populate the French colonies in North America. The idea of compulsory emigration had been there for some decades, and proved attractive even later on. Napoleon promoted the colonisation of newly-acquired Algeria with *enfants assistés*, and again in the 1860s, the French government considered sending pauper children to colonise Algeria.[23] The British authorities sent children to the colonies: Australia, the Cape in South Africa, Canada and New Zealand. There was not much difference in the procedure between the transportation of convicted children and the state emigration of poor or workhouse children. Australia, short of women, wanted girls as servants. In the Cape, boys were wanted for cattle herding, which had been the work of older slaves before the emancipation, but which nobody was willing to do now. Most of the children sent to the colonies were evidently apprenticed as servants or labourers. Some faced harsh treatment from their masters, being flogged for trivial offences.[24]

The authorities in early twentieth-century Europe grew increasingly anxious about labour migration and migration in general. The traffic in women and children was one of the concerns of the first International Labour Conference, for example.[25] Similarly, present-day historical writing on labour migration highlights the hazards faced by migrants.[26] These and the sad stories of forced labour migration by children were one side of the coin. On the other side there were country children and adolescents for whom migration to the city was rather like grasping an opportunity not available at home.

Working in sight: children in the street

Boys and girls in search of coins were a familiar sight in the streets of rapidly growing nineteenth-century cities. Like their present-day counterparts, children in the street and public places may have been truly deprived, or just ordinary working-class children who saw the street as their rightful environment for work and play. Their very visible activities drew much negative reaction from the better-off, and made the authorities intervene in the form of heavy-handed measures, including compulsory work. In present-day historical writing, such reactions appear disproportionate to the deeds, while children in the streets of working-class neighbourhoods are considered to have had several functions in the community networks.[27] The encounter between children in the street and the authorities and others controlling them is discussed below with the help of two kinds of examples, first, children who were regarded as street children, and second, those who engaged in money-making activities out of school hours or after leaving school.

There was much learned rhetoric about the importance of the family for the child in nineteenth-century western Europe, but in practice the authorities do not seem to have had any scruples about separating working-class children from their families. According to Anna Davin, the authorities in London responsible for outdoor relief would commonly tell a widow with young children that 'some must go to the workhouse, on the grounds that she would not be able to manage with more than one or two'. Even charitable bodies provided relief only on condition that some of the children were sent to orphanages. Hostility to the workhouse was widespread, thus, 'neighbours would try to protect children from being sent there by providing temporary refuge'. Impoverished mothers endured privations rather than give up their children. Under such circumstances there was a use for every penny that the children might come by.[28] Nonetheless, in the end mothers were still liable to lose their children to a reformatory or industrial school, since many of the ways in which children tried to get some money were regarded as offences.

On the streets of London, children of the very poor sold low-priced wares, swept mud from street crossings, at times combining this work with acrobatic tumbling, or they performed small services in order to get some coins. They delivered newspapers, milk or bread, and ran errands. When out of school, one south London boy used to collect a sackful of broken-up wood from flower boxes at Covent Garden, and then walk to Tenison Street to sell it to households for twopence. Children frequenting the streets may have belonged to households, have paid for their lodging, or have slept rough like the homeless. Sometimes they stole apples and oranges, brass buttons, purses, fuel for their home, or whatever was useful or saleable. If they were caught, children charged with an offence risked being sentenced to prison, flogging or transportation, or later on being sent to reformatory or industrial schools.[29]

In the 1820s and 1830s the *gamins* of Paris had, as Colin Heywood writes, 'a quick eye for the little services required by those with money in their pockets. The commercial sector provided jobs as messengers, delivery boys and street traders. The rich could be tapped an odd coin by opening carriage doors … the public at large by street singing, acrobatics and travelling circuses'.[30] However, such skills were not appreciated by the authorities who applied the severe laws forbidding begging to 'small vagabonds'. According to a law of 1850, all detained juveniles were to be sentenced to agricultural work, although in practice industrial work was also used. It was estimated that there were about 10,000 *vagabonds* aged between ten and sixteen in Paris in the 1870s. In 1876, the police arrested a total of 1,754 boys and girls, of whom 302 were returned to their families, while the rest were presented as children in need of preventive measures, meaning industrial school. The agricultural colony of Mettray, near Tours, opened in 1840, housed almost exclusively urban children and youth.[31] Mettray was widely imitated. H. Kylberg, the head of the new Swedish agricultural colony of Hall, visited it in 1875. He was critical of the too-large 'families' (each with 40 boys), for example, but fully agreed with the use of prison punishment and the principle of education through hard work.[32]

Deprived Spanish children from seven years up were sent to beg alone in the early nineteenth century. Nonetheless, the majority of the some 800 'urchins' (*golfos*), as they were called in Madrid, were adolescents aged between fourteen and eighteen. Children engaged in any activities on the streets were readily seen as potential delinquents and risked being treated as such. The Spanish Penal Code of 1822 lowered the minimum age for being regarded as delinquent to seven years (it was raised to nine years in 1848) from the previous ten or twelve for girls and fourteen for boys in cases of indecency. New kinds of penal institutions for juveniles included agricultural colonies, while a separate prison department, with a school and a workshop, remained the only 'reformatory school' for the rest of the century.[33]

A new charity institution, Allunato dell'Annunziata, was established in Naples in 1840 for deprived and abandoned children aged between five and seven. The institution frequently placed children in fosterage in or out of the city, and it was self-evident that boarded-out children of tender years were set to work. When they turned seven they were moved to the poor house, Albergo dei poveri, to learn a trade. The Annunziata also acted as a foundling home, with a *ruota*, a revolving, windowlike aperture in the building. According to a stipulation from 1739, only children who were delivered through the *ruota* were entitled to care in the foundling hospice. Thus porters in neighbouring streets specialised in pressing children aged between eight and ten, and sometimes as old as eleven, through the small, quadrangular mouth of the *ruota*. The children were oiled or greased to make their passage easier, but many of them had broken bones when they came through.[34] These children were a living witness of desperate urban poverty.

In Russia urban poverty was extensive but at first street children do not seem to have caused moral alarm. Around 1840, J.G. Kohl, a German traveller, spent time watching children earning coins in the haymarket in St Petersburg. He wrote that, between the rows of heaps of hay, 'poor women and little girls and boys creep ... to sweep up with little brooms and collect in their aprons the scattered halms ... As soon as they have gleaned a mouthful for a horse, they run with it to the street to dispose of it to the iswoschtschiks [droshkies], and to earn a mouthful for themselves'. In the evenings he saw coachmen's outriders in front of theatres, 'boys no more than twelve years old, who have not yet learned to keep awake till midnight, sit dozing upon their horses, or, twisting the bridle round their arm, stretch themselves on the frozen snow of the street-pavement'.[35] Perhaps at that time the aristocratic establishment in Russia still felt less threatened by the hordes of urban poor than the bourgeois establishment in Western Europe. By 1880 reformatory schools had been introduced in Russia. In his childhood memories, Maxim Gorky (Aleksei Peshkov) wrote about his friend Kostroma who, at the age of thirteen, 'hung himself in a home for juvenile delinquents to which he had been sent for stealing a pair of pigeons'.[36]

Maxim Gorky, or Aleksei, was about ten when he began to earn money in the late 1870s in Nijni Novgorod: 'Early Sunday mornings I would take a sack and go through the streets and yards collecting old bones, rags, nails, and paper. The junkman would pay us twenty kopeks a pood for rags or paper or metal, and eight or ten kopeks a pood for bones. I collected junk after school during the week as well, and every Saturday I earned from thirty to fifty kopeks (or even more if it had been a particularly successful week).' He gave the kopeks to his grandmother who maintained them by making bobbin lace. However, Aleksei and his friends (the ten-year-old son of a Mordovian beggarwoman, a twelve-year-old Tatar boy, the eight-year-old son of a gravedigger, the son of a widowed seamstress, and 'the waif Kostroma') made their best earnings by selling boards and poles that they stole from a lumberyard. When he turned eleven, Aleksei was employed in a shop.[37]

In Western Europe, as well as in Russia, there was good reason for children to earn money and to find work out of school hours and right after leaving school. Many families had difficulties making ends meet, and children's earnings were needed. Moreover, for the children themselves, the little extra they earned may have been the only money over which they could decide for themselves.

Compared to the Russian boys above, a twelve-year-old German boy, Paul Löbe, a future politician, had more and better options for earning money in Freiburg during the 1880s. He was employed as an errand boy in a shoe shop, but he also delivered bread in the morning before school, in between doing some shoe polishing, delivering newspapers in the evening, carrying travellers' suitcases in the railway station, and dragging around 50-kilo sacks of coal for a coal trader in the house in which his family lived. In addition, he was expected to do home-industry work in the evening (see below). It is no wonder that sleep was the most scarce commodity for a boy of his age.[38] However, Aleksei and his friends did have their counterparts in Scandinavia. In Stockholm, where begging children were still a common sight in the 1890s, empty bottles, iron scrap and bones could be changed into money, which children then used to buy candy or food for themselves. Occasionally boys stole items of little value from stalls and stands, something they could easily pawn or sell. The police kept an eye on poor-looking boys, and many of them were caught and brought to the police station. Pompous reports were then drawn up and catalogued on 'criminal minors' who had stolen, say, a few apples, pins, empty bottles, a piece of soap or at most a pullover, as Eva-Lis Bjurman sarcastically puts it. Parents and teachers were informed, and corporal punishment awaited at school. If the teacher was also otherwise discontented with the boy, a sentence to a reformatory loomed large.[39]

Anecdotal information suggests that in Danish towns and cities, even children aged seven or eight might succeed in getting part-time work out of school hours as errand boys or girls, as assistants (doing floor sweeping, for instance) in bakeries, retail-trade shops, laundries, and the like. Some even managed to become milk-deliverers who were usually expected to have reached the age of ten. In Aarhus, Denmark, Alfred Jensen (born in 1903) delivered newspapers in his neighbourhood, starting on weekdays at four o'clock in the morning, and on Sundays two or three hours later. He earned 1.75 crowns, of which he kept 25 øre for himself and took 1.50 crowns home. Many girls were part-time child minders or domestic servants. In 1889, one ten-year-old girl, Elvine, went every morning before school to a widowed lady's home. Her job was to light a fire in the tiled stoves and polish footwear, and in the afternoon, after school hours, she was expected to wash the floor and windows and scrub the kitchen table white.[40]

According to a small-scale survey, conducted in Kristiania (Oslo) in Norway around the turn of the twentieth century, covering some 30 working-class boys and 20 girls, only one of the boys had not worked before confirmation. Most of them had their first jobs at the age of twelve or thirteen, and the youngest one had started around the age of seven doing part-time work in a factory. Six boys delivered or sold newspapers, two were errand boys, one did shoe polishing, and seven had garden work, while the rest worked in factories. Half of some 20 working-class girls had work outside of the home, seven in a factory, two as errand girls, one as a maid-of-all-work, and three had garden work. In general, factory work was more rare in Norway than running errands was for boys and child minding for girls. Much of girls' work consisted of unpaid child care and household work, since they were more likely than boys to avoid paid work before confirmation.[41]

A Swedish inquiry on children's work out of school hours found that, in Stockholm, children delivered newspapers to subscribers' homes early in the morning, before school hours. They started at five or six o'clock, running up and down staircases until it was time to get to school for eight o'clock. The school day lasted until one o'clock in the afternoon, and many children then had another job. Delivering newspapers and selling printed matter, flowers and haberdashery in the streets or in public places or premises before eight o'clock in the morning and after eight o'clock in the evening had been prohibited in Stockholm since 1891 for children under fifteen.[42]

A corresponding Finnish inquiry in 1906, covering some 20,000 children in public primary schools in the four largest cities, found that the great majority of children had no paid work out of school hours. Only 14 per cent of school boys aged under fifteen and six per cent of school girls of the same age had work away from home, while less than three per cent of boys and girls worked in home industries.

Children who did work had very little free time and slept fewer hours than other schoolchildren. Those with paid work did less well at school, but contrary to what one might expect, girls did better than boys, with or without paid work. Many children were paid in food only, girls more often than boys. Delivering newspapers to subscribers' homes was about equally common among boys and girls, while boys were more likely to have jobs carrying shopping and other goods to customers' homes. A third of boys and a tenth of girls with work away from home sold newspapers or, less often, cigarettes, candy, shoe laces, postcards and the like, on the streets. Such forms of child labour were known throughout Europe, as were most of the more miscellaneous jobs reported by Finnish children:

> Rowing, fishing, assisting in handwork and handicraft, assisting in selling food, cutting firewood and carrying it in schoolrooms or in a workhouse, taking care of other's children, tending other's livestock and helping in agriculture, picking and selling berries, carrying out bread, milk and food, cleaning up or serving in other people's homes, cleaning up railway wagons, assisting in a barber's shop, assisting in a restaurant, working as a pin boy in a bowling alley, delivering advertisements and theatre programmes, hunting rats, looking after the graves, helping the blind in going out and in selling their products, assisting artisan masters in scribal work, carrying out bills, delivering clean or ironed laundry, delivering mail, working as a message boy or girl, carting loads, lighting of lamps, working as a hand in the harbour and other places, carrying up bricks and mortar in building places, 'taking out a gentleman's dog'.[43]

The Finnish inquiry showed a consistent and unambiguous relationship between the family background and the likelihood of work out of school hours. The children may, of course, have underreported their work activities – but given that there was no compulsory education they did not have pressing reasons for this – yet it is unlikely that any underreporting would have produced such consistent results. Virtually no children from a middle-class background, few in number in public primary schools, were engaged in any work out of school hours, and even among working-class children, the more regular the father's income, the more seldom the child had to work out of school hours. This held true even when the mother was the sole provider (5,900 cases). For example, six in twenty children of washer women, but only three in twenty of those of female factory workers, had work away from home out of school hours.[44] This is in line with what Jane Humphries found from British working-class autobiographies from the time of industrialisation.[45]

That the Finnish situation was in line with the British one is also implied in Arnold Freeman's survey on 'boy labour' in Birmingham in 1912. Freeman categorised the boys in his sample into 'Class I: Apparently Destined for Skilled Work; Class II, Apparently Destined for Unskilled Work; and Class III:

Apparently Destined for "Unemployables". Only six boys out of 71 qualified as 'first class'. Their fathers were skilled workers, and none of these 'superior' boys had been engaged in any employment when still at school.[46] This suggests that English boys from comfortable homes may have been less likely to have work out of school hours than other working-class boys.

To keep children off the streets, charitable organisations in Scandinavia established day work centres for school children (*arbetsstugor*). The first such centres were established in Denmark in the 1870s, followed in the 1880s by Norway, Sweden and Finland, where they were first called workhouses (*arbetshus*). Children working out of school hours in work centres earned the meals they were served there. Children in Sweden were occupied in making various kinds of brushes, baskets and toys for sale. For boys there was carpentry and metal work, for girls cooking. Children from the countryside in northern Sweden were boarded for the whole school term in urban *arbetsstugor*. Some historians have described such boarding in idyllic terms, while others have told a more dismal story, echoed in contemporary reports.[47] Entry into the Finnish *arbetshus* for primary-school children was voluntary and had to be applied for, but the attendance of those who were enrolled was controlled by daily roll calls and absence was reported to the children's guardians. In Helsinki a number of children 'at risk' were sentenced to spend their free time in an *arbetshus* for children. The work by girls consisted mainly of sewing, by boys of carpentry, tailoring and shoe repairing. An *arbetshus* in Helsinki served as a subcontractor for the match industry in the 1880s, and in one winter children made 31,000 matchboxes. The regulations forbade talking during meals and when working. Thus Martta Hellstedt – a widow's daughter and a future politician who attended an *arbetshus* in Helsinki in 1901–1905 – liked Wednesdays best. On Wednesdays children sat in the kitchen peeling potatoes for Thursday's soup, and there the housekeeper let them chat freely.[48]

Scandinavian work centres for children, remotely related to English industrial day schools and German *Arbeitsschule für Knaben*, shared the characteristics of many charity and disciplinary institutions of the time. As a rule, the training prepared children for a lowly social role, with a narrow range of occupational options – girls were taught sewing and domestic-service skills, boys tailoring, carpentry, basketmaking, rugmaking, shoemaking and repairing. Regardless of whether they were at an institution for the disabled, for the deprived or for the poor, children were forced to use out-of-date methods to make a narrow range of old-fashioned products (virtually the same irrespective of the country, and unmistakably recognised as charity work) that sold badly compared with commercial consumer goods.⁴⁹ The children themselves may have gained very little from the whole process.

Why, then, did the authorities and reformers choose such an outmoded range of products and poorly-paid skills? Was there a hidden curriculum to depress or discourage urban children 'with a quick eye', in order to keep them from later taking better opportunities from under the noses of less inventive middle-class youth? This would be in line with the fact that reformatories and other such institutions seldom provided children with more than the minimum curriculum of compulsory education. In any case, the authorities' ideas of suitable work for these children did not conform with the jobs they sought and found in the open labour market. Reminiscences of urban working-class childhood support the overall impression that the jobs children did away from home were at best exciting, at worst dangerous, but in any case had some variety. As such, they were the very opposite of the deadly boring and monotonous work children performed in sweated trades or outworkers in putting-out industries.

The extent of child labour in agricultural colonies, reformatories and in day industrial schools and work centres proves that the authorities and reformers saw work as a prime preventive or corrective measure concerning children on the streets. This undermines the plausibility of the kind of argument suggesting that child labour became regarded as a social evil because it did not conform to the new sensitivity towards children, or to the new ideal of a 'proper' or 'normal' childhood.

Out of sight: workshops and putting-out work

Much of urban child labour was carried out indoors, out of sight, in small workshops and in homes as putting-out, or outwork. We could presume that, while industrial child labour decreased in mills and factories, some of it returned via the back door in homes and tiny workshops – too small to be included in the industrial statistics. The use of children in urban putting-out and sweated trades seemed to raise relatively little concern on the part of the authorities. Yet there is nothing to suggest that this kind of work was any lighter than children's work in public places or factories. Urban home industries and small workshops in fact involved long working hours and low pay for women and children.

'As soon as a product came to be made for a mass market, its manufacture was liable to become sweated' (L.D. Schwarz). In early-eighteenth-century London low-paid labour by women and children was prevalent in several trades, such as clothing and shoe manufacturing. The falling prices of cotton and wool yarn in the nineteenth century, for instance, made the great expansion of the clothing business possible. According to the 1851 census of London, 17 per cent of girls aged between ten and fourteen with an occupation were engaged in needlework. Many crafts had little to offer in the second half of the century.[50] Traditional routes from apprentice to journeyman to master artisan had long been in decline, even though corporate traditions and legislation survived in France, Germany and Sweden long into the nineteenth century. Around 1820 in Sweden apprentices constituted just cheap labour for masters, corporate rules notwithstanding, but few of them were children. For example, less than a tenth of those in Malmö in southern Sweden were aged under fifteen. About ten per cent of journeymen progressed to master each year. Nonetheless, the number of life-long journeymen was small due to the constant flow of apprentices and journeyman away from the trade. In the London drapery trade, however, the costs of entry made it unlikely that assistants would be able to start on their own. Likewise, despite 'a high degree of self-exploitation in the struggle to defend the craft', *canut* families' children in late nineteenth-century Lyon could no longer look forward to continuing in the silk industry.[51]

In the nineteenth century, the 'proto-industrial' production of consumer goods increasingly moved from the countryside, or were established in towns and cities, because urban areas offered better transport logistics and larger markets for luxury and mass-consumption goods. Agnete Raaschou-Nielsen suggests that the fact that 'many workers, male and female, certainly avoided the factory if at all possible' contributed to the availability of cheap urban labour for putting-out production.[52] The extensive division of production into standard components facilitated mechanisation while retaining several routine manual procedures that lent themselves to putting-out home industry.

In the 1860s, at Pirna by the River Elbe in Saxony, almost 60 poor girls and a dozen boys stood nearly all day on a board, occupied in the monotonous work of knotting woollen yarn for the then fashionable shawls. Their break from this was the two or three hours when they sat down at school. The job was known as 'wool and knotting work' (*Woll- und Knüpfarbeit*). Children worked 50 to 60 hours a week and earned only 5 to 15 *Neugroschen*.[53] In 1881, the mother of an eleven-year-old German girl, Adelheid Popp, took her away from school to start learning a trade. Since the girl was still of compulsory school age, she was not apprenticed to a professional seamstress, but to a woman who was a putter-out, or an outwork agent (*Zwischenmeisterin*). For twelve hours a day, without a break, Adelheid made decorations from pearls and silk ribbons for ladies' dresses. When she had finished one item, her mistress counted the hours she took, and always paid the same per hour. Thus the more the girl gained in skill, the less she earned, since it then took her less time to make an item. Her mother cherished the idea that the girl would one day have a decent income if only she was skilled and industrious.[54]

It did not look any brighter for girls in Paris. Girls and women working in ready-to-wear clothing had highly seasonal employment, low wages and monotonous work. Girls aged between thirteen and fifteen had the lowest wages, and could count on a maximum of 160 days' work a year, just like other semi-skilled workers. Girls were hired for the day, sometimes for a week, but never for a whole month. No wonder that charitable organisations found it necessary to provide seamstresses in downtown Paris with meals at reduced prices. There were vocational schools for clothes making for girls aged between thirteen and sixteen. In one such school, after six months' training in stitch patterns, the girls would begin to sew clothes for the poor. The municipal vocational school offered them the opportunity to generate some earnings which the school then saved on their behalf until they had successfully finished their training. The training was supposed to bring the young seamstresses double the wages of semi-skilled seamstresses.[55]

Much of the *petite industrie* in Paris involved sweated labour for young and semi-skilled workers. Boys were legally eligible for apprenticeship in bakeries and culinary trades at the age of fourteen, but were too young for the heavy work in bakeries in the eyes of other workers. Apprenticeship offered no other wage than 'dungarees and towels, and one kilo of bread a day'. The youngest workers in confectionery lived in their master's home, often 'badly nourished and badly accommodated', while the masters were advised to keep the boys isolated. The trade typically required night working and work on Sundays and feast days. In addition, competition from *grande industrie* and the new machines loomed large for small entrepreneurs. Piecework had already been introduced in confectionery, and new apprentices were not quaranteed any future since workers would eventually be replaced by mechanisation.[56]

In spring 1906, Martta Hellstedt from Helsinki (whom we met above) finished the full six years of primary school at the age of fourteen. After school she worked first as a part-time domestic servant, but started in the autumn at a small bookbinding workshop, earning ten marks a month, of which she gave 9.50 to her mother and kept the rest for herself. Apprentices should have turned fifteen, but Martta's master ignored such rules. He resorted heavily to cheap, young labour in order to compete with the more mechanised and efficient large printing and bookbinding houses. Nonetheless, as Martta would later realise, the large printing houses applied an advanced division of labour, so new beginners learned a very limited scope of skills, whereas in the non-mechanised small workshop where she was they became Jacks- and Jills-of-all-trades who learned every component of the profession.[57]

Before the First World War most boys in Birmingham, 'the first manufacturing town in the world', still went after school to various kinds of workshops, some worked in distribution, and a few in other services. The six boys whom Arthur Freeman classified as 'first-class' boys in his study on 'boy labour' (see above) started by doing various jobs. The son of a stamper worked in pattern-making, modelling and designing in brass while also attending evening classes for two years. The first job of a hairdresser's son was cleaning up in a shop, labouring, whitewashing and getting the men's teas, after which he started in a jewellery works, then assisted an engineer in a factory, then tried working at a printer's. A cabinet maker's son first ran errands for six months in a factory, then went to a motor works, then obtained 'jobbing work with a plumber'. The son of a slater worked first as a messenger boy in a post office, then by a capstan-lathe. The son of a commercial traveller learned the trade of silversmith for nine months, then became a page in a railway dining saloon. The son of a travelling actor wanted to follow in his father's footsteps, so while training he had about fifteen jobs, all equally irrelevant to his plans. Other boys in Freeman's sample worked as van-boys, for plumbers and printers, in brass factories and the like, doing polishing, filing, drilling, soldering or 'dogging up', for instance. One 'second-class' boy seriously trained for the stage in order to follow his father as a music-hall entertainer.[58]

Writing during the First World War, the Spanish factory inspector Adsuar Moreno explained that boys or girls, be they children of the patron or not, never learned a trade in small urban domestic workshops doing subcontracted outwork, or putting-out work, for larger enterprises. In more or less miserable conditions they did monotonous piecework in great quantities, and the long working day left no time for school. The worst off were girls in sewing, under pressure of time, poorly paid and forced to sit still for hours on end.[59]

If children's jobs in workshops were monotonous, outwork or putting-out home industries were exhausting, judging from reminiscences of working-class childhood. Paul Löbe from Freiburg, whom we met above, had to sit long into the night with his mother making caps, hoods and shawls for a clothing factory. He gladly left this work to his younger sisters, preferring to work away from home.[60] In the 1880s, a small boy in Copenhagen sat the whole night with his mother making fuses (a kind of match). The mother promised the son a two-øre Danish pastry if only he would continue. By dawn they had managed to make 500 fuses, for which they would get 25 øre, enough to buy a quarter of a loaf of rye bread and some fat for cooking.[61] In the mid-1890s, Hanna Bergendahl sat with her mother and elder sister from morning to evening in Pori (Björneborg), a Finnish coastal town, without moving from the spot, making inner boxes for matchboxes for the largest Finnish match factory located in the neighbourhood. They received 40 pennies for more than 1,100 boxes, enough for one kilo of salted Baltic herrings, the staple diet of the poor.[62] A Vienese coachman's daughter Thekla, being the eldest child (born in 1899), had to assist her mother in hosiery work late into the evening. Home-industry income seemed to have been badly needed for making ends meet in this large family.[63]

All over Europe, from Birmingham to Aarhus and Freiburg, mothers and children were sitting long hours and late into the night around the kitchen table making thousands of matchboxes, wrapping thousands of hairpins in paper, bending thousands of tin clasps round safety pins, sewing numerous tangled hooks and eyes onto cards, assembling toys, sewing, knitting and trimming countless identical parts of clothes, stockings or footwear, making lace, rolling up lower-quality cigars.[64] These mothers and children were industrious, not in order to be able to buy more new consumer goods – as the theory of the industrious revolution suggests – but in order to be able to buy their daily bread. There are references to the 'self-exploitation' of smallholder peasant families in the history books, but the 'self-exploitation' of mothers and children in urban home industries may have been on a par with it.

The service sector

Boys and girls moving around the city and making money from the urban lifestyle appear more modern than the boys and girls stuck in urban workshops or at the kitchen table doing putting-out work. The former anticipated the future consumer society, while the latter were there only because that particular phase of the production process had not yet been mechanised. Nonetheless, the preferences of urban consumers shaped both forms of child labour. The emergence of a status-conscious, middle-class life style, together with increasing purchasing power, led to a growing demand for commercial consumer goods as well as for more and novel services. This could be seen in the demand for domestic servants, on the one hand, and for shop assistants and the like on the other. How did all this affect children? What were their terms of employment like in the service sector?

Domestic service enjoyed the reputation of being an occupation of easy entry, but not every poor girl became a servant. For example, at the turn of the nineteenth century in a school for poor girls in London, three quarters of those aged between nine and thirteen could not sew, and none could sew well enough to make a dress. Knitting and spinning were equally alien to them. According to a contemporary judgement, they were 'plainly disqualified for domestic servants'.[65]

The feminisation of domestic service generally spread over Europe, and was accompanied by a shift in the class-composition of masters, with more servants being hired in middle-class and petite bourgeoisie households.[66] Did they hire girls or women? They often hired both in nineteenth-century Madrid, since many lone women with children offered themselves for service for no other pay than board and lodging for themselves and their children. This led to a demand for widows who should bring with them a young daughter who knew how to cook, iron and sew. In Cuenca, young girls from kindred families, such as nieces, were employed as servants, although daughters of well-to-do families were far less likely than those of day labourers and artisans to move away from home. Furthermore, there was both a supply of and demand for young girls and boys in the servant labour market of Madrid. They may have received no other pay than maintenance, perhaps complemented with such education as masters felt they owed their young servants. In 1800, an eleven-year-old girl from the Basque country who knew to read and write, sew and embroider, offered herself as a nursemaid and servant for a lady with children. In 1859, a father wished to have his eleven-year-old daughter, who had lost her mother, employed for seven or eight years as a nursemaid (*niñera*) or in a vocation (*oficio*). In 1860, a respectable family wanted an orphaned boy aged between ten and twelve as a servant, promising to see to his education. However, frequent announcements by masters concerning the whereabouts of deserted children suggest that servant life was often hard on children.[67]

English working-class girls were often employed in small households as poorly paid maids-of-all-work. According to the 1851 census for London, 13 per cent of girls aged between ten and fourteen were employed, 45 per cent of them in service, and almost 60 per cent of the young women aged between fifteen and nineteen who were employed, 49 per cent of them were in service.[68] In the whole of England, girls under fifteen comprised eight per cent of all female indoor servants, and their number grew more quickly than that of female servants aged over fifteen. By 1871, girls comprised ten per cent of female servants, and for the first time their number exceeded that of male servants. However, the number of young girls in domestic service fell during the next ten years, while the number of other female servants kept growing, so by 1881 the proportion of girls was back to eight per cent.[69] According to the 1881 census, industry employed slightly less girls than domestic service (Tables 4.3 and 5.1). This did not last, however, and by 1911, manufacturing work in textiles or clothing was more common for girls.[70]

In Italy, children aged under fifteen comprised nine per cent of all domestic servants in 1901. The proportion of boys of male servants was exactly the same as that of girls of all female servants. Nonetheless, since the number of female servants was five times that of males, five times more girls than boys worked as domestic servants. There were clear differences between the regions. Children comprised between five and six per cent of all domestic servants in northern Italy, and about 17 to 19 per cent in the south. Yet, judging from the census returns, children in domestic service were but a tenth of children in the manufacturing industry, which employed five times the number of girls and 20 times that of boys in domestic service.[71]

It was rare in Stockholm to find girls aged under fifteen, the former minimum age for living-in farm servants, in domestic service. In 1880–1881, the number of female domestic servants peaked at the age-group 20–24 years, and only a few were younger than fifteen. Domestic servants were clearly less numerous in Stockholm in 1900 than they had been two decades earlier, but they were on average slightly younger, since the peak had moved down to 20 years.[72] Likewise in Denmark, young girls aged under fifteen or, more precisely, who had not been confirmed, seldom worked as full-time domestic servants, even though they may have worked as part-time helpers or child minders. Three-fifths of female domestic servants in 1901 were in the 15–25 age group.[73]

Very young servants were rare in the two Russian metropolises, even though employers preferred 'fresh country girls', and metropolitan families who could not afford proper nursemaids for their children hired young girls. According to the 1869 census for St Petersburg, young girls aged under fourteen comprised as little as one per cent (under ten-year-olds 0.15%) and girls aged between fourteen and fifteen less than two per cent of female domestic servants. Boys aged under fourteen comprised less than two per cent (under ten-year-olds 0.13%) and those between fourteen and fifteen two per cent, of all male servants. Girls aged under thirteen comprised ten per cent of domestic servants in 1898–1900 in the Moscow district, whereas in the city, servants aged under ten had virtually disappeared by the 1902 census, while boys and girls aged under fifteen comprised one and two per cent respectively of servants. Contemporary observers agreed that domestic service was 'the most degrading of all women's work'. A leading social-democratic newspaper was concerned about the vulnerability of young servant girls, and this fear may not have been groundless.[74] A survey was carried out in the 1890s among prostitutes in St Petersburg concerning their life course. The 150 returns tell of a former servant girl who had been raped at the age of ten by a tradesman, two former servant girls who had been raped at the age of eleven, one by an officer and the other by a soldier, and a former servant girl who had experienced the same fate at the age fourteen at the hands of a manservant.[75]

The question of the extension of child labour to urban domestic service must remain open, since systematic information is lacking. Nonetheless, the impression gained from the above is that the incidence of young girls as domestic servants may have been partly associated with whether or not there was a tradition of young servants. As mentioned above in the context of life-cycle service and indentured servants, Sweden and Russia lacked the tradition of indoor servants in rural households, even though in both countries the practice of using 'outside' girls for domestic chores spread in the late nineteenth century. In contrast, in England, Italy and Spain it had long been common practice to have children from other families as domestic servants.

Information about child labour in urban public and commercial services is not as extensive as that about manufacturing, which is no wonder, given the contemporary interest in industrial child labour. Census returns presumably leave a lot to be desired as regards part-time or casual child labour, nonetheless they may still be indicative. For example, English census returns imply that the absolute dominance of domestic service as the occupation of girls aged under fifteen remained intact from 1851 to 1861, but after that other services began to encroach, and continued to increase even after the number of girls in domestic service had declined (Table 5.1).

Italian census returns suggest that the proportion of child employees in commercial services increased from 1882 to 1901, except in the banking trade. According to an authoritative contemporary explanation, these children were looking for means of subsistence. As in the case of domestic service, the south (Sicily, Calabria and Campania) was characterised by higher-than-average numbers of child workers, apparently because of the sparse primary-school education and weakly developed commercial, manufacturing and agricultural trades. Lower-than-average proportions of child labour in commercial services were found in the central and northern areas (Umbria, Liguria, Lazio, Tuscany and Lombardy). Over all of Italy, commercial and public services employed ten times more boys than girls aged under fifteen in 1901. More than five out of ten boys and as many as nine out of ten girls in service trades worked in 'goods and commodities' trade (*vendita di merci e derrate*) or in shops (*esercisi pubblici*), presumably as shop assistants or the like. Transport and communication were male-dominated, and accounted for four out of ten boys working in trades. For example, boys comprised four per cent (in 1882 it was two per cent) of all males in public transport and the like (*servizi di piazzi*). Boys also found jobs in the service of the Church, in money and banking, and in public and private administration.[76]

Boys in England were employed in various service jobs out of school hours, for example, as messengers, errand boys, delivery boys, van boys and barrow boys for milkmen, while many were occupied in street trading. Some boys may have worked very long hours in barbers' shops – five hours after school in the evenings, fifteen hours on Saturdays and six or eight hours on Sundays.[77] Contemporary moralists saw running errands as a dead-end job, but this was not necessarily the case. Einar Olsson, aged fourteen, was hired in 1912 as an errand boy and telephone responder in the office of Kockums machinery factory in Malmö, Sweden, and retired from the same firm 51 years later.[78]

It was customary in Denmark for boys to start with full-time work after confirmation, after five to seven years of primary school. Christian Kampmann started in Aarhus as an apprentice at the ironmonger dealer Viggo L. Rahr in 1896, working in the office and the storeroom. The working day in the storeroom started at exactly six o'clock in the morning, and an hour later at the office, although punctuality was not as strictly monitored there. A major disadvantage with the office work was that the length of the working day was dependent on the habits of the manager, since clerks and apprentices could not leave before their boss. At Rahr the manager usually left at seven or half past seven in the evening, but it was worse with Christian's next boss, a bachelor who used to stay in the office until nine or half past nine.[79]

If such flexibility was expected of employees, one wonders what amount of flexibility was expected of the shopkeeper's own children. According to Geoffrey Crossick and Heinz-Gerhard Haupt, in petite bourgeoisie shops 'family labour could … be coerced by pressures far beyond those to which wage labour was susceptible'. Keeping a respectable grocer's shop or café was a family affair that required endless work and unlimited working hours not only from the wife, husband and children, but also from their servants. The flexibility of the family members and domestic servants 'reduced the need for more than the minimum employed labour force'. The other side of the coin was that servants and employees, who ultimately gained nothing in return, frequently changed employer, while children may have learned to detest the work in the family shop. In fact, children generally turned first to wage employment before becoming shopkeepers themselves, if they ever did. Petite

Table 5.1. Children aged under 15 in service occupations in England and Wales, 1851, 1861, 1871 and 1881 (in thousands).

		1851	1861·	1871	1881
Dealing, raw materials	boys	0.8	1.5	2.7	0.9
	girls	0.2	0.5	0.4	0.1
Dealing, dress and clothing materials	boys	1.5	2.0	1.9	1.6
	girls	0.3	0.2	0.7	0.8
Dealing, food, drink and smoking	boys	5.2	6.7	7.8	8.0
	girls	0.5	0.5	0.7	0.8
Dealing, lodging and coffee houses	boys	..	..	0.1	..
	girls	..	..	0.1	..
Dealing, furniture, utensils and stationery	boys	1.3	2.0	2.5	2.5
	girls	..	0.2	0.3	0.3
General dealers and unspecified	boys	1.3	2.1	3.1	1.8
	girls	0.9	0.6	1.1	0.9
Industrial service, commercial	boys	1.3	2.2	3.7	6.3
	girls	..	..	..	0.1
Industrial service, general labour	boys	14.1	13.5	21.6	13.1
	girls	0.4	0.2	0.4	0.1
Public service and professional, administration	boys	0.1	1.2	2.5	2.6
	girls	..	..	0.1	0.1
Public service and professional, army and navy	boys	0.6	1.1	0.9	0.5
	girls	..	..	..	..
Public service and professional, law	boys	0.7	0.9	0.9	1.0
	girls	..	..	..	..
Public service and professional, medicine	boys	0.4	0.5	0.4	0.4
	girls	..	..	..	..
Public service and professional, art and amusement	boys	0.7	1.0	0.9	0.7
	girls	0.1	0.1	0.2	0.3
Public service and professional, education	boys	0.3	1.2	1.8	1.9
	girls	0.4	1.5	2.7	5.3
Domestic service, indoor	boys	6.3	8.0	8.2	6.2
	girls	61.4	86.7	111.1	98.9
Domestic service, outdoor	boys	0.6	1.4	1.2	2.6
	girls	..	..	..	..
Domestic service, extra	boys	1.5	1.2	0.9	0.8
	girls	1.0	1.1	1.4	1.5
ALL SERVICES	children	101.9	138.1	180.3	160.1
	boys	36.7	46.5	61.1	50.9
	girls	65.2	91.6	119.2	109.2
Other than domestic service	girls	2.8	3.8	6.7	8.8

Source: Occupation Censuses 1851–1881, published in Booth 1886, Appendix A.

bourgeoisie families had difficulties maintaining the same status for even the few children they could afford to have. To allay these fears, as with any parents with ambitions of upward mobility, one frequently chosen strategy was to provide their children with education. Most opportunities for petite bourgeoisie children equipped with secondary-school education were 'at the lower end of the white-collar occupational world', in clerical and postal work and in elementary-school teaching, in other words jobs offered by the bureaucratic state.[80]

These three mechanisms – urbanisation, the development of service trades, and education – seem to have fed each other. The impact of formal education on economic performance in manufacturing during the first and second industrial revolutions has remained a debated issue,[81] whereas the development of commercial and public service trades appears inseparably connected with the expansion of education.

Educational opportunities

Attitudes among the population were more favourable to education in urban areas and in the maritime districts than in the villages, as Colin Heywood observes concerning mid-nineteenth century France. He cites a French School Inspector who remarked in 1855:

> As a matter of fact, children in the towns are initiated at an early stage to all the ideas circulating around them, and participate in the intellectual movements which can be felt in the big centres of population. Knowing infinitely more than children in the countryside, they are better prepared for the instruction given in the schools.[82]

Such a sagacious insight does not seem to have been shared by the majority of educational professionals in Europe, however. Rather than appreciating how mentally quick precocious working-class children were, teaching staff in urban schools were inclined to see them as undisciplined, impertinent and malevolent. Boys from poorer homes were only too readily sentenced to institutions of forced education, such as industrial and reformatory schools. Thus instead of being places for learning and intellectual stimulus, classrooms became places of fear, humiliation and painful strokes of the cane, pointer or ruler for many working-class and pauper children.[83] Even if something of the same kind was experienced by middle-class boys or girls in their schools, at least they escaped the reformatory.

Making urban working-class children attend school was a more burning concern for the authorities than the education of the rural poor or even factory children. The image of lower-class or working-class youths roaming the streets unchecked loomed large in the contemporary discussion, motivating investments in compulsory education. The law of 1870 made free and compulsory education possible in England which brought with it many conflicts between parents and school concerning use of children's time. Girls in particular were often absent, usually because they were minding younger children at home or in the neighbourhood for pay. The minimum leaving age was successively raised from ten to twelve, and in London to thirteen. At that stage, working-class boys leaving school began to appear as a problem. There was not enough demand for such boys in the labour market, but the introduction of compulsory part-time day continuation classes for boys proved a failure.[84]

In Germany, as in many other countries, public elementary schools developed from urban pauper schools. In Berlin, for example, it was reasoned that children of the lower classes should be kept separated from those of other social classes. This led to a parallel school system, as in most of Europe. It was originally planned that schools for the lower classes would combine schooling and productive work, in the tradition of introducing lower-class children to work at an early age. Such a principle, which was difficult to put into practice, gave way to one emphasising the importance of preventing children's moral decline ('*sittliche Verwahrslosung*') and juvenile delinquency. Prussia introduced compulsory education in 1863, and by 1880 it had been implemented in all of Germany.[85]

'The Russian government oscillated between the Scylla of the demand for educated manpower in industry and business and the Charybdis of the preservation of a rigidly stratified society ...', as Arcadius Kahan wrote. The fear of education awakening social ambitions was shared by the establishment in other countries, but in Russia the establishment could point to precedents. The foundling hospitals of St Petersburg and Moscow had previously trained between 800 and 1,000 young women a year as governesses. They did not suit élite families, however, who only recruited West-European nurses and governesses. Thus young governesses from the foundling hospitals would 'mostly meet with not the most polished society', for which they 'had received too refined an education', as J.G. Kohl explained in 1843. The quality of education received by working-class children in one- or two-grade Russian elementary schools in the late nineteenth century was not likely to promote social ambitions, but the schools did promote literacy. Among the urban population in 1897, about 70 per cent of males and almost 60 per cent of females in the age-group 10–19 were literate, which was clearly more than in older age-groups or among rural populations of the same age-group. By then the Russian government had even yielded to a growing demand for educational facilities made by educated persons, who there as elsewhere entertained social ambitions concerning their offspring.[86]

1848 was a memorable year in European history, and it was the year in which the Norwegian educational system was reformed in the towns. From then on, community school (*folkskole*) was not only for the poor, but was for all children, rich and poor. Nevertheless, as Floyd Martinson remarks, this may only have intensified the desire for segregated education. In consequence, 'highly motivated, affluent families arranged for paid classes beyond the standard courses offered in the public schools. So there still remained two classes of students at the elementary level ...'.[87] Working-class boys in Stockholm who were close to the age of fourteen felt old enough to start working, and their parents probably agreed. Thus older boys were often increasingly reluctant to attend school. However, dropping-out or truancy were not tolerated. Teachers could resort first to corporal punishment to force boys to attend school, and the next step was to sentence them to reformatory or truant schools.[88] Denmark followed another kind of policy. Around the turn of the twentieth century, older children in urban areas had the right to go to school for only half the school day, that is for four hours before noon, so they could work in the afternoon. Occasionally their work lasted long into the night, and the children were then too tired to follow instruction the next morning.[89] Danish girls leaving school were only expected to have a decent job, such as domestic service, until marriage, while factory work was long regarded as unbecoming or injurious to girls.[90]

Unlike Danish girls, Finnish working-class girls preferred factory work to domestic service. In fact, girls had more to gain than boys from extra years at school, because they thus escaped becoming domestic servants, while a good school report could even open the way to a sought-after job as a shop-assistant. The urban public primary schools took in about as many or slightly more girls (51% in 1906) than boys, and generally only girls were found in continuation classes. Conflicts over children's time use were not an issue, since the relatively easy primary-school curriculum enabled them to work out of school hours and during the three-months summer vacation. It was then that well-off families moved to the countryside, which they believed was an integral part of having a proper childhood.[91]

If we are to trust the resumé presented by Baron Daru, educational experts attending in a congress in Frankfurt in 1857 were interested in questions concerning appropriate forms of religious education, while a speaker from Vienna forecast the ruin of middle-class families who could no longer afford the education of their too many children. It was a source of wonder to the participants that children's schools in Milan housed both children of popular classes and children of 'the most opulent classes'.[92] The present-day historian Marzio Barbagli offers us a key to the puzzle: 'If the Italian ruling class created a relatively open educational system ... this was because of the importance it attributed to the secondary school in building the new nation state and in giving a firm base to its own hegemony.'[93] In its choice of strategy, the Italian ruling class was surprisingly similar to the one in Russia until the 1890s, with an equally disadvantageous allocation of resources to popular primary education.

The role of the primary school was to turn the children of the popular classes from 'subjects into citizens' (E.J. Hobsbawm) without awakening their social ambitions. A parallel school system was applied in most of Europe in order to restrict the passage to higher levels, and thereby competition for white-collar occupations. According to Hobsbawm, as far as the state was concerned, the primary school was a 'powerful machinery ... to spread the image and heritage of a "nation" and to inculcate attachment to it'.[94] Twentieth-century nationalism proved the success of the primary school in this, whereas the parallel school system failed to hold back competition from working-class children.

Conclusion

Necessity was the mother of invention. In hindsight, the many ways by which urban working-class children strove to make money appear quite innovative, sometimes daring or even hazardous (children risked both their health and their freedom). These children were flexible, enterprising, quick to grasp a chance to earn some coins, and shunned no opportunity. Such characteristics would be appreciated in the labour market of today, but they shocked and frightened the authorities and the establishment of the time, who wanted steady workers capable of putting up with monotonous work. To use present-day jargon, these children responded adequately and without delay to consumer demand in a heavily competitive business environment. Urban children were also alert and active, as the French School Inspector in 1855 seems to have understood. In short, they anticipated the service-oriented, commercial urban economy of the twentieth century.

Hugh Cunningham poses the following question: 'How far the segregated child labour market of the late nineteenth and twentieth centuries, oriented to the service sector, was created by the attempts at curtailment of demand, with child labour and school enforcement laws being the most important of those attempts'.[95] Ingrid Peikert suggests that the implementation of compulsory education in Germany and the increasing consistency by which the child-labour laws were observed brought with them an unintended outcome ('*hatte ... einem – unbeabsichtigten – Verdrängungseffekt geführt*'): children now moved from factories to home industries and errand and delivery jobs.[96] By the turn of the twentieth century, industrial child labour in Germany had increasingly given way to urban service jobs and work in home industries. Pamphlet writers continued to see industrial child labour as their prime target, but the legislation was extended in 1903 to prohibit children from appearing on stage in the theatre (except in high-class performances) and banning the under-twelves from working in boarding houses and restaurants serving alcohol.[97]

I suggest that increasing engagement of children in service-sector jobs was connected with the growth of services in urban and national economies, and the legislation rather followed suit. The 1841 Census of London already bore witness to the importance of commercial services in the urban economy.[98] In the second half of the nineteenth century, according to Norman Gemmell and Peter Wardley, 'structural change in Britain involved principally a shift of resources from agriculture to services, rather than manufacturing'. In Britain the services (transport and communications, distributive trades, insurance, banking and finance, catering, domestic service, public and professional services, miscellaneous services) had surpassed manufacturing in total output by 1873, and in total employment by 1913. Services accounted almost 40 per cent of total output and 30 per cent of total employment in 1856, and almost 50 per cent and 45 per cent respectively in 1913. Labour productivity in 1856 was higher in transport and communications and distribution than in manufacturing. However, unlike in the other sectors (manufacturing, transport and communication, commerce), labour productivity evidently declined in distribution during the period 1873–1913.[99] Interestingly enough, in Britain the very sector that typically used child labour, such as van-boys, was distribution.

Paper making and newspapers illustrate the economic changes of the time. As noted above, paper began to be made from wood fibres and in mechanised large-scale production processes around 1870. Paper made from wood pulp was many times cheaper than that made from cloth and rag pulp. Cheap paper had many spin-off effects, one of which was the emergence of the cheap press in the course of the two decades before the First World War. Newspaper boys and girls soon appeared on the streets selling and delivering cheap newspapers. The new large-scale paper-making process employed hardly any children, whereas the old system used children and women in rag sorting, which was very dirty work and caused nasty infections. In this respect, the fact that children sorting rags for paper were replaced by children in rags selling newspapers was an improvement. The changes did not stop there, however. As the circulation figures rose, poor-looking children in the streets selling newspapers exposed to the rain and snow were not efficient enough and did not contribute to the image of the product. Thus Britain and France were among the first to witness the emergence of chain stores in newspaper distribution,[100] which meant that children became redundant.

Errand running was another example of how closely child labour was related to changes in technology and the economy. As the Norwegian historian Floyd Martinson remarks, running errands was especially prevalent before the introduction and widespread use of the telephone as a means of communication.[101] Similarly girls and boys crying 'Telegram!' disappeared from the streets once superior news transmission by radio broadcasting came along.

Finally, did not the consumer-oriented urban life style as such embrace characteristics that promoted cheap labour and informal arrangements? As far as consumer end goods and services were concerned, the entrepreneur always felt the pressure to cut costs by cutting labour costs. The poorest customer in the second-hand market haggled over pennies, the most opulent gentleman had no scruples when it came to paying the tailor, while seamstresses were sewing fine dresses for a mere pittance for his lady. The sewing machine was a great invention, but still needed someone to use it. Taylorism (scientific management) seemed to be a solution in the case of mass-produced consumer goods, but with growing purchasing power, customers demanded more sophisticated products. In the course of the twentieth century entrepreneurs in consumer goods and services came up with several ways of cutting labour costs. Self-service was a significant invention, but offered no universal solution. Other solutions included the recruitment of cheap labour from abroad, taking on more women, and starting production or business where labour was cheaper. Child labour also returned to urban consumer goods and services during the last decades of the twentieth century.

Notes

1. Arbaiza Vilallonga 1998; Assion 1987; Bideau and Brunet 1996; Camps i Cura 1996, p. 62; Duroux 2001; Goubert 1986, p. 108; Jorde 1995, pp. 65–80; Mathias 1995, p. 198; Moch 1992, pp. 12, 37–48; Perrot 1997, p. 86; Postel-Vinay 1994; Sarasúa 1994, pp. 23–29, 235–237; Wall 2001; Weber-Kellermann 1979, pp. 93–94.
2. Ehmer 1997; Zucchi 1992, p. 18.
3. Niccoli 2000, pp. 175–192.
4. Nadaud 1948, pp. 19, 66–77.

5. Quoted in Lönnqvist 1992, p. 217.
6. Anderson, M. 1971, pp. 39–40, 53–55, 125–127.
7. Walton 1990, p. 396.
8. Heywood 1988, pp. 122–123.
9. Rahikainen 2002b.
10. Olsson, L. 1980, pp. 94–95.
11. Åström 1951.
12. Tissot 1882, pp. 315–320, quotation p. 320n.
13. Bater 1976, pp. 2–3, 51–59, 91–114, 300–303; Kirby 1995, pp. 52–53, 141, 165–167; Moch 1992, p. 103; Ransel 1988, pp. 114, 145.
14. Semyonova Tian-Shanskaia 1993 [1914], pp. 141–142.
15. D. Zhbankov, quoted in Tugan-Baranovsky 1970 [1907], pp. 409–410.
16. [Kanatchikov] 1986, [1929], pp. 5–9. See also Gatrell 1986, pp. 92–93.
17. Rustemeyer 1996, pp. 66–68, 100.
18. Wall 2001.
19. Kaltwasser 1987; Moch 1992, pp. 48, 89.
20. Engman 1983, pp. 370–373; Engman 1992; Åström 1951. See also Rahikainen 2001a.
21. Daru and Bournat 1875, pp. 402–405.
22. Zucchi 1992, pp. 17–40, quotations pp. 17, 37.
23. Boucheron 1869, pp. 146–149; Farge and Revel 1991, pp. 8–33. See also Daru and Bournat 1875, pp. 448–450.
24. Henrick 1994, pp. 80–83; Pinchbeck and Hewitt 1973, pp. 546–580.
25. International Labour Conference 1922, pp. 688–689.
26. E.g. Duroux 2001; Moch 1992, pp. 81, 92–3.
27. E.g. Bjurman 1995, pp. 73–91, 109–110, 139–142; Lis and Soly 1993, pp. 21–29; Rahikainen 1995a; Trinidad Fernández 1996, pp. 477–479.
28. Davin 1996, pp. 38–39.
29. Davin 1984; Davin 1996, p. 105, 157–163, 185–186; Dewar 1910, pp. 31, 36–41; Hopkins 1994, pp. 192–200; Thompson, P. 1975, pp. 34–35.
30. Heywood 1988, p. 128.
31. Boucheron 1869, pp. 150–178; Daru and Bournat 1875, pp. 410, 434, 454; Robin 1879, pp. 1–11.
32. Bjurman 1995, pp. 153–160.
33. Borderies-Guereña 1996, p. 43; Trinidad Fernández 1996, pp. 468–476.
34. Guidi 1986, pp. 112–113, 129.
35. Kohl 1842, pp. 118, 151.
36. Gorky 1950, p. 414.
37. Gorky 1950, pp. 409–417. One *pood* equals 40 *funts*, or 16.38 kilogramme.
38. Peikert 1986, p. 206.
39. Bjurman 1995, pp. 19–33.
40. Martinson 1992, p. 91; Søreide 1991, pp. 92–93.
41. Andersen 1985, pp. 66, 166–172; Sigsgaard 1995, p. 65.
42. Bjurman 1995, p. 39.
43. Markkola 1997; Snellman 1908, quotation p. 23.
44. Snellman 1908, pp. 28–42.
45. Humphries 2003.

46. Freeman 1914, pp. 5, 21–22.
47. Hierta-Retzius 1897; Johansson, J-E. 1986, pp. 14–36; Lundemark 1980; Markkola 1997, pp. 89–90; Olsson, O. 1999, pp. 71, 156–64.
48. M. Salmela-Järvinen [Hellstedt] 1965, cited in Rahikainen 1998.
49. Humphries and Gordon 1992, pp. 118–123; Rahikainen 1995a.
50. Schwarz 1992, pp. 47, 180–207, quotation p. 206.
51. Crossick and Haupt 1995, pp. 32–37, 81–89, quotation p. 98; Edgren 1986, pp. 368–371; Strumingher 1977.
52. Cerman 1993, pp. 284–285; Raaschou-Nielsen 1993, p. 13.
53. Lange 1978, pp. 186–189.
54. Quoted in Weber-Kellermann 1979, p. 159.
55. [Du Maroussem] 1894, pp. 308–309, 394, 573, 660–679.
56. [Du Maroussem] 1893, pp. 48–52, 91–109, 130–133, 170–89, quotations pp. 49, 131.
57. M. Salmela-Järvinen [Hellstedt] 1966, cited in Rahikainen 2001, p. 134.
58. Freeman 1914, pp. 5, 15–21, 29–49.
59. Adsuar Moreno 1916, pp. 9–13.
60. Peikert 1986, p. 206.
61. Quoted in Sigsgaard 1995, p. 65.
62. Quoted in Rahikainen 2001c, pp. 131–132.
63. Quoted in Papathanassiou 1999, p. 135.
64. Andersen 1985, p. 63; Davin 1996, pp. 157–164, 174; Peikert 1986; Raaschou-Nielsen 1993; Sigsgaard 1995, p. 63.
65. Schwarz 1992, pp. 45–46.
66. E.g. Rustemeyer 1996, pp. 90–99; Sarasúa 1994, pp. 4–6, 37–44, 71–73.
67. Sarasúa 1994, pp. 221–222, 226–228, 237–242; Dubert 1999; Reher 1990, p. 229.
68. Schwarz 1992, p. 47.
69. Census returns of 1851–1881, published in Booth 1886, Appendix A.
70. Horn 1989, p. 134. See also Hopkins 1994, pp. 224–233.
71. Censimento della popolazione ... d'Italia 1901:IV, Tavola 1B; 1901:V, p. xcviii.
72. Jorde 1995, p. 27.
73. Andersen 1985, p. 182.
74. Eklof 1986, Table 40; Rustemeyer 1996, pp. 100–103, 167–171; quotations from Glickman 1984, 60–61.
75. Fedorow 1897, pp. 19–22.
76. Censimento della popolazione ... d'Italia 1901:IV, Tavola IB; 1901:V, p. xcviii.
77. Davin 1984; Davin 1996, pp. 164–173; Hendrick 1992; Hopkins 1994, pp. 201–204, 223–233; Horn 1989, pp. 126–131.
78. Greiff 1992, pp. 220–221.
79. Quoted in Andersen 1985, p. 56.
80. Crossick and Haupt 1995, pp. 77–107, quotations pp. 85, 98.
81. E.g. Cassis 1997, p. 235; Kocka 1994; Landes 1991 p. 9; Locke, R.R. 1984, pp. 56–59; Tortella 2000, p. 49.
82. Heywood 1988, p. 203.
83. See, e.g., Andersen 1985, pp. 163–165; Bjurman 1995, pp. 34–47, 62–66; Hendrick 1994, pp. 30–33; Heywood 2001, pp. 165–169; Thompson, P. 1975, pp. 32–33.

84. Davin 1984; Davin 1996, pp. 86–111, 142–43; Freeman 1914; Hendrick 1980; Hendrick 1994, p. 29; Lavalette 1994, pp. 208–210.
85. Meyer 1971, pp. 228–243, 292–297, quotation p. 241; Peikert 1986.
86. Kahan 1989, pp. 168–178, quotation p. 173; Kohl 1843, p. 76.
87. Martinson 1992, pp. 119–123, quotation pp. 121–122.
88. Bjurman 1995, pp. 49–50.
89. Andersen 1895; Degnbol 1991.
90. Andersen 1985, pp. 63, 181; Ehlers 1991.
91. Markkola 1997; Rahikainen 2002b; Snellman 1908, pp. 5, 16–17.
92. Daru and Bournat 1875, pp. 120, 132–146.
93. Barbagli 1982, pp. 61–62. For selection, see also Roggero 1999, pp. 269–297.
94. Hobsbawm 1991, p. 91.
95. Cunningham, H. 2000, quotation pp. 419–420.
96. Peikert 1986, quotation p. 207.
97. Agahd 1902; Agahd 1904; Mooser 1986; Weber-Kellermann 1979, pp. 156–159. The German law of 1903 is reprinted, e.g., in Deutsch 1907, pp. 45–53.
98. Barnett 1998, pp. 197–201.
99. Gemmell and Wardley 1990, pp. 300–307, quotation p. 302.
100. For newspapers, see Cassis 1997, pp. 23–29, 53. For rag sorting, see Heywood 1988, p. 316.
101. Martinson 1992, p. 91.

CHAPTER 6

Twentieth-Century Child Labour

Child labour on the wane

The short twentieth century, as E.J. Hobsbawm called the period from the First World War to the fall of the Soviet Union, became the century of school children. There were differences in timing between countries, as between the urban and rural worlds, but broadly speaking, the developments followed a similar path. After the First World War, enrolment was firmly in progress, although far from all children of school age went to school. After the Second World War, all or almost all children of school age went to school, at least for a few years, and child labour became a marginal phenomenon, associated with family farms and particular population groups or regions. What remains to be explained is why the trend in child labour turned upwards towards the end of the short twentieth century. The following discussion starts from the assumption that, until this upturn, child labour in Europe could be considered 'old-type' child labour on the wane, although the decline may have been interrupted by the war.

When the Great War broke out in 1914, farmers in England were quick to resort to child labour, which was much cheaper than the scarce adult male labour. According to Pamela Horn, in fact, many farmers had never liked the idea that their labourers' children would receive a better school education, which would only make them reluctant to accept the low wages in farm work. As a response to pressure from farmers, local educational committees permitted boys as young as ten and eleven to leave school in order to work on farms. During the war years, several hundred thousand children at elementary school may have abandoned it for farm work.[1]

By the outbreak of the war in the summer, *Schwabenkinder* were already herding for farmers in Upper Swabia. They had been hired in March in the child market (*Kindermarkt*) at Friedrichshafen, on the northern coast of the Bodensee, where some 200 children had gathered. The children had walked more than 300 kilometres from about thirty villages in the Tyrol mountains. This turned out to be the last *Kindermarkt* of migrant children, even though later, almost by a way of an epilogue, Swabian farmers took to maintaining hundreds of children in their homes for eight to ten weeks: in 1920 they took more than 1,300 and in 1921 some 700 children from Voralberg, which had suffered badly during the war. However, as Otto Uhlig observes, the farmers hardly allowed these children to remain idle, but probably set them to work like the *Schwabenkinder* before them, although now without a wage, save board, lodging and perhaps clothes.[2] In any case, the Great War put an end to the labour migration of Alpine children, the first signs of which can be traced three centuries back to the Thirty Years' War.

The old systems lingered on in many parts of the German countryside. In Kiebingen, a Catholic village of smallholders, children of landowning farmers, 'peasant children', stayed within the village sphere of production and had relatively secure life-changes, whereas those from families of day-labourers and building workers had to cope with absolute insecurity. They left the village at the ages of thirteen to fifteen to seek work in Upper Swabia, Switzerland, or in the factory towns of Württemberg.[3] Contemporary statistics suggest that, in the whole of Germany, the number of children aged under fourteen occupied in agriculture fell from 515,600 in 1907 to 390,600 in 1925, while their proportion of the total agricultural labour force fell from four to less than three per cent. The German child-labour legislation distinguished between the master's own 'inside' (*eigene*) children and 'outside' (*fremde*) children. The number of 'outside' children in agriculture declined relatively more than that of 'inside' children, thus in 1925 nine out of ten belonged to the latter category, compared with less than eight out of ten in 1907.[4]

Child labour in Hessen increased during the First World War, then declined, but the decline was not linear. For example, during the economically favourable years 1924–1927, more families than previously could afford newspapers, which led to increasing numbers of children delivering them. The numbers of 'inside' children were double those of 'outside' children in 1913 and 1922, and the two groups had slightly different profiles. For example, in 1913, two-fifths of 'inside' children but only little over a tenth of 'outside' children were aged under twelve. A decade later, the age composition of the former was still the same, while the latter had become on average younger, more than a quarter of them being now aged under twelve. In 1913, nine out of ten children in both groups were engaged in delivering, and in 1922 almost all of the 'inside' children were in delivering, while nearly one-fifth of 'outside' ones now had other kinds of jobs in workshops, for example.[5] In Hessen, many country girls and boys who left school at the age of fourteen still started work as servants in a farm house, but on the whole, farm servants were few in number compared to family labour: in Limburg, non-family labour accounted for five per cent of the labour force in holdings of five or more hectares in 1925 and 1933.[6]

Sweden stayed outside the Great War, so life continued as usual. In 1915, Bror Jönsson, the son of a *statare* farm labourer from Skåne (Scania) in southern Sweden, began to help to thin out root crops at the age of eight, and at nine he began to help his mother working in the landowner's beet fields. After turning ten, he began to work for a day wage, but he also had the opportunity to go to primary school, as compulsory education had already been effectively implemented. Bror finished school in May 1919, at the age of thirteen. He had by then already hired himself out to a farmer. His master was a kind man whose farmhands were given good food, and even the bedclothes in their lodgings were kept clean. All this meant that Bror later remembered that spring and summer as the best time of his childhood. However, this farmer hired farmhands only for the summer, and so Bror started at another farm in the autumn, but there everything was badly run. When he had served his year out, he again changed master, and now had better luck.[7] Similarly, girls and boys in the Danish and Norwegian countryside continued to hire themselves out from the age of twelve up, often after confirmation. Girls worked as 'little servants', mostly indoors, but also outdoors washing laundry, milking cows and potato picking, while boys worked as 'little farm-hands' outdoors. Hired girls and boys were either housed separately from the master's family or, as in Trøndelag in Norway, together with the master's children.[8]

Finland was not directly involved in the war, but Finnish industry supplied the imperial Russian army with different kinds of provisions. An outcome of this was that child labour increased in some manufacturing sectors, peaking in 1916, while in 1917, after the Revolution in Russia, supplies were no longer needed for the army, and child-labour requirements followed suit. After the Finnish Civil War of 1918, the number of children in Helsinki in manufacturing temporarily increased, as the severe food shortage and the thousands of war orphans from the losing side (the Reds) meant that many children were desperately short of bread. Nonetheless, the demand for children remained limited in the urban labour market. By way of compensation, in the 1920s and 1930s the municipal authorities of Helsinki licensed the YMCA to organise shoe-polishing work in public places for boys from poor families.[9]

Another consequence of the Finnish Civil War was that the establishment now opted for 'social control by education', to cite Marzio Barbagli, and compulsory education was introduced in 1921. For many country children it was a true reform. Hilda Salomaa, from the rural parish of Kauhajoki, was twelve years old at the coming of compulsory education. She had lost her father in the Civil War, and started working for farmers in the summer of 1918, herding in summer and in winter as a child minder. Now, for the first time, her master had to let her attend school. She loved to learn, so she completed the four-year primary-school curriculum in three years, while earning her maintenance and second-hand clothes from farmer families by teaching their children reading and arithmetic.[10] The implementation of compulsory education advanced slowly in the sparsely populated countryside, and it was not until the end of the 1930s that all Finnish country children attended primary school. Likewise primary school become a fully established institution only in the 1930s in the outlying parishes in northern Sweden, despite the fact that compulsory education had been formally introduced in Sweden 90 years earlier. According to Marianne Liliequist, primary education then also succeeded in disseminating middle-class ideas of child-rearing among local farmers and cottagers.[11]

The implementation of primary school education faced similar difficulties in outlying French mountain villages. Émilie Allais, a newly-qualified primary-school teacher (whom we met above as a child) was assigned as a substitute teacher in a mountain village in the autumn of 1923. After an arduous 20-kilometre climb, she reached the desolated and poverty-stricken village. It soon turned out that none of the inhabitants was willing to send any child to the school, despite it being obligatory. Their vague excuse was that all children were committed to the autumn's work, 'the cows, the sheep, the hay, they're all at it'.[12]

Anna from Montevarchi in Tuscany, had something of the same attitude as those in the French mountain village. She was impatient to find an opportunity to start work in a factory. Compulsory schooling remained largely meaningless for girls in Tuscan sharecropping families who were themselves eager to start as soon as possible in the local silk mills or felt and hat factories. Thus, in the way of many other girls, in 1925, at the age of eleven, Anna gave a dozen eggs as a bribe to the teacher to write a certificate that she had finished compulsory schooling, and then she started work in a felt and hat factory. It was not until several years later that Anna and other girls realised that they had been exposed to mercury in the felt and hat factory.[13]

Children in inter-war Italy still lived in a world in which 'an eleven-year-old girl could look for a job without her mother's knowledge, in order to tell her triumphantly: "Quite soon you no longer will have to work"', as Chiara Saraceno recalled about the childhood of her mother.[14] The Industrial and Commercial Census of 1927 reported more than 112,000 boys and nearly 83,000 girls aged under fifteen in manufacturing, and a further 16,400 boys and 3,600 girls in commercial services. Boys comprised six per cent of the total male labour force, and girls nine per cent of the total female labour force, in manufacturing and commercial services. The higher proportion of girls than of boys was a result of the large proportion of girls in the textile industry (10%), and particularly in clothing (15%). These two sectors employed more than eight out of ten girls in manufacturing and commercial service. The range of industries was wider for boys; the three largest employers, the mechanical, food and clothing industries, together covered five out of ten boys.[15]

The Spanish countryside presented a somewhat similar picture to the Italian one. In 1930, three-quarters of the youngest boys and girls, aged between six and eleven in Villamanta, in the province of Madrid, were at school. Nearly a third of boys, but only a tenth of girls aged between twelve and fourteen were still in education, the rest were working. However, not all those who were enrolled always went to school. Absenteeism rates among children of functionaries (*servicios*) remained low throughout the school year, whereas the rates among children of wage earners, craftsmen and agricultural labourers increased in the spring and summer in response to the labour needs of agriculture. The increase in absenteeism was most drastic in the case of children aged thirteen, but all age groups showed largely similar jumps in March and April. As in Italy, school enrolment was higher in the northern than in the southern provinces. According to José Borrás Llop, child labour contributed to these differences, as it brought with it delayed schooling (*escolarización tardía*), while many rural children left school at the age of ten or eleven.[16] Nonetheless, from one cohort to the next, literary rates among all age groups improved. Taking Spain as a whole, around 1930 literacy acquisition at an early age began to take off, even though the rates were still somewhat lower for females than for males.[17]

Primary school attendance was no longer regarded as a problem in the urban world, while primary-school leavers were still seen as such. The reluctance of working-class boys to go to school at an age when they could be gainfully employed was often overcome by providing evening schools. In contrast, compulsory day continuation schools for boys risked failure, as in the case of the reform in British compulsory part-time day schools for adolescents.[18] Likewise, vocational education advanced more slowly than the authorities liked to pretend. The depression years in the early 1930s provoked a series of efforts to increase vocational training and apprenticeship, including the system of 'pre-apprenticeship'.[19] In hindsight, it is clear that an incentive was the need to limit the flow of young people to the unemployment-plagued labour market.

More women and occasionally children were employed during the Second World War. For example, within a month of the outbreak of war, there was evidence that some British rural educational authorities planned to permit children to be withdrawn from school. By 1941, magistrates in some agricultural districts had begun to turn a blind eye to the illegal employment of school children. In April 1942, those aged twelve and upward were legally allowed to miss up to 20 days of school, and more if necessary, to work on the land. Farmers began to think that they could 'get child labour for the asking', and they had every reason to ask, since children were cheap and 'flexible'. In sum, the war years witnessed a widespread use of child labour in Britain.[20] The number of children in manufacturing in Finland rose in the peak year 1943 to the same level at which it had been in 1900. As an ally of Germany, Finland imitated German work programmes. Evacuee boys were sent to forestry work camps, for instance. There were also plans to evacuate all children from Helsinki for the summer, and those old enough were expected to work on the farms.[21] A parallel with Britain during the two World Wars is evident: as men were at the front, farmers suffered from acute shortages of labour and schoolchildren provided it.

After the Second World War child labour was largely a rural phenomenon in many countries. Women who migrated for seasonal farm work to a German village in the French occupation zone took their children with them to help with the harvest work in the bean fields of the *Hof*, a large estate. These migrant women were professionals who knew that the strips in the middle gave the best harvest, while local children worked on the strips at the sides, and found it difficult to keep up the work pace. Older schoolgirls worked in the local cardboard box factory during the longer school holidays, where village women also worked. There were many labour-intensive work stages. In the 1950s, Maria Wimmer, still a schoolgirl, was made to gum together ready-cut box parts, pressing them together with her fingers. In the end she was up to her elbows in stinking glue.[22]

Child labour was relatively common in Italy in the early 1950s. Boys aged between ten and thirteen comprised nine per cent of the labour force, less in the north and more in the southern provinces and in regions with little industry. According to the statistics, there were some 90,000 economically active girls, and 120,000 boys, aged between ten and fourteen. While the land reform of 1947 (abolishing sharecropping) had brought with it schools and roads, the way to school may have remained too long before the appearance of school buses, and rural children may have been teased at school for being 'peasants'. In 1960, many boys left school after the third year of primary education, that is at the age of nine or ten, and another third left around the age of eleven, so that less than a third of boys aged fourteen were in any education. Most of the boys who left school at an early age were rural children who were trained in agricultural work on the farm in the old way, learning by doing, and then only learned the traditional methods, as Dina Bertoni Jovine argued in 1963.[23] Literacy rates were in inverse relation to child labour. In 1951, illiteracy rates among children of school age, that is between six and fourteen, were low (2.8%) in the northern provinces, while south of Rome more than a tenth of children were illiterate (the rates ranging from 10.8% to 15.1%).[24]

Agricultural child labour was also an issue in (West) Germany, where the use of the labour of own, or 'inside', and 'outside' (*fremde*) children was well established, and the use of kindred children was understood to be permitted by law. A member of parliament in the *Bundestag* of 1956 proposed a total prohibition of all forms of child labour, including agriculture, but the new law of 1960 maintained that children aged twelve years or more could work in agriculture, while German farmers continued to lobby for keeping their right to use their children's labour.[25]

What kind of and how much work did German children of school age (between six and fourteen years) do in agriculture? The following example is from the early 1950s in the region of Marburg, Hessen. The family farm in question used no outside labour. Their eight-year-old daughter did not work, while the fifteen-year-old daughter, who was still at school, did. She helped her mother with indoor work and in the garden, and was responsible for poultry. Otherwise the main contribution came from two sons, aged eleven and thirteen. They helped their father in the fields during the busiest working periods, and more regularly by feeding and watering the animals, spreading straw for bedding and clearing the stable of dung. In the spring they worked in the fields with root crops and potato planting, and in the autumn with potato picking. Their working day was seven or eight hours long during school vacations.[26] If the range of jobs of these two German brothers is compared with that of the two Danish brothers of the same age a century previously (see p. 102 above), the overall picture is not that different, save that mechanisation had removed some of the heaviest jobs, such as threshing, from the range of male farm work.

In the region of Marburg, the youngest school children, aged six or seven, very seldom helped on other farms, while two-fifths of boys and a third of girls helped on the parental farm. In farming families, girls aged eight or nine were of more help than boys of the same age, presumably because they were already able to help with domestic tasks, while typical boys' work outdoors required more muscular strength. From the age of ten up, boys and girls from farming families helped about as much on the parental farm, while more boys than girls were prepared to leave for other farms (Table 6.1). Klaus Beltzer estimated that child labour comprised no more than 1.25 per cent of total agricultural labour. In his view, the significance of schoolchildren's labour lay not in its magnitude, but in its role as a flexible workforce that was there when needed in the busy times, so farmers did not have to hire seasonal labour, which was expensive and difficult to come by. Children also worked on neighbours' farms, and even a whole school class might come to help. Potato picking in particular was a regular autumn job for schoolchildren.[27]

As in Germany, work by rural children was taken for granted in Finland, too. A comparison with Italy suggests that it was not regarded as any problem whatsoever, because all children completed at least the minimum primary-school curriculum, enough to make them literate. Moreover, it was generally socially accepted, and completely legal, for boys or girls to start with wage work the year they turned fourteen, by which time compulsory school was over as a rule. In fact, this was the very argument for maintaining the minimum age at fourteen years in the committee report of 1949 on the protection of young workers. Nonetheless, the great majority of fourteen-year-olds were still at school, while those who had left school for work were mostly rural children. In 1950, eight out of ten, and in 1960 nine out of ten economically active boys aged fourteen were occupied in agriculture and forestry, while in the same years, 1950 and 1960, six and five, respectively, out of ten economically active girls in the same

Table 6.1. A sample of schoolboys and girls by age and the work contribution by schoolchildren from farming families on the parental farm and other farms in Marburg, Hessen, in the early 1950s.

	all schoolchildren				of whom schoolchildren from farming families					
							proportion of whom help on			
							parental farm		other farms	
age	boys	%	girls	%	boys	girls	boys	girls	boys	girls
							%	%	%	%
6–7	898	21.8	889	22.3	228	241	42.5	34.9	2.2	0.4
8–9	861	20.9	777	30.9	264	212	76.1	85.4	13.3	11.3
10–11	992	24.1	946	23.8	347	351	87.6	86.6	27.4	22.8
12 +	1,367	33.2	1,369	34.4	562	523	90.0	91.6	43.6	38.0
		100		100						
N	4,118		3,981		1,401	1,327	1,113	1,048	380	304

NB. The summed percentages by age and sex of schoolchildren from farming families do not equal 100 because not all children worked or because some worked both on the parental farm and other farms.

Source: Baltzer 1957, Table 4.

years worked in agriculture, or more precisely, in animal husbandry. The great majority of economically active rural boys and girls worked on the family farm and, in the case of boys, with their fathers at lumbering sites or in logging.[28]

Notwithstanding the general acceptability of many forms of child labour, the Scandinavian belief in the blessings of work for social engineering was disappearing in official circles. Before the war, day work-centres for schoolchildren, *arbetsstugor* had changed their focus from productive work to hobby-like activities, and had given up selling the products made by the children (which had never been profitable). After the war, *arbetsstugor* became 'free-time centres', or were closed. The last Finnish 'work-centre for children' was closed in 1946, and the last Swedish residential *arbetsstugor* were closed in the 1950s. Correspondingly, in the 1950s, Finnish reformatory schools abandoned the commercial agriculture that had formed the core of compulsory work by the boys who were sent there.[29] In short, productive work had lost its credibility as the remedy for 'idle' or 'delinquent' boys.

In the 1950s, the big question in Europe concerning children was not child labour, even though it was still on the agenda in relation to compulsory education,[30] but the post-war baby boom. Most countries made plans and took special measures in order to move the high numbers of young people smoothly from school to work. An anonymous ILO expert proposed that that countries should make an effort 'to check the influx of young people into crowded fields, such as office work, where there is little future ...'. The problem in France was thought to be the young school leavers 'who are put to work directly in spite of their success at school'. Behind that was believed to be 'an attitude which favours speedy entry into employment', which was prevalent among parents and children.[31] Denmark was not alone in seeing extended compulsory education as a solution:

> The [Danish] Committee considered that the introduction of an eighth year of compulsory school attendance, now under consideration, might, if it were to take place at the peak of the influx of young people into the employment market (1960–62), assist greatly in solving the problem at hand.[32]

In contrast, in 1957, the shortage of young workers was considered the problem in Britain. This was attributed not only to the low birth rates before the baby boom, but also to the fact that the school-leaving age had been raised from fourteen to fifteen in 1947, 'which reduced the quota of young workers entering the employment market by the full number of persons normally becoming available in one year'.[33]

Such statements presume a continuation of demand for young persons in the labour market. However, some typical first jobs for school leavers, such as errand work, were rapidly disappearing.

The rationalisation and standardisation of office work along the principles of Taylorism had been going on since the First World War. For example, clerical work had been broken down into minimal stages in two large Swedish firms, where a smooth flow of documents as on an assembly line was one of the leading principles. This brought young women into offices to do monotonous clerical work, and several errand boys who were part of the fully synchronised logistics. Nevertheless, from the very beginning there were efforts to replace live (and therefore unpredictable) errand boys by technology.[34] This succeeded only after the Second World War. By 1960 'the office boy [had] vanished almost completely' from Britain, and ten years later also from Finland.[35]

Nothing similar seems to have taken place in domestic service, the most typical first job for girls. For example, many girls moving from the countryside to Madrid in the 1950s found shelter with their relatives, but worked for their keep as servants: 'At the age of twelve I left school and came to Madrid to serve at my cousin's', one former servant recalled.[36] Likewise in Helsinki, which was plagued by the scarcity of housing after the war, employment as a domestic servant or living-in child minder meant a place to stay, and hence the job enabled a large number of girls to move from the countryside; no such solution was available to boys. From 1950 to 1970, domestic service was the leading occupation for girls under fifteen, as well as for young women. Work as shop assistants came second for girls, and as messengers third. The most common urban job in 1950 and 1960 for boys under fifteen was that of an errand boy, while that of shop assistant came second. More girls than boys were economically active in Finnish towns and cities because of the high demand for domestic servants and child minders.[37]

The school reforms undertaken in most of Europe in the course of the economically favourable post-war decades took as their model lower-secondary schools, that is schools preparing children for middle-class occupations, while vocational education appeared to be the loser. The slogans of the time were 'equal opportunities' and 'reserve of talent', and the school reforms generally strove to increase the comprehensiveness of the educational system. The lengthening of compulsory education also served to delay entry into the labour market.[38]

There was much concern in the 1970s about the growing reluctance of the young 'to make a career in manual or unskilled jobs'. Filling the gap 'by using immigrant labour and implanting certain industries in less-developed countries' was seen merely as a remedy for the moment. Even quite drastic measures were proposed for breaking down this reluctance. The more conventional ones included life-long education and 'making production work part of the school'. In hindsight, the justification appears almost presumptuous and therefore worth quoting. The proposed changes for enhancing the value of manual work 'would, in the long run, give the advanced countries their only chance of maintaining if not their leadership, at least a certain cultural presence not confined to technology only, in the rest of the world'.[39] Among the critics of 'an expensive school reform' was also an Italian expert, who was concerned about the declining numbers of economically active juveniles, because the young now stayed longer at school.[40] Such concerns proved premature, as economically active juveniles and child manual workers reappeared soon enough.

Nobody in the 1960s and 1970s doubted the ultimate victory of school, or that child labour was a bygone phase in European history. The 138th ILO convention of 1973 recommended that the minimum working age should not be less than the age of the completion of compulsory education, and in any case not less than fifteen years. By 1980, half of the ten countries considered here had ratified the convention: Finland, Germany, Norway, Russia (the USSR) and Spain.[41] One of the reasons why Sweden did not ratify the 138th convention was that Sweden had no minimum age for employment in domestic service or the like (*husligt arbete*), and hesitated to introduce one.[42] At that time, child labour had reappeared on the international agenda, but was thought to be a problem confined to poor countries. There was still some child labour in Europe, but since the children involved rather resembled their predecessors, and also did most of the jobs they performed, it was clear to everyone that it would end once such 'backward' cases caught up with the modern way of life. The future proved to be different.

The return of child labour

Affluent Western consumer societies witnessed the return of child labour as reports on new practices or the expansion of old ones began to appear in the 1980s. Given the time needed for implementing the 'expensive school reforms', it seems that child labour began to increase in Europe at most a decade after the reforms. Eventually street children also returned, in Russia and Germany, for example. It was not only the alert working-class boys and girls delivering newspapers or advertisements who were involved, but also the unfortunate, living miserably on begging, prostitution and small crimes, and seeking shelter in railway stations.[43] Even occupational accidents among children again gave reason for concern.[44]

How, then, can this development, which was clearly unexpected and contrary to received ideas that child labour was connected with poverty, be explained? It seems to me that it might be useful to recall that shortly before, the emergence of newly-industrialising countries (NICs) had also been unexpected and contrary to the then prevailing theories of economic development. Some deny any parallels between the abusive child labour in poor countries and the new child labour in rich countries: '*Ou'y a-t-il de commun entre un petit garçon, souvent rachitique, travaillant douze heures par jour dans un fabrique de tapis pakistanais, et un solide adolescent de nos pays glissant des revues sous les portes, quelques heures par semain? Rien, absolutement rien ...*'.[45] On the contrary, I suggest that we start looking for parallels.[46]

After the Second World War, clothing companies, 'in search of domestic low-cost labour', had started by relocating their operations to areas with access to cheap labour. Thus some Italian peripheral areas witnessed a considerable expansion of the clothing industry. Most of the stages of production within textiles had been mechanised or automated, while sewing still needed women. Compared with other stages, sewing remained extremely labour intensive, and was therefore farmed out to low-wage regions or countries, such as Italy, Finland and Portugal, in Europe.[47]

One Catholic organisation estimated that the number of children aged eight to fourteen employed illegally in the south of Italy in 1988 may have been around 90,000. Even in 1990 hosiery was characterised as a domestic industry in Carpi, in previous centuries the same region had been known for its domestic production of straw hats.[48] In 1996, a study group of the Council of Europe suggested that children in Italy dropped out of school before reaching the age of fourteen because of 'work either at home for their families or illegally in the private sector'.[49] In the 1970s, a US multinational firm in the footwear industry subcontracted exclusive models requiring much manual work to village craftsmen in Spain, many of whom had formerly been independent entrepreneurs.[50] The government of Portugal reported in 1994 to the UN that 'there have been numerous cases of clandestine child labour ... especially in the clothing, footwear, housing, furniture, and textiles industries'.[51]

One is struck by the fact that, in early modern Europe, precisely these two, clothing and footwear, were among the first to be transformed into 'sweated' urban home industries, in which masters' wives and children provided the cheap labour.[52] Is history repeating itself here, but now, as was the case in early modern 'proto-industry', with the dispersion of manufacturing to the countryside? Do we again have mothers and children doing long hours of monotonous outwork, or putting-out work, today called subcontracting? The study group of the Council of Europe has no doubts about the use of child labour in home industries in Mediterranean countries:

> Subcontracting of industrial products from private companies to families is an important part of the picture here. This seems to be an accepted way for manufacturing: providing economic benefit both for private companies as well as for poor families. The losers are the children, kept home from school to increase family income, or given work late at night with little time for homework and play, and too little sleep before the next day at school.[53]

Structural changes in the economy and major transformation in society were experienced in Europe during the decades when child labour returned. This suggests a complex set of factors behind the new child labour. Poverty may explain some of it, but the relationship is not clear. For instance, relative poverty among children did not change much in Spain from 1973 to 1990. This is also supported to some extent by the fact that primary-school enrolment ratios rose from 85 per cent to 100 per cent by 1975.[54] Poverty cannot be ruled out either, since many countries have witnessed the re-emergence of child poverty in the last few decades. For example, the rapid spread of unemployment and low-paid jobs, and the declining purchasing power of national child allowances are presented in a UNICEF report as explanations for the increasing child poverty in eastern Europe.[55]

In a cross-country comparison of poverty trends, Bruce Bradbury and Markus Jäntti found that 'the dominant trend is one of increasing relative child poverty, with the most dramatic increases in Russia, Hungary, Italy and the UK'. In Germany, too, the relative incidence of child poverty increased from 1973 to 1994. Among countries with decreases were Denmark, Norway, Spain and Finland, while it remained on the same level in Sweden and France. According to Bradbury and Jäntti, 'variations in the market incomes received by the families of disadvantaged children are more important' in explaining child poverty across nations than 'differences in welfare state institutions and social transfer outcomes'.[56]

Children's work out of school hours, which must have been there all the time, also became the subject of renewed interest. In the Federal Republic of Germany, the only major exemptions to the law forbidding employment among children under the age of fourteen, or still attending school, included in 1988 work in agriculture, delivering newspapers and helping with sports activities. A survey on child labour in 1988 found that nearly nine per cent of children aged thirteen were engaged in work allowed by law, while 23 per cent had work that was not allowed. The corresponding figures for children aged fourteen were 14 and 22 per cent. An-Margit Jensen and Angelo Saporiti conclude that, in industrialised countries, 'children are found at the marginal, but still quite extensive, parts of the labour market'.[57]

There is principally, although not universally, a favourable attitude to children's work out of school hours in the Nordic countries, evidently because there are few drop-outs from compulsory education.[58] Danish children aged under ten were not allowed to work at all in the 1980s, and children aged under fifteen were not allowed to work full-time. Typical jobs for children were newspaper and advertisement delivery, cleaning, babysitting, taking care of animals, and working in shops. In 1987, the proportion of children with some kind of job rose with each additional year of age, from seven per cent for ten-year-olds to 45 per cent for fourteen-year-olds, and 62 per cent for fifteen-year-olds. The difference in hours worked per week was much smaller: ten-year-olds worked on average 5.5 hours, fifteen-year-olds 9.1.[59]

In five years (1986–1989 and 1991) 276 children aged between ten and fourteen met with occupational accidents in Denmark, a quarter of these were school children. Six of the children died, while 100 of them were seriously injured. Children's jobs as such do not appear accident-prone. They include delivering advertisements and newspapers (87), learning a trade or assisting (53), while only five were errand boys or girls. During the same five years, 23 children aged thirteen or fourteen were diagnosed with work-related diseases. Among these were three restaurant dish washers, a cook's helper, a grill-kiosk worker, some garden helpers, newspaper deliverers, cleaning assistants, and one metal cleaner, one industrial lacquer worker and one glue worker.[60]

Child labour returned to Finland in the 1980s, when the country was more affluent than ever before. A survey carried out in 1989 in Helsinki showed that schoolboys and girls were engaged in delivering advertisements, or had temporary or part-time jobs in fast-food restaurants, for example. A great majority of the pupils in the Finnish survey said that they used their earnings for their own consumption, consisting of typical teenager commodities, while only very few said that they worked because their family needed the money, or that they had to earn their living. The new child labour appeared for many, including the legislators, as a positive and welcome phenomenon. It would teach the school children of a consumer society the value of work and money. Ten years later, schoolchildren's jobs were by and large the same, but the increase in casual and short-tenure jobs appeared somewhat less harmless.[61]

By then Finland had been through a major economic depression, and had learned to live with permanent mass unemployment. Even unemployed adults were now offered casual, short-term delivery jobs, previously thought of as typical teenagers' jobs.[62]

Drawing together the results of several British surveys, Michael Lavalette concludes: 'The extent of child labour was found to be relatively similar when compared within, and across, a number of regions', and that the 'results confirm that children are an important source of labour in modern British society'. In 1988, a survey on the extent and form of child labour was undertaken in Scotland among secondary-school pupils approaching the end of their compulsory education. The returns gave a list of typical jobs for boys and girls, which appears like an up-dated version of the jobs children had a century ago: delivery, sales (retail), catering, farm (animals), hairdressing, manual work, cleaning. Since the types of tasks were fairly similar, irrespective of the locality, 'there is a relatively constant amount of and type of employment available to children', which indicates that child labour may be 'a structural feature of the British economy' (M. Lavalette).[63] At around the same time, it was estimated that about two million children in Britain had jobs. In Birmingham, for example, perhaps nearly 2,000 children aged ten to sixteen were working, three quarters of them in jobs that were not allowed by law.[64]

Lavalette is right in remarking that 'children are a particularly "flexible" and "casual" source of labour power'.[65] However, in a country like Britain, with its extensive immigrant labour force, they were and are not the only source of 'flexible' and 'casual' labour. If children are just filling some niches in segmented labour markets, should we not take a closer look at the changes in the labour market as a whole? Perhaps the question 'why children?' should be reformulated to 'why labour market flexibility?'.

Conclusion

There was an increase in short-term and insecure employment in Britain in the 1980s, a sign that employers were aiming towards a more flexible labour use. Flexibility has become the rule in the deregulated labour markets in Europe today, and permanent employment something of a privilege.[66] Gijsbert van Liemt wondered, in the conclusion of his 1992 study on 'industry on the move', whether what we were seeing was the beginning of a trend. If so, then 'tapping cheaper sources of labour no longer needs a relocation of activities abroad, but rather calls for intensified use of domestic subcontracting or of intensified contacts with labour in the unofficial sector'.[67]

With hindsight, the expansion of new 'flexible' and 'casual' child labour appears to have anticipated a breakdown of the world of work in which secure jobs and permanent employment contracts were the norm, in favour of the unregulated use of labour. This suggests an analogy with the developments in early modern Europe, when the expansion of non-guild systems, such as manufacturing and putting-out production, and the increased use of the non-guild labour of women and children, anticipated the erosion of established craftsmen's solid economic status. At that time, the monopoly of artisan masters was broken by capital moving to the countryside in order to tap 'cheaper sources of labour', while in today's world the monopoly of skilled Western workers, male and female, has been broken by capital moving to other countries and continents, and by technology that enables distance control of scattered producers.

In short, it seems that the successful quest for cheaper labour implies child labour. Previously, increasing competition made profitability a priority over low labour costs, and this, as I have argued, tended to counteract the use of low-productive child labour. It remains to be seen whether the globalising economy will follow suit, or whether it will mould and eventually abandon the prevailing rules of the game.

Phillip Mizen, Angela Bolton and Christopher Pole are critical of the research that has so far been undertaken concerning present-day child labour in the West. It is easy to agree with them that the US approach, which positions work as an aspect of child development 'necessarily leads to a denial of work as a rational response on the part of many children to the specific (and changing) social conditions of childhood'. They also 'reject claims that children's work is best understood in relation to their consumer aspirations'.[68]

What is more relevant here is their discussion of children as a group of marginal workers, and of the evidence suggesting that child labour has become more extensive. They argue, plausibly I think, that there are no children's jobs, since newspaper delivery, for example, a job usually identified with working children, is also done by 'other groups of marginal workers like pensioners or the unemployed'. Perhaps they should have stopped there for a moment. How long have such marginal workers been around in Britain? Were they there in the 1960s, or 1970s? There was a time when newspaper delivery was a proper job and not something done by 'marginal workers'. There was a time when it, as other such service jobs, was not in the domain of the cheapest possible labour. If such labour, including children, now abounds in 'undercapitalised and intensely competitive areas of the service sector', does this not give us reason to look more closely at the changing needs of the mode of production, something that Mizen, Bolton and Pole dismiss as an 'overly deterministic' line of argument? They refer to the 'willingness to employ school age labour [which] has been met with an increase in supply', but then turn to children's motivations for working.[69] Thus they skip the question how this willingness to employ school-age labour came about. It was not there thirty years ago.

Michael Lavalette offers another critical contribution to the theorising on children at work. He sets out to explain 'the process whereby children moved from occupying full-time jobs working alongside, or occasionally in competition with, adult workers ... to occupying, overwhelmingly, part-time out of school work'. He identifies three linked elements, the re-creation of the working-class family, the role of the state in the regulation of family life and childhood, and 'transformations to the employment structure and the opportunities and restrictions these place on children's employment'.[70] It is the last one which is of interest here. After glossing over the familiar history of the working-class family and child labour in nineteenth- and early twentieth-century Britain in a dozen pages, Lavalette arrives at an interesting conclusion. He argues 'that the transition to a capitalist market system and the commodification of labour power that came with it marked a significant intensification in child labour exploitation ...'.[71]

Today we seem again to be witnessing an intensification of child labour, perhaps of exploitation, too. Would Lavalette's conclusion help us to achieve a better understanding of the reasons for this? The commodification of labour power is a relatively recent phenomenon in poor countries, and parallels to British and European history thus readily present themselves. But what is going on in Europe? Is a partial de-commodification of adult labour power on the way, since so many people have fallen outside of the labour market? Is this then balanced by the expansion of child labour, in other words, by the commodification of children's energy?

Notes

1. Horn 1976, p. 86; Horn 1984, pp. 162–181; Hendrick 1992, p. 60.
2. Uhlig 1978, pp. 275, 288–291.
3. Kaschuba 1986, pp. 238, 251–252.
4. Strauss 1932, pp. 31–32.
5. von Westerhagen 1932, pp. 58–72.
6. Koch 1987, pp. 214–216.
7. Quoted in Olsson, L. 1985, pp. 93–98.
8. Sigsgaard 1995, pp. 135–137; Slettan 1978, pp. 91–95, 113–116.

9. Rahikainen 1996.
10. Quoted in Rahikainen 2003, p. 167.
11. Liliequist, M. 1991, pp. 12, 111, 137.
12. Carles 1991, pp. 85–91, quotation p. 89.
13. Karvinen 2001, pp. 121–123, 135–137.
14. Saraceno 1991, p. 457.
15. Censimento industriale e commerciale 1927, Volume IV, Tavola III.
16. Borrás Llop 2000, Tabla 2, Grafico 4. 5. and 6; Borrás Llop 2002, pp. 390–393.
17. de Gabriel 1998, Graph 2. and 3.
18. Hendrick 1980, passim.
19. E.g. International Labour Conference 1938, Report I, passim.
20. Cunningham, S. 1999, pp. 155–158, quotation p. 158.
21. Children in Bondage 1943, pp. 120–121; Rahikainen 1996, pp. 338–339; Rahikainen 2003, pp. 171–175.
22. Wimmer 1979, pp. 54–56, 93–94.
23. Bertoni Jovine 1963, pp. 136–137, 157–169; Pratt 1994, pp. 60, 100, 107.
24. Salvemini 1962, Tab. 2.
25. Becker 1986, pp. 40–41.
26. Baltzer 1957, pp. 9–15.
27. Baltzer 1957, pp. 24–25.
28. Rahikainen 1999. See also Abrahams 1991, pp. 160–193.
29. Lundemark 1980, p. 203; Olsson, O. 1999, pp. 182–189; Rahikainen 1995a; Rahikainen 1998.
30. E.g. International Labour Review 1951, pp. 462–472.
31. International Labour Review 1957, pp. 344, 352.
32. International Labour Review 1957, p. 343.
33. International Labour Review 1957, p. 346.
34. Greiff 1992, pp. 21–29, 172–174.
35. Dale 1962 p. 82; Rahikainen 1999, Table 5.
36. Quoted in Sarasúa 1994, p. 4n.
37. Rahikainen 1999, Table 5.
38. For the school reforms, see, e.g. Degnbol 1991, pp. 60–61 (Denmark); Genovesi 1998, pp. 190–192 (Italy); Härnqvist 1992, pp. 360–366 (Sweden).
39. Visalberghi 1986 [1979], quotations p. 48.
40. Mingione 1981, pp. 19–25.
41. Ruxton 1996, pp. 462–463; Standing 1982; Children and work in Europe 1996, p. 14.
42. Minderårigas tillträde till arbetslivet 1989, pp. 22–27, 34.
43. E.g. Pfennig 1995; Mansurov 2001.
44. Children and work in Europe 1996, pp. 64–65.
45. Rimbaud 1980, p. 8.
46. See Rahikainen 2001a.
47. Mingione 1981, p. 23. Spinanger 1992, quotation p. 109.
48. Belfanti 1993, p. 260.
49. Children and work in Europe 1996, p. 27.
50. Bernabé Maestre 1976, pp. 76–78.
51. Cited in Ruxton 1996, p. 459.

52. Schwarz 1992, pp. 180–207.
53. Children and work in Europe 1996, p. 27.
54. Cantó-Sánchez and Mercader-Prats 1998, pp. 5, 16.
55. Cited in Children and work in Europe 1996, p. 15. See also Mizen, Bolton and Pole 1999, pp. 429–431.
56. Bradbury and Jäntti, 1999, pp. 2, 22, 70–72, quotations p. 1.
57. Jensen and Saporiti 1992, pp. 59–60, quotation p. 59.
58. E.g. Children and work in Europe 1996, pp. 24–25. The Nordic countries include Denmark, Finland, Island, Norway and Sweden.
59. Jensen and Saporiti 1992, pp. 59–60.
60. Bilag til Betænkning 1993, pp. 8–12, 41–43, Tables 1.2, 1.6, 1.10.
61. Kouvonen 2000, pp. 40–46, 90–112.
62. Rahikainen 1999.
63. Lavalette 1994, pp. 67–92, quotations pp. 74, 84; Mizen, Bolton and Pole 1999.
64. Hopkins 1994, p. 233.
65. Lavalette 1994, p. 77.
66. E.g. Atkinson 1987; Kühl 1990; Standing 1982.
67. van Liemt 1992, p. 314.
68. Mizen, Bolton and Pole 1999, quotations p. 424.
69. Mizen, Bolton and Pole 1999, quotations pp. 424, 428, 435.
70. Lavalette 1999, p. 45.
71. Lavalette 1999, pp. 53–67, quotation p. 66.

Conclusions

Today, historical child labour seems different from what it appeared to be when historians believed it belonged to the past. This was still the case in the 1960s when E.P. Thompson and E.J. Hobsbawm wrote their interpretations of nineteenth-century industrial child labour.[1] Now we are faced with the task of explaining historical child labour in terms that would also encompass its return.

If the history of child labour can no longer be told as a story ending with its disappearance, then how should it be told? Much what has been written about it in Europe must be rewritten. It seems to me that the best way to start is to go back in time to the genesis of modern child labour in order to determine whether there was something that was ignored when the happy end was so clearly in sight. Demand for child labour is taken here as a starting point on the journey through four centuries of child labour.

The formative centuries of modern child labour and modern childhood were characterised by frequent and destructive warfare. The wars in early modern Europe drew heavily on human and material resources, which contributed to pauperism and, as it seems, to the harsh policy of forcing the poor to work. One could well imagine how attractive to the poor-relief authorities the new compulsory work schemes must have appeared. For centuries to come, these authorities stubbornly refused to give up the idea that compulsory work could be made profitable. However, reality always proved them wrong.

It is difficult to see any principal difference between the treatment of pauper children and adults in early modern or even early nineteenth-century Europe. The Establishment of the time could not conceive of any other incentives for work than poverty, and if poverty alone was not enough, compulsion. The compulsion applied to deprived children seems to have differed from that applied to adults only in its extreme forms.

Children in workhouses and in orphanages resembling workhouses were mostly engaged in spinning, but so were women and men. If they had a better option, free men and even women would not spin for a living. At least people strove to avoid going to the manufactory, and preferred to spin for it at home. Spinning was a skill so commonly mastered that it carried a very low price. It was hardly even understood as a skill, since a child could do it, as contemporary authorities liked to think. (The skill of writing is an example of the opposite development: it was once a rare and exclusive skill, but today it is so universal in Europe that it has no price and is seldom thought of as a skill, since even a child can do it.) Spinning was one of the most labour-intensive phases of textile production, which was evidently an important factor behind the efforts to push or force more women and children to do it.

The division of labour applied in the manufactories was another factor that explains the increasing use of children and women. Early manufactories did not differ much from workhouses, but if a child working there had a father or mother in the same one, he or she may have escaped the worst conditions. The principle of the division of labour also spread to the crafts. Parish apprentices formed a new proletarian labour force, distinct from the boys who were learning the craft to become master in the traditional way.

The English case has dominated the picture of rural child labour in early modern Europe. First, pauper children in early modern England who were not set to work in orphanages and workhouses were sentenced to work as parish apprentices or indentured servants in the countryside. In contrast, in most of Europe putting deprived children into indentured service or fosterage in the countryside did not became a mass phenomenon until the nineteenth century. Second, it seems to have been common practice since Tudor times in England to send children at a relatively early age to work as servants in another household. It is suggested here that the same may not have been the case generally in Europe, although without proper, quantitative data many questions must remain open. In any case, there are enough detailed studies of parishes in different parts of Europe to suggest that farm servants, as a rule, were more usually in their mid-teens or over than in their early teens. Neither should we ignore the possibility that even such a common practice as life-cycle service may not have been universally accepted. Advancing social stratification and downward social mobility seem to have been accompanied with a reluctance to go into service.

According to the proto-industrial theory, the cottage-industry phenomenon has served as an explanation for large families and poverty among the landless, as children provided the labour from an early age. Again, detailed studies of communities or regions in various parts of Europe paint a more varied picture. In rural areas where money was difficult to come by, proto-industry may have offered a welcome opportunity to earn it. What is more interesting here is the fact that, in different parts of Europe, children in home industries were producing a surprisingly similar range of products, and this is taken to suggest that customer preferences deserve a large role in the discussion on home industries.

With the commercialisation of agriculture, nineteenth-century and early twentieth-century Europe witnessed very labour-intensive forms of agricultural production. Even though peasant farmers' own children contributed to the work in their parental household, farmers around Europe saved labour costs by using 'outside' children. Such children were taken from foundling homes, or they were farmed-out parish pauper children. Landless families took such foster children because of the cash premiums paid by the foundling hospital or the poor-relief authorities. Another source of cheap labour was the children of the landless, who worked for trifling sums, or even for board and lodging only. Children of underlings and tenant farmers also served the landlord, providing an extremely flexible labour reserve. The labour burden and treatment of 'outside' children even involved exploitation.

As far as nineteenth-century manufacturing industry was concerned, the demand for child labour in the countries considered here was concentrated around a dozen industries, depending on how they are grouped. This could be taken as an indication that explaining the demand for child labour is of primary importance. To begin with, the demand for factory children stemmed from the recruitment problems of the early entrepreneurs, and in some places pauper children may have been about the only labour force available. As long as profit margins remained high, productivity was not an issue, but entrepreneurs preferred the cheapest possible labour. After the mechanisation in British textiles, expectations of labour productivity were raised to an unforeseen level. Textile entrepreneurs' efforts to cut labour costs, even if productivity suffered, led to the hiring of children and women. In order to attract children and young women, they even incurred extra costs, such as building dormitories. As far as the other industries discussed here are concerned, that is mining, metal-work and machinery, paper, glass and brick making, tobacco and match manufacture, it appears that the employment of child labour depended on various aspects, such as the labour-intensive character of the trade, the need to adjust production to seasonal or cyclical variations in consumer demand, and the seasonal nature of the production itself.

I suggest that, in explaining the decline in industrial child labour that started in the decades around 1880 in most countries discussed here, we should consider the impact of the growing productivity-consciousness of employers, and possibly also of the improving managerial competence, both fuelled by the profitability challenges during the long deflationary period of the 1870s and 1880s. A critical look at nineteenth-century child-labour laws and contemporary statements gives little support to the idea, common in popular as well as in historical writing, that the first laws would have been intended as successive steps towards the total abolition of industrial child labour. Furthermore, since it is seldom argued that the laws restricting women's work brought about a decline in their contribution to the industrial labour force, the question remains why the laws restricting children's labour should have been crucial. Nevertheless, these laws evidently anticipated reforms in the terms of employment of adult workers.

Children as labour migrants were found in several parts of Europe, from Italy to Scandinavia and Russia. A particularly vulnerable group comprised those covering long distances without their parents. There was even some forced labour migration. Nevertheless, once in the city, children seem to have adapted relatively soon to the urban lifestyle, making use of any opportunity to earn money. Urban working-class children were engaged in work outside of school hours on their own initiative, although this may not have been typical of children from solid families of skilled workers. These practices were strikingly similar irrespective of country. In some countries, primary-school schedules adapted somewhat to children's work out of school hours.

Keeping urban working-class children off the streets and away from 'idleness' was behind many determined, even harsh public and private initiatives of the time, which in hindsight appear disproportionate. The measures included compulsory education and work organised by the authorities or reformers for children in the street. Such a work was often reminiscent of urban outwork, or putting-out work.

Irrespective of the country, child labour, particularly in putting-out production in urban home industries and small workshops, such as sewing and baking, generally consisted of very monotonous, endless tasks described as the most exhausting type of work. It even involved self-exploitation by mothers and children. In contrast, the jobs done by boys and girls engaged in urban service trades, such as running errands and delivery work, appear innovative, albeit of necessity. They could also be taken as anticipating the consumption-oriented lifestyle of the twentieth century.

Until recently, the history of child labour in Europe was, implicitly or explicitly, the story of its disappearance. By the time the ILO agreed the child labour convention of 1973, all of the ten countries considered here had reached the same point where child labour largely appeared to belong to the past. Even today, many forms of child labour, as well as adult labour, do seem past and gone. Yet, the last few decades have shown that child labour is a phenomenon that cannot be explained by poverty alone, as was once thought. It is rather that the expansion of new 'flexible' and 'casual' child labour appears to have anticipated the breakdown of the world of work in which secure jobs and permanent employment contracts were the norm.

In the midst of our affluent societies, children are again engaged in the streets in various ways of making money, and children are again running up and down staircases delivering papers and advertisements. These children make a mockery of the idea of progress, as it was understood just a few decades ago. In the same vein Pierre Caspard raises the question of progress by asking whether the crisis 'currently experienced by school is perhaps, fundamentally, a crisis of the idea or ideology of progress'.[2] Child labour in the age of globalisation challenges the idea of progress. Do we see the partial de-commodification of adult labour power on the way, since so many people have fallen outside of the labour market? Does the expansion of child labour indicate the commodification of children's energy?

What conclusions may be drawn from the four centuries of child labour, as illustrated by patchy evidence from different parts of Europe? It should be pointed out that neither child-labour laws nor any new concept of childhood present themselves as indispensable components of the story as it is told above. Starting with child labour – opportunities for education will be covered later – three tentative conclusions may be drawn.

First, child labour has been closely connected with adult workers' freedom of choice. Children were used in the kind of work that adults were not willing to do, if only they could escape it. Women had, as a rule, fewer choices than men, thus in this respect they have often been closer to children than to men. There have, of course, been various and shifting reasons why men and women have avoided some occupations or jobs. In so far as productivity was ignored by masters or employers, cheap and docile child labour was an acceptable substitute, particularly for women. Children were readily replaced by more productive adult labour, again particularly by women, when adults no longer had a choice, either because they had to accept any work on any terms to keep body and soul together, or because they had no other means of livelihood save wage labour.

Second, child labour and the child labour market seem to have anticipated changes in adult labour and the adult labour market. Children were the first group of workers for whom the law stipulated, for example, the maximum working day, the right to breaks and protection against occupational diseases and accidents. It was only later that corresponding stipulations were extended to adult workers. Children were the first group of workers to be rationalised away from industrial production: in time, this affected one group after the other, and there seems to be no end to it, save full automation or the end of production. In the offices, errand boys and girls were the first to disappear in the wake of the rationalisation and mechanisation of office routines, and since then various clerical jobs, particularly those engaging women, have vanished with further mechanisation and then computerisation.

The urban economy offers other types of example. Many of the service jobs brought into being by the urban way of life, such as selling newspapers on the streets, were first typically a way for children to earn some coins, and it was only later that they became jobs for adults. In an analogous way, casual and 'dead-end' jobs that were still thought of as typical teenager jobs a few decades ago, have since then became adult jobs as well. This is not to say that masters or employers deliberately used children as guinea pigs, or that children themselves would have strived to be pioneers. However, children and school pupils have been easy to hire and dismiss, and as they seldom need to make their living or support a family, or to pay taxes, they have accepted low pay, short and insecure contracts, and otherwise poor terms of employment.

Third, child labour has been intimately connected with children who never worked. The lives of working children and children who never worked were directly connected with each other in upper-class and middle-class households. Children working as servants worked for the well-being of their master's children too, and girls who were hired as child minders carried around babies who would grow up into their future superiors, masters or employers. There were more sublime connections too: working children represented one resource among many to be exploited for the benefit of the social ambitions of masters' children.

Reading about the development of education takes us to the familiar story of modern Western childhood. In the strictly hierarchical societies of the *ancien régime*, quite straightforward arguments were put forward against school education for the children of the labouring population, even in the celebrated age of the Enlightenment. Then, as usual, deeds spoke even louder than words. Public money was allocated to the confinement of children of the poor to workhouses and orphanages, which did not much differ from workhouses, while private charity and ecclesiastic money was needed for establishing schools for the children of the common people.

The principles of the proper education of children of high birth, which Erasmus and Rousseau tried to formulate, were adopted, albeit on the classroom scale, by the bourgeoisie and the middle class as the proper education for their children. This proved a most successful strategy for gaining and maintaining middle-class hegemony in increasingly bureaucratic societies. The traditional secondary-school curriculum, generally applied in Europe, was ideally suited to producing neatly-dressed functionaries for all kinds of neatly-written paperwork. This was a world away from dung heaps, cowsheds and hard labour in the fields, which awaited uneducated rural children; and it was a world away from the greasy and often dangerous work at an increasing pace on factory shop floors, with its ear-splitting noise and polluted air, which awaited uneducated urban children.

The Norwegian anthropologist Jan Brøgger nicely captures the essentials of the middle-class family strategy that distinguished the upwardly mobile from the rest. Most fishermen families in a Portuguese fishing community lived in the late 1970s the life of 'pre-bureaucratic Europeans', as Brøgger calls them. The average fishermen's sons moved around freely with their friends, without letting school bother them too much, up to the age of fourteen when they were considered old enough to follow men to the dangerous fishing grounds at sea. Their sisters went to work as servants in middle-class families at around the age of ten. What was clear to all of them was that, among them, were some modern families with bourgeois aspirations. These families were distinguished from the others by their 'concern for scholastic performance' of their children, 'the care they invested in their children', who were 'subject to more strict supervision', and also 'better groomed and dressed than the average fishermen's children'.[3]

The rhetoric was different from the reality of education. Establishing even very modest schools in the sparsely populated countryside is costly (as we know from present-day developing countries). Children in the countryside were thought to pose a small risk to the social order, so why bother? As a consequence, resources were allocated to their education only sparingly and tardily. In contrast, children in urban areas and factory towns appeared potential rebels, and thus very expensive parallel systems were created: schools for compulsory education, and reformatory schools and the like for those who could not be disciplined in ordinary schools.

Depending on the options and prospects for élite and middle-class children, the gates of secondary education, monopolised by the middle and upper class, were closed or opened for children of the underprivileged. Skilful law makers did not resort to crude methods when it became necessary to close the gates; a few neat ordinances were enough. The gates could be opened wide when new options for middle-class jobs and careers abounded. This took place generally in Europe after the Second World War. Most countries instituted school reform that extended the compulsory education to at least nine years, and which in practice soon became twelve years (which kept juveniles away from the labour market longer). In the post-war decades of economic growth it was deemed that all children should have the right to a middle-class childhood. All children were to be offered 'equal opportunities', even if, as it turned out, some had more equal opportunities than others.

Today the competition has become harder and the future more insecure. The élite close ranks, while the middle class strives to keep its children from social downslide. In a situation such as this, we can expect that the gateways to the decent occupations will become narrower. A few neat measures will be enough: vouchers so that parents may choose freely among schools, more private schools, smaller governmental grants for public schools. The slogan of 'equal opportunities' has been replaced by 'excellence in schools'. When the children of the privileged and the underprivileged no longer meet in the same classroom, when their worlds separate, will it again, as under the *ancien régime*, appear natural that some children must work for the benefit of the more fortunate ones? Would this explain, at least in part, why there are again intellectuals who advocate child labour? They even use the same modifiers, such as 'industrious' and 'useful', as their predecessors in the overtly unequal societies of the past. 'In the eyes of the rich between 1790 and 1830', E.P. Thompson wrote, 'factory children were "busy", "industrious", "useful".'[4]

✳ ✳ ✳

Le sentiment de la famille, le sentiment de classe, et peut-être ailleurs le sentiment de race, appraissent comme les manifestations de la même intolerance à diversité, d'un même souci d'uniformité.

The concept of the family, the concept of the class, and perhaps elsewhere the concept of race, appear as manifestations of the same intolerance towards variety, the same insistence of uniformity.

Philippe Ariès 1960, 1962

Reading Ariès in present-day Europe is embarrassing. More than ever, it reads like a history of the genesis of middle-class childhood: what was part of middle-class childhood was part of childhood. When Ariès finished his study, middle-class childhood was still an expanding project. At that time European children, especially middle-class children, wore clothes that were clearly distinct from those of adults. It was then only natural that Ariès stressed the fact that this was not the case in medieval Europe. Today, Western children and adults again wear more or less similar clothes, and Ariès' arguments appear puzzling (Do we no longer have a clear concept of childhood? Should we have one?).

Another example is offered by education. At the time Ariès wrote his book, schooling and education were for children, so he argued that in medieval times, when this was not the case, people failed to distinguish between children and adults: 'Like the pedagogues of the Middle Ages, they [the humanists of the Renaissance] confused education with culture, spreading education over the whole span of human life, without giving a special value to childhood or youth.'⁵ Hardly had his book come into print when UNESCO launched the idea of life-long education, and today the OECD propagates life-long learning for all. Where is the difference between children and adults?

The United Nations Convention on the Rights of the Child of 1989 defines in principle children as persons aged under eighteen, and similarly in present-day western European child-welfare laws, the upper age limit for the child is often eighteen years, while the age of majority is generally eighteen as well.⁶ Will such formal or judicial age limits be read by future historians as evidence that, at the turn of the twenty-first century in Europe, people thought that children moved directly from childhood to adulthood?

As Ariès indicated, modern childhood was born with the bourgeoisie: 'There is accordingly a remarkable synchronism between the modern age group and the social group: both originated at the same time, in the late eighteenth century, and in the same milieu – the middle class.'⁷ Hugh Cunningham explains: 'By the middle of the nineteenth century an ideology of childhood had become a powerful force in middle-class Europe and North America', and he continues: 'At the heart of that ideology lay a firm commitment to the view that children should be reared in families'. Following the path laid down by Ariès, Cunningham declares: 'What holds the period [1500–1900] together is a heightened sense of the importance of childhood …'. With romanticism this developed into a 'sanctification of childhood'.⁸ Is this not to accept as proof the rhetoric produced by and the self-image of the middle class itself? Is it not more than likely that appearances are deceptive?

Ellen Key's *The Century of the Child* (first published in 1900 in Swedish) is often offered as proof of the breakthrough of the new concept of childhood. The book became a best seller, translated into all major European languages. In her book Key prophesied that the twentieth century would become the century of the child. However, the title is deceptive. She had adopted it from the then popular play 'A Lion's Whelp', in which an older man explained to a younger one that the next century would be the century of the child, and added that a man must think carefully if and when he had the right to create life. Key concluded that the first right of the child is the right to chose its parents. This was to argue for what became known as eugenics, but that she referred to as Darwinism. She had pronounced ideas on the proper ways of bringing up children: 'a large, sunny nursery', and some regular household chores so that they would not always resort to servants, but also firm discipline, absolute obedience and punishment by isolation, but never corporal punishment. She had nothing to offer street children but reformatories.[9]

Perhaps it was symptomatic that the two most single-minded adherents to the evolutionary history of European childhood, Lloyd deMause and Edward Shorter, wrote their contributions in the 1970s in the USA.[10] After the horrors that had taken place in Europe during the Second World War, when children faced the same atrocities as adults, Europeans, including Ariès, were more cautious. It may also be symptomatic that the two most single-minded advocates of child labour, Viviana Zelizer and Clark Nardinelli, wrote their apologies in the USA at the point of time at which the monetarist market economy (the utopia of a self-adjusting market, as Karl Polanyi called it[11]) was about to come off victorious from the Cold War.

In the midst of changes on a global scale it is difficult to follow Carlo Ginzburg's good advice of 'making things strange'.[12] If we try, what do we see in recent sociological contributions to European childhood,[13] if we read them as documents of European societies at the end of the twentieth century?

What first captures the reader's attention is the Scholastic character of the discourse on the extent to which childhood is or is not a social or cultural construction. Is this debate not reminiscent of the medieval discourses of representatives of the Scholastic schools of nominalism, realism and conceptualism? When Aristotelian thinking was added to Scholasticism, a moderating school was born in between the rival extremes. Today, the role of the moderator between rival sociological schools seems to fall to historians.

The second characteristic of sociological contributions is that they echo the linguistic turn (even that reminiscent of Scholastic interest in analysing linguistic expressions). Compared with what was written just a few decades ago, they represent another paradigm. Paradigm changes are more than academic battles. It takes fundamental changes in society for paradigms to change in sciences dealing with society.

Until the linguistic turn, sociologists – whether they liked it or not, or whether they intended it or not – were providing material for social engineering, which was part of what we now, in hindsight, call the modern project. Sociological studies used to reveal what was behind phenomena that were called social problems. Sociologists mailed thousands of inquiries, interviewed thousands of people, in depth or breadth, calculated correlation and drew fourfold tables with headings such as 'social background'. The children they were interested in were called 'working-class children', 'deprived', 'destitute', deviant' or 'delinquent' children. The childhood of these children was thought to be something very concrete, an object of reforming or civilising measures. The linguistic turn in sociology brought with it a change in terms of whose childhood was being conceptualised. In the new contributions, the surveying eye is turned towards middle-class childhood, which is debated in terms of social or cultural construction. Some North-American developmental psychologists speak of 'the elusive historical child', claiming that, after the linguistic turn, social historians and developmental psychology 'are converging upon the notion of "the invented child"'.[14]

I suggest that the replacement of the working-class child of flesh and blood with the elusive, constructed (but still middle-class) child is more than a sociological paradigm shift. It seems to me that it tells of a major turn whereby the Establishment conceded defeat and abandoned the modern project of a middle-class childhood for all.

For three centuries now, if we start from John Locke, the bourgeoisie and the middle class have enjoyed ideological hegemony in terms of the proper education of children, developing middle-class family life and childhood to certain standards, and making the middle-class family strategy the winner. In the last decades of the twentieth century, middle-class childhood asserted itself as the precarious childhood. Today, as poverty and abusive child labour are again on the agenda, a middle-class childhood appears to be a privileged one.

Modern childhood is an age-mate of nationalism. A decade ago, Eric Hobsbawm thought it a good sign that the owl of Minerva was circling around nations and nationalism.[15] Is it also circling around modern European childhood? Hegel thought that the owl of Minerva flies out at dusk. If he was right, then the numerous childhood studies since Ariès would indicate that the middle-class family strategy, for centuries so very successful, is past its peak. For whom is it a good sign, and for whom is it a bad sign, if the owl of Minerva is circling around European childhood today?

Notes

1. Hobsbawm 1974 [1964], pp. 292–293, 310–312, 322; Thompson, E.P. 1980 [1963], pp. 366–384.
2. Caspard 1998, p. 710.
3. Brøgger 1989; pp. 43–44.
4. Thompson, E.P. 1980, p. 377.
5. Ariès 1962, p. 330.
6. E.g. Children and work in Europe 1996, Table 1.
7. Ariès 1962, p. 336. 'Il existe donc un remarquable synchronisme entre la classe d'âge moderne et la classe sociale : l'une et l'autre sont nées en même temps à la fin du XVIIIe siècle, dans le même milieu : la bourgeoisie.' (Ariès 1960, p. 376.)
8. Cunningham, H. 1995, pp. 41, 77.

9.   Key 1900a, pp. 44–81; Key 1900b, pp. 18–49. Key also supported the ideas of Malthus
     and Galton (Key 1900a, pp. 29–31, 135; Key 1900b, pp. 168–179). For a review of Key's
     book, see Cunningham, H. 1995, pp. 163–164.
10. deMause 1974, pp. 1–6, 51–54 and passim; Shorter 1977.
11. Polanyi 1971, p. 3.
12. Ginzburg 1996.
13. The sociological contributions I have in mind are the following: Gittins 1998; Goldson
     1997; Jenks 1996; James and Prout (eds) 1990; Qvortrup 1993; Qvortrup et al. 1994. See
     also Lavalette 1999, pp. 16–19, 55.
14. Cahan et al. 1993, p. 192.
15. Hobsbawm 1991, p. 183.

Bibliography

N.B. Letters **å, ä, æ, ø, ö** appear last in the alphabetical order and **ü** is alphabetised as **y**.

I

Censimento della popolazione del Regno d'Italia al 31 dicembre 1881, Relazione generale, Ministero di Agricoltura, Industria e Commercio, Roma.

Censimento della popolazione del Regno d'Italia al 10 febrario 1901, Volume V. Relazione, Direzione Generale della Statistica, Roma.

Censimento industriale e commerciale al 15 ottobre 1927, Volume IV, Instituto Centrale di Statistica del Regno d'Italia, Roma.

European Historical Statistics 1750–1975 (1981), ed. B.R. Mitchell, Macmillan and Sijthoff and Noordhoff, London and Basingstoke and Alphen aan den Rijn.

Folketællingen i Kongeriket Norge 3 December 1900, Femte Hefte, Norges Officielle Statistik, Fjerde Række Nr. 111, Det Statistiske Centralbureau, Kristiania [Oslo].

Industristatistik 1887 and *1907, Finlands Officiella Statistik XVIII:4 and XVIII:24.*

Resultaterne af Folketællingen i Norge i Januar 1876, C. No. 1, Det Satistiske Centralbureau, Kristiania [Oslo].

Statistique de la France [1861–1865] (1873): *Industrie: Résultats généraux de l'enquête effectuée dans les années 1861–1865, Deuxieme série, Tome XIX*, Nancy.

Statistiske opgaver til belysning af Norges industriella forholde I: Aarene 1870–1875, C. No. 13, Departementet for det indre, Christiania [Oslo].

Svod otchetov fabrichnykh inspektorov za 1901 god (1903), Ministerstvo Finansov, S.-Peterburg.

Table de mortalité des ouvriers mineurs 1923–1928 (1933), Statistique Générale de la France, Paris.

II

Aapola, S. and Kaarninen, M. (eds) (2003), *Nuoruuden vuosisata: Suomalaisen nuorison historia*, Suomalaisen Kirjallisuuden Seura, Helsinki.

Abrahams, R. (1991), *A place of their own: Family farming in eastern Finland*, Cambridge University Press, Cambridge.

Adolphs, L. (1972), *Industrielle Kinderarbeit im 19. Jahrhundert unter Berücksichtigung des Duisburger Raumes*, Duisburger Forschungen 15, Walter Braun Verlag, Duisburg.

Adsuar Moreno, J. (1916), *El niño en la industria: Condiciones en que trabaja, medidas de protección existentes en España y cuáles deberían adoptarse para que esta protección fuera más efectiva*, Sociedad Española de de Higiene, Madrid.

Agahd, K. (1902), *Kinderarbeit und Gesetz gegen die Ausnutzung kindliche Arbeitskraft in Deutschland*, Verlag von Gustav Fischer, Jena.

Agahd, K. (1904), 'Kinderarbeit und Kinderschutz', *Sozialer Fortschritt*, No. 4, pp. 1–15.

Albertini, R. (1996), *La scuola dei poveri: Ragazze povere e orfane adette ai lavorizi di seta e di lino nei territori della Città, Pretura e Capitanato circolare di Rovereto nella primera metà dell'800*, Manfrini Editori, Trento.

Alexandre-Bidon, D. and Closson, M. (1985), *L'Enfant à l'ombre des cathédrales*, Presses Universitaires de Lyon, Lyon.

Alexandre-Bidon, D. and Lett, D. (1997), *Children in the Middle Ages, Fifth–Fifteenth Centuries*, The University of Notre Dame Press, Notre Dame, Indiana.

Allen, R.C. (1988), 'The Growth of Labor Productivity in Early Modern English Agriculture', *Explorations in Economic History*, vol. 25:2, pp. 117–146.

Allen, R.C. (1991), 'Labor Productivity and Farm Size in English Agriculture before Mechanization: Reply to Clark', *Explorations in Economic History*, vol. 28:4, pp. 478–492.

Amstrong, W.A. (1990), 'The countryside', in Thompson, F.L.M. (ed) (1990), pp. 87–153.

Andersen, S.A. (1985), *Salt og brød gør kinden rød. Arbejderliv i Århus 1870–1940*, Universitetsforlaget i Århus, Århus.

Anderson, M. (1971), *Family structure in nineteenth century Lancashire*, Cambridge University Press, Cambridge.

Anderson, M. (1980), *Approaches to the History of the Western Family, 1500–1914*, The Macmillan Press, London and Basingstoke.

Anderson, M.S. (1988), *War and Society in Europe of the Old Regime, 1618–1789*, Fontana Press, London.

Anderson, P. (1993), *Lineages of the Absolutist State*, Verso, London and New York.

Arbaiza Vilallonga, M. (1998), 'Labour Migration During the First Phase of Basque Industrialization: The Labour Market and Family Motovations', *The History of the Family*, vol. 3:2, pp. 199–219.

Ariès, P. (1962), *Centuries of Childhood: A Social History of Family Life*, Vintage Books, New York. Original: Ariès P. (1960), *L'enfant et la vie familiale sous l'ancien régime*, Librairie Plon, Paris.

Assion, P. (1987), 'Die Gesindeverhältnisse im hinteren Odenwald', in Becker and Matter (1987), pp. 101–124.

Atkinson, J. (1987), 'Flexibility or fragmentation? The United Kingdom labour market in the eighties', *Labour and Society*, vol. 12:1, pp. 87–105.

Audoux, M. (1936 [1910]), *Marie-Claire*, Arthème Fayard, Paris.

Bahamonde, Á. and Martínez, J.A. (1994), *Historia de España siglo XIX*, Catedra, Madrid.

Baltzer, K. (1957), *Probleme der bäuerlichen Kinderarbeit*, Inaug.-Diss., Phillipps-Universität zu Marburg, Marburg.

Bardet, J.-P. (1987), 'L'Enfance abanonnée au cœur des interrogations sociales', *Histoire, Economie et Societé*, vol. 6:3, pp. 291–299.

Barbagli, M. (1982), *Educating for Unemployment: Politics, Labour Markets, and the School System – Italy, 1859–1973*, Columbia University Press, New York.

Barbagli, M. (1984), *Sotto lo stesso tetto: Mutamenti della famiglia in Italia dal XV al XX secolo*, Il Mulino, Bologna.

Barbagli, M. (1991), 'Marriage and the family in Italy in the early nineteenth century', in Davis and Ginsborg (ed) (1991), pp. 92–127.

Barnett, D. (1998), *London, Hub of the Industrial Revolution: A Revisionary History 1775–1825*, Tauris Academic Studies, London.

Bater, J.H. (1976), *St Petersburg: Industrialization and Change*, Edward Arnold, London.

Becchi, E. and Julia, D. (eds) (1998), *Histoire de l'enfance en Occident, Tome 2: Du XVIIIe siècle à nos jours*, Éditions du Seuil, Paris.

Becchi, E. and Julia, D. (1998), 'Histoire de l'enfance, histoire sans parole?', in Becchi and Julia (eds) (1998), pp. 7–39.

Becker, S. (1986), *Arbeit und Gerät als Zeichensetzung bäuerlicher Familienstrukturen: Zur Stellung der Kinder im Sozialgefüge landwirtschaftlicher Betriebe des hessischen Hinterlandes zu Beginn des 20. Jahrhunderts*, Inaug.-Diss., Phillips-Universität Marburg/Lahn, Marburg.

Becker, S. and Matter, M. (eds) (1987), *Gesindewesen in Hessen: Studien zur historischen Entwicklung und sozialkulturellen Ausprägung ländlicher Arbeitsorganisation*, Hessische Blätter für Volk- und Kulturforschung 22, Jonas Verlag, Marburg.

Belfanti, C.M. (1993), 'Rural manufactures and rural proto-industries in the "Italy of the Cities" from the sixteenth through the eighteenth century', *Continuity and Change*, vol. 8:2, pp. 253–280.

Benjamin, W. (1987), *Berliner Kindheit um neunzehnhundert*, Suhrkamp Verlag, Frankfurt am Main.

Berg, M. (1994), *The Age of Manufactures, 1700–1820: Industry, innovation and work in Britain*. Routledge, London and New York.

Berg, M. and Bruland, K. (eds) (1998), *Technological Revolutions in Europe*, Edward Elgar, Cheltenham and Northhampton.

Bergqvist, K., Petersson, K. and Sundkvist, M. (eds) (1995), *Korsvägar: En antologi om möten mellan unga och institutioner förr och nu*, Symposion, Stockholm/Stehag.

Berlin, M. (1997), '"Broken all in pieces": artisans and the regulation of workmanship in early modern London', in Crossick (ed) (1997), pp. 75–91.

Bernabé Maestre, J.M. (1976), *La industria del calzado en el Valle del Vinalopó*, Universidad de Valencia,Valencia.

Bertoni Jovine, D. (1963), *L'alienazione dell'infanzia: Il lavoro minorile nella società moderna*, Editori Riuniti, Roma.

Betänkande 1877: *Betänkande angående minderårigas antagande och användande i fabrik, handtverk eller annan handtering*, Stockholm.

Betänkande 1892: *Betänkande afgivet den 11 mars 1892 af komitén för revision af förordningen den 18 november 1881 angående minderårigas användande i arbete vid fabrik, handtverk eller annan handtering, m.m.*, Stockholm.

Bideau, A. and Brunet, G. (1996), 'Stay or Leave? Individual Choice and Family Logic: The Destinations of Children Born in the Valserine Valley (French Jura) in the Eighteenth and Nineteenth Centuries', *The History of the Family*, vol. 1:2, pp. 159–168.

Bierer, W. (1913), *Die hausindustrielle Kinderarbeit im Kreise Sonneberg: Ein Beitrag zur Kritik des Kinderschutzgesetzes*, Verlag von J.C.B. Mohr, Tübingen.

Bilag til Betænkning om børn og unges erhvervsarbeijde (1993), *Betænkning 1257*, Copenhague.

Bjurman, E.L. and Olsson, L. (eds) (1979), *Barnarbete och arbetarbarn*, Nordiska museet, Stockholm.

Bjurman, E.L. (1979), 'Barnarbete i 1892 års betänkande', in Bjurman and Olsson (eds) (1979), pp. 26–40.

Bjurman, E.L. (1995), *Barnen på gatan*, Tidens förlag, Stockholm.

Bjørn, C. (ed) (1988a), *Det danske landbrugs historie II*, Landbohistorisk Selskab, Odense.

Bjørn, C. (ed) (1988b), *Det danske landbrugs historie III*, Landbohistorisk Selskab, Odense

Bjørn, C. (ed) (1998), *The Agricultural Revolution Reconsidered*, Landbohistorisk Selskab, Odense.

Blanchard, I. (1984), 'Industrial employment and the rural labour market 1380–1520', in Smith, R.M. (ed) (1984), pp. 227–276.

Blaug, M. (1961), 'The Productivity of Capital In The Lancashire Cotton Industry during the Nineteenth Century', The Economic Hisrory Review, vol. 13:3, pp. 358–381.

Blum, J. (1972), *Lord and Peasant in Russia, From the Ninth to the Nineteenth Century*, Princeton University Press, Princeton.

Boje, P. (2000), 'Ledelse og ledere i dansk industri 1870–1970', in Rostgaard and Wagner (eds) (2000), pp. 61–90.

Boli, J. (1989), *New Citizens for a New Society: The Institutional Origins of Mass Schooling in Sweden*, Pergamon Press, Oxford.

Bolin-Hort, P. (1989), *Work, Family and the State: Child Labour and the Organization of Production in the British Cotton Industry, 1780–1920*, Lund University Press, Lund.

Bonnaissie, P. (1975), *La organizacion del trabajo en Barcelona a fines del siglo XV*, Universidad de Barcelona, Instituto de Historia Medieval, Barcelona.

Boot, H.M. (1995), 'How skilled were Lancashire cotton factory workers in 1833?', *Economic History Review*, vol. 48:2, pp. 283–303.

Booth, C. (1886), 'Occupations of the People of the United Kingdom, 1801–81', *Journal of the Statistical Society*, vol. 49 (June), pp. 314–439.

Borderies-Guereña, J. (1996), 'Niños y niñas en familia', in *Historia de la infancia* (1996), pp. 19–66.

Borrás, J.M. and Cohen, A. (1990), 'Aproximation al trabajo infantil y juvenil en la mineria española (1868–1930)', in *XV Simposi d'anàlisi econòmica, Vol. I*, Dpt. d'Economia i d'Història Econòmica, Universitat Autònoma de Barcelona, pp. 57–66.

Borrás Llop, J.M. (1995), 'Actitudes patronales ante la regularization del trabajo infantil, en el tránsito del siglo XIX al XX: Salarios de subsistencia y economías domésticas', *Hispania*, vol. 55:2, pp. 629–644.

Borrás Llop, J.M. (1996), 'Zagales, pinches, gamenes... aproximaciones al trabajo infantil', in *Historia de la infancia* (1996), pp. 227–309.

Borrás Llop, J.M. (1999), 'El trabajo infantil en la industria de Barcelona según el Censo Obrero de 1905', *Historia Social*, No. 33, pp. 25–48.

Borrás Llop, J.M. (2002), 'El trabajo infantil en el mundo rural español (1849–1936): Genero, edades y ocupaciones', in Martínez Carrión (ed) (2002), pp. 497–547.

Boucheron, M. (1869), *Les enfants assistés et la famille*, Paul Dupont, Paris.

Bowen, H.V. (1998), *War and British society 1688–1815*, Cambridge University Press, Cambridge.

Bradbury, B. and Jäntti, M. (1999), *Child Poverty Across Industrialized Nations*, UNICEF International Child Development Centre, Florence.

Braun, R. (1990), *Industrialisation and Everyday Life*, Cambridge University Press, Cambridge.

Brown, J.C. (1995), 'Imperfect Competition and Anglo-German Trade Rivalry: Market for Cotton Textiles before 1914', *The Journal of Economic History*, vol. 55:3, pp. 494–527.

Brembeck, H. (1986), *Tyst, lydig, arbetsam: Om barnuppfostran på den västsvenska landsbygden under senare delen av 1800-talet*, Etnologiska Föreningen i Västsverige, Göteborg.

Brockmann, J-L. (1987), 'Mareleis, die letzte Scweinehirtin von Wasenberg (1871–1945), in Becker and Matter (eds) (1987), pp. 145–167.

Brugger von Nesslau, M. (1991), *Kindheit im zaristischen Russland des 19. Jahrhunderts*, ADAG Administration & Druck, Zürich.

Bruland, K. (ed) (1991), *Technology Transfer and Scandinavian Industrialisation*, Berg, New York and Oxford.

Bruland, K. (1989), *British Technology and European Industrialization: The Norwegian textile industry in the mid nineteenth century*, Cambridge University Press, Cambridge.

Bruland, K. (1991), 'The Norwegian Mechanical Engineering Industry and the Transfer of Technology, 1800–1900', in Bruland (ed) (1991), pp. 229–293.

Bruland, K. (1998), 'Skills, Learning and International Diffusion of Technology: A Perspective on Scandinavian Industrialisation', in Berg and Bruland (eds) (1998), pp. 161–187.

Brøgger, J. (1989), *Pre-bureaucratic Europeans*, Norwegian University Press, Oslo.

Bull, E. (1982), 'Industrial Boy Labour in Norway', in Thompson and Burchard (eds) (1982), pp. 223–231.

Bull, E. (1984), 'Barn i industriarbeid', in Hodne and Sogner (eds) (1984), pp. 76–86.

Burke, P. (1994), *Popular Culture in Early Modern Europe*, Scolar Press, Aldershot.

Büttner, C. and Ende, A. (eds) (1984), *Jahrbuch der Kindheit 1: Kinderleben in Geschicte und Gegenwart*, Beltz Verlag, Weinheim and Basle.

Cahan, E., Mechling, J., Sutton-Smith, B. and White, S.H. (1993), 'The elusive historical child: Ways of knowing the child history and psychology', in Elder, Modell and Parke (eds) (1993), pp. 192–223.

Camps i Cura, E. (1996), 'Family Strategies and Children's Work Patterns: Some Insights from Industrializing Catalonia, 1850–1920', in Cunningham and Viazzo (eds) (1996), pp. 57–71.

Camps-Cura, E. (1998), 'Transitions in Women's and Children's Work Patterns and Implications for the Study of Family Income and Household Structure: The Case Study From the Catalan Textile Sector (1850–1925), *The History of the Family*, vol. 3:2, pp. 137–153.

Cantó-Sánchez, O. and Mercader-Prats, M. (1998), *Child Poverty in Spain: What Can Be Said?*, UNICEF International Child Development Centre, Florence.

Capul, M. (1983), *Internat et internement sous l'ancien régime: Contribution à l'histoire de l'éducation spéciale, Tome 1*, Centre technique national d'études et de recerces sur les handicaps et les inadaptations, Paris.

Capul, M. (1984), *Internat et internement sous l'ancien régime: Contribution à l'histoire de l'éducation spéciale, Tome 2*, Centre technique national d'études et de recerces sur les handicaps et les inadaptations, Paris.

Carles, É. (1991), *A Wild Herb Soup: The Life of a French Countrywoman*, as told to R. Destanque, Victor Gollancz, London.

Caron, J.C. (1997), 'Young People in School: Middle and High School Students in France and Europe', in Levi and Schmitt (eds) (1997), pp. 117–173.

Casey, J. (1999), *Early Modern Spain: A Social History*, Routledge, London and New York.

Caspard, P. (1998), 'The School in Crisis, Crisis in the Memory of School: School, Democracy and Economic Modernity in France from the late Middle Ages to the Present Day', *Paedagogica Historica*, vol. 34:3, pp. 691–710.

Cassis, Y. (1997), *Big Business: The European Experience in the Twentieth Century*, Oxford University Press, Oxford.

Casson, M. (1999), 'The Economics of the Family Firm', *Scandinavian Economic History Review*, vol. 47:1, pp. 10–23.

Castles, F.G. (ed) (1993), *Families of Nations: Patterns of Public Policy in Western Democracies*, Darthmouth, Aldershot.

Caty, R. (ed) (2002), *Enfants au travail: Attitudes des élites en Europe occidentale et méditerranéenne aux XIXe et XXe siècles*, Publications de l'Université de Provence, Aix-en-Provence.

Caunce, S. (1975), 'East Riding Hiring Fairs', *Oral History*, vol. 3:2, pp. 45–52.

Cavallo, S. (1990), 'Patterns of poor relief and patterns of poverty in eighteenth-century Italy: the evidence of the Turin Ospedale di Carità', *Continuity and Change*, vol. 5:1, pp. 65–98.

Cerman, M. (1993), 'Proto-industrialization in an urban environment: Vienna, 1750–1857', *Continuity and Change*, vol. 8:2, pp. 281–320.

Cerutti, S. (1991), 'Group strategies and trade strategies: the Turin tailors' guild in the late seventeenth and early eighteenth centuries', in Woolf (ed) (1991), pp. 102–147.

Chapman, S.D. and Chassagne, S. (1981), *European Textile Printers in the Eighteenth Century: A Study of Peel and Oberkampf*, Heineman Educational Books, London.

Chassagne, S. (1998), 'Le travail des enfants au XVIIIe et XIXe siècles', in Becchi and Julia (eds) (1998), pp. 224–272.

Chayanov, A.V. (1966 [1925]), *The Theory of Peasant Economy*, eds. D. Thorner, B. Kerblay and R.E.F. Smith, The American Economic Associaltion and Richard D. Irwin, Homewoods, Ill.

Children and work in Europe (1996): *Report prepared by a study group 1994–95 programme of co-ordinated research in the employment field*, Steering Committee for employment and Labour (CDEM), Council of Europe, Strasbourg.

Children in Bondage (1943), *Children in Bondage: A Survey of Child Life in the Occupied Countries of Europe and in Finland*, Save the Children Fund, London.

Chiri, M. (1990 [1908]), *Il lavoro dei fanciulli nell'industria in Italia*, L'Associazione Internazionale per la Protezione Legale dei Lavoratori, Roma, repr. L. Ponzio, Pavia.

Christensen, D.C. (1998), 'The agricultural revolution – reconsidered: Technological and institutional innovations 1750–1820', in Bjørn (ed) (1998), pp. 35–47.

Christensen, J. (1988), 'Den nye landbokultur', in Bjørn (ed) (1988b), pp. 383–410.

Christensen, J.P. (2002), *Fabriksarbejdere og funktionærer 1870–1972: Dansk industri efter 1879, Bind 6*, Odense Universitetsforlag, Odense.

Cipolla, C.M. (1981), 'Economic Fluctuations, the Poor and Public Policy (Italy, 16th and 17th Centuries)', in Riis (ed) (1981), pp. 65–77.

Cives, G. (ed) (1994), *La scuola italiana dall'unita ai nostri giorni*, La Nuova Italia, Firenze.

Cives, G. (1994), 'La scuola elementare e popolare', in Cives (ed) (1994), pp. 55–103.

Clark, G. (1991), 'Labor Productivity and Farm Size in English Agriculture before Mechanization: A Note', *Explorations in Economic History*, vol. 28:2, pp. 248–257.

Clark, G. (1994), 'Factory Discipline', *The Journal of Economic History*, vol. 54:1, pp.128–163.

Cohen, A. (2002), 'Le travail des enfants entre droit et pratiques sociales: Un observatoire médico-patronal en Andalousie minière (1902–1920), in Caty (ed) (2002), pp. 253–265.

Coignet, J-R. (1923 [1851]), *Les Cahiers du Capitaine Coignet*, ed. Lorédan-Larchey, Librairie Hachette, Paris.

Collected Works of Erasmus (1985): *Literary and Educational Writings 3*, ed. J.K. Sowards, University of Toronto Press, Toronto.

Colli, A. and Rose, M.B. (1999), 'Families and Firms: The Culture and Evolution of Family Firms in Britain and Italy in the Nineteenth and Twentieth Century', *Scandinavian Economic History Review*, vol. 47:1, pp. 24–47.

Cooter, R. (ed) (1992), *In the Name of the Child: Health and welfare, 1880–1940*, Routledge, London and New York.

Crafts, N.F.R. and Mills, T.C. (1994), 'Trends in Real Wages in Britain, 1750–1913', *Explorations in Economic History*, vol. 31:2, pp. 176–194.

Craig, L.A. and Fisher, D. (1992), 'Integration of the European Business Cycle: 1871–1910', *Explorations in Economic History*, vol. 29:2, pp. 144–168.

Crossick, G. (ed) (1997), *The Artisan and the European Town, 1500–1900*, Ashgate, Aldershot.

Crossick, G. and Haupt, H-G. (1995), *The Petite Bourgeoisie in Europe 1780–1914: Enterprise, Family and Independence*, Routledge, London and New York.

Crouzet, F. (1994), 'England and France in the eighteenth century: a comparative analysis of two economic growths', in O'Brien (ed) (1994b), pp. 46–77.

Cunningham, H. (1990), The Employment and Unemployment of Children in England c. 1680–1851, *Past & Present*, No. 126, pp. 115–150.

Cunningham, H. (1992), *The Children of the Poor: Representations of Childhood since the Seventeenth Century*, Blackwell, Cambridge, Mass.

Cunningham, H. (1995), *Children & Childhood in Western Society since 1500*, Longman, London and New York.

Cunningham, H. (1996), 'Combating Child Labour: The British Experience', in Cunningham and Viazzo (eds) (1996), pp. 41–55.

Cunningham, H. (2000), 'The Decline of child labour: labour markets and family economies in Europe and North America since 1830', *The Economic History Review*, vol. 53:3, pp. 409–428.

Cunningham, H. and Viazzo, P.P. (eds) (1996), *Child Labour in Historical Perspective, 1800–1985: Case Studies from Europe, Japan and Colombia*, UNICEF International Child Development Centre and Instituto degli Innocenti, Florence.

Cunningham, S. (1999), 'The Problem that Doesn't Exist? Child Labour in Britain 1918–1970', in Lavalette (ed) (1999), pp. 139–172.

Czap, P. Jr. (1983), '"A large family: the peasant's greatest wealth": serf households in Mishino, Russia, 1814–1858', in Wall (ed) (1983), pp. 105–151.

Dale, J.R. (1962), *The Clerk in Industry: A survey of the occupational experience, status, education, and vocational training of a group of male clerks employed in industrial companies*, Liverpool University Press, Liverpool.

Daru, C. and Bournat, V. (1875), *Adoption éducation et correction des enfants pauvres, abandonnés, orphelins ou vicieux*, Libraires-Éditeurs, Paris.

Davin, A. (1982), 'Child Labour, the Working-Class Family, and Domestic Ideology in 19th Century Britain', *Development and Change*, vol. 13:4, pp. 633–652.

Davin, A. (1984), 'Working or Helping? London Working-Class Children in the Domestic Economy', in Smith, J., Wallerstein and Evers (eds) (1984), pp. 215–232.

Davin, A. (1996), *Growing Up Poor: Home, School and Street in London 1870–1914*, Rivers Oram Press, London.

Davis, N.Z. (1983), *The Return of Martin Guerre*, Harvard University Press, Cambridge, Mass. and London.

Davis, N.Z. (1975), *Society and Culture in Early Modern France*, Stanford University Press, Stanford, California.

Davis J. and Ginsborg, P. (eds) (1991), *Society and Politics in the Age of the Risorgimiento*, Cambridge University Press, Cambridge.

de Coninck-Smith, N., Sandin, B. and Schrumpf, E. (eds) (1997), *Industrious Children: Work and Childhood in the Nordic Countries 1850–1990*, Odense University Press, Odense.

de Gabriel, N. (1998), 'Literacy, Age, Period and Cohort in Spain (1900–1950)', *Paedagogica Historica*, vol. 34:1, pp. 29–62.

Degnbol, L. (1991), 'Rig/fattig og dreng/pige i børnens skole: Træk af delingens historie i skolen', in Haue et al. (eds) (1991), pp. 51–62.

deMause, L. (ed) (1974), *The History of Childhood*, The Psychohistory Press, New York.

deMause, L. (1974), 'The Evolution of Childhood', in L. deMause (ed) (1974), pp. 1–73.

Deutsch, J. (1907), *Die Kinderarbeit und ihre Bekämpfung*, Verlag von Rascher & Co, Zürich.

de Viguerie, J. (1978), *L'institution des Enfants: L'éducation en France XVIe – XVIIe siècle*, Calmann-Lévy, Paris.

Devine, T.M. (ed) (1984), *Farm Servants and Labour in Lowland Scotland, 1770–1914*, John Donald Publishers, Edinburgh.

Devine, T.M. and Dickson, D. (eds) (1983), *Ireland and Scotland, 1600–1850*, John Donald Publishers, Edinburgh.

Devreese, D.E. (1999), 'The International Working Men's Association (1864–1876) and Workers' Education: An Historical Approach', *Paedacogica Historica*, vol. 35:1, pp. 15–21.

de Vries, J. (1994a), 'The Industrial Revolution and the Industrious Revolution', *The Journal of Economic History*, vol. 54:2, pp. 249–270.

de Vries, J. (1994b), 'How did pre-industrial labour markets function?', in Grantham and MacKinnon (eds) (1994), pp. 39–63.

Dewar, D. (1910), *The Children Act, 1908 and Other Acts Affecting Children in the United Kingdom*, William Green & Sons, Edinburgh and London.

Dixon, S. (1999), *The Modernisation of Russia 1676–1825*, Cambridge University Press, Cambridge.

Dokka, H.-J. (1967), *Fra allmueskole til folkeskole: Studier i den norske folkeskolens historie i det 19. hundreåret*, Universitetsforlaget, Bergen.

Dosi, G., Giannetti, R. and Toninelli, P.A. (eds) (1992), *Technology and Enterprise in a Historical Perspective*, Clarendon Press, Oxford.

Dribe, M. (2000), *Leaving Home in a Peasant Society: Economic Fluctuations, Household Dynamics and Youth Migration in Southern Sweden, 1829–1866*, Almqvist & Wiksell International, Stockholm.

Dubert, I. (1999), 'Domestic service and social modernisation in urban Galicia, 1752–1920', *Continuity and Change*, vol. 14:2, pp. 207–226.

Duffy, P. (2000), *The skilled compositor, 1850–1914: An Aristocrat among Working Men*, Ashgate, Aldershot.

[Du Maroussem, P.] (1893), *La petite industrie, Tome I: L'alimentation à Paris*, Imprimerie Nationale, Paris.

[Du Maroussem, P.] (1894), *La petite industrie, Tome II: Le vêtement à Paris*, Imprimerie Nationale, Paris.

Dupin, C. (1840), *Du travail des enfants qu'emploient les ateliers, les usines et les manufactures, considéré dans les intérêts mutuels de la société, des familles et de l'industrie*, Bachelier, Paris.

Duroux, R. (2001), 'The Temporay Migration of Males and the Power of Females in a Stem-Family Society: The Case of Nineteenth-Century Auvergene', *The History of the Family*, vol. 6:1, pp. 33–49.

Dönhoff, M.G. (1988), *Kindheit in Ostpreussen*, Siedler Verlag, Berlin.

Edgren, L. (1986), 'Crafts in transformation?: Masters, journeymen, and apprentices in a Swedish town, 1800–1850', *Continuity and Change*, vol. 1:3, pp. 363–383.

Edvardsen, E. (1992), *Den gjenstridige allmue: Skole og levebrod i et nordnorsk kystsamfunn ca. 1850–1900*, Solum, Oslo.

Ehlers, S. (1991), 'Veje til voksenlivet: Overvejelser vedrørende den konfirmerade ungdoms historie', in Haue et al. (eds) (1991), pp. 63–74.

Ehmer, J. (1997), 'Worlds of mobility: migration patterns of Viennese artisans in the eighteenth century', in Crossick (ed) (1997), pp. 172–199.

Eklof, B. (1986), *Russian Peasant Schools: Officialdom, village culture, and popular pedagogy, 1861–1914*, University of California Press, Berkeley and Los Angeles.

Elder, G.H., Modell, J. and Parke, R.D. (eds) (1993), *Children in time and space: Developmental and historical insights*, Cambridge University Press, Cambridge and New York.

Ellena, V. (1879), 'La Statistica di alcune Industrie italiane', in *Archivo di Statistica, Anno IV, Fase III*, Rome, pp. 359–511.

Enders, L. (1995), 'On social interaction within the family', in Larsson and Myrdal (ed) (1995), pp. 106–108.

Engel, B.A. (1978), 'Mothers and Daughters: Family Patterns and the Female Intelligentsia', in Ransel (ed) (1978), pp. 44–59.

Engman, M. (1983), *S:t Petersburg och Finland: Migrationen och influens 1703–1917*, Societas Scientarum Fennica, Helsinki.

Engman, M. (ed) (1992), *Ethnic Identity in Urban Europe: Comparative Studies on Governments and Non-Dominant Ethnic Groups in Europe, 1850–1940*, European Science Foundations and New York University Press, Dartmouth.

Engman, M. (1992), 'The Finns in St Petersburg', in Engman (ed) (1992), pp. 99–130.

Erdozáin-Azpilicueta, P. and Mikelarena-Peña, F. (1998), 'Labor Power, Social and Economic Differentials and Adaptive Strategies of Peasant Households in Stem-Family Regions of Spain', *The History of the Family*, vol. 3:2, pp. 155–172.

Eriksson, I. and Rogers, J. (1978), *Rural Labor and Population Change: Social and Demographic Developments in East-central Sweden during the nineteenth Century*, Uppsala University, Uppsala.

Evans, C. and Rydén, G. (1998), 'Kinship and the Transformation of Skills: Bar Iron Production in Britain and Sweden, 1500–1860', in Berg and Bruland (eds) (1998), pp. 188–206.

Evans, R.J. and Lee, W.R. (eds) (1986), *The German Peasantry: Conflict and Community in Rural Sociaty from the Eighteenth to the Twentieth Centuries*. Croom Helm, London.

Farge, A. and Revel, J. (1991), *The Vanishing Children of Paris: Rumour and Politics before the French Revolution*, Harvard University Press, Cambridge, Mass.

Farge, A. (1992), *Vivre dans la rue à Paris au XVIIIe siècle*, Gallimard, Paris.

Farr, J.R. (1997), 'Cultural analysis and early modern artisans', in Crossick (ed) (1997), pp. 56–74.

Fauve-Chamoux, A. (1996), 'Beyond Adoption: Orphans and Family Strategies in Pre-Industrial France', *The History of the Family*, vol. 1:1, pp. 1–13.

Fedorow, A.J. (1897), *Grundzüge der polizei-ärztlichen Beaufsichtigung der Prostitution in St. Petersbutg*, W. Köhne & Co., St. Petersburg.

Feinstein, C. (1991), 'A New Look at the cost of living 1870–1914', in Foreman-Peck (ed) (1991), pp. 151–179.

Fellman, S. (2001), *Uppkomsten av en direktörsprofession: Industriledarnas utbildning och karriär i Finland 1900–1975*, Finska Vetenskaps-Societeten, Helsinki.

Fellman, S. and Hjerppe, H. (2001), 'The Strengberg Tobacco Company – An Early Succesful Finnish Multinational', in Henrekson, Larsson and Sjögren (eds) (2001), pp. 257–275.

Fineschi, F. (1993), 'I "Monelli" della Quarconia: Controllo pubblico e disciplinamento dei fancioulli in un instituto fiorentino del Seicento', in Niccoli (ed) (1993), pp. 252–286.

Finucane, R.C. (1997), *The Rescue of the Innocents: Endangered Children in Medieval Miracles*, Macmillan, London.

Fitch, N. (1986), '"Les Petits Parisiens en Provence": The Silent Revolution in the Allier, 1860–1900', *Journal of Family History*, vol. 11:2, pp. 131–155.

Flandrin, J-L. (1980), *Families in former times: Kinship, household and sexuality*, Cambridge University Press, Cambridge.

Florén, A. (1994), 'Social Organisation of Work and Labour Conflicts in Proto-Industrial Iron Production in Sweden, Belgium and Russia', *International Review of Social History*, vol. 39, Supplement 2, pp. 83–113.

Florén, A. and Rydén, G. (1992), *Arbete, hushåll och region: Tankar om industrialiseringspro cesser och den svenska järnhanteringen*, Uppsala universitet, Uppsala.

Foreman-Peck, J. (ed) (1991), *New Perspectives on the late Victorian economy: Essays in Quantitative Economic History 1860–1914*, Cambridge University Press, Cambridge.

Fossen, A.B. (1989), *Nordens eldste barneskole: Christi Krybbe skoler 1740–1990*. J.W. Eides Forlag, Bergen.

Frandsen, K-E. (1988), '1536–ca. 1720', in Bjørn (ed) (1988a), pp. 9–209.

Fraser, R. (1984), *In Search of the Past: The Manor House, Amnersfield, 1933–1945*, Verso, London.

Freeman, A. (1914), *Boy Life & Labour: The Manufacture of Inefficiency*, P.S. King & Son, London.

Fremdling, R. (1991), 'Productivity Comparision between Great Britain and Germany, 1855–1913', *Scandinavian Economic History Review*, vol. 39:1, pp. 28–42.

Friedländer, E. (1887), *Die Frage der Frauen- und Kinderarbeit: Eine Studie*, Verlag von Robert Hupher, Forbach.

Fuchs, R.G. (1984), *Abandoned Children: Foundlings and Child Welfare in Nineteenth-Century France*, State University of New York Press, Albany.

Fuchs, S. (1981), 'Die Laufstelle: Interviews zur Kinderarbeit in Bremen', in *Kindheiten, Teil 2: Schüler, Schule, Kinderarbeit. Beiträge zur Sozialgeschichte Bremens, Heft 3*, Universität Bremen, Bremen, pp. 101–160.

Furth, C. (1995), 'From Birth to Birth: The Growing Body in Chinese Medicine', in Kinney (ed) (1995), pp. 157–191.

Gadd, C-J. (2000), *Det svenska jordbrukets historia: Den agrara revolutionen 1700–1870*, Natur och Kultur/LTs förlag, Stockholm.

Gatrell, P. (1986), *The Tsarist Economy, 1850–1917*, B.T. Batsford, London.

Gaunt, D. (1977), 'Pre-Industrial Economy and Population Structure: The elements of variance in early modern Sweden', *Scandinavian Journal of History*, vol. 2:3, pp. 183–210.

Gaunt, D. (1983), *Familjeliv i Norden*, Gidlunds, Stockholm.

Gavitt, P. (1997), 'Charity and State Building in Cinquecento Florence: Vincenzio Borghihini as Administrator of the Ospedale degli Innocenti', *Journal of Modern History*, vol. 69:2, pp. 230–270.

Gemmell, N. and Wardley, P. (1990), 'The Contribution of Services to British Economic Growth, 1856–1913', *Explorations in Economic History*, vol. 27:3, pp. 299–321.

Genovesi, G. (1998), *Storia della scuola in Italia dal Settecento a oggi*, Editori Laterza, Roma-Bari.

Gerger, C. (1992), *Där nöden var som störst: En studie av fattigdom och fattigvård i en småländsk landsbygdssocken åren 1815–1935*, Kulturgeografiska institutionen, Stockholms universitet, Stockholm.

Giffin, F.C. (1967), 'In Quest of an Effective Program of Factory Legislation in Russia: The Years of Preparation, 1859–1880', *The Historian* (Kingston), vol. 29 (February), pp. 175–185.

Giffin, F.C. (1977), 'Improving the Conditions of Child Labour in Russia: The Law of 12 June 1884', *European Studies Review*, vol. 7, pp. 359–370.

Ginzburg, C. (1996), 'Making Things Strange: The Prehistory of a Literary Device', *Representations*, No. 56 (Special Issue), pp. 8–28.

Gittins, D. (1998), *The Child in Question*, Macmillan Press, Basingstoke.

Glickman, R.L. (1984), *Russian Factory Women: Workplace and Society, 1880–1914*, University of California Press, Berkeley.

Goldson, B. (1997), '"Childhood": An Introduction to Historical and Theoretical Analyses', in Scraton (ed) (1997), pp. 1–27.

Gorky, M. (1950), *Childhood*, Foreign Language Publishing House, Moscow.

Gormsen, G. (1995), 'The family cycle: inheritance, descendants and matrimony', in Larsson and Myrdal (eds) (1995), pp. 109–114.

Goubert, P. (1986), *The French Peasantry in the Seventeenth Century*, Cambridge University Press, Cambridge.

Grantham, G. and MacKinnon, M. (eds) (1994), *Labour market evolution: The economic history of market integration, wage flexibility and the employment relation*, Routledge, London and New York.

Greiff, M. (1992), *Kontoristen: Från chefens högra hand till proletär: Proletarisering, feminisering och facklig organisering bland svanska industritjänstemän 1840–1950*, Bokförlaget Mendocino, Lund.

Griffiths, T., Hunt, P.A. and O'Brien, P.A. (1992), 'Inventive Activity in the British Textile Industry, 1700–1800', *The Journal of Economic History*, vol. 52:4, pp. 881–906.

Grubb, F. and Stitt, T. (1994), 'The Liverpool Emigrant Servant Trade and the Transition to Slave Labour in the Chesapeake, 1697–1707: Market Adjustments to War', *Explorations in Economic History*, vol. 31:3, pp. 376–405.

Guéhenno, J. (1973), *Changer la vie: Mon enface et ma jeunesse*, Grasset, Paris.

Guereña, J.L. (1996), 'Infancia y escolarización', in *Historia de la infancia* (1996), pp. 347–418.

Guidi, L. (1986), 'Parto e maternità a Napoli: carità e solidarietà spontanee, beneficenza instituzionale (1840–1880)', *Sanità scienza e storia*, vol. 3:1, pp. 111–148.

Guidi, L. (1991), *L'onore in pericolo: Carità e reclusione femminile nell'ottocento napoletano*. Liguori Editore, Napoli.

Guidi, L. (1999), 'La storia dell'infanzia in Italia: Studia recenti, zone oscure, questioni aperte', *Società e storia*, No. 86 (vol. 22), pp. 847–874.

Guillaumin, E. (1983 [1904]), *The Life of a Simple Man*, ed. E. Weber, University Press of New England, Hanover, New Hampshire.

Hajnal, J. (1983), 'Two kinds of pre-industrial household formation system', in Wall (ed) (1983), pp. 65–104.

Hamon, M. and Perrin, D. (1993), *Au cœur du XVIIIᵉ siècle industriel: Condition ouvrière et tradition villagenoise à Saint-Gobain*, Éditions P.A.U., Paris.

Hansen, N. (1987), *Fabrikkinder: Zur Kinderarbeit in schleswig-holsteinischen Fabriken im 19. Jahrhundert*, Karl Wachholtz Verlag, Neumünster.

Hanssen, B. (1976), 'Hushållens sammansättning i österlenska byar under 300 år', *Rig*, vol. 59:2, pp. 33–60.

Hanssen, B. (1978), 'The Oikological Approach', in Åkerman, Johansen and Gaunt (eds) (1978), pp. 147–158.

Hareven, T.K. (1975), 'Family Time and Industrial Time: Family and Work in a Planned Corporation Town, 1900–1924', *Journal of Urban History*, vol. 1.3, pp. 365–389.

Harnesk, B. (1990), *Legofolk: Drängar, pigor och bönder i 1700- och 1800-talens Sverige*, Umeå universitet, Umeå.

Harnisch, H. (1986), 'Peasants and Markets: The Background to the Agrarian Reforms in Feudal Prussia East of Elbe, 1760–1807', in Evans and Lee (eds) (1986), pp. 37–70.

Hassell Smith, A. (1989a and 1989b), 'Labourers in late sixteenth-century England: a case study from north Norfolk [Part I] and [Part II]', *Continuity and Change*, vol. 4:1 and 4: 3, pp. 11–52 and 367–394.

Haue, H., Hvidt, K., Markussen, I. and Nørr, E. (eds) (1991), *Skole, Dannelse, Samfund*, Odense Universitetsforlag, Odense.

Heckscher, E.F. (1936), *Sveriges ekonomiska historia från Gustav Vasa: första delen, andra boken*, Albert Bonniers Förlag, Stockholm.

Heckscher, E.F. (1955), *Mercatilism, Volume Two*, George Allen & Unwin, London.

Heikkinen, S. (1997), *Labour and the Market: Workers, Wages and Living Standards in Finland, 1850–1913*, The Finnish Society of Sciences and Letters, Helsinki.

Hélias, P-J. (1975), *Le cheval d'orgueil: Mémoires d'un Breton du pays bigouden*, Librairie Plon, Paris.

Henderson, J. and Wall, R. (eds) (1994), *Poor Women and Children in the European Past*, Routledge, London and New York.

Hendrick, H. (1980), '"A Race of Intelligent Unskilled Labourers": The Adolescent Worker and the Debate on Compulsory Part-Time Day Continuation Schools, 1900–1922', *History of Education*, vol. 9:2, pp. 159–173.

Hendrick, H. (1990), 'Construction and Reconstruction of British Childhood: An Interpretative Survey, 1800 to the present', in James and Prout (eds) (1990), London, pp. 35–59.

Hendrick, H. (1992), 'Child labour, medical capital and the School Medical Service', in Cooter (ed) (1992), pp. 45–71.

Hendrick, H. (1994), *Child Welfare, England 1872–1989*, Routledge, London and New York.

Hendrick, H. (1997), *Children, childhood and English society, 1880–1990*, Cambridge University Press, Cambridge.

Hendrickx, F.M.M. (1997), 'Economic Change and Demographic Continuity: The Demography of Borne and Wierden (the Netherlands) in the Period of Proto- and Factory Industry, 1800–1900', *The History of the Family*, vol. 2:4, pp. 425–450.

Henrekson, M., Larsson, M. and Sjögren, H. (eds) (2001), *Entrepreneurship in Business and Research: Essays in Honour of Håkan Lindgren*, Handelshögskolan i Stockholm, Stockholm.

Hertrich, E. (1986), 'Vom Wandel der Erwerbsmöglichkeiten: Die innere Striktur der Arbeiterschaft', in Ruppert (ed) (1986), pp. 93–103.

Herzig, A. (1983), 'Kinderarbeit in Deutschland in Manufaktur und Proto-Fabrik (1750–1850)', *Archiv für Sozialgeschichte XXIII. Band*, pp. 311–375.

Heywood, C. (1981a), 'The Market for Child Labour in Nineteenth-Century France', *History*, vol. 66, No. 216, pp. 34–49.

Heywood, C. (1981b), 'The Launching of an "Infant Industry"? The Cotton Industry of Troyes under Protectionism, 1793–1860', *The Journal of European Economic History*, vol. 10:3, pp. 553–581.

Heywood, C. (1988), *Childhood in nineteenth-century France: Work, health and education among the classes populaires*, Cambridge University Press, Cambridge.

Heywood, C. (1992), *The development of French economy, 1750–1914*, Cambridge University Press, Cambridge.

Heywood, C. (2001), *A History of Childhood: Children and Childhood in the West from Medieval to Modern Times*, Polity, Cambridge.

Hierta-Retzius, A. (1897), *Arbetsstugor för barn: En sammanfattande framställning af arbetsstugeverksamheten i Sverige*, P.A. Norstedt, Stockholm.

Historia de la infancia en la España contemporánea 1834–1936 (1996), Ministerio de Trabajo y asuntos sociales and Fundación German Sánches Ruipérez, Madrid.

Hobsbawm, E.J. (1974 [1964]), *Labouring Men: Studies in the History of Labour*, Weidenfeld and Nicolson, London.

Hobsbawm, E.J. (1991), *Nations and Nationalism Since 1780: Programme, Myth, Reality*, Cambridge University, Cambridge.

Hodne, B. and Sogner, S. (eds) (1984), *Barn av sin tid: Fra norske barns historie*, Universitetsforlaget, Oslo.

Hoffman, P.T., Jacks, D., Levin, P.A. and Lindert, P.H. (2002), 'Real Inequality in Europe since 1500', *The Journal of Economic History*, vol. 62:2, pp. 322–355.

Holley, J.C. (1981), 'The Two Family Economies of Industrialism: Factory Workers in Victorian Scotland', *Journal of Family History*, vol. 6:1, pp. 57–69.

Holmes, C. and Booth, A. (eds) (1991), *Economy and Society: European Industrialisation and its social consequences*, Leicester University Press, Leicester and London.

Hopkins, E. (1989), *Birmingham: The First Manufacturing Town in the World, 1760–1840*, Weidenfeld & Nicolson, London.

Hopkins, E. (1994), *Childhood transformed: Working-class children in nineteenth-century England*, Manchester University Press, Manchester.

Hoppe, R. (ed) (1958), *Geschichte der Kinderarbeit in Deutschland 1750–1939, Band II. Dokumente*, Verlag Neues Leben, Berlin.

Horn, P. (1976), *Labouring Life in the Victorian Countryside*, Gill and Macmillan, Dublin.

Horn, P. (1978), *Education in Rural England, 1800–1914*, St. Martin's Press, New York.

Horn, P. (1980), *The Rural World, 1780–1850: Social change in the English Countryside*, St. Martin's Press, New York.

Horn, P. (1984), *Rural Life in England in The First World War*, Gill and Macmillan, New York.

Horn, P. (1989), *The Victorian and Edwardian Schoolchild*, Alan Sutton, Gloucester.

Hornby, O. and Oxenbøll, E. (1982), 'Proto-Industrialisation before Industrialisation? The Danish Case', *Scandinavian Economic History Review*, vol 30:1, pp. 3–33.

Horrell, S. and Humphries, J. (1992), 'Old Questions, New Data, and Alternative Perspectives: Families' Living Standards in the Industrial Revolution', *The Journal of Economic History*, vol. 52:4, pp. 849–880.

Horrell, S. and Humphries, J. (1995), '"The Exploitation of Little Children": Child Labor and the Family Economy in the Industrial Revolution', *Explorations in Economic History*, vol. 32:4, pp. 458–516.

Horrell, S. and Humphries, J. (1999), 'Child Labour and British Industrialisation', in Lavalette (1999), pp. 76–100.

Horrell, S. and Oxley, D. (1999), 'Crust or crumb? Intrahousehold resource allocation and male breadwinning in late Victorian Britain', *The Economic History Review*, vol. 52:3, pp. 494–522.

Houston, R.A. (2002), *Literacy in Early Modern Europe*, Longman, Harlow.

Huberman, M. (1991), 'How Did Labor Markets Work in Lancashire? More Evidence on Prices and Quantities in Cotton Spinning, 1822–1852', *Explorations in Economic History*, vol. 28:1, pp. 87–120.

Humphries, J. (2003), 'At what cost was pre-eminence purchased? Child labour and the first industrial revolution', in Scholliers and Schwarz (eds) (2003), pp. 251–268.

Humphries, S. and Gordon, P. (1992), *Out of Sight: The Experience of Disability, 1900–1950*, Northcote House, Plymouth.

Hung, W. (1995), 'Private Love and Public Duty: Images of Children in Early Chinese Art', in Kinney (1995), pp. 79–110.

Hyldtoft, O. (1991), 'Foreign Technology and the Danish Brick and Tile Industry', in Bruland (1991), pp. 201–227.

Härnqvist, K. (1992), 'En SOU-forskarens hågkomster', in Selander (ed) (1992), pp. 358–370.

Höck, A. (1987), 'Knecht und Magd auf Zeit: Bauernkinder als Gesinde bei Eltern und Verwandten in Oberhessen', in Becker and Matter (eds) (1987), pp. 125–129.

Industri, servizi e scuola, (1962) Editori Laterza, Bari.

International Labour Conference (1922), *Fourth Session, Volume I*, International Labour Office, Geneva.

International Labour Conference (1938), *Twenty-Fourth Session, Report I*, International Labour Office, Geneva.

International Labour Review (1951), vol. 64, 'Child Labour in Relation to Compulsory Education', pp. 462–472.

International Labour Review (1957), vol. 75, 'The Influx of Young People into the Employment Market in Western and Northern Europe', pp. 335–353.

Iradiel Murugarren, P. (1974), *Evolucion de la industria textil castellana en los siglos XIII–XVI: Factores de desarrollo, organización y costes de la producción manufacturera an Cuenca*, Acta Salamanticensia 84, Salamanca.

Isacson, M. and Magnusson, L. (1987), *Proto-industrialisation in Scandinavia: Craft Skills in the Industrial Revolution*, Berg Publishers, Leamington Spa.

Jacobsson, M. (2000), *'Att Blifva Sin Egen': Ungdomars väg in i vuxenlivet i 1700- och 1800-talens övre Norrland*. Umeå universitet, Umeå.

Jamerey-Duval, V. (1981 [1747]), *Mémoires: Enfance et éducation d'un paysan au XVIIIe siècle*, ed. J.M. Goulemot, Editions Le Sycomore, Paris.

James, A. and Prout, A. (eds) (1990), *Constructing and Reconstructing Childhood: Contemporary Issues in the Sociological Study of Childhood*, The Falmer Press, London.

Jansson, J-O. (1990), *Arbetsorganisationen vid Motala verkstad 1822–1843: Den engelska tiden*, Almqvist & Wiksell International, Stockholm.

Jenks, C. (1996), *Childhood*, Routledge, London and New York.

Jensen, A.-M. and Saporiti, A. (1992), *Do Children Count? Childhood as a Social Phenomenon. A Statistical Compendium*, Eurosocial Reports 36/17, Vienna.

Johansen, H.C. (1988), *Industriens vækst og vilkår: Dansk industri efter 1870, Bind 1*, Odense Universitetsforlag, Odense.

Johansson, E. (1991), '"Läser själva orden. Läser i book": Barnens läsning i Bygdeå 1640 med några vidare utblickar', in Haue et al. (eds) (1991), pp. 131–137.

Johansson J-E., (1986), *Från arbetsstuga till fritidshem: Ett bidrag till fritidshemmets historia*, Liber, Stockholm.

Johansson, P.G. (2001), *Gods, kvinnor och stickning: Tidig industriell verksamhet i Höks härald, Halland ca 1750–1870*, Lunds universitet, Lund.

Jones, M.G. (1938), *The Charity School Movement: A Study of Eighteenth Century Puritanism in Action*, Cambridge University Press, Cambridge.

Jones, P.M. (1988), *The Peasantry in the French Revolution*, Cambridge University Press, Cambridge.

Jorde, T.S. (1995), *Stockholms tjenestepiker under industrialiseringen: Tjenestepikeyrkets funksjon i individets livsløp og i en ekspanderende storby*, Stockholms universitet, Stockholm.

Joyce, J. (1993 [1916]), *A Portrait of the Artist as a Young Men*, ed. R.B. Kershner, Bedford Books of St. Martin's Press, Boston.

Julia, D. (1998), 'L'enfance aux débuts de l'époque moderne', in Becchi and Julia (eds) (1998), pp. 286–372.

Jutikkala, E. (1986), 'Labour Policy and the Urban Proletariat in Sweden and Finland during the Pre-Industrial Era', in Riis (ed) (1986), pp. 133–142.

Jutikkala, E. (1990), 'La pauvreté en Finland de 1500 à 1800', in Riis (ed) (1990), pp. 41–63.

Jütte, R. (1996), 'Poverty and Poor Relief', in Ogilvie (1996), pp. 377–404.

Jörberg, L. (1994), 'Structural Change and Economic Growth in Sweden in the Nineteenth Century', in O'Brien (ed) (1994), pp. 411–454.

Jørgensen, H. (1990), 'L'assistance aux pauvres au Danemark jusqu'à la fin du XVIIIe siècle', in Riis (ed) (1990), pp. 9–34.

Kaelble, H. (1979), 'L'évolution du recrutement du patronat en Allemagne comparée à celles des Etats-Unis et de la Grande-Bretagne depuis la révolution industrielle', in Levy-Leboyer (ed) (1979), pp. 15–36.

Kahan, A. (1989), *Russian Economic History: The Nineteenth Century*, ed. R. Weiss, The University of Chicago Press, Chigaco and London.

Kaltwasser, I. (1987), 'Gesindewanderung nach Frankfurt in freistädtisher Zeit', in Becker and Matter (eds) (1987), pp. 85–99.

[Kanatchikov] (1986 [1929]), *A radical Worker in Tsarist Russia: The Autobiography of Semën Ivanovich Kanatchikov*, ed. R.E. Zelnik, Stanford University Press, Stanford.

Karvinen, M. (2001), *Regular, Honest and Diligent Lives: Female Life Histories in a Tuscan Town*, University of Helsinki, Helsinki.

Kaschuba, W. (1986), 'Peasants and Others: The Historical Contours of Village Class Society', in Evans and Lee (eds) (1986), pp. 235–264.

Katajisto, K. (2000), *Vale-Jaakko: Suomalainen huijaritarina 1700-luvulta*, Edita, Helsinki.

Kennard, Howard P. (1908), *The Russian Peasant*, J.B. Lippincott Company, Philadelphia.

Kermann, J. (1972), *Die Manufakturen im Rheinland 1750–1833*, Rheinisches Archiv 82, Ludwig Röhrscheid Verlag, Bonn.

Kerridge, E. (1973), *The Farmers of Old England*, George Allen & Unwin, London.

Kerridge, E. (1985), *Textile manufactures in early modern England*, Manchester University Press, Manchester.

Kertzer, D.I. (1977), 'European Peasant Household Structure: Some Implications from a Nineteenth Century Italian Community', *Journal of Family History*, vol. 2:4, pp. 333–349.

Kertzer, D.I. (1999), 'Age Structuring and the Lives of Abandoned Children', *The History of the Family*, vol. 4:1, pp. 5–15.

Key, E. (1900a and 1900b), *Barnets århundrade I* and *II*, Albert Bonniers Förlag, Stockholm.

Kiel, A. and Mjøset, L. (1990), 'Wage Formation in the Norwegian Industry 1840–1985', *Scandinavian Economic History Review*, vol. 38:1, pp. 19–49.

Kinney, A.B. (ed) (1995), *Chinese Views of Childhood*, University of Hawai'i Press, Honolulu.

Kinney, A.B. (1995), 'Dyed Silk: Han Notions of the Moral Development of Children', in Kinney (1995), pp. 17–56.

Kirby D. (1995), *The Baltic World 1772–1993: Europe's Northern Periphery in an Age of Change*, Longman, London.

Kjellman, M. (1997), *Bondens dagbok: En studie baserad på bondedagböcker avseende barns/ungas socialisering, åldringarnas deltagande i gårdsarbetet och kvinnan i 1800-talets svenska bondsamhälle*, Institutet för folklivsforskning, Stockholm.

Klapisch-Zuber, C. (1985), *Women, Family, and Ritual in Renaissance Italy*. The University of Chicago Press, Chicago.

Klingnéus, S. (1997), *Bönder blir vapensmeder: Protoindustriall tillverkning i Närke under 1600- och 1700-talen*, University of Uppsala, Uppsala.

Koch, G. (1987), '"We keine Arbeit hat, der nimmt sich niemend" – Gesindeleben im Limburger Raum', in Becker and Matter (eds) (1987), pp. 213–222.

Kocka, J. (1979), 'Les entrepreneurs salariés dans l'industrie allemande à la fin du XIXe et au début du XXe siècle', in Levy-Leboyer (1979), pp. 85–100.

Kocka, J. (1994), 'Capitalism and Bureaucracy in German Industrialization before 1914', in O'Brien (ed) (1994b), pp. 3–17.

Kohl, J.G. (1842), *Russia and the Russians, in 1842, Vol. I: Petersburg*, Henry Colburn, London (facsimile by University Microfilms International, Ann Arbor, Mich. 1987).

Kohl, J.G. (1843), *Russia and the Russians, in 1842, Vol. II*, Henry Colburn, London (facsimile by University Microfilms International, Ann Arbor, Mich. 1987).

Korkiakangas, P. (1996), *Muistoista rakentuva lapsuus: Agraarinen perintö lapsuuden työnteon ja leikkien muistelussa*, Suomen Muinaismuistoyhdistys, Helsinki.

Kouri, E. and Jansson, T. (eds) (forthcoming), *Cambridge History of Scandinavia, Vol. II*, Cambridge University Press, Cambridge.

Kouvonen, A. (2000), *Lapset ja nuoret palkkatyössä*, Työministeriö, Helsinki.

Kraack, D. (2002), 'The *Memorial und Jurenal* of Peter Hansen Hajstrup (1624–1672): Literacy as a Precondition for Leaving the Peasants' World', in Lorenzen-Schmidt and Poulsen (eds) (2002), pp. 50–76.

Krausman Ben-Amos, I. (1988), 'Service and the coming of age of young men in seventeenth-century England', *Continuity and Change*, vol. 3:1, pp. 41–64.

Krausman Ben-Amos, I. (1991), 'Women apprentices in the trades and crafts of early modern Bristol', *Continuity and Change*, vol. 6:2, pp. 227–252.

Kriedte, P. (1983), 'Proto-Industrialiserung und grosses Kapital', *Archiv für Sozialgeschicte XXIII. Band*, pp. 219–266.

Kriedte, P., Medick, H. and Schlumbohm, J. (1981), *Industrialization before Industrialization: Rural Industry in the Genesis of Capitalism*. Cambridge University Press and Éditions de la Maison des Sciences de l'Homme, Cambridge and Paris.

Kriedte, P., Medick, H. and Schlumbohm, J. (1993), 'Proto-industrialization revisited: demography, social structure, and modern domestic industry', *Continuity and Change*, vol. 8:2, pp. 217–252.

Krogh, T. (1987), *Staten og de besiddelsesløse på landet 1500–1800*. Odense Universitetsforlag, Odense.

Krötzl, C. (1989), 'Parent-Child relations in Medieval Scandinavia According to Miracle Collections', *Scandinavian Journal of History*, vol. 14:1, pp. 21–37.

Kuczynski, J. (1958), *Geschichte der Kinderarbeit in Deutschland 1750–1939, Band I. Geschichte*, Verlag Neues Leben, Berlin.

Kuisma, M. (1992a and 1992b), *Helsinge sockens historia II* and *III*, Vanda stad, Vantaa.

Kussmaul, A. (1981), *Servants in husbandry in early modern England*, Cambridge University Press, Cambridge.

Kuusanmäki, L. (1954), *Elämänmenoa entisaikaan*, WSOY, Porvoo and Helsinki.

Kühl, J. (1990), 'New deal and new forms of employment', *Labour and Society*, vol. 15:2, pp. 237–255.

Lagerlöf-Génetay, B. (1990), *De svenska häxprocessernas utbrottsskede 1668–1671: Bakgrund i Övre Dalarna. Social och ecklesiastic kontext*. Stockholms universitet, Stockholm.

Laine, K. (1935), *Otavalan pellavanviljely- ja kehruukoulu: Ruotsi-Suomen pellavanviljely- ja kehruupolitiikkaa 1700-luvulla*, Suomen Historiallinen Seura, Helsinki.

Landes, D.S. (1991), 'Does it pay to be late?', in Holmes and Booth (eds) (1991), pp. 3–23.

Landsteiner, E. (1999), 'Household, Family and Economy among Wine-Growing Peasants: The Case of Lower Austria in the First Half of the Nineteenth Century', *The History of the Family*, vol. 4:2, pp. 113–135.

Lange, S. (1978), *Zur Bildungssituation der Proletarierkinder im 19. Jarhhundert: Kinderarbeit und Armenschulwesen in der sächsicchen Elbestad Pirna*, Monumenta Paedagogica, Band XVIII, Volk und Wissen Volkseigener Verlag, Berlin.

Larsson, B. and Myrdal, J. (eds) (1995), *Peasant Diaries as a Source for the History of Mentality*, Nordiska museet, Stockholm.

Larsson, B. (1995), 'Deaths of children as reflected in peasant diaries', in Larsson and Myrdal (eds) (1995), pp. 141–147.

Laslett, P. (1965), *The World we have lost*, Methuen & Co., London.

Laslett, P. (1977), 'Characteristics of the Western Family Considered over Time', *Journal of Family History*, vol. 2:2, pp. 89–115.

Lavalette, M. (1994), *Child Employment in the Capitalist Labour Market*, Avebury, Aldershot.

Lavalette, M. (ed) (1999), *A Thing of the Past? Child Labour in Britain in the Nineteenth and Twentieth Centuries*, St. Martin's Press, New York.

Lavalette, M. (1999), 'The Theoretical Context of Child Labour Research', in Lavalette (ed) (1999), pp. 9–68.

Leontief, W. (1906), *Die Lage der Baumwollarbeiter in St. Petersburg, die Geschicte der Industries und die Fabrikgesetzgebung*, Ernst Reinhard Verlagsbuchhandlung, München.

Le Roy Ladurie, E. (1990 [1978]), *Montaillou: Cathars and Catholics in a French Village, 1294–1324*, Penguin Books, Harmondsworth.

Levi, G. (1988), *Inheriting Power: The Story of an Exorcist*, Chicago University Press, Chicago.

Levi, G. and Schmitt, J-C. (eds) (1997), *A History of Young People, Volume Two: Stormy Evolution to Modern Times*, Harvard University Press, Cambridge, Mass. and London.

Levine, D. (1977), *Family Formation in an Age of Nascent Capitalism*, Academic Press, New York.

Levy-Leboyer, M. (ed) (1979), *Le patronat de la seconde industrialisation*, Les Éditions Ouvrières, Paris.

Lext, G. (1968), *Mantalskrivningen i Sverige före 1860*, Meddelanden från Ekonomisk-historiska institutionen vid Göteborgs universitet 13. Göteborg.

Liliequist, J. (1991), 'Peasants Against Nature: Crossing the Boundaries between Man and Animal in Seventeenth- and Eighteenth-Century Sweden', *Journal of the History of Sexuality*, vol. 1:3, pp. 393–423.

Liliequist, M. (1991), *Nybyggarbarn: Barnuppfostran bland nybyggare i Frostvikens, Vilhelmina och Tärna socknar 185–1920*, Almqvist & Wiksell International, Stockholm.

Lindberg, F. (1989), *Hantverk och skråväsen under medeltid och äldre vasatid*, Bokförlaget Prisma, Stockholm.

Lindegren, J. (1980), *Utskrivning och utsugning: Produktion och reproduktion i Bygdeå 1620–1640*, Uppsala universitet, Uppsala.

Lindegren, J. (1985), 'The Swedish "Military State", 1560–1720', *Scandinavian Journal of History*, vol. 10:4, pp. 305–336.

Lindemann, M. (1990), *Patriots and Paupers: Hamburg, 1712–1830*. Oxford University Press, Oxford.

Linebaugh, P. (1992). *The London Hanged: Crime and Civil Society in the Eighteenth Century*, Cambridge University Press, Cambridge.

Lis, C. and Soly, H. (1993), 'Neighbourhood Social Change in West European Cities', *International Review of Social History*, vol. 38:1, pp. 1–30.

Locke, J. (1988 [1693]), *Some Thoughts concerning Education*, Claredon Press, London.

Locke, R.R. (1984), *The End of Practical Man: Entrepreneurship and Higher Education in Germany, France and Great Britain, 1880–1940*, Jai Press, Greenwich.

Lorenzen-Schmidt, K-J. (1998), 'Modern agriculture since 1200 – the Holsteinian Elbmarshes', in Bjørn (ed) (1998), pp. 11–24.

Lorenzen-Schmidt, K-J. and Poulsen, B. (eds) (2002), *Writing Peasants: Studies on Peasant Literacy in Early Modern Northern Europe*, Landbohistorisk Selskab, Odense.

Loriga, S. (1997), 'The Military Experience', in Levi and Schmitt (eds) (1997), pp. 10–36.

Lundemark, E. (1980), *Arbetsstugorna*, Tornedalica, Luleå.

Lundh, C. (1999), 'The social mobility of servants in rural Sweden, 1740–1894', *Continuity and Change*, vol. 14:1, pp. 57–89.

Lundsjö, O. (1975), *Fattigdomen på den svenska landsbygden under 1800-talet*, Stockholms universitet, Stockholm.

Löfgren, O. (1974), 'Family and Household among Scandinavian Peasants: An Exploratory Essay', *Ethnologia Scandinavica*, vol. 4, pp. 7–52.

Löfgren, O. (1978), 'The Potato People: Household Economy and Family Patterns among the Rural Proletariat in Nineteenth Century Sweden', in Åkerman, Johansen and Gaunt (eds) (1978), pp. 95–106.

Lönnqvist, B. (1992), *Ting, rum och barn: Historisk-antropologiska studier i kulturella gränser och gränsöverskridande*, Finska fornminnesförening, Helsinki.

Machiavelli, N. (1980 [1514]), *The Prince*, Penguin Books, Harmondsworth.

Macfarlane, A. (1984), 'The myth of the peasantry: family and economy in a northern parish', in Smith, R.R. (ed) (1984), pp. 333–349.

Magnac, T. and Postel-Vinay, G. (1997), 'Wage Competition between Agriculture and Industry in Mid-Nineteenth Century France', *Explorations in Economic History*, vol. 34: 1, pp. 1–26.

Malmberg, B. and Sommestad, L. (2000), 'The Hidden Pulse of History. Age Transition and Economic Change in Sweden, 1820–2000', *Scandinavian Journal of History*, vol. 25: 1–2, pp. 131–146.

Malmstedt, G. (1994), *Helgedagsreduktionen: Övergången från ett medeltida till ett modernt år i Sverige 1500–1800*, Göteborgs universitet, Gothenburg.

Mansurov, V. (2001), *Criminal Employment of Children and Teenagers in Russia*, Paper presented in the Fifth Conference of the European Sociological Association, Helsinki, 1st September 2001 (unpublished).

Manzione, C.K. (1995), *Christ's Hospital of London, 1552–1598: "A Passing Deed of Piety"*, Susquehanna University Press and Associated University Press, Selinsgrove and London.

Marcello, L. (1993), 'Andare a bottega. Adolescenza e apprendistato nelle arti (se. XVI–XVII)', in Niccoli (ed) (1993), pp. 231–251.

Markkola, P. (1997), '"God wouldn't send a child into the world without a crust of bread": Child labour as part of working-class family economy in Finland 1890–1920', in de Coninck-Smith, Sandin and Schrumpf (eds) (1997), pp. 79–105.

Martínez Carrión, J.M. (ed) (2002), *El nivel de vida en la España rural, siglos XVII–XX*, Universidad de Alicante, Alicante.

Martinius, S. (1977), *Peasant Destinies: The History of 552 Swedes Born 1810–12*, Almqvist & Wiksell International, Stockholm.

Martinson, F.M. (1992), *Growing Up in Norway, 800 to 1990*, Southern Illinois University Press, Carbondale and Edwardsville.

Mathias, P. (1995), *The First Industrial Nation: An Economic History of Britain 1700–1914*, Routledge, London and New York.

Matikainen, O. (2002), *Verenperijät: Väkivalta ja yhteisön murros itäisessä Suomessa 1500–1600-luvulla*. Suomalaisen Kirjallisuuden Seura, Helsinki.

Mayhew, G. (1991), 'Life-cycle service and the family unit in early modern Rye', *Continuity and Change*, vol. 6:2, pp. 201–226.

McCracken, G. (1983), 'The Exchange of Children in Tudor England: An Anthropological Phenomenon in Historical Context', *Journal of Family History*, vol. 8:4, pp. 303–313.

McIntosh, M.K. (1988), 'Local responses to the poor in late medieval and Tudor England', *Continuity and Change*, vol. 3:2, pp. 209–245.

Medick, H. (1976), 'The proto-industrial family economy: the structural functions of household and family during the transition from peasant society to industrial capitalism', *Social History*, vol. 1:3, pp. 291–315.

Mendels, F.F. (1972), 'Proto-industrialization: The First Phase of the Industrialization Process', *The Journal of Economic History*, vol. 32:1, pp. 241–261.

Meyer, A.H.G. (1971), *Schule und Kinderarbeit: Das Verhältniss von Schul- und Sozialpolitik in der Entwicklung der preussischen Volkschule zu Beginn des 19. Jahrhunderts*, Diss., Universität Hamburg, Hamburg.

Minderårigas tillträde till arbetslivet (1989). *Betänkande 1 angivet av arbetsgruppen (A 1987: D) för översyn av vissa bestämmelser i arbetsmijölagen*, Ds 1989:1, Arbetsmarknadsdepartement, Stockholm.

Mingione, E. (1981), *Mercato del lavoro e occupazione in Italia dal 1945 ad oggi*, Celuc libri, Milano.

Mitterauer, M. (1990), 'Servants and Youth', *Continuity and Change*, vol. 5:1, pp. 11–38.

Mitterauer, M. (1993), *A History of Youth*, Blackwell, Cambridge, Mass. and Oxford.

Mizen, P., Bolton, A. and Pole, C. (1999), 'School Age Workers: Paid Employment of Children in Britain', *Work, Employment & Society*, vol. 13:3, pp. 423–438.

Moch, L.P. (1992), *Moving Europeans: Migration in Western Europe since 1650*, Indiana University Press, Bloomington and Indianapolis.

Moen, E. (1991), 'Norway's Entry into the Age of Paper: The Development of the Pulp and Paper Industry in the Drammen District', in Bruland (ed) (1991), pp. 363–386.

Molas Ribalta, P. (1988), *Edad Moderna (1474–1808): Manual de Historia de España 3*, Espasa-Calpe, Madrid.

Molinas, C. and Prados de la Escosura, L. (1989), 'Was Spain Different? Spanish Historical Backwardness Revisited', *Explorations in Economic History*, vol. 26:4, pp. 385–402.

Monroe, P. (1999 [1904]), *Thomas Platter and the Educational Renaissance of the Sixteenth Century*, D. Appleton and Company, New York (reprinted by Thoemmes Press, Bristol and Maruzen Co, Tokyo).

Mooser, J. (1986), 'Familienarbeit und Arbeiterfamilie: Kontinuität und Wandel seit 1900', in Ruppert (ed) (1986), pp. 106–116.

Moring, B. (1993), 'Household and Family in Finnish Coastal Societies 1635–1895', *Journal of Family History*, vol. 18:4, pp. 395–414.

Moring, B. (1994), *Skärgårdsbor: Hushåll, familj och demografi i finländsk kustbygd på 1600-, 1700- och 1800-talen*, Finska Vetenskaps-Societen, Helsinki.

Moring, B. (1996), 'Marriage and social change in south-western Finland, 1700–1870', *Continuity and Change*, vol. 11:1, pp. 91–113.

Moring, B. (1999), 'Land, Labour and Love: Household Arrangements in Nineteenth Century Eastern Finland – Cultural Heritage or Socio-Economic Structure?', *The History of the Family*, vol. 4:2, pp. 159–184.

[Munsterhjelm] (1970, orig. 1799–1801), *Jacobina Charlotta Munsterhjelms dagböcker 1799–1801*, ed. B. Lönnqvist, Svenska litteratursällskapet i Finland and Munksgaard, Helsinki and Copenhagen.

Musgrave, E. (1997), 'Women and the craft guild in eighteenth-century Nantes', in Crossick (ed) (1997), pp. 151–171.

Musgrave, P. (1999), *The Early Modern European Economy*, Macmillan, Basingstoke.

Müller, J. (1906), *Fattigvård i Stockholm från äldre till nyare tid jämte beskrifning af Stockholms stads arbetsinrättningar med anledning af den nya arbetsinrättningens fullbordan*, Kungl. hofboktryckeriet, Stockholm.

Myllyntaus, T. (1990), 'Education in the Making of Modern Finland', in Tortella (1990), pp. 153–171.

Myrdal, J. (1981), 'Betingsläror och arbetsåtgång i lantbruket', *Rig*, vol. 64:2, pp. 41–57.

Myrdal, J. (ed) (1988), *Gustaf Perssons liv och arbete: Ur en värmländsk bondedagbok 1809–1833*, Nordiska museet, Stockholm.

Myrdal, J. (1994), 'Kulturhistoriska fragment', in Myrdal and Bäärnhielm (eds) (1994), pp. 12–90.

Myrdal, J. (2002), 'Erik Axel Karlfeldt: the Farmer's Son who Kept a Diary and Won the Nobel Prize', in Lorenzen-Schmidt and Poulsen (eds) (2002), pp. 239–251.

Myrdal, J. and Bäärnhielm, G. (ed) (1994), *Kvinnor, barn & fester i medeltida mirakelberättelser*, Skaraborgs länsmuseum, Skara.

Nadaud, M. (1948), *Mémoires de Léonard, ancien garçon maçon*, Egloff, Paris.

Nardinelli, C. (1980), 'Child Labor and the Factory Acts', *The Journal of Economic History*, vol. 40:4, pp. 739–755.

Nardinelli, C. (1990), *Child Labor and the Industrial Revolution*, Indiana University Press, Bloomington and Indianapolis.

Nevéus, C. (1974), *Trälarna i landskapslagarnas samhälle, Danmark och Sverige*, Uppsala universitetet, Uppsla.

Niemelä, J. (1989), *Punkalaitumen historia 2. vuoteen 1985*, Punkalaitumen historiatoimikunta, Punkalaidun.

Niccoli, O. (1995), *Il seme della violenza: Putti, fanciulli e mammoli nell'Italia tra Cinque e Seicento*, Editori Laterza, Roma and Bari.

Niccoli, O. (2000), *Storie di ogni giorno in una città del Seicento*, Editori Laterza, Roma and Bari.

Niccoli, O. (ed) (1993), *Infanzie: Funzioni di un gruppo liminale dal mondo classico all'Età moderna*, Ponte alle Grazie, Firenze.

Nikula, O. (1962), *Strengbergs 1762–1962*, Oy Ph. U. Strengberg, Jakobstad-Pietarsaari.

Nikula, O. (1972), *Åbo stads historia 1721–1890, Band II*, Åbo stad, Turku.

Nilsson, A. (1999), 'What do Literacy Rates in the 19th Century Really Signify? New Light on an old Problem from Unique Swedish Data', *Paedacogica Historica*, vol. 35:2, pp. 275–296.

Nilsson, A. and Pettersson, L. (1990), 'Some Hipotheses Regarding Education and Economic Growth in Sweden During the First Half of the 19th Century', in Tortella (ed) (1990), pp. 209–222.

Niskanen, K. (1995), *Godsägare, småbrukare och jordbrukets modernisering: Södermanlands län 1875–1935*, Almqvist & Wiksell International, Stockholm.

Nordström, E. and Nordström, G. (1966), *Pojo sockens historia, del III*, Pojo kommun, Pojo-Pohja.

Nyberg, K. (1992), *Köpes: Ull, Säljes: Kläde: Yllemanufakturens företagsformer i 1780-talets Stockholm*, Uppsala universitet, Uppsala.

Nyberg, K. (1999), *Kommersiell kompetens och industrialisering: Norrköpings ylleindustriella tillväxt på Stockholms bekostnad 1780–1846*, Uppsala universitet, Uppsala.

Nyberg, K., Jonsson, P., Fagerberg, M. and Lindberg, E. (1998), 'Trade and Marketing: Some Problems Concerning the Growth of Market Institutions in Swedish Industrialisation', *Scandinavian Economic History Review*, vol. 46:1, pp. 85–102.

Nygård, T. (1989), *Suomen palvelusväki 1600-luvulla: Palkollisten määrä, työ, palkkaus ja suhteet isäntäväkeen*, Suomen Historiallinen Seura, Helsinki.

O'Brien P.K. (ed) (1994a and 1994b), *The Industrial Revolution in Europe, I and II: The Industrial Revolutions, Vols. 4 and 5*, Blackwell, Oxford.

O'Brien, P.K. (1994), 'Introduction', in O'Brien (1994a), pp. IX–LVIII.

Ogilvie, S. (1986), 'Coming of age in a corporate society: Capitalism, Pietism and family authority in rural Württemberg, 1590–1740', *Continuity and Change*, vol. 1:3, pp. 279–331.

Ogilvie, S. (ed) (1996), *Germany: A New Social and Economic History, Volume 2, 1630–1800*, Arnold, London.

Ogilvie, S. (1997), *State corporatism and proto-industry: The Württemberg Black Forest, 1580–1797*, Cambridge University Press, Cambridge.

Olsson, L. (1980), *Då barn var lönsamma: Om arbetsdelning, barnarbete och teknologiska förändringar i några svenska industrier under 1800- och början av 1900-talet*, Tidens Förlag, Stockholm.

Olsson, L. (ed) (1985), *Skånska statare och lantarbetare berättar*, Tidens förlag, Stockholm.

Olsson, O. (1999), *Från arbete till hobby: En studie av pedagogisk filantropi i de svenska arbetsstugorna*, Linköping university, Linköping.

O'Rourke, K.H. and Williamson, J.G. (1995), 'Education, Globalization and Catch-Up: Scandinavia in Swedish Mirror', *Scandinavian Economic History Review*, vol. 43:3, pp. 287–309.

Orr, A. (1984), 'Farm Servants and Farm Labour in the Forth Valley and South-East Lowlands', in Devine (ed) (1984), pp. 29–54.

Ortaggi Cammarosano, S. (1991), 'Labouring women in northern and central Italy in the nineteenth century', in Davis and Ginsborg (eds) (1991), pp. 152–183.

Orwell, G. (1953), '*Such, Such Were the Joys*', Harcourt, Brace and Company, New York.

Ottenjann, H. (1995), 'Private written sources relating to everyday history and popular culture in rural environments', in Larsson and Myrdal (eds) (1995), pp. 18–24.

Outram, Q. (2002), 'The Demographic Impact of Early Modern Warfare', *Social Science History*, vol. 26:2, pp. 245–272.

Overton, M. (1996), *Agricultural revolution in England: The transformation of the agrarian economy 1500–1850*, Cambridge University Press, Cambridge.

Ozment, S. (1983), *When Fathers Ruled: Family Life in Reformation Europe*, Harvard University Press, Cambridge, Mass. and London.

Ozment, S. (1990), *Three Behaim Boys: Growing up in Early Modern Germany*, Yale University Press, New Haven and London.

Palacio Atard, V. (1988), *Edad Contemporánea I (1808–1898): Manual de Historia de España 4*. Espasa-Calpe, Madrid.

Papathanassiou, M. (1999), *Zwischen Arbeit, Spiel und Schule: Die ökonomische Funktion der Kinder ärmerer Schichten in Österreich 1880–1939*, Verlag für Geschichte und Politik and R. Oldenbourg Verlag, Vienna and München.

Parikka, R. (ed) (1999), *Korvesta konttoriin: Suomalaisen työn historiaa*, Suomalaisen Kirjallisuuden Seura, Helsinki.

Parmer, T. (1991), 'How Industrial Technology First Came to Norway', in Bruland (ed) (1991), pp. 37–57.

Pastor, R. (1994), 'Jóvenes campesinos de las pequeñas explotaciones: Entra reproduccion y el trabajo. Reino de Castilla, siglos XII–XIV', *Revista d'Història Medieval*, No. 5, pp. 41–54.

Peikert, I. (1986), '"… manchmal ein leises Weh …": Die Arbeit im Leben proletarisher Kinder', in Ruppert (ed) (1986), pp. 206–214.

Peltonen, M. (forthcoming), 'Agricultural Development in Scandinavia (c. 1800–1850)', in Kouri and Jansson (eds) (forthcoming).

Perrier, S. (1998), 'The Blended Family in *Ancien Régime* France: A Dynamic Family Form', *The History of the Family*, vol. 3:4, pp. 459–471.

Perrot, M. (1997), 'Worker Youth: From the Workshop to the Factory', in Levi and Schmitt (eds) (1997), pp. 66–116.

Persson, B. and Öberg, L. (1996), 'Foster-Children and the Swedish State 1785–1915', in Tedebrand (ed) (1996), pp. 51–81.

Persson, C. (1992), *Jorden, bonden och hans familj: En studie av bondejordbruket i en socken i norra Småland under 1800-talet, med särskild hänsyn till jordägande, sysselsättning och familje- och hushållsbildning*, Stockholms universitet, Stockholm.

Persson, C. (1993), *Stockholms klädesmanufakturer 1816–1846*, Almqvist & Wiksell International, Stockholm.

Persson, C. (1997), 'Land Ownership, Farm Structure and the Economy: Some Examples of Farm Sub-Division in Sweden, 1780–1862', *Scandinavian Economic History Review*, vol. 45:1, pp. 70–89.

Petschauer, P. (1984), 'Mädchenjahre deutscher Frauen im 18 Jahrhundert', in Büttner and Ende (eds) (1984), pp. 177–193.

Pettersson, L. (1996), 'Reading and Writing Skills and the Agrarian Revolution: Scandinavian Peasants During the Age of Enclosure', *Scandinavian Economic History Review*, vol. 44:3, pp. 207–221.

Peukert, K. (1986), 'Industrialiserung des Bewusstseins? Arbeitserfahrung von der Ruhrbergleuten in 20. Jahrhundert', in Tenfelde (ed) (1986), pp. 92–119.

Pfennig, G. (1995), *Strassenkinder in Deutchland: Eine Herausforderung für die Pädagogik*, Inaug.-Diss., Universität zu Köln, Köln.

Pierrard, P. (1987), *Enfants et jeunes ouvriers en France XIXe–XXe siècle*, Les Éditions ouvrières, Paris.

Pietsch, U. (1979), *Stockelsdorfer Fayencen: Geschichte und Leistung einer holsteinischen Manufaktur im 18. Jahrhundert*, Museum für Kunst und Kulturgeschicte der Hansestadt Lübeck, Lübeck.

Pinchbeck, I. and Hewitt, M. (1969), *Children in English Society Volume I: From Tudor Times to the Eighteenth Century*, Routledge & Kegan Paul, London.

Pinchbeck, I. and Hewitt, M. (1973), *Children in English Society Volume II: From the Eighteenth Century to the Children Act 1948*, Routledge & Kegan Paul, London.

Plakans, A. (1978), 'Parentless Children in Soul Revisions: A Study of Methodology and Social Fact', in Ransel (ed) (1978), pp. 77–102.

Plakans, A. (1983), 'The familial context of early childhood in Baltic serf society', in Wall (ed) (1983), pp. 167–206.

[Platter] (1999 [1572]), 'The autobiography of Thomas Platter', reprinted in Monroe (1999 [1904]), pp. 77–227.

Plaul, H. (1986), 'The Rural Proletariat: The Everyday Life of Rural Labourers in the Magdeburg Region, 1830–1880', in Evans and Lee (eds) (1986), pp. 102–128.

Polanyi, K. (1971), *The Great Transformation*, Beacon Press, Boston.

Pollack, E.G. (2002), 'The Childhood We Have Lost: When Siblings Were Caregivers, 1900–1970', *Journal of Social History*, vol. 36:1, pp. 31–53.

Pollard, S. (1968), *The Genesis of Modern Management: A Study of the Industrial Revolution in Great Britain*, Penguin Books, Harmondsworth.

Pollard, S. (1981), *Peaceful Conquest: The Industrialization of Europe 1760–1970*, Oxford University Press, Oxford.

Pollard, S. (1992), 'The Concept of Industrial Revolution', in Dosi, Giannetti and Toninelli (eds) (1992), pp. 29–62.

Pollard, S. and Holmes, C. (eds) (1968), *Documents of European Economic History, Volume One: The Process of Indistrialization, 1750–1870*, Edward Arnold, London.

Pollock, L. (1983), *Forgotten Children: Parent–Child Relations from 1500 to 1800*, Cambridge University Press, Cambridge.

Pollock, L. (1989), '"Teach her to live under obedience": the making of women in the upper ranks of early modern England', *Continuity and Change*, vol. 4:2, pp. 231–258.

Poole, R. (1995), '"Give Us Our Eleven Days": Calendar Reform in the Eighteenth-Century England' *Past & Present*, No. 149, pp. 95–139.

Poulsen, B. (1995), 'Seventeenth century peasants of Schleswig and Holstein, their writings and their worlds', in Larsson and Myrdal (eds) (1995), pp. 58–73.

Postel-Vinay, G. (1994), 'The dis-integration of traditional labour markets in France: From agriculture *and* industry to agriculture *or* industry', in Grantham and MacKinnon (ed) (1994), pp. 64–83.

Pratt, J. (1994), *The Rationality of Rural Life: Economic and Cultural change in Tuscany*, Harwood Academic Publishers, Chur.

Pris, C. (1973a and 1973b), *La manufacture royale des Glaces de Saint-Gobain: Une grande enterprise sous l'Ancien Régime, Tome I* and *III*, Thèse, Universite de Paris IV, Paris.

Prost, A. and Vincent, G. (eds) (1991), *A History of Private Life V: Riddles of Identity in Modern Times*, The Belknap Press, Cambridge, Mass. and London.

Pullan, B. (1988), 'Support and redeem: charity and poor relief in Italian cities from the fourteenth to seventeenth century', *Continuity and Change*, vol. 3:2, pp. 177–208.

Pulma, P. (1985), 'The Riksdag, the State Bureaucracy and the Administration of Hospitals in Eighteenth-Century Sweden', *Scandinavian Journal of History*, vol. 10:2, pp. 119–141.

Quataert, J.H. (1985), 'Combining Agrarian and Industrial Livelihood: Rural Households in the Saxon Oberlausitz in the Nineteenth Century', *Journal of Family History*, vol. 10: 2, pp. 145–162.

Qvortrup, J. (ed) (1993), *Childhood as a Social Phenomenon: Lessons from an International Project*, Eurosocial Report 47/19, Vienna.

Qvortrup, J., Bardy, M., Sgritta, G. and Wintersberger, H. (eds) (1994), *Childhood Matters: Social Theory, Practice and Politics*, Avebury, Aldershot.

Raaschou-Nielsen, A. (1990), 'Danish Agrarian Reform and Economic Theory', *Scandinavian Economic History Review*, vol. 38:3, pp. 44–61.

Raaschou-Nielsen, A. (1993), 'The Organizational History of the Firm: The putting-out system in Denmark around 1900', *Scandinavian Economic History Review*, vol. 41:1, pp. 3–17.

Rahikainen, M. (1995a), 'The Fading of Compulsory Labour: The Displacement of Work by Hobbies in the Reformatory Schools of Twentieth-Century Finland', *Scandinavian Economic History Review*, vol. 43:2, pp. 251–262.

Rahikainen, M. (1995b), 'Hyttipoikia: Lasten työnteko Suomen lasitehtaissa 1844–1944', *Historiallinen Aikakauskirja*, vol. 93:2, pp. 117–124.

Rahikainen, M. (1996) 'Arbete eller skola? Om minderårigas arbete i Finland under mellankrigstiden', *Historisk Tidskrift för Finland*, vol. 81:3, pp. 323–342.

Rahikainen, M. (1998), '"Ingen mat utan arbete": Arbetshusen för barn i Helsingfors [Helsinki] 1883–1945', *Historisk Tidskrift för Finland*, vol. 83:2, pp. 289–307.

Rahikainen, M. (1999), 'Kaupunkilaisnuorten töitä 1950- ja 1960-luvulla', in Parikka (ed) (1999), pp. 335–369.

Rahikainen, M. (2001a), 'Historical and present-day child labour: is there a gap or a bridge between them?', *Continuity and Change*, vol.16:1, pp. 137–155.

Rahikainen, M. (2001b), 'Children and "the Right to Factory work": Child Labour Legislation in Nineteenth-Century Finland', *Scandinavian Economic History Review*, vol. 46:1, pp. 41–62.

Rahikainen, M. (2001c), 'Herrasväki, työväki ja palkkatyö toimeentulon lähteinä kaupungissa', in Rahikainen and Räisänen (eds) (2001), pp. 118–145.

Rahikainen, M. (2002a) 'Compulsory Child Labour: Parish Paupers as Indentured Servants in Finland, c. 1810–1920', *Rural History*, vol. 36:2, pp. 163–178.

Rahikainen, M. (2002b), 'First-Generation Factory Children: Child Labour in Textile Manufacturing in Nineteenth-Century Finland', *Scandinavian Economic History Review*, vol. 50:2, pp. 71–95.

Rahikainen, M. (2003), 'Nuorena töihin: Lasten ja nuorten työnteko 1900–1970', in Aapola and Kaarninen (eds) (2003), pp. 161–185.

Rahikainen, M. and Räisänen, T. (eds) (2001), *'Työllä ei oo kukkaan rikastunna'. Naisten töitä ja toimeentulokeinoja 1800- ja 1900-luvulla*, Suomalaisen Kirjallisuuuden Seura, Helsinki.

Ramsay, A. (1949 [1904]), *Från barnaår till silverhår*, Söderström, Helsinki.

Ransel, D.L. (ed) (1978), *The Family in Imperial Russia: New Lines of Historical Research*, University of Illinois Press, Urbana.

Ransel, D.L. (1988), *Mothers of Misery: Child Abandonment in Russia*, Princeton University Press, Princeton.

Rapports annuels des inspecteurs de fabriques (1912 and 1915), *Rapports annuels des inspecteurs de fabriques. Année 1911* and *Année 1914* (*Svod otchetov fabrichnykh inspektorov*), Ministère du Commerce et de l'Industrie de l'Empire de Russie, Division de l'Industrie, St. Petersburg.

Raussi, E. (1966, orig. c.1850), *Virolahden kansanelämää 1840-luvulla*, Suomalaisen Kirjallisuuden Seura, Helsinki.

Reay, B. (1996), *Microhistories: demography, society and culture in rural England, 1800–1930*, Cambridge University Press, Cambridge.

Reeder, L. (1998), 'Women in the Classroom: Mass Migration, Literacy and the Nationalization of Sicilian Women at the Turn of the Century', *Journal of Social History*, vol. 32:1, pp. 101–124.

Reher, D.S. (1990), *Town and Country in Pre-Industrial Spain: Cuenca, 1550–1870*, Cambridge University Press, Cambridge.

Reher, D.S. (1998), 'Family Ties in Western Europe: Persistent Contrasts', *Population and Development Review*, vol. 24:2, pp. 203–234.

Reininghaus, W. (1986), 'Arbeit im städtishen Handwerk an der Wende zur Neuzeit', in Tenfelde (ed) (1986), pp. 9–31.

Rétif de La Bretonne, N-E., (1989 [1797]), *Monsieur Nicolas, volume I*, ed. P. Téstud, Gallimard, Paris.

Reuter, O. (1961), *Die Manufaktur im Fränkischen Raum*, Gustav Fischer Verlag, Stuttgart.

Reybaud, L. (1856), *L'Industrie en Europe*, Michel Lévy Freres, Paris.

Riis, T. (ed) (1981), *Aspects of Poverty in Early Modern Europe, I*, Klett-Cotta, Stuttgart.

Riis, T. (ed) (1986), *Aspects of Poverty in Early Modern Europe II: Les réactions des pauvres à la pauvreté*, Odense University Press, Odense.

Riis, T. (ed) (1990), *Aspects of Poverty in Early Modern Europe III: La pauvreté dans les pays nordiques 1500–1800*, Odense University Press, Odense.

Rimbaud, C. (1980), *52 millions d'enfants au travail*, Plon, Paris.

Ritter, G.A. and Tenfelde, K. (1992), *Arbeiter im Deutschen Kaiserreich 1871 bis 1914*, Verlag J.H.W. Dietz Nachf., Bonn.

Robin, E. (1879), *Des écoles industrielles et de la protection des enfants insoumis ou abandonnés*, J. Bonhoure, Paris.

Robson, M. (1984), 'The Border Farm Worker', in Devine (ed) (1984), pp. 71–96.

Roggero, M. (1999), *L'alfabeto conquistato: Apprendere e insegnare nell'Italia tra Sette e Ottocento*, Il Mulino, Bologna.

Roggero, M. (2000), 'State and Education in Eighteenth Century Italy: The School System of Turin', *Paedagogica Historica*, vol. 36:2, pp. 539–569.

Romano, R. (1992), *L'industria cotoniera lombarda dall'Unità al 1914*, Banca Commerciale Italiana, Milano.

Roper, L. (2000), '"Evil Imaginings and Fantasies": Child-Witches and the End of the Witch Craze', *Past & Present*, No. 167, pp. 107–139.

Rose, M.B. (2000), *Firms, Networks and Business Values: The British and American Cotton Industries since 1750*, Cambridge University Press, Cambridge.

Rossi, G. (1985), *L'Agro di Roma tra '500 e '800: Condizioni de vita lavoro*, Edizioni di storia e letteratura, Roma.

Rostgaard, M. and Wagner, M. (eds) (2000), *Lederskab i Dansk Industri og Samfund 1880–1960*, Historiestudiet, Aalborg Universitet, Aalborg.

Rostgaard, M. (2000), 'Patriarkalisme og industriledelse i Danmark ca. 1880–1910', in Rostgaard and Wagner (eds) (2000), pp. 91–128.

Roth, R. (2001), 'Child Murder in New England', *Social Science History*, vol. 25:1, pp. 101–147.

Ruppert, W. (ed) (1986), *Die Arbeiter: Lebensformen, Alltag und Kultur von Frühindustrialiserung bis zum "Wirtschaftswunder"*, Verlag C.H. Beck, München.

Rustemeyer, A. (1996), *Dienstboten in Petersburg und Moskau 1861–1917. Hintergrund, Alltag, soziale Rolle*, Franz Steiner Verlag, Stuttgart.

Ruxton, S. (1996), *Children in Europe*, NCH Action For Children, London.

Salvemini, T. (1962), 'L'instruzione nel Mezzogiorno con particolare riguardo all'instruzione professionale', in *Industri, servizi e scuola*, Editori Laterza, Bari, pp. 519–567.

Sandberg, L.G. and Steckel R.H. (1988), 'Hard Times in 19th-Century Sweden: A Reply', *Explorations in Economic History*, vol. 27:1, pp. 114–121.

Sandberg, L.G. and Steckel R.H. (1990), 'Overpopulation and Malnutrition Rediscovered: Hard Times in 19th-Century Sweden', *Explorations in Economic History*, vol. 25:1, pp. 1–19.

Sandin, B. (1988), 'Education, popular culture and the surveillance of the population in Stockholm between 1600 and the 1840s', *Continuity and Change*, vol. 3:3, pp. 357–390.

Sandin, B. (1995), 'Skapandet av det normala barnet', in Bergqvist, Petersson and Sundkvist (eds) (1995), pp. 55–64.

Sandin, B. (1997), '"In the Large Factory Towns": Child Labour Legislation, Child Labour and Scool Compulsion', in de Coninck-Smith, Sandin and Schrumpf (eds) (1997), pp. 17–46.

Saraceno, C. (1991), 'The Italian Family: Paradoxes of Privacy', in Prost and Vincent (eds) (1991), pp. 451–501.

Sarasúa, C. (1994), *Criados, nodrizas y amos: El servico doméstico en la formación del mercado de trabajo madrileño, 1758–1868*, Siglo Veintiuno de España Editores, Madrid.

Sarasúa, C. (1998), 'Understanding intra-family inequalities: The Montes de Pas, Spain, 1700–1900', *The History of the Family*, vol. 3:2, pp. 173–197.

Sarasúa García, C. (1995), 'La industria del encaje en el Campo de Calatrava', *Arenal: Revista de historia de las mujeres*, vol. 2:2, pp. 151–174.

Sarasúa Garcia, C. (2000), '¿De la vagancia al paro? Las raíces históricas de un concepto', *Revista de Occidente*, vol. 235, pp. 65–84.

Sarasúa García, C. (2002), 'El acceso de niños a los recursos educativos en la España rural del siglo XIX', in Martínez Carrión (ed) (2002), pp. 549–609.

Sarti, R. (2002), *Europe at Home: Family and Material Culture, 1500–1800*, Yale University Press, New Haven and London.

Saul, S.B. (1989), *The Myth of the Great Depression, 1873–1896*, Macmillan, Basingstoke and London.

Scharfe, M. (1986), '"Gemütliches Knechtschaftsverhältnis?". Landarbeitserfahrungen 1750–1900', in Tenfelde (ed) (1986), pp. 32–50.

Scholliers, P. and Schwarz, L. (eds) (2003), *Experiencing Wages: Social and cultural aspects of wage forms in Europe since 1500*, Berghahn Books, New York and Oxford.

Schlumbohm, J. (ed) (1983), *Kinderstuben: Wie Kinder zu Bauern, Bürgern, Aristokraten wurden 1700–1850*, Deutscher Taschenbuch Verlag, München.

Schlumbohm, J. (1994), *Lebensläufe, Familien, Höfe: Die Bauern und Heuerleute des Osnabrückischen Kirchspiels Belm in proto-industriellen Zeit, 1650–1860*, Vandenhoeck & Ruprecht, Göttingen.

Schlumbohm, J. (1996), 'Micro-History and the Macro-Models of the European Demographic System in Pre-Industrial Times: Life Course Patterns in the Parish of Belm (Northwest Germany), Seventeenth to the Nineteenth Centuries', *The History of the Family*, vol. 1:1, pp. 81–95.

Schubert, E. (1996), 'Daily Life, Consumption, and Material Culture', in Ogilvie (ed) (1996), pp. 350–376.

Schulte, R. (1986), 'Peasant farms and Farmers' Maids: Female Farm Servants in Bavaria at the End of the Nineteenth Century', in Evans and Lee (eds) (1986), pp. 158–173.

Schön, L. (1982), 'Proto-indistrialization and factories. Textiles in Sweden in the mid-nineteenth century', *Scandinavian Economic History Rewiew*, vol. 30:1, pp. 57–72.

Schwartz, R.M. (1988), *Policing the Poor in Eighteenth-Century France*, The University of North Carolina Press, Chapel Hill.

Schwarz, L.D. (1992), *London in the age of industrialisation: Entrepreneurs, labour force and living conditions, 1700–1850*, Cambridge University Press, Cambridge.

Scraton, P. (ed) (1997), *'Childhood' in 'Crisis'*, UCL Press, London.

Selander, S. (ed) (1992), *Forskning om utbildning: En antologi*, Symposion, Stockholm and Skåne.

Semyonova Tian-Shanskaia, O. (1993 [1914]), *Village Life in Late Tsarist Russia*, ed. D. Ransel, Indiana University Press, Bloomington.

Sen, G. (1995), *The Military Origins of Industrialisation and International Trade Rivalry*, Pinter, London and New York.

Sergene, A. (1972 [1963]), *La Manufacture de Sèvres sous l'Ancien Régime, T. I*, Thèse, Paris and Nancy.

Shahar, S. (1992), *Childhood in the Middle Ages*. Routledge, London and New York.

Sharpe, P. (1991), 'Poor children as apprentices in Colyton, 1598–1830', *Continuity and Change*, vol. 6:2, pp. 253–270.

Shorter, E. (1977), *The Making of the Modern Family*, Basic Books, New York.

Sicsic, P. (1994), 'Establishment Size and the Economies of Scale in 19th-Century France', *Explorations in Economic History*, vol. 31:4, pp. 453–478.

Sigsgaard, E. (1995), *Om børn og deres virkelighed – før og nu*, Hans Reitzels Forlag, Copenhagen.

Simon, C. (1994), 'Labour Relations at Manufactures in the Eighteenth Century: The Calico Printers in Europe', *International Review of Social History*, vol. 39, Supplement 2, pp. 115–144.

Simon, J. (1875), *L'instruction gratuite et obligatoire*, Librairie de la Bibliothèque Démocratique, Paris.

Simonton, D. (1998), *A History of European Women's Work, 1700 to the Present*, Routledge, London.

Sjöberg, M. (1996), *Att säkra framtidens skördar: Barndom, skola och arbete i agrar miljö. Bolstads pastorat 1860–1920*, Linköpings Universitet, Linköping.

Sjöberg, M. (1997), 'Working Rural Children: Herding, child labour and childhood in the Swedish Rural Environment 1850–1950', in de Coninck-Smith, Sandin and Schrumpf (eds) (1997), pp. 106–128.

Slettan, D. (1978), *Dreng og taus i Verdal: Eksperiment med en kollektiv sjølbiografi*, Universitetsforlaget, Oslo.

Slettan, D. (1982), 'Farmwives, Farm Hands and the Changing Rural Community in Trøndelag, Norway', in Thompson and Burchardt (eds) (1982), pp. 144–153.

Slettan, D. (1984), 'Barnearbeid i jordbruket', in Hodne and Sogner (eds) (1984), pp. 64–75.

Smith, A. (1973 [1776]), *The Wealth of Nations, Books I–III*, ed. A. Skinner, Peguin Books, Harmondsworth.

Smith, H. (1984), 'Family and Class: The Household Economy of Languedoc Winegrowers, 1830–1870', *Journal of Family History*, vol. 9:1, pp. 64–87.

Smith, J., Wallerstein, I. and Evers, H-D. (eds) (1984), *Households and the World-Economy*, Sage Publications, Beverly Hills.

Smith, R.M. (ed) (1984), *Land, Kinship and Life-Cycle*, Cambridge University Press, Cambridge.

Smith, R.M. (1984), 'Some issues concerning families and their property in rural England 1250–1800', in Smith, R.M. (1984), pp. 1–86.

Snell, K.D.M., (1992), *Annals of the Labouring Poor: Social Change and Agrarian England, 1660–1900*, Cambridge University Press, Cambridge.

Snellman, G.R. (1908), *Undersökning af folkskolebarnens i Helsingfors* [Helsinki], *Åbo* [Turku], *Tammerfors* [Tampere] *och Viborg* [Vyborg] *arbete utom skolan*, Arbetsstatistik V, Industristyrelse, Helsinki.

Solberg, A. (1990), 'Negotiating Childhood: Changing Constructions of Age for Norwegian Children', in James and Prout (eds) (1990), pp. 118–137.

Sonnino, E. (1994), 'Between the home and the hospice: The plight and fate of girl orphans in seventeenth- and eighteenth-century Rome', in Henderson and Wall (eds) (1994), pp. 94–116.

Soreau, E. (1935), 'Note sur le travail des enfants dans l'Industrie pendant la Révolution', *Revue des Études Historiques*, avril-juin, pp. 159–163.

Spinanger, D. (1992), 'The impact on employment and income of structural and technological changes in the clothing industry', in van Liemt (ed) (1992), pp. 83–116.

Sprauten, K. (1992), *Oslo bys historie, Bind 2: Byen ved festningen. Fra 1536 til 1814*. J.W. Cappellens Forslag, Oslo.

Spufford, M. (1995), 'Sources for studying ordinary people in the sixteenth and seventeenth century England', in Larsson and Myrdal (eds) (1995), pp. 8–17.

Standing, G. (1982), 'State Policy and Child Labour: Accumulation Versus Legitimation?', *Development and Change*, vol. 13:4, pp. 611–631.

Strauss, R. (1932), *Das arbeitende Kind in der Unfallsbesicherung der Reichsversicherungsord nung*, Inaug.-Diss., Universität Tübingen, Tübingen.

Strumingher, L.S. (1977), 'The Artisan Family: Traditions and Transition in Nineteenth-Century Lyon', *Journal of Family History*, vol. 2:3, pp. 211–222.

Strømstad, P. (1991), 'Artisan Travel and Technology Transfer to Denmark, 1750–1900', in Bruland (ed) (1991), pp. 135–156.

Szabó, M. (1971), 'Barnarbete i agrarsamhället', *Fataburen 1971*, Nordiska museet and Skansen, Stockhom, pp. 19–38.

Söderberg, J. (1978), *Agrar fattigdom i Sydsverige under 1800-talet*, Almqvist & Wiksell International, Stockholm.

Söderberg, J. (1989), 'Hard Times in 19th-Century Sweden: A Comment', *Explorations in Economic History*, vol. 26:4, pp. 477–491.

Söderberg, J., Jonsson, U. and Persson, C. (1991), *A stagnating metropolis: the economy and demography of Stockholm, 1750–1850*, Cambridge University Press, Cambridge.

Söderberg, J. and Myrdal, J. (2002), *The Agrarian Economy of Sixteenth-Century Sweden*, Almqvist & Wiksell International, Stockholm.

Søreide, E. (1991), *Arbeiderbarns oppveksts i Kristiania 1890–1914*, Hovedfagsoppgave i historie våren 1991, Universitetet i Trondheim (unpublished masters thesis).

Tausendpfund, A. (1975), *Die Manufaktur im Fürstentum Neuburg*, Schriftenreihe des Stadtarchivs Nürnberg, Nürnberg.

Tedebrand, L-G. (ed) (1996), *Orphans and Foster Children: A Historical and Cross-Cultural Perspective*, Umeå University, Umeå.

Tenfelde, K. (ed) (1986), *Arbeit und Arbeitserfahrung in der Geschichte*, Vandenhoek & Ruprecht, Göttingen.

Therborn, G. (1993), 'The Politics of Childhood: The Rights of Children in Modern Times', in Castles (ed) (1993), pp. 241–291.

Thompson, E.P. (1967), 'Time, Work-Discipline, and Industrial Capitalism', *Past & Present*, No. 38, pp. 56–97.

Thompson, E.P. (1980 [1963]), *The Making of the English Working Class*, Penguin Books, Harmondsworth.

Thompson, F.M.L. (ed) (1990), *The Cambridge Social History of Britain, 1750–1850, Volume 1. Regions and Communities*, Cambridge University Press, Cambridge.

Thompson, P. (1975), 'The War with Adults', *Oral History*, vol. 3:2, pp. 29–38.

Thompson, P. and Burchardt, N. (eds) (1982), *Our Common History: The Transformation of Europe*, Humanities Press and Pluto Press, Atlantic Highlands and London.

Tiana Ferrer, A. (1996), 'The Workers' Movement and Popular Education in Contemporary Spain (1868–1939), *Paedacogica Historica*, vol. 32:3, pp. 647–684.

Tissot, V. (1882), *La Russie et les Russes: Indiscrétions de voyage*, E. Dentu, Paris.

Toniolo, G. (1990), *An Economic History of Liberal Italy, 1850–1918*, Routledge, London and New York.

Torstendahl, R. (1979), 'Les chefs d'entreprise en Suède de 1880 à 1950: sélection et milieu social', in Levy-Leboyer (ed) (1979), pp. 37–50.

Tortella, G. (2000), *The Development of Modern Spain: An Economic History of the Nineteenth and Twentieth Centuries*, Harvard University Press, Cambridge, Mass. and London.

Tortella, G. (ed) (1990), *Education and Economic Development since the Industrial Revolution*, Generalitat Valenciana, València.

Tourgueneff [Turgenev], N. (1847), *La Russie et les russes, Tome II: Tableau politique et social de la Russie*, Imprimeurs Unis, Paris.

Tovrov, J. (1976), 'Mother-Child Relationship among Russian Nobility', in Ransel (ed) (1978), pp. 15–43.

Tranberg, A. (1996), 'Forretningsjordbruk på Hedmarken før 1850', in Tranberg and Sprauten (eds) (1996), pp. 13–30.

Tranberg, A. and Sprauten, K. (eds) (1996), *Norsk bondeøkonomi 1650–1850*, Det Norske Samlaget, Oslo.

Trinidad Fernández, P. (1996), 'La infancia delincuente y abandonada', in *Historia de la infancia* (1996), pp. 459–521.

Tugan-Baranovsky, M.I. (1970 [1907]), *The Russian Facory in the 19th Century*, eds. D. Thorner, B. Kerblay and R.E.F. Smith, The American Economic Associaltion and Richard D. Irwin, Homewoods, Ill.

Turgenev, see Tourgueneff.

Tweedie, Mrs. A. [E.B.] (1897), *Through Finland in Carts*, Adam and Charles Black, London.

Tønsberg, J. (1997), 'Børnearbejde i dansk tekstilindustri: Brede Klædefabrik ca. 1870–1913', *Arbejderhistorie*, Nr. 3, pp. 33–50.

Uhlig, O. (1978), *Die Schwabenkinder aus Tirol und Voralberg*, Universitätsverlag Wagner and Konrad Theiss Verlag, Innsbruck, Stuttgart and Aalen.

Ure, A. (1967 [1835]), *The Philosophy of Manufactures, or an Exposition of the Scientific, Moral, and Commercial Economy of the Factory System of Great Britain*, Frank Cass & Co., London.

Utterström, G. (1957a and 1957b), *Jordbrukets arbetare: Levnadvillkor och arbetsliv på landsbygden från frihetstiden till mitten av 1800-talet, Första* and *Andra delen*, Tidens förlag, Stockholm.

Utterström, G. (1978), *Fattig och föräldralös i Stockholm på 1600- och 1700-talen*, Umeå universitet, Umeå.

Vainio-Korhonen, K. (2000), 'Handicrafts as Professions and Sources of Income in the Late Eighteenth and Early Nineteenth Century Turku (Åbo): A Gender Viewpoint to Economic History', *Scandinavian Economic History Review*, vol. 48:1, pp. 40–63.

van Liemt, G. (ed) (1992), *Industry on the move: Causes and consequences of international relocation in the manufacturing industry*, International Labour Office, Geneva.

van Liemt, G. (1992), 'Summary and conclusions', in van Liemt (ed) (1992), pp. 309–312.

Vassberg, D.E. (1984), *Land and Society in Golden Age Castile*, Cambridge University Press, Cambridge.

Vassberg, D.E. (1998), 'Orphans and Adoption in Early Modern Castilian Villages', *The History of the Family*, vol. 3:4, pp. 441–458.

Verdon, N. (2002), 'The rural labour market in the early nineteenth century: women's and children's employment, family income, and the 1834 Poor Law Report', *Economic History Review*, vol. 55:2, pp. 299–323.

Viazzo, P.P. (1994), 'Family structures and the early phase in the individual life cycle: A southern European perspective', in Henderson and Wall (ed) (1994), pp. 31–50.

Vilkuna, K.H.J. (1996), *Arkielämää patriarkaalisessa työmiesyhteisössä: Rautaruukkilaiset suurvalta-ajan Suomessa*, Suomen Historiallinen Seura, Helsinki.

Villermé, M. [L.R.] (1840a and 1840b), *Tableau de l'état physique et moral des ouvriers employés dans les manufactures de coton, de laine et de soie, Tome premier* and *second*, Jules Renouard et Cie, Libraires, Paris.

Villstrand, N.E. (1992), *Anpassning eller protest: Lokalsamhället inför utskrivningarna av fotfolk till den svenska krigsmakten 1620–1679*, Åbo Akademins förlag, Turku.

Virrankoski, P. (1963), *Myyntiä varten harjoitettu kotiteollisuus Suomessa autonomian ajan alkupuolella (1809 – noin 1865)*, Suomen Historiallinen Seura, Helsinki.

Visalberghi, A. (1986 [1979]), 'Education and division of labour in the developed world', in Z. Morsy (ed) (1986), *Learning and working*, Unesco, Paris, pp. 31–49.

von Westerhagen, A. (1932), *Kinderarbeit und Kinderschutz in dem ehemaligen Grossherzogentum, jetzigen Volkstaat Hessen während der letzten 30 Jahre*, Philipps-Universität zu Marburg, Marburg.

Wales, T. (1984), 'Poverty, poor relief and the life-cycle: some evidence from seventeenth-century Norfolk', in Smith, R.M. (ed) (1984), pp. 351–404.

Wall, R. (1978), 'The Age at Leaving Home', *Journal of Family History*, vol. 3:2, pp. 181–202.

Wall, R. (1987), 'Leaving home and the process of household formation in pre-industrial England', *Continuity and Change*, vol. 2:1, pp. 77–101.

Wall, R. (2001), 'The Family Circumstances of Women Migrating Permanently or Temporarily to Sundsvall in the Nineteenth Century', *Scandinavian Economic History Review*, vol. 49:3, pp. 46–61.

Wall, R. (ed) (1983), *Family forms in historic Europe*, Cambridge University Press, Cambridge.

Walton, J.K. (1990), 'The north-west', in Thompson, F.L.M. (ed) (1990), pp. 355–414.

Walton, J.K. (1998), 'The Agricultural Revolution and the Industrial Revolution: the case of Nort-West England, 1780–1850', in Bjørn (ed) (1998), pp. 65–88.

Weber, E. (1976), *Peasants into Frenchmen: The Modernization of Rural France, 1870–1914*, Stanford University Press, Stanford.

Weber-Kellermann, I. (1979), *Die Kindheit: Kleidungen und Wohnen, Arbeit und Spiel. Eine Kulturgeschicte*, Insel Verlag, Frankfurt am Main.

Weber-Kellermann, I. (1987), *Landleben im 19. Jahrhundert*, Verlag C.H. Beck, München.

Weiner, M. (1991), *The Child and the State in India: Child Labour and Education Policy in Comparative Perspective*, Princeton University Press, Princeton.

Weissbach, L.S. (1989), *Child Labour Reform in Nineteenth-Century France: Assuring the Future Harvest*, Louisiana State University Press, Baton Rouge.

Whyte I.D. and Whyte, K.A. (1983), 'Some Aspects of the Structure of Rural Society in Seventeenth-Century Lowland Scotland', in Devine and Dickson (eds) (1983), pp. 32–45.

Williamson, J.G. (1995), 'The Evolution of Global Labor Market since 1830: Background Evidence and Hypotheses', *Explorations in Economic History*, vol. 32:2, pp. 141–196.

Wimmer, M. (1979), *Die Kindheit auf dem Lande*, Rowohlt, Hamburg.

Wilmi, J. (1991), *Isäntäväet ja palvelusväen pito 1600-luvulla ja 1700-luvun alkupuolella*, Jyväskylän yliopisto, Jyväskylä.

Winberg, C. (1978), 'Population Growth and Proletarianization: The Transformation of Social Structures in Rural Sweden during the Agrarian Revolution', in Åkerman, Johansen and Gaunt (ed) (1978), pp. 170–184.

Wirilander, K. (1982), *Herrskapsfolk: Ståndspersoner i Finland 1721–1870*, Nordiska Museet, Stockholm.

Woodward, D. (1995), *Men at Work: Labourers and building craftsmen in the towns of northern England, 1450–1750*, Cambridge University Press, Cambridge.

Woolf, S. (ed) (1991), *Domestic strategies: work and family in France and Italy, 1600–1800*, Cambridge University Press and Editions de la Maison des Sciences de l'Homme, Cambridge and Paris.

Wunder, Heide (1996), 'Agriculture and Agrarian Society', in Ogilvie (ed) (1996), pp. 63–99.

Ylikangas, H. (1990), *Mennyt meissä: Suomalaisen kansanvallan historiallinen analyysi*, WSOY, Porvoo and Helsinki.

Zelizer, V.A. (1985), *Pricing the Priceless Child: The Changing Social Value of Children*, Basic Books, New York.

Zelnik, R.E. (1971), *Labour and Society in Tsarist Russia: The Factory Workers of St. Petersburg, 1855–1870*, Stanford University Press, Stanford.

Zelnik, R.E. (1995), *Law and Disorder on the Narova River: The Kreenholm Strike of 1872*, University of California Press, Berkeley and Los Angeles.

Zucchi, J.E. (1992), *The Little Slaves of the Harp: Italian Child Street Musicians in Nineteenth-Century Paris, London, and New York*, McGill-Queen's University Press, Montreal, Kingston and London.

Åkerman, S., Johansen, H.C. and Gaunt, D. (eds) (1978), *Chance and Change: Social and Economic Studies in Historical Demography in the Baltic Area*, Odense University Press, Odense.

Åström, S.-E. (1951), 'Den s.k. barnexporten från östra Finland till Petersburg i mitten av 1800-talet', *Historisk Tidskrift för Finland*, vol. 36:3, pp. 116–125.

Österberg, E. (1991), *Mentalities and Other Realities: Essays in Medieval and Early Modern Scandinavian History*, Lund University Press and Chartwell Bratt, Lund.

Østerud, Ø. (1978), *Agrarian Structure and Peasant Politics in Scandinavia: A Comparative Study of Rural Response to Economic Change*, Universitetsforlaget, Oslo

Index

N.B. Letters å, ä, æ, ø, ö appear last in the alphabetical order and ü is alphabetised as y.

For Product Safety Concerns and Information please contact our
EU representative GPSR@taylorandfrancis.com Taylor & Francis
Verlag GmbH, Kaufingerstraße 24, 80331 München, Germany